MAGILL'S LITERARY ANNUAL 2018

*Essay-Reviews of 150 Outstanding Books
Published in the United States During 2017*

With an Annotated List of Titles

Volume I
A-K

Edited by
Jennifer Sawtelle

SALEM PRESS
A Division of EBSCO Information Services, Inc.
Ipswich, Massachusetts

GREY HOUSE PUBLISHING

Cover photo: Việt Thanh Nguyễn, photo by David Levenson/Getty Images

Magill's Literary Annual, 2018, published by Grey House Publishing, Inc., Amenia, NY, under exclusive license from EBSCO Information Services, Inc.

∞ The paper used in these volumes conforms to the American National Standard for Permanence of Paper for Printed Library Materials, Z39.48-1992 (R2009).

Publisher's Cataloging-In-Publication Data
(Prepared by The Donohue Group, Inc.)

Names: Magill, Frank N. (Frank Northen), 1907-1997, editor. | Wilson, John D., editor. | Kellman, Steven G., 1947- editor. | Goodhue, Emily, editor. | Poranski, Colin D., editor. | Akre, Matthew, editor. | Spires, Kendal, editor. | Toth, Gabriela, editor. | Sawtelle, Jennifer, editor.

Title: Magill's literary annual.

Description: <1977->: [Pasadena, Calif.] : Salem Press | <2015->: Ipswich, Massachusetts : Salem Press, a division of EBSCO Information Services, Inc. ; Amenia, NY : Grey House Publishing | Essay-reviews of ... outstanding books published in the United States during the previous year. | "With an annotated list of titles." | Editor: 1977- , F.N. Magill; <2010-2014>, John D. Wilson and Steven G. Kellman; <2015>, Emily Goodhue and Colin D. Poranski; <2016>, Matthew Akre, Kendal Spires, and Gabriela Toth; <2017->, Jennifer Sawtelle. | Includes bibliographical references and index.

Identifiers: ISBN 9781682176801 (2018 edition : set) | ISBN 9781682176825 (2018 edition : vol. 1) | ISBN 9781682176832 (2018 edition : vol. 2) | ISSN: 0163-3058

Subjects: LCSH: Books--Reviews--Periodicals. | United States--Imprints--Book reviews--Periodicals. | Literature, Modern--21st century--History and criticism--Periodicals. | Literature, Modern--20th century--History and criticism--Periodicals.

Classification: LCC PN44 .M333 | DDC 028.1--dc23

CONTENTS

CONTENTS

PUBLISHER'S NOTE

Magill's Literary Annual, 2018 follows a long tradition, beginning in 1954, of offering readers incisive reviews of the major literature published during the previous calendar year. The *Magill's Literary Annual* series seeks to critically evaluate 150 major examples of serious literature, both fiction and nonfiction, published in English, from writers in the United States and around the world. The philosophy behind our selection process is to cover works that are likely to be of interest to general readers that reflect publishing trends, that add to the careers of authors being taught and researched in literature programs, and that will stand the test of time. By filtering the thousands of books published every year down to notable titles, the editors have provided librarians with an excellent reader's advisory tool and patrons with fodder for book discussion groups and a guide for choosing worthwhile reading material. The essay-reviews in the *Annual* provide a more academic "reference" review of a work than is typically found in newspapers and other periodical sources.

The reviews in the two-volume *Magill's Literary Annual, 2018* are arranged alphabetically by title. At the beginning of each volume is a complete alphabetical list of all covered books that provides readers with the title and author. In addition, readers will benefit from a brief description of each work in the volume. Every essay is approximately four pages in length. Each one begins with a block of reference information in a standard order:

- Full Book Title, including any subtitle
- *Author:* Name, with birth year, and death year when applicable
- *First published:* Original foreign-language title, with year and country, when pertinent
- Original language and translator name, when pertinent
- Introduction, Foreword, etc., with writer's name, when pertinent
- *Publisher:* Company name and city, and the number of pages
- *Type of work* (chosen from standard categories):

Anthropology	Fine arts
Archaeology	History
Autobiography	History of science
Biography	Language
Current affairs	Law
Diary	Letters
Drama	Literary biography
Economics	Literary criticism
Education	Literary history
Environment	Literary theory
Essays	Media
Ethics	Medicine
Film	Memoir

Miscellaneous	Psychology
Music	Religion
Natural history	Science
Nature	Short fiction
Novel	Sociology
Novella	Technology
Philosophy	Travel
Poetry	Women's issues

- *Time:* Period represented, when pertinent
- *Locale:* Location represented, when pertinent
- Capsule description of the work
- *Principal characters* (for novels, short fiction) or *Principal personages* (for bibliographies, history): List of people, with brief descriptions, when pertinent

The text of each essay-review analyzes and presents the focus, intent, and relative success of the author, as well as the makeup and point of view of the work under discussion. To assist readers further, essays are supplemented by a list of additional "Review Sources" for further study in a bibliographic format. Every essay includes a sidebar offering a brief biography of the author or authors. Thumbnail photographs of book covers and authors are included as available.

Three indexes can be found at the end of volume II:

- Category Index: Groups all titles into subject areas such as current affairs and social issues, ethics and law, history, literary biography, philosophy and religion, psychology, and women's issues.
- Title Index: Lists all works reviewed in alphabetical order, with any relevant cross references.
- Author Index: Lists books covered in the Annual by each author's name.

A searchable cumulative index, listing all books reviewed in *Magill's Literary Annual* between 1977 and 2018, as well as in *Magill's History Annual* (1983) and *Magill's Literary Annual, History and Biography* (1984 and 1985), can be found at online.salempress.com.

Our special thanks go to the outstanding writers who lend their time and knowledge to this project every year. The names of all contributing reviewers are listed in the beginning of Volume I, as well as at the end of their individual reviews.

COMPLETE ANNOTATED LIST OF CONTENTS

VOLUME I

Paul Auster's first novel in seven years, 4 3 2 1, is a sprawling family saga focusing on the capricious nature of fate, as illustrated through the trials endured by four alternative, parallel versions of the life of a youthful protagonist.

This is a collection of sixteen stories, previously published in literary magazines, focusing on young women living in an uneasy limbo of loveless relationships while yearning for order and normality.

Omar El Akkad's debut novel, American War, *imagines a future in which the United States is embroiled in a bloody civil war over the use of fossil fuels.*

An American Sickness, the first book by Dr. Elisabeth Rosenthal, examines the shortcomings of the modern American health-care system and provides readers a guide for navigating those shortcomings.

An Extraordinary Union is a historical romance set during the American Civil War. Protagonist Ellen Burns is a Union spy with a perfect memory. She poses as a slave in Virginia to acquire sensitive military information, but a romance with a white man threatens to upend her mission.

Ali Soufan offers an overview of Islamic terrorism, focusing on how the death of Osama bin Laden led to the splintering of his al-Qaeda organization and the rise of newer groups such as the Islamic State of Iraq and Syria (ISIS). While the book suggests this cycle of terrorism will continue, it provides valuable insight into the people and processes involved.

In Anything Is Possible, *author Elizabeth Strout loosely links nine short stories with connections to Lucy Barton, the character in her previous novel, My Name Is Lucy Barton. People in Lucy's hometown of Amgash, Illinois, read and reflect on Lucy's memoir while dealing with the everyday pain, loss, and love in their own lives.*

cocaine and opioids. Ohler's groundbreaking book sheds new light on the depravity of the Third Reich.

The Blood of Emmett Till *provides an account of the murder of Emmett Till, a black fourteen-year-old who was killed near Money, Mississippi, after he allegedly insulted a white woman. Timothy B. Tyson examines the case itself but also its immediate background and its ongoing legacy.*

Part memoir, part history, Charles Campisi's Blue on Blue: An Insider's Story of Good Cops Catching Bad Cops *provides a treasure trove of New York City cop lore and constitutes a valuable source of information from an authority on law-enforcement efforts to reduce police corruption and misconduct.*

In A Book of American Martyrs, *Joyce Carol Oates examines a volatile, divisive issue. She dramatizes the aftereffects of a violent confrontation between a fundamentalist antiabortion activist and a sympathetic doctor dedicated to the pro-choice cause, and humanizes those whose lives are forever changed by events beyond their control.*

In The Book That Changed America: How Darwin's Theory of Evolution Ignited a Nation, *author Randall Fuller traces the relationship between the reception of Charles Darwin's 1859 book On the Origin of Species and the abolitionist movement in the United States. Fuller situates the reception of the text in the intellectual circle of Ralph Waldo Emerson, Henry David Thoreau, and the Alcott family, emphasizing its widespread and deeply felt influence on the development of the American intellectual community.*

In the desolate landscape of a derelict metropolis, a handful of ragged humans in a battle for survival scavenge for food while dodging bioengineered monsters created by a now-defunct firm known as the Company. Amid the rubble, a young woman finds and nurtures a creature she calls Borne, which looks like a plant, acts like an animal, and strives to become human.

In The Brain Defense, *Kevin Davis presents an illuminating study of the ways in which modern neuroscience is becoming a contested tool in American jurisprudence. He focuses on the bellwether case of Herbert Weinstein, whose brutal murder of his wife was attributed by his defense to the effects of a brain tumor. Davis evenhandedly explores the debate over whether brain injuries negate free will and personal responsibility in criminal cases.*

Portia Carmichael is determined to remain single and to open her own business, but when an old family friend arrives, her plans are challenged by an unexpected attraction to Kent Randolph. As the two get to know each other, they face challenges that could undermine their growing relationship.

Nina Riggs wrote The Bright Hour: A Memoir of Living and Dying *as she struggled with the repercussions of a cancer diagnosis that would eventually take her life. In this memoir, she shares the everyday moments that people often take for granted as well as the difficulties of living with and through a terminal illness.*

Having previously published a nonfiction book about creatures that feed on blood, zoologist and biology professor Bill Schutt next examines the phenomenon of animals—from insects to humans—that consume their own kind. Filled with interesting facts, helpful illustrations, and characteristic humor, Cannibalism: A Perfectly Natural History *provides a wealth of information about a largely understudied and misunderstood topic in the science world.*

Noted scholar Richard Rothstein provides an exhaustively researched look at the official and unofficial governmental policies that led to a long history of highly segregated housing in the United States and argues that because these policies were both official and unconstitutional, the government has a responsibility to make things right today.

The Cooking Gene *excavates the history of African American foodways from the earliest eras of slavery in the American South to the present day. The book fuses the genres of history and autobiography to trace the intertwined stories of food, culture, and bloodlines in the South.*

Drabble explores the varied issues of aging in this character study about several people who are moving into the golden years of their lives.

Jennie Melamed's debut novel.

   Ginny Moon is the story of an autistic teen who struggles with being understood as her adoptive parents prepare for the birth of a child.

   A fierce indictment of warmakers and peace negotiators entangled in the complex politics of the Middle East, The Girl in Green *spans more than two decades of sectarian conflict. The taut, sometimes farcical narrative demonstrates both the ultimate senselessness of war, as well as the opportunity for personal redemption for individuals swept up in the chaos of battle.*

   Glass House *traces the rise and fall of an "all-American" corporate town through the complexities of the conjoined fates of the Anchor Hocking corporation and the town of Lancaster, Ohio. The narrative opens when town and corporation had a local and at least somewhat symbiotic relationship. Author Brian Alexander traces the economic, social, and psychological fallout for Lancaster following the shattering of this paradigm by international investment models.*

   Armand Gamache is confronted with a murder in his small town of Three Pines, but murder is the least of his problems as he and his team plot to take down at least one major case of criminal activity in Québec.

   The distinguished German philosopher and biographer Rüdiger Safranski presents a comprehensive and compelling biography of Johann Wolfgang von Goethe. A multifaceted literary genius, over a long career Goethe produced novels, poetry, and plays, including his most celebrated masterpiece Faust (1808–32). Safranski argues that Goethe worked to make his life as much a work of art as he did his writings.

   Francis Spufford's first novel, Golden Hill, *about power, artifice, and race, vividly conjures the city of New York in the years before the American Revolution.*

   Set in the United States during the presidency of Barack Obama, Salman Rushdie's twelfth novel, The Golden House, *follows the fortunes of a real-estate developer from India as he and his sons relocate to Manhattan.*

COMPLETE ANNOTATED LIST OF CONTENTS

VOLUME II

Amber Patterson has her sights set on rich and handsome Jackson Parrish, but he is married to the seemingly perfect Daphne. Amber's schemes to replace Daphne lead to a surprising twist, and only the best woman will win.

Lisa Ko's debut novel, The Leavers, *is a coming-of-age story that explores identity, immigration, and motherhood.*

An octogenarian walks the streets of New York City, reliving moments from her illustrious past as a poet, advertising copywriter, wife, and mother. She speaks to everyone she meets along the way and is determined to live life on her own terms.

Award-winning short-story writer George Saunders's first novel melds historical fiction with earnest metaphysical inquiry as he considers the post-death fate of Abraham Lincoln's son Willie and the other souls that exist in a limbo between the world of the living and the afterlife.

In July 1965, Ruth Malone, separated from her husband, becomes the prime suspect in the murder of her two children, largely because she is young, attractive, and does not behave according to society's expectations of a mother. Pete Wonicke, a reporter fascinated by both the enigmatic Ruth and the case, works tirelessly to learn the truth, but the intrigue and obstacles mount.

Little Fires Everywhere, *Celeste Ng's second novel, tells the interconnected stories of the Richardson family, living a privileged life in a comfortable suburb, and Mia and Pearl Warren, a single artist and her daughter whose arrival triggers conflicts within the family and the larger community.*

Written by Yale Law School professor James Forman Jr., Locking Up Our Own: Crime and Punishment in Black America *explores how black civic leaders unwittingly contributed to the mass incarceration of black people.*

The Lonely Hearts Hotel, *a love story set in the seedy underworld of early-twentieth-century Montreal, follows the lives of two talented orphans.*

The Ministry of Utmost Happiness *examines India's changing sociopolitical landscape during the second half of the twentieth century. It is award-wining Indian writer Arundhati Roy's second novel.*

Mississippi Blood *is the sixth book in Greg Iles's Penn Cage series and the final novel in a trilogy that began with Natchez Burning (2014). Mayor Penn Cage, a former prosecutor, seeks to defend his father, Dr. Tom Cage, for the supposed murder of Viola Turner, the elder Cage's former nurse. The revelations that come out in this final installment have devastating repercussions for Cage and his city.*

The Mountain *is made up of six stylized stories about people in a variety of times and places, from post–World War II France to late-twentieth-century China, displaced from their homes and distanced from reality.*

Coretta Scott King, widow of civil rights leader Dr. Martin Luther King Jr., shares the story of her life as a wife, single mother, civil rights leader, and peace activist with Rev. Dr. Barbara Reynolds.

Award-winning journalist Patrick Kingsley follows the present-day odyssey of Syrian refugee Hashem al-Souki while reporting on the larger refugee crisis in Europe in The New Odyssey: The Story of the Twenty-First Century Refugee Crisis.

In her eighth novel, Alice McDermott follows the lives of poor Irish Catholic immigrant families living in Brooklyn, New York, in the early twentieth century and the group of nuns who assist them.

Pulitzer Prize–winning journalist and author Ron Powers writes movingly of a family tragedy and a national crisis in his book No One Cares About Crazy People.

Just before his death, Shimon Peres, who was a significant figure in the founding of the modern state of Israel and served the Israeli government in various capacities throughout his life, finished his memoir. It details his political career and his thoughts on war, peace, entrepreneurship, and the future of the Middle East.

The Potlikker Papers *offers a history of food in the American South that pairs food history with social history. Civil rights, race violence, politics, and gentrification are here effectively intertwined with food consumption, distribution, and service.*

Naomi Alderman's novel The Power *imagines a world in which women develop the ability to generate powerful electric shocks through a muscle in their bodies. This electric power alters the power balance of the world.*

Priestdaddy *is a memoir by poet Patricia Lockwood in which she chronicles her atypical life as the daughter of a married Catholic priest. Lockwood examines tradition and belief from the viewpoint of a nonbeliever while questioning whether a person can ever escape the world they have been raised in.*

In Protestants: The Faith That Made the Modern World, *Alec Ryrie provides a survey of the first five hundred years of Protestantism, focusing on central themes and individual leaders rather than a strict chronological history, with considerable attention to Protestant movements outside of Europe and North America.*

Part historical fiction, part Cold War thriller, and part police procedural mystery, Philip Kerr's twelfth entry in his popular Bernie Gunther series, Prussian Blue, *follows two separate but closely related plotlines set seventeen years apart to reach equally exciting conclusions.*

The Radium Girls: The Dark Story of America's Shining Women *is Kate Moore's historical account of the lives of the young women who painted watch faces with glowing radium paint and succumbed to radium poisoning; they fought a fierce legal battle with their former employers to get some measure of justice.*

This collection of eight stories, published in periodicals before Nguyễn's novel The Sympathizer *won the 2016 Pulitzer Prize in Fiction, focuses on Vietnamese refugees navigating the differences between their homeland and their new home in the United States.*

Reincarnation Blues *follows a hapless human named Milo on a journey across thousands of years and millions of miles as he burns through ten thousand lives in a quest for perfection entwined with the pursuit of a love affair with Death, in the form of a beautiful, dark-haired woman called Suzie.*

Rest in Power: The Enduring Life of Trayvon Martin *chronicles the life and death of Trayvon Martin, an unarmed African American teenager who was shot and killed in Sanford, Florida, by a neighborhood watch volunteer. His parents, Tracy Martin and Sybrina Fulton, recall the terrible days following their son's death but also the civil rights movement that sprang from it.*

This latest biography of Richard M. Nixon, thirty-seventh president of the United States, offers a wealth of valuable detail about the life and career of this controversial leader.

In The Road to Camelot, *the authors argue that John F. Kennedy's campaign for the Democratic presidential nomination began in the fall of 1956; they trace the history of this five-year effort through research in primary sources and personal interviews with some of those involved.*

Brad Parks's thriller Say Nothing *presents a plot that could be ripped from the newspaper headlines. A public official is caught on the horns of a dilemma: if he does not exactly follow the orders of a sinister group, he will lose those most precious to him.*

Sarah Schmidt's debut novel, See What I Have Done, *delves into the interior lives of the Borden family in August 1892, the month in which the notorious axe murders of patriarch Andrew Borden and his second wife, Abby, were committed. Andrew's daughter Lizzie was charged with and eventually acquitted of these real-life murders. Schmidt's fictional story creates compelling psychological portraits of the family members while exploring their daily lives, which were filled with small hurts and petty jealousies that may have inspired one of them to commit murder.*

When eleven-year-old Polly McClusky's mother is murdered by gang members under orders from their leader, an imprisoned man who is an enemy of her recently released and long-estranged father, she embarks on a crime spree and life on the run with him in an effort to avoid either of them meeting a similar fate and, ultimately, to avenge the death.

   The Signal Flame *is a novel that explores the nature of loss. It is the sequel to American author Andrew Krivák's award-winning book The Sojourn (2011).*

   Sing, Unburied, Sing *is a novel that follows an African American family living on the Gulf Coast in Mississippi that is haunted by the past. It is American writer Jesmyn Ward's third novel.*

   Roddy Doyle's novel Smile, *though darker and more downbeat in tone than much of his previous work, contains familiar elements: blunt and folksy dialogue, well-drawn characters, and forgotten memories of events from the past that, once remembered, resonate in unexpected ways in the lives of those trapped in the present.*

   A critically acclaimed experimental novel, Solar Bones *creatively presents the thoughts, memories, and philosophical musings of a small-town civil engineer in western Ireland. Marcus Conway draws strength from the bonds of family and takes comfort in the mathematical certainty of science in the process of navigating an increasingly complicated and chaotic world.*

   Jenny Zhang's debut short-story collection, Sour Heart, *explores young womanhood and the Chinese immigrant experience through the eyes of various narrators.*

   Ayobami Adebayo's debut novel, Stay with Me, *tells the story of a Nigerian marriage.*

   In The Tea Girl of Hummingbird Lane, *Lisa See deploys intimate themes of destiny and chance, motherhood and custom, to explore the enigmatic albeit prevailing boundaries between the historical forces of timeworn tradition and inescapable change.*

   Adopting the format of a sermon, academic and ordained Baptist minister Michael Eric Dyson delivers a moving polemic against American racism, urging his audience to examine their beliefs and take steps to change.

reestablishes herself as a woman, intellectual, and mother.

dystopian allegories and traditional fables.

CONTRIBUTING REVIEWERS

Pegge Bochynski

Matthew J. Bolton

Jeremy Brown

Joy Crelin

Chris Cullen

Robert C. Evans, PhD

Jack Ewing

Melynda Fuller

Molly Hagan

Ashleigh Imus, PhD

Frank Joseph

Mark S. Joy, PhD

Kathryn Kulpa

Charles E. May

Laurence W. Mazzeno

Daniel Murphy

Daniel P. Murphy

Marybeth Rua-Larsen

Andrew Schenker, MLIS

Julia A. Sienkewicz

Theresa L. Stowell, PhD

Emily Turner

Kenrick Vezina, MS

Tom Willard

4 3 2 1

Author: Paul Auster (b. 1947)
Publisher: Henry Holt and Company (New York). 880 pp.
Type of work: Novel
Time: 1947 to mid-1970s
Locales: Newark, New Jersey, and environs; New York City, New York; Paris, France, and environs

Courtesy of Henry Holt & Company, Inc.

Paul Auster's first novel in seven years, 4 3 2 1, is a sprawling family saga focusing on the capricious nature of fate, as illustrated through the trials endured by four alternative, parallel versions of the life of a youthful protagonist.

Principal characters

ARCHIBALD ISAAC "ARCHIE" FERGUSON, an intelligent, athletic young man who aspires to become a writer
ISAAC REZNIKOFF, a.k.a. Ichabod Ferguson, his paternal grandfather, a Russian Jew who emigrated to the United States in 1900
STANLEY FERGUSON, his father, a furniture and appliance businessman
ROSE ADLER FERGUSON, his mother, the proprietor of a photography studio
DANIEL "DAN" SCHNEIDERMAN, the son of the man who taught Rose photography
AMY SCHNEIDERMAN, Daniel's pretty daughter, Archie's love interest

On its surface, Paul Auster's epic *4 3 2 1* bears little resemblance to his early work. The three novels that first brought him to public notice—the New York Trilogy's *City of Glass* (1985), *Ghosts* (1986), and *The Locked Room* (1986)—were concise, suspenseful, and stark explorations into the question of identity, the meaning of life, and the essence of reality, set against a backdrop of hard-boiled mystery. The novel *4 3 2 1*, at nearly nine hundred pages, is anything but concise. But the topics under examination by the main character—questions such as "Who am I?" "What is my destiny?" "What changes would occur if I chose a different directions at each of life's major crossroads?"—have remained essentially the same as those Auster focused on in his previous novels. These probing questions are all communicated by *4 3 2 1*'s unusual structure and the narrative choices made by the author.

4 3 2 1 begins with a relatively brief passage—titled 1.0, similar to the first release of a computer program—that lays the foundation for the protagonist's family history. In the early twentieth century, a Russian Jew named Isaac Reznikoff arrives in New York City. As he waits to be processed at the immigration center on Ellis Island, he talks with a countryman who remarks that Reznikoff needs a more American-sounding surname to adapt to his new life and suggests "Rockefeller" as a substitute. However, when Reznikoff reaches the head of the line and is asked his name, he does not remember what his fellow immigrant said and mutters in Yiddish, *"Ikh hob fargessen,"* or, "I have forgotten." The official writes down what he thought he heard: Ichabod Ferguson.

Ichabod Ferguson marries and fathers three sons (Lew, Arnold, and Stanley). Stanley Ferguson marries Rose Adler; he forms a partnership with his brothers in a furniture and appliance business; and, in 1947, fathers a son named Archie who will take his place as the novel's major protagonist and usual viewpoint character.

At this point in the narrative, Auster, in keeping with the underlying theme of life decisions affecting outcomes, presents a conundrum. He creates four versions of Archie's life and splits the novel's construction into four differing plotlines. He labels the versions 1.1, 1.2, 1.3, and 1.4, progressing to 2.1, 2.2, 2.3, and 2.4 and maintaining this structure throughout the book. This structural device allows readers to choose whether to read alternate versions of Archie's life in chronological order or to skip ahead to follow the complete life of 1.1 to its conclusion before returning to the second, third, and fourth permutations of Archie Ferguson.

All the Archies are almost identical in physical appearance, personality, interests, and ambitions; like the author, they were all born in 1947 and grew up in or around Newark and South Orange, New Jersey. They are all personable, intelligent, and sensual (one is decidedly heterosexual, one is bisexual, and another is asexual). They are all individuals who excel at sports, enjoy reading and watching films, and aspire to become a writer. The Archies all have dreams that are alternately unfulfilled or realized in unforeseen ways: one Archie becomes a newspaper reporter, while another becomes a fledgling novelist. One Archie, like Auster, graduates from Columbia University and lives in Paris as a translator of French literature. What separates one version of Archie from another version is the specific conditions he happens to encounter, particularly the relationships he establishes with the sets of characters he meets, which combine to influence the action of that segment of the story.

Like the protagonist, many of the minor characters appear in each of the four parts, though their personalities are subtly different in each section. Archie's parents, Stanley and Rose, for example, are important throughout, and their occupations—store owner and photographer, respectively—are constant. However, in one version of Archie's life, it is Rose who is dominant and Stanley who is subservient, while in another version their roles are reversed. Stanley's business in the various sections ranges from being a marginal enterprise to being a thriving chain of stores, and the family's economic situation is affected accordingly. One version of Stanley dies violently at the age of thirteen, while another becomes wealthy. Other characters—Aunt Mildred, his grandfather Benjy Adler, Noah Marx—are brought forward or recede into the background depending upon their importance to that particular plotline.

Of special note is the character of Amy Schneiderman, the granddaughter of the man who taught photography to Rose, who appears in all four sections of the narrative as an object of affection for Archie. Sometimes that affection is returned (in one version of the story Archie and Amy become passionate lovers for a time); sometimes it is unrequited (in another version, Archie's mother divorces and marries Amy's father, so the two youngsters become stepsiblings, making a physical relationship taboo).

Current events of the period, woven into the narrative, are significant as the four versions unfold. Some incidents serve to define character (such as one Archie's fascination for President John F. Kennedy). Some help the reader fix the timeframe of a story segment. Other events are instrumental to the plot. For example, Archie loses two fingers in a car accident and becomes exempt from serving in the Vietnam War.

In another version of Archie's life, a friend suddenly dies. For those readers who are aware of Auster's past works and personal life, this event recalls how the author in his youth witnessed his friend getting struck by lightning. The unpredictability of death, as well life, is a theme. Certain historical incidents, such as the 1967 Newark riots and the 1968 takeover of campus buildings at Columbia University in protest of the Vietnam War, are autobiographical, as well. They reflect how parts of Auster's own life become

Courtesy of Lotte Hansen

The author of twenty novels and numerous other works, Paul Auster first gained acclaim for his series of novels in the New York Trilogy. He has been awarded the Prince of Asturias Award for Literature (2006), the Prix Médicis étranger (1989), an Independent Spirit Award for best first screenplay (1996), and many other honors.

the model for his fictional four-part hero and underscore the relationship of an author creating and editing versions of oneself in the act of creating fiction.

Though the cast of characters has been greatly expanded from the author's first novels and the scope of the plot has been extended in both place and time, the pace of Auster's storytelling has been considerably slowed by the incorporation of more internal and external material. The incorporation of dialogue without employing quotation marks to signal a new speaker presents an additional challenge for readers. This deviation from conventional formatting is economical, but it further slows the pacing.

Though the book is lengthy and demands concentration from the reader to navigate the four plotlines, *4 3 2 1* is consistent in its underlying message about issues of fate and chance in the development of an individual's life. That theme echoes throughout much of Auster's other works and is reflected in *4 3 2 1* in the approach to the characters' different outcomes and Auster's strategic integration of autobiographical details.

Highly anticipated because of the author's long hiatus from fiction, *4 3 2 1* has received mixed reviews. Auster's keen eye for characterization, his descriptive skills, and clarity of vision in particular have been highlighted among the book's major strengths. In a review for NPR Books, critic Michael Schaub called *4 3 2 1* "a stunningly ambitious novel, and a pleasure to read." Schaub elaborated, writing, "Auster's writing is joyful, even in the book's darkest moments, and never ponderous or showy."

On the other hand, Auster's inclusion of a multitude of extraneous details and his unwillingness to self-edit were noted on the negative side. In a scathing review of the novel for the *Los Angeles Times*—in which she derisively referred to *4 3 2 1* as a "doorstopper"—Michelle Dean criticized Auster's equivocations and asides, writing, "Even the most devoted Auster fan, the sort of reader who enjoys the struggle of keeping track in a book like this, seems very likely to lose the thread." Dean also criticized the relatively straightforward plotline, asserting, "There isn't enough ambition in the narrative message to justify the page length."

Whatever its perceived strengths and weaknesses, critic Tom Perrotta aptly described the general critical reception of *4 3 2 1* in his review for the *New York Times*, writing, "Despite [its] flaws, it's impossible not to be impressed—and even a little awed—by what Auster has accomplished. *4 3 2 1* is a work of outsize ambition and remarkable craft." In spite of the diverging critical opinions of its merit, *4 3 2 1* has been recognized as a major accomplishment and was short-listed for the 2017 Man Booker Prize.

Jack Ewing

Review Sources

Dean, Michelle. "For a Doorstopper, Paul Auster's *4 3 2 1* Is Surprisingly Light." *The Los Angeles Times*, 2 Feb. 2017, www.latimes.com/books/jacketcopy/la-ca-jc-auster-4321-20170202-story.html. Accessed 26 Sept. 2017.

Miller, Laura. "Paul Auster's Novel of Chance." Review of *4 3 2 1*, by Paul Auster. *The New Yorker*, 30 Jan. 2017, www.newyorker.com/magazine/2017/01/30/paul-austers-novel-of-chance. Accessed 19 Aug. 2017.

Morrison, Blake. "A Man of Many Parts." Review of *4 3 2 1*, by Paul Auster. *The Guardian*, 27 Jan. 2017, www.theguardian.com/books/2017/jan/27/4321-by-paul-auster-review. Accessed 19 Aug. 2017.

Perrotta, Tom. "One Young Man's Life Served Up Four Ways." Review of *4 3 2 1*, by Paul Auster. *The New York Times*, 31 Jan. 2017, www.nytimes.com/2017/01/31/books/review/4-3-2-1-paul-auster.html. Accessed 19 Aug. 2017.

Schaub, Michael. "4 Lives in Parallel Run through Ambitious *4 3 2 1*." Review of *4 3 2 1*, by Paul Auster. *NPR Books*, 1 Feb. 2017, www.npr.org/2017/02/01/512042685/four-lives-in-parallel-run-through-ambitious-4-3-2-1. Accessed 26 Sept. 2017.

Ulin, David L. "Paul Auster's *4 3 2 1* Offers Four Parallel Versions of One Life." Review of *4 3 2 1*, by Paul Auster. *The Washington Post*, 24 Jan. 2017, www.washingtonpost.com/entertainment/books/paul-austers-4321-offers-four-parallel-versions-of-one-life/2017/01/24/c2e85b0a-e18e-11e6-a547-5fb9411d332c_story.html. Accessed 19 Aug. 2017.

Always Happy Hour

Author: Mary U. Miller (ca. 1977)
Publisher: Liveright/Norton (New York). 256 pp.
Type of work: Short fiction
Time: Present day
Locale: The American South

Courtesy of W.W. Norton

This is a collection of sixteen stories, previously published in literary magazines, focusing on young women living in an uneasy limbo of loveless relationships while yearning for order and normality.

Joyce Carol Oates describes Mary Miller's characters as "affably directionless young women" who are world-weary, estranged from society, and "preoccupied with their own small, vacuous lives." In an interview, Miller has said her characters are rebelling against a previous generation when women were expected to be teachers, nurses, and secretaries, and then stay-at-home moms making homes for their families. But the recurring conflict in this collection of sixteen stories is that while most of the central characters seem to reject social stability in their actions, Miller shows them yearning for what they imagine is a "normal" life.

Many of the stories focus on the interior worlds of female narrators as they grapple with romance and the direction of their lives in their early adulthood. For example, in the opening story, "Instructions," a woman wakes up in her boyfriend's apartment to find some drawings he has left her, one of which is a headstone with the line: "Everything Was Beautiful and Nothing Hurt." The epitaph makes her think about people who have been hurt, and she wonders how so few words can be so meaningful when she does not believe in them. She worries that she offends people and yet expects them to love her for her inappropriateness When her boyfriend's cat knocks her razor off the edge of the bathtub and she cannot find the blade, she feels miserable because she imagines her boyfriend cannot trust her—she must be provided with clear instructions. She recalls a dream her boyfriend told her about being caught in a great storm and piranhas eating his arms as he tried to paddle ashore. On the phone, she reassures him that everything is fine, but in this story as in many of the others, there remains a constant atmospheric unease that seems to be primarily caused by characters who need instructions on how to live a happy life.

In "The House on Main Street," a graduate teaching assistant lives with her female roommate in southern Louisiana. She is divorced and miserable, and resentful of her roommate, who has loud sex, eats a lot of meat, and, in the protagonist's estimation, seems to look down on her for being racist and unsophisticated. When the protagonist

Courtesy of Lucky Tucker

Mary Miller is a professor of creative writing at Mississippi University for Women. Her first collection of short stories, Big World, was published in 2009. She has also published a novel, The Last Days of California (2014).

learns that a man she once dated has died, she thinks that for every man who commits suicide, there must be a dozen women who think that they were the only one with the power to save him, and they failed. She climbs out on the roof, thinking that if she crashed through, she would fall into the living room of a man who lives with his dead lover's son, making them come running to stand over her, "eager to see what new tragedy had befallen them"—a metaphor for the woman's sense that her only value is to fall disastrously into the lives of others.

In "Proper Order," a woman is working as a writer-in-residence at a university for a year. She is supposed to be working on her second novel, but is stalled, not knowing whether she wants to be a writer anymore, not sure why she is writing or if she has any talent. She has been divorced for eight years, and during that time she has felt that there is no "proper order" in her life. Every time she thinks she loves someone and they love her, something comes along and ruins it; her exes think that *she* is that something that destroys the relationship. She is sexually drawn to one of her students, but she knows he loves another student with whom he will do things in the "proper order." She wants to tell him not to make any mistakes, because once you start to do that, she feels, there comes a point at which you do not know how to do anything. Living in fear of making the wrong choice seems to be the state all the women characters in Miller's collection seem to suffer from.

In "Big Bad Love," a married woman works at a temporary shelter for abused and neglected children, and is especially attached to a seven-year-old child named Diamond, who keeps getting sent back from foster homes. She wants to take the child out of the place and find a nice little house in a nice little town, where she can forget about her husband, and where Diamond can forget about all the bad things that have happened to her. She wonders if Diamond will remember that someone loved her once or if she will have any memories of the protagonist at all. This is the one story in the collection when a woman looks outside of herself and really cares for another person; but the narrator in "Big Bad Love" is as helpless as many of Miller's other female characters to do anything about it.

Three of the stories in the collection focus on women who exist on the edge of decency and the law. The woman in "Uphill" lives in an RV with a man who is hired by a drug dealer to take a picture of a woman to identify her as a murderer. The main character in "Uphill" claims this is not her life or the life she is supposed to be living. However, she also knows that every day she lives this life it becomes the real one, while the one she imagines she is supposed to be living moves further from her reach, until eventually it will be gone forever. She thinks she is going to be involved in a murder and there is no voice to tell her that what she is doing is wrong. She looks at her face in a bathroom mirror and thinks if she could see her ugliness all her problems might be solved. She tries to be as unlikeable as possible, thinking that the perfect man will allow her to be as ugly as she wants. When her boyfriend takes the photo, she thinks that when she gets back to her apartment, she will not answer his calls; she will get a restraining order and will move away to another state where he will not find her. Yet, even as she tells herself this is not her life, she continues to cling to him.

"Dirty" is the story of a woman whose boyfriend makes videos of them having sex. The woman is unemployed, and her boyfriend pays her by taking her out to eat and providing a place to sleep for helping him clean the low-income rental units he owns. The only person the couple interacts with is a character called Coach, an alcoholic with a chronic cough. At the end of the story, the woman says the only way she and her boyfriend survive is by surrounding themselves with disabled people and drunks, "attaching our lives to the sad, impermanent lives of others." In "Hamilton Pool," another story of extreme dysfunction, a woman lives with her boyfriend who has been in prison where he was the leader of a gang. He tells her one day they will get married, have children, live in a little house on a quiet street, and have their own chickens. Like most of the protagonists in this collection, this character thinks there is plenty of time to make mistakes and begin again before "she has to figure out a different way of being in the world."

In "He Says I Am a Little Oven," a woman is on an ocean cruise with her boyfriend and his mother and father. She uses a vibrator and thinks it is better than having sex with her boyfriend, and observes that it is confusing the way thinking about a thing can be better than the thing itself. Her boyfriend tells her she is so warm that she is good in winter, like a little oven, but she wonders if he still loves her. At the end of the story, she stands at the front of the cruise ship and throws her arms out as she imagines the scene in the movie *Titanic*. He takes a picture of her, and she wonders how many people have posed in exactly the same way. For a moment, she likes the idea of being exactly like everyone else, and he takes a series of pictures of them together until they are "perfectly centered and happy, until he gets it exactly right."

"Where All of the Beautiful People Go" is one of the shortest stories in the collection, taking place in a single setting—a swimming pool owned by a woman named Aggie who has recently lost her mother, but not before taking out several credit cards in her mother's name and recklessly using them. Aggie has a son and the narrator imagines that if he were hers, she would give him a better life—wean him off sugared cereal, take him to an upscale grocery store so he could experience something grander than the circumstances his family provides. The narrator also yearns for something different. She wants a dog, but never follows through on adopting one. She thinks about the dogs she saw at the pound and recalls her favorite, who did not pull at the leash but stayed by her side and wagged his tail, "no doubt in his mind that all of his troubles were in the past, already forgotten."

In "Love Apples," the most elliptical and satirical story in the collection, an unhappily married woman meets a man in an internet chat room who sends her explicit photos and asks for her to send him a used article of her clothing. The woman has heard an anecdote about soldiers' wives presenting their men with apples before they go to war. The men will later eat the apples. The woman decides that sending her clothing to her chat-room boyfriend has an acceptable precedent. She decides to get a divorce and asks her parents to come and retrieve her and her possessions. Meanwhile, she fantasizes about being in San Francisco with her new boyfriend. She is riding on the handlebars of his bike, thin and beautiful, and excited about her new life, "even though there is nothing to be excited about," as far as she can tell, "at least not immediately."

In "The 37," perhaps a metaphor for of all the female characters in this collection, the central character has dropped out of a PhD program; broken up with her boyfriend; moved out of her house, leaving her roommate in a bind; and gone back to live with her mother. The narrator gets lost in the city and helplessly confused about how to get the Number 37 bus to get home. Meanwhile, she thinks longingly about learning to be more at ease in the city, adopting better health habits by becoming a vegetarian, and discovering more tips about how to better navigate her life. She thinks she will meet a young man who might become the love of her life, "like he would in a good story, in a story I couldn't write."

As this collection indicates, a "happily ever after" story is not the kind of story that Miller writes. Her narrators struggle with their circumstances, decisions, and discontent. While they yearn for positive change it seems unlikely and just out of reach. Still, Miller's women have specific visions of better lives and do not quite resign themselves fully to worlds of missed opportunities.

Charles E. May

Review Sources

McCrory, Charles Ramsey. "Ex Marks the Spot." Review of *Always Happy Hour*, by Mary Miller. *American Short Fiction*, 21 Feb. 2017, americanshortfiction. org/2017/02/21/ex-marks-spot-review-mary-millers-always-happy-hour/. Accessed 25 Oct. 2017.

Moss, Hilary. "Short Stories." Review of *Always Happy Hour*, by Mary Miller. *The New York Times*, 20 Jan. 2017, www.nytimes.com/2017/01/20/books/review/short-stories.html. Accessed 25 Oct. 2017.

Oates, Joyce Carol. "Postcards from the Edge." Review of *Always Happy Hour*, *The Last Days of California*, and *Big World*, by Mary Miller. *The New York Review of Books*, 20 Apr. 2017, www.nybooks.com/articles/2017/04/20/mary-miller-post-cards-from-the-edge/. Accessed 25 Oct. 2017.

Review of *Always Happy Hour*, by Mary Miller. *Booklist*, 1 Dec. 2016, www.book-listonline.com/Always-Happy-Hour-Mary-Miller/pid=8370085. Accessed 25 Oct. 2017.

Review of *Always Happy Hour*, by Mary Miller. *Kirkus*, 19 Sept. 2016, www.kirkus-reviews.com/book-reviews/mary-miller/always-happy-hour/. Accessed 25 Oct 2017.

American War

Author: Omar El Akkad (b. 1982)
Publisher: Alfred A. Knopf (New York).
352 pp.
Type of work: Novel
Time: Late twenty-first through early twenty-second centuries
Locale: United States

Omar El Akkad's debut novel, American War, *imagines a future in which the United States is embroiled in a bloody civil war over the use of fossil fuels.*

Principal characters

SARA T. CHESTNUT, a.k.a. Sarat Chestnut, the protagonist, a young girl who becomes a vigilante leader of the Free Southern State
DANA CHESTNUT, her twin sister
SIMON CHESTNUT, her older brother
BENJAMIN CHESTNUT, Simon's son, a historian and the book's narrator
MARTINA CHESTNUT, Sarat's mother

Omar El Akkad's debut novel, *American War*, is set in the late twenty-first and early twenty-second centuries. Told in retrospect—through memories and scraps of fictional newspaper articles, oral histories, and government documents—by a narrator who is an elderly historian and the nephew of the protagonist, it imagines the United States embroiled in a Second Civil War. The story begins in 2075, when the novel's protagonist, Sarah T. Chestnut, or Sarat, as she prefers to be called, is six years old. She lives with her parents; older brother, Simon; and twin sister, Dana, in a salvaged shipping container in St. James, Louisiana, on the banks of the Mississippi River. Louisiana, its coastlines flooded by rising seas, is neutral territory wedged between the Mexican Protectorate (which swallows West Texas and most of the American Southwest) and the secessionist Free Southern State, or the Mag, which includes Mississippi, Alabama, and Georgia.

A combination of factors led to this geographical configuration. As the effects of climate change altered the face of the country, the US government imposed a ban on fossil fuels. The ban threw the country into turmoil. President Daniel Ki was assassinated by a suicide bomber in 2073 and the proud South—the Mag, with the sympathies of the surrounding states—seceded in 2074, which is approximately when El Akkad's story begins.

Despite these new circumstances, Sarat and her siblings recall their makeshift early existence as a happy one spent swimming in the river in the sweltering summer season, which lasts from March to mid-December. One day, the children's father journeys up North to find work and is killed by a suicide bomber. The event is a harbinger of things to come. As the war progresses in later years, its southern participants are largely insurrectionists and guerilla warriors supported by China and the Bouazizi Empire, a nation made up of smaller states across the Middle East and North Africa. Solar-powered drones called Birds patrol the Southern skies, unleashing death and destruction at random. An attack from one of these Birds forces Sarat's mother, Martina, to leave St. James with her children for a refugee camp called Camp Patience near the Tennessee border.

Omar El Akkad is an award-winning Egyptian Canadian journalist. A former staff reporter for The Globe and Mail, American War *is his first novel.*

In the refugee camp, Sarat comes of age. She is an awkward girl, over six feet tall, with a penchant for reckless behavior. This combination of traits brings her to the attention of a man named Albert Gaines. Gaines is a shadowy figure, offering Sarat real honey (as opposed to slimy apricot gel rations) in exchange for running messages to the various corners of the camp. He shows her books and teaches her about history, but he has a larger vision for his protégé. He is carefully grooming Sarat as a human weapon of war, an intent made more clear after a terrible massacre kills Martina and almost kills Simon. The rest of the book traces Sarat's emotional journey from resistance leader to prisoner of war.

American War is Omar El Akkad's first novel. He was born in Cairo, Egypt, and grew up in Doha, Qatar. He later moved to Canada and joined the staff of the *Globe and Mail*, covering the war in Afghanistan, the military trials in Guantanamo Bay, the Arab Spring uprising in Egypt, and the Black Lives Matter movement in Ferguson, Missouri. In interviews, El Akkad has said that real events inspired him to write *American War*. He said that in writing the novel, he sought to portray the emotional fallout of war and how suffering can inspire brutal acts of revenge. The novel includes drone strikes, suicide bombers, and torture, but also the hellish existence of a refugee camp and the pretensions of more powerful countries. It explores the mythology of war long after fossil fuels are no longer economically viable (the entire world in the novel is powered by alternate sources of energy). The people of the South weave their grievances into a kind of protective blanket as they continue to champion their resistance to the Sustainable Future Act, which prohibits the use of fossil fuel. There are no clearly defined agents of good and evil in *American War*, and El Akkad does not ask for sympathy for his characters.

American War has a place in the larger literary canon of dystopian novels. *New York Times* book critic Michiko Kakutani favorably compared it to Cormac McCarthy's *The Road* (2006), a Pulitzer Prize–winning vision of a postapocalyptic America, and Philip Roth's historical revisionist novel *The Plot Against America* (2004). She also compared it to more recent young-adult series such as the Hunger Games (2008–10) and Divergent (2011–13), in which a young female protagonist, shaped by a cruel world, must "prove herself as a warrior," as Kakutani put it. These comparisons are apt but do not fully capture the unique (if only intermittently successful) tone of El Akkad's novel.

American War is a parable about American hubris. It is a thought experiment centered around what might happen if American fighting abroad came home. The newspaper clippings and other ephemera scattered between chapters feel alarmingly real. Unsurprisingly, given his journalistic background, El Akkad's vision of a war-torn country is one of the book's most successful features. *American War* is peppered with seemingly authentic narrative details—like the hand-me-down T-shirts that arrive by the boatload from the Bouazizi Empire and the Texas-centric imagery of the Southern resistance. However, the book is even more thought-provoking when it comes to the complexity of what a civil war in the modern United States would look like, with a retaliatory escalation followed by a stagnation that gives way to a protracted guerilla war. In El Akkad's vision, a Southern terrorist unleashes a terrible plague on the country after the end of the war in 2095. According to the book's narrator, at that point in the narrative, eleven million died in the war, but more than one hundred million died in the plague.

Outwardly, El Akkad's vision is strikingly realistic, but elements of his future give rise to distracting questions. For one thing, there is a curious lack of technology in the world he has created. The words *computer* and *internet* do not appear in the book at all. El Akkad's world is extrapolated from the partisan politics of the mid-2010s, but there is no engagement with the content of these ideological differences outside of a very narrow clash related to climate change. Fossil fuels are no longer profitable, but the South structures a mythology around the worthless product to further the war. In reality, the American South already has a mythology, largely shaped by the actual American Civil War, but El Akkad structures his story based on conflicts elsewhere in the world, where grievances are shaped over hundreds and sometimes thousands of years. This approach begs the question of whether the inhabitants of the South in 2075 have any understanding of slavery in relation to the American Civil War.

Such nagging details hinder the enjoyment of a book that is otherwise a very good rendering of the mental and emotional costs of war. Sarat, a smart and curious child, is slowly broken over time. She hardens after the Camp Patience massacre when her mother dies, but Sugarloaf, where she is held as a prisoner of war, robs her of her humanity. Both experiences inspire her to commit terrible acts of revenge, which, as El Akkad suggests, is the engine that powers most conflicts. Worse, Sarat is trapped in this painful mechanism. For her, there is no true escape from the pain of the war. In one early scene, Sarat, then a young teenager, and her friend Marcus discuss the relative safety of the North. If Sarat had the opportunity to go North, Marcus asks if

Sarat would go. The question gives her pause. "It seemed sensible to crave safety, to crave shelter from the bombs and the Birds and the daily depravity of war," she thinks. "But somewhere deep in her mind an idea had begun to fester—perhaps the longing for safety was itself just another kind of violence—a violence of cowardice, silence, submission. What was safety, anyway, but the sound of a bomb falling on someone else's home?"

American War received generally positive reviews when it was published in early 2017. Kakutani wrote that it was "surprisingly powerful," though she conceded that it contained "considerable flaws." She took issue with El Akkad's melodramatic plot and dialogue. Ron Charles, reviewing the book for the *Washington Post*, focused on the transformation of Sarat and the "cycles of vengeance" so carefully depicted by El Akkad. Anthony Cummins, reviewing the book for the *Guardian*, was less impressed; in that critic's view, *American War* was too "schoolmasterly" to be enjoyable, likely referring to the density of expository information revealed through the newspaper clippings woven into the narrative. Overall, the book elicited a wide range of opinion and is worth an exploration on the part of the curious reader, particularly a reader who is a fan of the dystopian genre.

Molly Hagan

Review Sources

Review of *American War*, by Omar El Akkad. *Kirkus Reviews*, 23 Jan. 2017, p. 1.

Review of *American War*, by Omar El Akkad. *Publishers Weekly*, 20 Feb. 2017, p. 56.

Charles, Ron. "*American War* Follows Today's Vitriol to a Dystopian Future." Review of *American War*, by Omar El Akkad. *The Washington Post*, 3 Apr. 2017, www.washingtonpost.com/entertainment/books/american-war-follows-todays-vitriol-to-a-dystopian-future/2017/04/03/79ac6952-186d-11e7-bcc2-7d1a0973e7b2_story.html. Accessed 3 Oct. 2017.

Cummins, Anthony. Review of *American War*, by Omar El Akkad. *The Guardian*, 10 Sept. 2017, www.theguardian.com/books/2017/sep/10/american-war-omar-el-akkad-review. Accessed 3 Oct. 2017.

Kakutani, Michiko. "A Haunting Debut Looks Ahead to a Second American Civil War." Review of *American War*, by Omar El Akkad. *The New York Times*, 27 Mar. 2017, www.nytimes.com/2017/03/27/books/review-american-war-omar-el-akkad.html. Accessed 3 Oct. 2017.

An American Sickness
How Healthcare Became Big Business and How You Can Take It Back

Author: Elisabeth Rosenthal (b. 1956)
Publisher: Penguin Press (New York). 416 pp.
Type of work: Current affairs, medicine
Time: Twentieth and twenty-first centuries
Locale: United States

An American Sickness, the first book by Dr. Elisabeth Rosenthal, examines the short-comings of the modern American health-care system and provides readers a guide for navigating those shortcomings.

Courtesy of Penguin Press

Few people are as qualified as Elisabeth Rosenthal to write about the American health-care system. A physician who graduated from Harvard Medical School in 1986, Rosenthal quit practicing medicine in 1994 to begin covering the health and hospital beat for the *New York Times*. In the years that followed, she worked around the world as a medical journalist and consultant, eventually focusing exclusively on the Affordable Care Act (ACA), or "Obamacare."

It is this well-curated expertise that makes Rosenthal's debut book, *An American Sickness: How Healthcare Became Big Business and How You Can Take It Back*, so compelling. An in-depth look at all the moving parts that make up the US health-care system, *An American Sickness* chronicles the historical events and forces that led to today's age of industrialized medicine. The book's central argument is that health care has become a money-making industry rather than a wellness one. In other words, the priority of medical professionals is no longer to provide patients with the treatment and cures necessary to improve their quality of life, but rather to maximize revenue for hospitals, doctors, and pharmaceutical companies. For Rosenthal, this is unacceptable. In order for the nation's health to improve, she argues, there must be a return to affordable, evidence-based care that puts patients, not profit, first.

In its criticism of the existing health-care industry, *An American Sickness* feels both radical and galvanizing. Rosenthal describes what is wrong with modern American health care in a straightforward and unapologetic style. To this end, between the book's introduction and its first chapter, she provides readers with a list of ten corrupt tenets, labeled "Economic Rules of the Dysfunctional Medical Market," that the existing system operates on as a kind of guide. In addition to providing a wake-up call for readers, this list functions as a succinct outline of the topics explored in later chapters. For example, the first rule states, "More treatment is always better. Default to the most expensive option." Throughout *An American Sickness*, Rosenthal cites these rules in bolded parenthetical statements when she describes scenarios in which they apply, such as (for rule 1) when a patient finds themselves undergoing unnecessary surgeries or is hit with excessive charges. The frequency at which such rules as "a lifetime of treatment is preferable to a cure" (rule 2) recur throughout the book's text is alarming.

Rosenthal uses true patient stories to illustrate the dysfunctional way in which the American health-care system operates. These stories prove to be a powerful tool, one that allows readers to connect emotionally with the topic at hand. It is near impossible to read innumerable accounts of poor, sick people being victimized by their health-care providers without feeling empathy or concern. The effectiveness with which Rosenthal leverages these stories to make her point is especially evident in the story of fifty-year-old widow Wanda Wickizer, who underwent brain surgery after a sudden subarachnoid brain hemorrhage. Although she was fortunate enough to survive, her luck soon took a turn for the worse. Just a few months into her recovery, Wickizer received numerous medical bills totaling nearly $500,000. When she told the University of Virginia Health System that she could not afford to pay but they could take the entire $100,000 in her retirement fund, they refused her offer, suggesting instead that either she agree to pay $5,000 per month—far more than she could conceivably afford—or the hospital could put a lien on her house. Wickizer, who was still cognitively impaired due to the hemorrhage and surgery, had to seek help from pro bono lawyers and billing specialists. After combing through her bill, the specialists found over $80,000 in errors. Ostensibly, Rosenthal references the story of Wickizer to demonstrate how dangerous it is that the United States does not regulate and set medical costs, but rather allows hospitals to charge patients whatever they want. It is also a criticism of the American medical billing code system, which is so complex and convoluted that it is near impossible for the average person to tell whether they are being overcharged. Beyond that, however, Rosenthal cites this case because it is deeply unjust and upsetting; no readers are likely to believe that a widow suffering from brain damage should have to pay half a million dollars to a hospital when the actual costs of her medical expenses were a mere fraction of that amount.

To prevent the book's dozens of patient stories from becoming overwhelming, Rosenthal doles them out strategically across the chapters. *An American Sickness* is divided into two sections, a structure that proves to be effective at facilitating narrative flow while also maximizing comprehension. The first section of breaks downs the major entities within the health-care industry and the ways that they have evolved over the past century or so to become the profit-driven entities they are today. Each chapter in this section focuses on an individual entity, among them insurance companies, hospitals, physicians, pharmaceutical companies, billing contractors, and ultimately, the ACA. Rosenthal works hard to ensure that readers have a clear understanding of each component and how they function together to form a greedy, corrupt ecosystem.

As the American health-care system is highly complex, it would be easy for any writing on the subject to be dull to readers from nonmedical backgrounds, but Rosenthal excels at discussing these issues in a way that is both clear and engaging. Her comprehensible writing can be attributed in part to her firsthand experience the medical-industrial complex as a doctor and an intimate understanding of how it harms patients.

© Nina Subin

A former emergency room physician, Elisabeth Rosenthal is the editor in chief of the Henry J. Kaiser Family Foundation. An American Sickness is her first book.

Furthermore, Rosenthal's years as a medical journalist have made her a deft writer. With a careful, evenhanded tone, she presents the facts to readers in straightforward language so that everyone can understand how their own lives and bank accounts are on the line.

Rosenthal's purpose in *An American Sickness* is to reveal that what hospitals, doctors, and pharmaceutical companies can get away with. She never employs hyperbole; the truth is harrowing enough to need no exaggeration. At one point, she describes an incident in which a woman went to the emergency room with a severe headache; upon performing a brain scan, the hospital discovered a tumor and insisted that she immediately have an emergency surgery to remove it, despite the fact that the on-call surgeon, who was an out-of-network subcontractor, had almost no experience with brain tumors. The surgeon "opened her skull, meddled with her brain, and stapled her skull flap back, leaving most of the tumor intact," according to the woman's mother—and yet the woman still received a bill for $97,000 for an "emergency" procedure that failed to achieve its sole objective. Elsewhere in the book, Rosenthal discusses how hospitals, which typically qualify as nonprofit institutions, have become big businesses that act more like luxury hotels than places of public service. She illustrates this point with the case of Providence Health & Services, a multihospital health-care system in the Pacific Northwest that began as a Catholic charity in the 1850s; in 2013, Providence earned $2.6 billion in revenue and owned about $2 billion in assets, and its chief executive officer receives an annual salary of around $3.5 million—all while retaining its status as a nonprofit institution. By relaying these incidents matter-of-factly, Rosenthal ensures that she cannot be accused by her critics of exaggerating or manipulating emotions to support her agenda for a new health-care system.

While the first section of *An American Sickness* provides readers with an in-depth explanation of how the American health-care system arrived at its current state, the second section aims to offer potential solutions. Although it maintains a similar tone to that of the first section, it arguably feels more optimistic. This is because Rosenthal posits that the American people truly have the power to take back their health care— they simply must resist complacency and begin demanding change. She counters the popular belief that the existing US health-care system is best suited for the country's economy and population size by providing examples of successful alternatives from around the world. The United States, she claims, could adopt the fee schedule system of Germany, which is similar to the existing (and successful) Medicare program; all it would require is for the government to start setting the prices of medicine and services rather than allowing businesses to make up their own. Additionally, this section offers practical advice to readers for navigating the current system and avoiding exorbitant bills. Rosenthal suggests that readers begin by preemptively researching and selecting fair doctors and hospitals before they get sick. Furthermore, she recommends that patients exercise their rights by refusing unnecessary treatment and medical equipment as well as negotiating outrageous hospital bills, as even clerks are allowed to approve discounts. *An American Sickness* begins as a shocking in-depth exposé on everything that is wrong in American health care today and ends as a guide to becoming an empowered patient.

Reviews for *An American Sickness* have been mixed. Positive reviews have extolled Rosenthal for writing such a thorough guide to a problem that affects hundreds of millions of Americans. In her review for the *Washington Post*, Juliet Eilperin wrote that the book is "an authoritative account of the distorted financial incentives that drive medical care in the United States." While examining each component of the health-care system, Rosenthal truly leaves no stone unturned—investigating every institution that affects patient costs, from the American Medical Association to the Food and Drug Administration and the pharmaceutical industry. Other critics have argued that the book does not provide enough insight as to why the American health-care system continues to operate as a profit-driven industry. Reviewer Jacob S. Hacker wrote for the *New York Times*, "Where Rosenthal's account falls short is in explaining why this deeply broken system persists," while the reviewer for *Kirkus Reviews* argued that *An American Sickness* is "a scathing denouncement, stronger in portraying the system's problems than in offering pragmatic solutions." It is true that the first section of the book is better researched and argued than the second section, and for many readers, the suggestion of introducing a single-payer system in the United States may seem a stale, uninspired, or unviable solution. Still, it is important to note that, as Rosenthal has stated in interviews, her primary purpose in writing about American health care has always been to start a dialogue. When viewed from this angle, her book is an undeniable success. *An American Sickness* is truly compelling and will likely inspire its readers to start demanding changes in how are treated as patients.

Emily Turner

Review Sources

Review of *An American Sickness: How Healthcare Became Big Business and How You Can Take It Back*, by Elisabeth Rosenthal. *Kirkus Reviews*, 13 Feb. 2017, www.kirkusreviews.com/book-reviews/elisabeth-rosenthal/an-american-sickness. Accessed 25 Jan. 2018.

Review of *An American Sickness: How Healthcare Became Big Business and How You Can Take It Back*, by Elisabeth Rosenthal. *Publishers Weekly*, 6 Feb. 2017, www.publishersweekly.com/978-1-59420-675-7. Accessed 25 Jan. 2018.

Hacker, Jacob S. "Why an Open Market Won't Repair American Health Care." Review of *An American Sickness: How Healthcare Became Big Business and How*

You Can Take It Back, by Elisabeth Rosenthal. *The New York Times*, 4 Apr. 2017, www.nytimes.com/2017/04/04/books/review/an-american-sickness-elisabeth-rosenthal.html. Accessed 25 Jan. 2018.

Eilperin, Juliet. "Gruesome Tales from a Dysfunctional Health Care System." Review of *An American Sickness: How Healthcare Became Big Business and How You Can Take It Back*, by Elisabeth Rosenthal. *The Washington Post*, 19 May 2017, www.washingtonpost.com/opinions/gruesome-tales-from-a-dysfunctional-health-care-system/2017/05/19/589e7f92-1fb2-11e7-ad74-3a742a6e93a7_story.html. Accessed 25 Jan. 2018.

Winter, Roberta E. Review of *An American Sickness: How Healthcare Became Big Business and How You Can Take It Back*, by Elisabeth Rosenthal. *New York Journal of Books*, 10 Apr. 2017, www.nyjournalofbooks.com/book-review/sickness. Accessed 25 Jan. 2018.

An Extraordinary Union

Author: Alyssa Cole
Publisher: Kensington Books (New York).
  258 pp.
Type of work: Novel
Time: 1861–62
Locale: Richmond, Virginia

An Extraordinary Union *is a historical romance set during the American Civil War. Protagonist Ellen Burns is a Union spy with a perfect memory. She poses as a slave in Virginia to acquire sensitive military information, but a romance with a white man threatens to upend her mission.*

Courtesy of Kensington Books

Principal characters
ELLEN "ELLE" BURNS, a freedwoman and
    Union spy
MALCOLM McCALL, Scottish Pinkerton detective
SUSIE CAFFREY, daughter of a Confederate senator

Alyssa Cole's Civil War–era romance *An Extraordinary Union* is the first novel in her Loyal League series, about Union spies. The protagonist, Ellen "Elle" Burns, was born into slavery, but freed, along with her parents, when she was a child. She grew up in the North, where she became an object of curiosity for abolitionists. Elle has an eidetic memory, an ability that allows her to memorize reams of complex information, accurately store it away, and recall it at will. As a child, she was shunted from meeting to meeting, required to recite long tracts from Sir Walter Scott and Shakespeare, to convince skeptical white people of African Americans' capacity for knowledge. The dehumanizing experience scarred Elle, and made her ashamed of her abilities, but after the outbreak of war, she decides to use her unique power to bring down the Confederacy as a Union spy as a member of a secret society called the Loyal League.

Elle's assignment in *An Extraordinary Union* is a difficult and dangerous one. She must infiltrate the Richmond, Virginia, house of a secessionist senator, posing as a hired-out, mute slave. It is humiliating and exhausting work, waiting hand and foot on the senator's cruel and spoiled daughter, Susie Caffrey, but Elle swallows her pride for the good of the Union. Her operation is running smoothly enough—with an assist from the house cook and the local grocer, who are also spies—when an ill-timed romance threatens to usurp her focus. Malcolm McCall is handsome, charming, and kind. He is a Pinkerton detective spying for the Union, but he is also a white man. Elle must wrestle with her feelings for Malcolm, her duty to her country, and the seeming impossibility of a world in which interracial love can thrive, unthreatened.

Cole is an award-winning historical romance and science-fiction writer who is best known for her historical novels, including *Let It Shine* (2015), an interracial love story set during the civil rights movement in the 1960s; *Let Us Dream* (2017), about a cabaret owner in 1917 Harlem; *Be Not Afraid* (2016), a novella about two enslaved African Americans vying for their freedom during the American Revolutionary War; and *Agnes Moor's Wild Knight* (2014), a novella about a black woman in the court of James IV in fifteenth-century Scotland. Cole is also known for *Mixed Signals* (2015), the third book in her critically acclaimed futurist-romance series, Off the Grid.

Cole's historical interests run the gamut of time and place. *An Extraordinary Union* combines her predominant focus on American history (and African Americans' struggles to reconcile their love for the country with slavery and oppression) and elements of Scottish history. Malcolm, Elle's love interest, is a Scottish immigrant, scarred by the horrors of the Highland Clearances of the mid-eighteenth to mid-nineteenth century, in which English aristocrats forced Scots from their homes to take their land. The Clearances were brutally violent; Malcolm still struggles with the memory of his mother's gang rape at the hands of their oppressors. This horrible episode changes the family's life forever, driving Malcolm's father to drink and eventually kill himself out of guilt and shame at his inability to protect his wife. Malcolm is scarred by the memory of his father's death as well. He promises himself that he will not fall in love so that he may be spared the pain that loves inevitably brings. This hard-heartedness makes McCall an excellent spy, adept at lying to women to gain information for the Cause, without a care as to the feelings he might be hurting in the process. Malcolm, through a combination of careful attention and charm, also has the uncanny ability to make people trust him—an ability that, naturally, gives Elle pause.

Cole's novel is both a romance and a spy thriller. The escalation of Elle and Malcolm's relationship comes in tandem with the growing urgency of their mission. Richmond, along with the rest of the Confederacy, is suffering under the Union blockade. Food and other necessary supplies are scarce, though it is hard to tell from the way Susie and her family live. As the poor starve, the rich throw lavish parties. Still, the secessionists are eager to break the blockade and Elle and Malcolm uncover clues suggesting that a plan to do so is in the works. This story line, and Elle and Malcolm's attempts to relay information to foil the plot to their superiors up north, becomes more urgent as the novel progresses, but the primary story here is the romance between Elle and Malcolm and the difficulty of maintaining their disguises as their love for each other grows. Elle's task is straightforward: she gathers information from the Caffreys as a member of their enslaved household staff. Malcolm's mission is more delicate. Posing as a Confederate soldier, he ingratiates himself with the Richmond elite. He plans to woo Susie to gain access to her father. His task is seriously complicated by his love for Elle, whom he must watch Susie abuse and dismiss. The queasy irony of these scenes drives home the crushing difficulty of the road ahead of Elle and Malcolm, should they and their love survive the war.

Though Elle and Malcolm both have histories of being oppressed, Elle must live her oppression as a black woman every day, whether she is disguised as a slave or living as a freedwoman. She is constantly underestimated, dismissed, and misunderstood, both by lecherous slave masters and well-meaning abolitionists. Her return to slavery dredges up complicated and contradictory emotions: horror, sympathy, fear, and shame. She is aware of her relative privilege as an interloper, but constant abuse contorts her feelings for Malcolm, making her wonder how she could possibly love someone who looks so much like her enemy, and how she can lie to the enslaved women who care about her at the house. Cole explores Elle's fractured emotional life with nuance. Her indecision about Malcolm feels real and rooted in anger and pain. Unfortunately, Malcolm's motivations are less clearly drawn. He falls in love with Elle the moment he sees her. His insta-love, a popular literary trope in romance fiction, short-circuits any tension that might arise from a relationship that grows over time.

Courtesy of Katana Photography

Alyssa Cole is an award-winning science-fiction, historical, and contemporary romance novelist. A Hope Divided, *the second in her* Loyal League *series, was published in November 2017.*

Elle's personal reservations aside, their union happens with relative speed and ease, aided by Malcolm's frustrating ability to always say the right thing. He seems to implicitly understand Elle's complex emotions, and her determination to begin their relationship on equal footing. This is admirable, but narratively questionable. Real romantic relationships, particularly heterosexual interracial ones, require partners to grapple with the realization that they can only know, to a certain point, what it is like to be their partner. Even this understanding requires patience, work, and time. Malcolm may be kind, and to use a contemporary phrase, relatively aware of his privilege in comparison to other white people of the time, but he cannot possibly truly know what is it like to be a black woman, especially one who is treated as a slave. Suggesting that he does undercuts Elle's complexity, and ultimately, prevents Malcolm from becoming a fully formed character. He often appears as a fantasy of a man rather than a complicated and flawed human being.

In consummating their relationship, Malcolm and Elle commit themselves to a partnership, and the novel becomes an adventure pitting them against the Confederacy. Obstacles to their love come in the form of villainous slavers, Southern belles, and Confederate spies—not Elle's own emotions. Cole packs a lot of plot into the last stretch of her short novel, a decision that did not sit well with some reviewers. Critics writing for the website *All About Romance* felt that the last third of the book became melodramatic, with Elle and Malcolm miraculously escaping peril in increasingly dubious ways. Reviewers for *Publishers Weekly* and *Kirkus*, however, were more enthusiastic about the book. "Cole's sparkling gem of a romance portrays love at its most practical and sublime; she writes with lyricism, intelligence, and historical accuracy," a *Publishers Weekly* reviewer wrote in a starred review. *An Extraordinary Union* is an imperfect novel, but is at its best when it is focused on Elle. For Elle, each moment is freighted with impossibly high stakes. Each choice, from her decision to glare at her "mistress," Susie, to her decision to kill a man in self-defense, brings with it the possibility of a terrible reckoning. How she makes these decisions and why makes for a gripping read.

Molly Hagan

Review Sources

Dyer, Shannon, and Em Wittmann. "Pandora's Box." Review of *An Extraordinary Union*, by Alyssa Cole. *All About Romance*, allaboutromance.com/book-review/an-extraordinary-union-by-alyssa-cole/. Accessed 9 Dec. 2017.

Review of *An Extraordinary Union*, by Alyssa Cole. *Kirkus Reviews*, 1 Feb. 2017, p.1. *Academic Search Complete*, search.ebscohost.com/login.aspx?direct=true&db=a9h&AN=121021905&site=eds-live. Accessed 9 Dec. 2017.

Review of *An Extraordinary Union*, by Alyssa Cole. *Publishers Weekly*, 20 Feb. 2017, p. 73. *Business Source Complete*, search.ebscohost.com/login.aspx?direct=true&db=bth&AN=121341402&site=eds-live. Accessed 9 Dec. 2017.

Ramsdell, Kristin. Review of *An Extraordinary Union*, by Alyssa Cole. *Library Journal*, 15 Apr. 2017, p. 67. *Education Resource Complete*, search.ebscohost.com/login.aspx?direct=true&db=ehh&AN=122467623&site=eds-live. Accessed 14 Dec. 2017.

Stec, Kristin. Review of *An Extraordinary Union*, by Alyssa Cole. *RT Book Reviews*, 28 Mar. 2017, www.rtbookreviews.com/book-review/extraordinary-union. Accessed 9 Dec. 2017.

Anatomy of Terror
From the Death of Bin Laden to the Rise of the Islamic State

Author: Ali Soufan (b. 1971)
Publisher: W. W. Norton (New York). 384 pp.
Type of work: Current affairs, history, psychology
Time: Primarily 2011–present, with context from mid-twentieth century
Locales: The Middle East, Africa

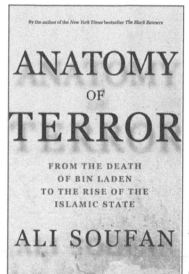

Ali Soufan offers an overview of Islamic terrorism, focusing on how the death of Osama bin Laden led to the splintering of his al-Qaeda organization and the rise of newer groups such as the Islamic State of Iraq and Syria (ISIS). While the book suggests this cycle of terrorism will continue, it provides valuable insight into the people and processes involved.

Principal personages
OSAMA BIN LADEN, founder of the al-Qaeda militant group
SAIF AL-ADEL, one of his top lieutenants
AYMAN AL-ZAWAHIRI, his successor as leader of al-Qaeda
ABU MUSAB AL-ZARQAWI, Jordanian jihadist aligned with al-Qaeda and founder of what would become the Islamic State of Iraq and Syria (ISIS)
ABU BAKR AL-BAGHDADI, leader of ISIS

Anyone seeking a clear, solid history of twenty-first century terrorism in the Middle East could hardly do better than to read the work of Ali Soufan. An expert consultant on terrorism and counterterrorism and a former FBI agent, he has advised on government policy, contributed to think tank panels and forums, and written for or been interviewed by numerous news outlets. His award-winning, best-selling first book, *The Black Banners: The Inside Story of 9/11 and the War against al Qaeda* (2011), earned praise for its insight into terror and counterterror efforts up to the killing of infamous terrorist leader Osama bin Laden. Now, with *Anatomy of Terror: From the Death of Bin Laden to the Rise of the Islamic State*, Soufan continues his analysis of the driving currents underlying Islamic terrorism.

In patient detail and clear phrasing, Soufan introduces readers to the key events, personalities, and issues that have stoked the rise of anti-Western (and especially anti-American) violence in the Middle East, Africa, and elsewhere—including the West itself. The book duly points out that the most numerous victims of Islamic terrorism

Courtesy of Laura Cutri

Ali Soufan, born in Lebanon, is a former FBI agent and leading expert on terrorism and counterterrorism. His book The Black Banners: The Inside Story of 9/11 and the War against al-Qaeda *(2011) won the 2012 Ridenhour Book Prize. He has contributed to many leading news outlets worldwide.*

have been always Middle Easterners themselves, but also addresses the concerns that most readers will have regarding attacks against Western targets. Striking a quite dire tone, Soufan acknowledges that such attacks have become more common since Bin Laden's death, and that an event as or more destructive than the September 11, 2001, terrorist attacks is an ongoing possibility. More importantly, he helps explain how things got to this point.

Soufan emphasizes the importance of specific personalities in creating the current threat. Broad religious views and ideological conflicts have of course played their parts, he suggests, but many acts of terrorism both before and after September 11 have been determined as much by who was in charge as by the existence of any specific groups. One of the book's main themes is how al-Qaeda splintered and lost influence following Bin Laden's death, but the rise of the Islamic State of Iraq and Syria (ISIS, also known as ISIL or IS) led to different forms and strategies of terror. And with ISIS seemingly on the verge of defeat (or at least temporary suppression) in Syria and Iraq as of the book's publication, Soufan predicts that new threats will arise with new leadership. *Anatomy of Terror* makes it clear that Islamic terrorism is a deeply engrained phenomenon that will not evaporate with the killing of any one figurehead or the defeat of one group. While Bin Laden himself is gone, "Bin Ladenism" remains a powerful force.

In setting the scene for the post–Bin Laden era of terrorism, Soufan patiently recounts the rise of al-Qaeda. While some readers may be familiar with this already heavily analyzed narrative, it is crucial in understanding what comes later. The story of Bin Laden's transition from early "freedom fighter" in Afghanistan to anti-American icon is carefully and clearly linked to the rise of ISIS. And Soufan further suggests that as the fortunes of ISIS fall, al-Qaeda is likely to experience a resurgence, making it all the more important to understand the group's history as fully as possible. The viciously cyclical nature of terrorist groups is emphasized: deaths of particular leaders often lead to leaders who are even worse; suppressions of violence in one form often lead to violence of even more massive and sickening proportions. While some counterterrorism operations seem successful, many worsen the problem or just push it into a new form.

Many readers will be especially interested in what Soufan has to say about the rapid spread of ISIS beginning around 2013—another subject already covered by many other works—thanks to his background in counterterrorism and direct experience interrogating terrorists. While ISIS's rise has often been blamed mainly on the power vacuum left by the withdrawal of US troops from Iraq during the presidency of Barack Obama, Soufan makes it clear that the roots of the group's success stretch to the initial US invasion of Iraq as well as mismanagement thereafter. In particular, he suggests that the decision to ban Ba'athists (members of Iraqi dictator Saddam Hussein's political party) from authority roles and breaking up the Iraqi Army sowed the seeds that grew into ISIS. Other mistakes were also made by the US and its allies, including the release from imprisonment of various terrorists who then went on to rejoin the fight. It is astonishing, in fact, to realize just how often these errors occurred.

Soufan presents such mistakes with the view that, as the struggle against terrorism inevitably continues, they should be studied and remembered in order to avoid similar errors. He also makes it clear that a better understanding of terrorists, and especially their leaders, is needed to have any hope of avoiding such mistakes. When Bin Laden was killed in 2011, many were optimistic that al-Qaeda would fall apart. But while the organization did change and fracture, it birthed offshoots such as ISIS that have swelled in size and in some cases proven even more brutal. What is important is Bin Laden's philosophy, which is more resilient than the man himself. While Bin Laden may have underestimated the US response to the September 11 attacks, he was in many ways correct that, as Soufan paraphrases, "A handful of militants might die, but they would perish as martyrs—the better to drum up fresh recruits seeking paths of glory." The thrust of *Anatomy of Terror* is that while a show of strength from the West can be successful to a degree, isolated military victories are not enough to stop the wheels of Bin Ladenism.

If understanding the enemy is the first and key step to victory, Soufan's firsthand experience in dealing with terrorists proves illuminating. He shows himself to be keenly aware of the psychology of not only terrorist leaders, but of the people drawn to them. The complex sociopolitical pressures that make terrorism viable are carefully considered, with an eye toward on-the-ground reality rather than theoretical speculation. Part of the value of Soufan's book results from its frank honesty—he does not expect idealistic Western concepts and values to transfer directly to Middle Eastern societies and end the problem of terrorism.

This is highlighted in discussion of the importance of the so-called Arab Spring, which many Westerners predicted would usher in a new era of liberal democracy in the Middle East. In contrast, Soufan writes knowingly that "the Arab world's tribal patriarchies, with zero history of liberalism, let alone participatory democracy, are simply not going to become Madisonian utopias any time soon." He further shows that Bin Laden and his successors understood this. Having seen such "democratic" movements rise and fall before, they fully expected that this new one would suffer the same fate.

Perhaps the most intriguing part of *Anatomy of Terror* is its final chapter. Here Soufan predicts the future of the Middle East and the impact it will have on the rest of the world. He especially foresees renewed power for al-Qaeda as the power of ISIS weakens. He expects that fighting among Muslims will be just as common as attacks by Islamic terrorists on the West. As he puts it (and as each day's headlines confirm), "Sunnis fight Shia, Persians battle Arabs, Turks struggle with Kurds, and on down to the tribal, communal, and even neighborhood level." Soufan shows that there are all sorts of "Islamic terrorists," with at least one group for each major division within Islam. Once again, he suggests that military responses to such complexities are not enough, even if insufficient military strength is also a problem.

Soufan does propose some nonmilitary solutions to the issue of terrorism, all rooted in the type of psychological and structural understanding of the enemy that he continually presents. While some readers may disagree with these solutions to varying degrees, the body of evidence throughout the book provides a compelling argument that he should be heard out. He suggests, for instance, the value of nation-building efforts, such as promoting education and reconstruction. Likewise, Soufan mentions various efforts to change the minds of young potential terrorists, remarking that such "programs may or may not achieve results right away, but at the very least they represent a step in the right direction." More detailed evidence of the results and achievements of such programs would have strengthened his argument, but in the absence of data Soufan's suggestions appear largely convincing.

Still, the suggestions of better strategies for combating terrorism cannot shake the ominous tone of *Anatomy of Terror*. Soufan urges immediate action, leaving readers with this warning:

> Someday, probably sooner rather than later, the fighting in Syria will end, and when that happens, some twelve thousand foreign fighters, their combat skills honed in the ranks of the Islamic State, al-Nusra, Ahrar al-Sham, and any number of other militant groups, will begin pouring out of the Levant. Some will simply move on to whatever they regard as the next Syria, be it Libya, Yemen, or elsewhere; but many will return home, some of them planning to bring the fight with them, others brutalized and traumatized by the death and maiming and disease and anarchy they have witnessed.

Only by working to end the dehumanizing process that has put these soldiers in this situation can anyone hope to break the cycle of violence. While this presents a massive challenge, it is one worth taking up. Soufan demonstrates that despite his grimly realistic, even jaded, knowledge of terrorism built on firsthand experience with terrorists, he retains faith in humanity.

The critical response to *Anatomy of Terror* was overwhelmingly positive. Reviewers praised Soufan's deep expertise, with many especially appreciating how he draws on his FBI experience to add new depth to the stories of the rise of al-Qaeda and ISIS. Others noted the strength of the prose itself, which guides the reader through an often tangled—and devastatingly brutal—narrative. As the reviewer for Kirkus stated, "In a dizzying scenario of violence, Soufan provides clarity and balance."

Robert C. Evans, PhD

Review Sources

Review of *Anatomy of Terror: From the Death of Bin Laden to the Rise of the Islamic State of Iraq and Syria*, by Ali Soufan. *Kirkus Reviews*, 7 Mar. 2017, www.kirkusreviews.com/book-reviews/ali-h-soufan/anatomy-terror/. Accessed 29 Jan. 2018.

Review of *Anatomy of Terror: From the Death of Bin Laden to the Rise of the Islamic State of Iraq and Syria*, by Ali Soufan. *Publishers Weekly*, May 2017, www.publishersweekly.com/978-0-393-24117-4. Accessed 29 Jan. 2018.

Kakutani, Michiko. "A Former FBI Agent on Terrorism since the Death of Bin Laden." Review of *Anatomy of Terror: From the Death of Bin Laden to the Rise of the Islamic State of Iraq and Syria*, by Ali Soufan. *The New York Times*, 29 May 2017, www.nytimes.com/2017/05/29/books/review-anatomy-of-terror-ali-soufan.html. Accessed 29 Jan. 2018.

Moyar, Mark. "After the Death of Bin Laden." Review of *Anatomy of Terror: From the Death of Bin Laden to the Rise of the Islamic State of Iraq and Syria*, by Ali Soufan. *The Wall Street Journal*, 24 July 2017, www.wsj.com/articles/after-the-death-of-bin-laden-1500937520. Accessed 29 Jan. 2018.

Sinai, Joshua. "Bringing Terror and Its Practitioners into Focus." Review of *Anatomy of Terror: From the Death of Bin Laden to the Rise of the Islamic State of Iraq and Syria*, by Ali Soufan. *The Washington Times*, 13 Sept. 2017, www.washingtontimes.com/news/2017/sep/13/book-review-anatomy-of-terror-from-the-death-of-bi/. Accessed 29 Jan. 2018.

Anything Is Possible

Author: Elizabeth Strout (b. 1956)
Publisher: Random House (New York). 272 pp.
Type of work: Novel
Time: Present day
Locales: Amgash, Illinois; various small towns and cities outside of Chicago and Peoria, Illinois

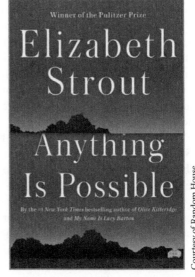

In Anything Is Possible, *author Elizabeth Strout loosely links nine short stories with connections to Lucy Barton, the character in her previous novel,* My Name Is Lucy Barton. *People in Lucy's hometown of Amgash, Illinois, read and reflect on Lucy's memoir while dealing with the everyday pain, loss, and love in their own lives.*

Courtesy of Random House

Principal characters

LUCY BARTON, a published author with a current best seller who spent her impoverished childhood in Amgash

PETE BARTON, her brother, who lives alone in the family house in Amgash

TOMMY GUPTILL, a retired custodian from her elementary school and former dairy farmer

PATTY NICELY, a widow and high school guidance counselor who was raised in and lives in Amgash

LINDA PETERSON-CORNELL, Patty's sister, patron of the arts, who lives outside of Chicago

CHARLIE MACAULEY, a veteran struggling in a bad marriage who develops a friendship with Patty

ABEL BLAINE, Lucy's cousin who grew up impoverished but became a successful businessman

Elizabeth Strout's sixth novel, *Anything Is Possible*, is much like her Pulitzer Prize–winning novel *Olive Kitteridge* (2008), in that the book is a series of interconnected short stories and not a traditional novel with a consistent protagonist and a clear narrative thread running throughout. In *Anything Is Possible*, Strout includes some of the characters and settings from her novel *My Name Is Lucy Barton* (2016), primarily the character Lucy and her numerous family members, as well as friends and acquaintances from Lucy's hometown of Amgash, Illinois. Furthermore, in *Anything Is Possible*, Strout's novel *My Name Is Lucy Barton* becomes Lucy's published memoir. What distinguishes *Anything Is Possible* from Strout's other work, however, is her emphasis on forbidden desires and sexual secrets. These themes, combined with Strout's simple and direct writing style and her ability to create characters who suffer the hurts of their past yet remain vulnerable, make the novel compelling and deserving of acclaim.

The nine stories in *Anything Is Possible* are connected through character and location. All the protagonists in the various stories have grown up in, lived in, or visited Amgash, Illinois, the town where Strout's former protagonist, Lucy Barton, spent her childhood. One of the premises of *Anything Is Possible* is that numerous characters encounter or read Lucy's memoir. Patty Nicely, in "Windmills," is deeply affected by Lucy's book. Tommy Guptill, Charlie Macauley, and Abel Blaine, who either discuss the book, consider purchasing it, or purchase it and meet Lucy at a public reading to have it signed, are also affected. Lucy herself makes an appearance in the story "Sister," where for the first time in seventeen years she returns to Amgash to visit her siblings. While readers do not need to have read *My Name Is Lucy Barton* to fully understand or appreciate *Anything Is Possible*, each novel is enriched by the reading of the other. Similarly, each of the short stories, while individually satisfying and able to stand alone, benefit greatly from their proximity to one another since numerous characters appear, or are referenced in, more than one other story. The linking contributes to the book's cohesiveness and depth.

As she has in past novels, Strout creates quiet characters with deep interior lives, characters who cling to past pain yet have moments of understanding. Tommy Guptill, for example, who is in his eighties and retired from his custodian job at a local elementary school, recalls his more prosperous past as a dairy farmer. In the novel's opening story, "The Sign," Tommy thinks about the night his life changed, when his farm burned down. Though he wondered about the cause of the fire, he accepted it as a sign from God. When Tommy checks in on his isolated neighbor Pete, who is Lucy Barton's brother, the reader learns that Pete thinks Tommy continues to check in to punish him for a past mistake. Pete thinks Tommy wants to remind him that his father, Ken, who was a troubled veteran Tommy employed on the farm, set the fire in retaliation for Tommy criticizing his behavior. Tommy never suspected this betrayal, and the revelation shatters his belief that the fire was a divine signal. When Tommy shares this betrayal with his wife, she easily accepts Ken's role in the fire as well as Tommy's belief that the fire was a sign from God. Though Tommy is relieved, it puts his relationship with God in question.

Strout's characters do not have lives of intrigue, and they are not generally interested in money or fame. She layers her characters with internal conflict and complexity that involve everyday matters of home, honesty, and meaningful relationships. While the points of tension, about whether the fire was accidental or set and messages from God, are not necessarily unusual, Strout makes them revealing and revelatory. Tommy questions past decisions and old assumptions, which are at once troubling and freeing. Pete sheds burdens he has shouldered for many years, and later in the novel, after the story "Sisters," he can see beyond his troubled past, showing how Strout's characters grow in small but significant ways.

While Strout's characters attempt to cope with an almost overwhelming amount of suffering, they also have moments of revelation. In "Windmills," Patty Nicely, a guidance counselor at the local high school, buys a copy of Lucy Barton's memoir at the local bookstore. Patty has been grappling with both the death of her husband, Sebastian, a wonderful man who suffered long-term effects from childhood rape, and the decline of her mother's health. Her mother broke up the family with an affair while Patty was in high school. Patty replays the details of her mother's affair and how much it changed their lives. Reading Lucy Barton's book, however, changes her perspective because she no longer feels alone, and that makes all the difference. Strout does not leave her characters hopeless, and Patty begins by making small changes in her life, such as buying flowers for her house. She starts to think of her life as "having a piece of yellow-colored candy, maybe butterscotch, tucked inside the back crevices of her mouth, she knew that private sweetness came from Lucy Barton's memoir." By the end of the novel, Patty has entered a new relationship, and the changes she made helped her find a new kind of happiness.

Strout's elegant prose serves her characters well. She writes with simple, direct language, utilizing metaphors that are both striking and easy to grasp. In "Gift," for example, the last story in the novel, Lucy's cousin Abel attends a local production of *A Christmas Carol* with his family, including his beloved granddaughter, Sophie. Sophie leaves her plastic pony in the theater and Abel returns to retrieve it, running into the much-panned lead actor, Linck McKenzie, who insists Abel stay and chat. Abel sees Sophie's pony hanging by the neck backstage, clearly a prank, and he acquiesces. During their conversation, McKenzie speculates that Abel has married into his money,

© Leonardo Cendamo

Elizabeth Strout is an award-winning writer and the author of six novels, including Olive Kitteridge *(2008), which won the Pulitzer Prize. Her last three novels,* The Burgess Boys *(2013),* My Name Is Lucy Barton *(2016), and* Anything Is Possible *(2017), were all* New York Times *best sellers.*

has a devoted secretary, and is a figurehead. Abel "says nothing. A private nail of shame was driven into his chest; he could feel himself perspire. He remembered how earlier he'd thought of people reciting a line, and he understood now that he was one of them." Abel realizes that despite his hard work to improve his life, he is in some sense acting, particularly in his marriage. Strout, through the imagery of the hanging pony and nail of shame, communicates the complexity of Abel's emotions. She allows readers to have a deeper understanding of Abel's life.

What separates this novel from Strout's earlier efforts is the sexual nature of the secrets many of the characters carry, which are often related to the struggles they endure. Patty Nicely's recently dead husband, for example, suffered from childhood rape, and due to Patty witnessing her mother's affair, she too is affected to the degree that neither she nor her husband wished to engage in sex. Patty talks about what a kind man Sebastian is, despite the trauma of all he experienced. That they both find love, however short-lived, after suffering these childhood traumas speaks to the title of the novel. Many of the characters dwell in either despair or difficult circumstances, yet opportunities occur that offer them hope.

Patty's sister, Linda Peterson-Cornell, for example, married a much more affluent husband, Jay, in the story "Cracked." They are financially secure, yet Linda states that she wished her husband would "simply disappear." She knows her husband is a voyeur. Linda is aware of her husband's proclivities but does nothing to stop him and sometimes assists him with his sexual fantasies. When there is a threat that those proclivities might be publicly revealed, Linda feigns ignorance of her husband's activities to save herself and keep their freedom. It is the compassion of a relative stranger, however, who helps her realize that going forward things must be different. Strout is adept at capturing those quiet, revealing moments when a character learns something about themselves, and the unburdening of the secret or the newfound strength to keep it private allows Strout's characters to transcend their circumstances.

Critics have uniformly praised *Anything Is Possible*, with *New York Times* reviewer Jennifer Senior writing, "You read Strout, really, for the same reason you listen to a requiem: to experience the beauty in sadness." Strout's characters are rarely happy people. They have been trod upon in childhood and suffered trauma, or they are in marriages that started strong and devolved into lovelessness and misunderstanding. Yet despite the trauma, they survive and often grow stronger. Patty Nicely, after reading Lucy Barton's memoir, sees life anew and embarks on a new relationship. Other characters share moments of compassion and understanding, which help them move forward. Strout, with simplicity and grace, offers the possibility that small hopes can bloom and thrive.

Marybeth Rua-Larsen

Review Sources

Day, Elizabeth. "Anything Is Possible by Elizabeth Strout: Masterful Chronicler of Small-Town America." Review of *Anything Is Possible*, by Elizabeth Strout. *The Guardian*, 23 Apr. 2017, www.theguardian.com/books/2017/apr/23/anything-is-possible-elizabeth-strout-review. Accessed 11 Sept. 2017.

Domestico, Anthony. "Anything Is Possible for Lives Seeking a Chance for Change." Review of *Anything Is Possible*, by Elizabeth Strout. *The Boston Globe*, 21 Apr. 2017, www.bostonglobe.com/arts/books/2017/04/20/even-darkest-most-complex-lives-chance-for-change/yDc61U6X9ZyJJSVzUYROAM/story.html. Accessed 11 Sept. 2017.

Merrell, Susan Scarf. "*Anything Is Possible* Demonstrates What Elizabeth Strout Does Best." Review of *Anything Is Possible*, by Elizabeth Strout. *The Washington Post*, 24 Apr. 2017, www.washingtonpost.com/entertainment/books/anything-is-possible-demonstrates-what-elizabeth-strout-does-best/2017/04/24/e2ea3a36-1df2-11e7-ad74-3a742a6e93a7_story.html. Accessed 11 Sept. 2017.

Senior, Jennifer. "Elizabeth Strout's Lovely New Novel Is a Requiem for Small-Town Pain." Review of *Anything Is Possible*, by Elizabeth Strout. *The New York Times*, 26 Apr. 2017, www.nytimes.com/2017/04/26/books/review-elizabeth-strout-anything-is-possible.html. Accessed 11 Sept. 2017.

Apollo 8
The Thrilling Story of the First Mission to the Moon

Author: Jeffrey Kluger (b. 1954)
Publisher: Henry Holt (New York). 320 pp.
Type of work: History
Time: 1961–68
Locales: United States, space

Providing a behind-the-scenes look at the 1968 Apollo 8 lunar mission, Jeffrey Kluger captures the trials and triumphs of the momentous event that led humans to leave Earth for the first time in its history.

Principal personages
FRANK BORMAN, commander of the Apollo 8 spacecraft
JIM LOVELL, command module pilot of the Apollo 8 spacecraft
WILLIAM "BILL" ANDERS, lunar module pilot of the Apollo 8 spacecraft
CHRISTOPHER C. KRAFT, Jr., director of the Manned Spacecraft Center
SUSAN BORMAN, wife of Frank Borman
MARILYN LOVELL, wife of Jim Lovell
VALERIE ANDERS, wife of Bill Anders

The year 1968 was marked by tumultuous and often tragic events. The escalation of the Vietnam War sparked nationwide protests which exposed deep political, social, and cultural divisions. In a contentious US presidential election, the candidacies of Richard Nixon, Hubert Humphrey, and Eugene McCarthy magnified those rifts. The assassinations of civil rights leader Martin Luther King Jr. and Senator Robert F. Kennedy just two months apart shook the nation to its core. Violent race riots ripped cities asunder. In the arts and entertainment industry, politically active artists, musicians, and television and movie stars fueled resistance against the establishment in Washington, DC. It was as though America was coming apart at the seams. Then, on Christmas Eve, the world was awestruck by a spectacular portrait of Earth beamed from the Apollo 8 spacecraft, which was orbiting the moon over 230,000 miles away. The serene blue ball covered in white swirling clouds floating in the blackness of space belied the tumult on the astronauts' home planet. For many, the breathtaking photograph symbolized the hope that relationships among Earth's people would one day mirror the tranquility captured in the image.

Earthrise, the photograph of the earth taken from the Apollo 8 spacecraft, is the most famous photograph associated with the Apollo 8 mission. But underlying the picture is the dramatic story of the individuals who made the first manned mission to the moon possible. In vivid prose, Jeffrey Kluger captures the danger, excitement, anxiety, and elation that defined the mission as the astronauts and the National Aeronautics and Space Administration (NASA) team struggled to accomplish their objective. Kluger is no stranger to writing about the American space program. A senior writer for *Time* magazine, he coauthored *Lost Moon: The Perilous Voyage of Apollo 13* (1994) with Jim Lovell, the commander of Apollo 13 and the command module pilot of Apollo 8. In *Apollo 8*, just as in *Lost Moon*, Kluger offers a gripping account of a pioneering flight to the moon. Yet while *Lost Moon* focused on the near disaster and eventual recovery of the Apollo 13 mission, *Apollo 8* provides a stirring chronicle of the flight that paved the way for future lunar trips.

The Apollo program, like its precursors the Mercury and Gemini programs, was inaugurated in response to President John F. Kennedy's vision of putting a man on the moon by the end of the 1960s. His mandate was motivated by the Cold War "space race" with the Russians, which the Russians were winning. When cosmonaut Yuri Gagarin became the first person to fly in space in 1961, the American public was stunned by the Soviet accomplishment. The United States space effort went into high gear with NASA's Mercury program, which included one-man flights piloted by Alan Shepard, Virgil "Gus" Grissom, and John Glenn. Following the success of the Mercury program, Project Gemini was established to develop a two-man craft designed to pursue the goals of space rendezvous, extravehicular activities, and extended mission duration. Grissom also took part in the Gemini program, along with Wally Schirra, Neil Armstrong, Edwin "Buzz" Aldrin, Frank Borman, and Jim Lovell. All these men subsequently became members of the Apollo astronaut team.

In the wake of the successful Mercury and Gemini projects, the reputation for American ingenuity took a tragic hit when disaster struck on January 27, 1967. The Apollo 1 spacecraft, crewed by Grissom, Roger Chaffee, and Ed White, burned up in a ground test, incinerating the astronauts. It was a devastating setback for NASA. With almost forensic precision, Kluger carefully dissects the causes of the fire. He notes that repairs being made to what he calls a "slapdash machine" were "patchwork affairs— workarounds and fixes made on top of earlier fixes, rather than the harder undertaking of ripping out the offending systems, redesigning them, and reinstalling them only when they worked right." The official determination of the cause was an electrical spark that flared out of control. Drawing on official transcripts, Kluger describes the last moments of the lives of the trapped astronauts in horrifying detail. Although the official story was that the men had died instantly, they actually lived twenty-one seconds into the fire, long enough to realize they were dying.

While the nation mourned the loss of Grissom, White, and Chaffee, NASA scrambled to get the program back on track. The space agency held the contractor, North American Aviation, to account and appointed a review board, which included Borman, an Air Force colonel and astronaut, to oversee the redesign and rebuilding of the spacecraft. Borman had both a professional and personal interest in serving on the board. He had lost his close friend Ed White in the accident, and he was scheduled to fly Apollo 9 in low-Earth orbit. He was determined that every safety detail be addressed. "Nobody's going to put anything in the spacecraft unless NASA management approves it,"

Courtesy of Audrey Kluger

Jeffrey Kluger is the overseer of Time *magazine's science and technology reporting. He has written or cowritten numerous books, including* Lost Moon: The Perilous Voyage of Apollo 13 *(1994);* Splendid Solution: Jonas Salk and the Conquest of Polio *(2004); and* The Sibling Effect *(2011).*

Kruger quotes Borman as saying.

Nonetheless, equipment defects and malfunctions continued to plague the Apollo program. Unmanned tests flights of the Saturn V rocket led NASA to address severe pogo oscillation—a dangerous longitudinal vibration—as well as other mechanical problems. In addition, there were problems with the lunar module. Since Apollo 8 was originally scheduled to test the module in low-Earth orbit with another crew, the plan was scrapped. To keep the program on track, NASA revamped the mission and, instead, decided to send the Apollo 9 (now redesignated Apollo 8) crewmen Borman, Lovell, and Anders to the moon using just the command and service module without the lunar module.

When Apollo 8 finally launched on December 21, 1968, the world watched as the Saturn V roared into space topped with a "comparatively spacious" 218 cubic-foot craft that would be the astronauts' home for six days. Kluger's penchant for detail is on full display as he chronicles the spacecraft's launch, the twenty-hour orbit journey around the moon, its return to Earth's atmosphere, and its splashdown on December 27. Drawing on "dump tapes" recorded during the mission, he recreates the conversations the astronauts had between themselves, as well as their communications with mission control. The result is a narrative that puts readers inside the capsule with the men as they deal with the mission's challenges.

The "you-are-there" feeling is further enhanced by Kluger's skillful storytelling. Although the result of the Apollo 8 mission is known, Kluger creates suspense by highlighting what could have happened during crucial times in the flight. For example, two hours and fifty minutes into the mission, mission control was scheduled to execute a difficult maneuver called the trans-lunar injection (TLI) burn. Kluger explains the technical aspects fully but in an understandable way, emphasizing the incredible precision required. The purpose of the burn was to put the craft on a trajectory to the moon. If the maneuver was miscalculated, the craft could be lost in the expanse of space. If the maneuver was successful, three human beings would leave Earth's gravity and enter the moon's gravitational field, something that had never been done before.

The mission included several other firsts. In addition to leaving Earth's gravity behind, the astronauts were the first humans to enter the Van Allen radiation belt, the first to see the far side of the moon, and the first to see their home planet "floating alone, unsupported in space" rather than just making up the horizon. The beauty of the Earth seen from the moon moved all three men. Another first was not as romantic as viewing Earth from space, however. Kluger describes Borman's brief bout of vomiting and diarrhea. Initially, NASA physicians were puzzled by Borman's symptoms and then later chalked them up to motion sickness. The effects of Borman's illness highlights the unpleasant difficulties of three people living in cramped quarters hundreds of thousands of miles from home.

As the astronauts adapted to life in space, their wives and children carried on at home. While this historic flight was a first for the human race, it was also a first for Susan Borman, Marilyn Lovell, and Valerie Anders, whose husbands had routinely courted danger as military pilots. The women generally accepted that danger as part of the job, but going to the moon was several steps beyond the risks their husbands had faced in airplane cockpits. In the prologue to the book, Kluger tells a story about how Susan Borman reacted when Frank told her about the Apollo 8 mission. She had some understanding of what could happen if the lunar mission failed. However, she decided to talk to Chris Kraft, the director of flight operations, to clarify the risks. When she asked him to level with her concerning the odds that her husband would return safely, he answered, "How's fifty-fifty?" Although the dangers of the mission weighed on them, the women publicly managed their children, their households, their guests, and the ever-present press with grace, courage, and stoicism. Privately, they spent sleepless nights wondering whether their husbands would be coming home.

The astronauts' families—along with the rest of the world—looked forward to the three television broadcasts from Apollo 8 in which Borman, Lovell, and Anders shared their impressions of their lunar journey. The most memorable—and most watched—broadcast took place on Christmas Eve. After Anders set up a movie camera to capture the crater-covered surface of Earth's natural satellite, the three men offered personal observations of their odyssey. When the lunar sunrise came into view, Anders turned to the last page of the flight plan and began to read, "In the beginning, God created the heaven and the Earth." As each man took turns reading the first nine verses from the book of Genesis, the lunar landscape slid below them.

Subsequent Apollo missions have been well covered by writers and historians—most notably Apollo 11, with which Neil Armstrong was the first person to set foot on the moon. However, none of those missions would have happened without the groundbreaking journey undertaken by Borman, Lovell, and Anders. *Apollo 8* has received strong reviews, with critics agreeing that in Kluger's capable hands, the full story of this crucial mission takes it rightful place in history.

Pegge Bochynski

Review Sources

Review of *Apollo 8: The Thrilling Story of the First Mission to the Moon*, by Jeffrey Kluger. *Kirkus Review*, vol. 85, no. 8, 2017, p. 59, 2 Apr. 2017, www.kirkusreviews.com/book-reviews/jeffrey-kluger/iapollo-8i/. Accessed 23 Feb. 2018.

Review of *Apollo 8: The Thrilling Story of the First Mission to the Moon*, by Jeffrey Kluger. *Publishers Weekly*, 20 Mar. 2017, vol. 264, no. 12, 2017, p. 64, www.publishersweekly.com/978-1-62779-832-7. Accessed 23 Feb. 2018.

Gawrylewski, Andrea. "Daring *Apollo 8* Astronauts, Rediscovering a Forgotten Math Genius and Other New Science Books." Review of *Apollo 8: The Thrilling Story of the First Mission to the Moon*, by Jeffrey Kluger, et al. *Scientific American*, vol. 316, no. 5, 1 May 2017, p. 74, www.scientificamerican.com/article/daring-apollo-8-astronauts-rediscovering-a-forgotten-math-genius-and-other-new-science-books/. Accessed 23 Feb. 2018.

Goedeken, Ed. Review of *Apollo 8: The Thrilling Story of the First Mission to the Moon*, by Jeffrey Kluger. *Library Journal*, vol. 142, no. 1, 1 Apr. 2017, p. 72, *Literary Reference Center Plus*, search.ebscohost.com/login.aspx?direct=true&db=lkh&AN=122230194&site=lrc-plus. Accessed 23 Feb. 2018.

Herrell, Keith. "Apollo 8: Stepping Bravely into the Unknown." Review of *Apollo 8: The Thrilling Story of the First Mission to the Moon*, by Jeffrey Kluger. *BookPage*, 16 May 2017, www.bookpage.com/reviews/21285-jeffrey-kluger-apollo-8#.WpA7nK6nFEY. Accessed 23 Feb. 2018.

Millard, Doug. "First Mission to the Moon: The Real Lesson." Review of *Apollo 8: The Thrilling Story of the First Mission to the Moon*, by Jeffrey Kluger. *New Scientist*, 24 May 2017, www.newscientist.com/article/2132000-first-mission-to-the-moon-the-real-lesson/. Accessed 23 Feb. 2018.

Astrophysics for People in a Hurry

Author: Neil deGrasse Tyson (b. 1958)
Publisher: W.W. Norton (New York). 224 pp.
Type of work: Science

Renowned astrophysicist and popular science communicator Neil deGrasse Tyson explains current scientific understanding of the cosmos and describes scientific and cultural problems that remain to be solved in a succinct manner meant for facilitated comprehension.

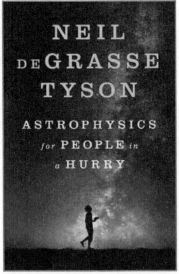

Courtesy of W.W. Norton

For readers who want to understand the latest scientific thinking on the cosmos but lack the time to master esoteric concepts such as cosmic microwave backgrounds and dark matter, *Astrophysics for People in a Hurry* just might come to the rescue. Maintaining a place on the New York Times Best Sellers list for several weeks, the book was written by astrophysicist Neil deGrasse Tyson, who, as director of the Hayden Planetarium at the American Museum of Natural History and a science communicator with frequent television and media appearances, has achieved both professional excellence and significant popularity among the public. True to its author's talent for making difficult concepts appealing and understandable, the book presents key ideas about the universe with regular doses of humor and entertainment. As a brief yet meaningful introduction to current conceptions of the cosmos, the book successfully outlines the most interesting problems that astrophysicists have addressed. That said, some ideas can still be hard to follow, and the connections between the key concepts are not always clear. Even less successful is Tyson's attempt to tackle thorny cultural issues, such as how to approach people who reject scientific rigor and empirical thinking.

The best parts of the book elucidate terms that readers may have encountered in popular media yet do not fully understand. A case in point: dark matter. Tyson draws the reader in by laying out the problem as a mystery waiting to be solved by the likes of a modern Sir Isaac Newton (1643–1727) or Albert Einstein (1879–1955); just as the latter refined the former's groundbreaking theory of gravity, people now need someone to explain the puzzle of dark matter. Says Tyson, "We've now been waiting nearly a century for somebody to tell us why the bulk of all the gravitational force that we've measured in the universe—about eighty-five percent of it—arises from substances that do not otherwise interact with 'our' matter or energy." The problem, Tyson elaborates, is that dark matter cannot be seen; the only way to detect it is through its undeniable effect, or gravitational pull, on matter that cannot be seen. This fact creates a host of new questions. Does the "excess gravity" truly come from matter and energy or from something else? Is the matter itself the thing to be investigated, or is there more about gravity that needs to be revealed? The answers remain elusive, and until someone finds them, dark matter remains, in Tyson's words, "our frenemy."

In addition to his often-lovely prose, such as, "We are stardust brought to life, then empowered by the universe to figure itself out," Tyson's embrace of popular culture terms such as "frenemy" is part of the book's appeal. His writing is clear and avoids unnecessarily difficult terms. He also keeps the discussion fun and engaging, including frequent doses of humor. Distinguishing between erroneous past predictions claiming that "'we will never fly'" or "'we will never break the sound barrier'" and the true statement that nothing can overcome the speed of light, he jokes that if "interstellar travelers of the future" were to encounter highway signs, they would clarify that the speed of light is a law rather than just an idea. Tyson also shows how one can use physics in everyday encounters. Further proving his ability to successfully incorporate anecdotes (both personal and historical) into the text, he describes a trip to a dessert shop, where he ordered hot chocolate with whipped cream only to find no cream topping his drink. He then recounts how he disproved the waiter's claim that the cream had simply sunk to the bottom. After explaining that whipped cream has low density and always floats on all liquids that humans ingest and the waiter still expressed disbelief, he conducted an impromptu experiment that proved the server wrong. Concluding the chapter, Tyson preens, "What better proof do you need of the universality of physical law?"

Despite Tyson's talent for clarity and entertainment, there are hints that readers might not be the only ones in a hurry. The book begins with a dramatic narration of the big bang, or the phenomenon theorized as responsible for the origin of the universe. Particularly breathtaking is Tyson's conveyance of the speed with which the event occurred. But within the first two pages, he plunges the reader into a discussion of the formal incompatibility between Einstein's theory of relativity and quantum mechanics. Here, he writes as if his audience already understands his terms—a mistake for an introductory book. A bit more context for how these concepts and others, such as the Planck era, relate to the larger topic would be helpful for beginners. This hurried and at times disjointed style recurs throughout and, as some reviewers also noted, might be a by-product of the book having been compiled and adapted from a series of essays that he had previously written for *Natural History* magazine between 1998 and 2007. Examples of this occur in the discussion of cosmic microwave backgrounds in chapter 3 and in the explanation of omega in the chapter on dark energy (which is different from dark matter). Also not entirely clear is the relationship among some of the key concepts covered in each chapter. The book does a good job of explaining the elements comprising the universe, and chapter 7, dedicated to the Periodic Table of elements, effectively sketches some of the ways in which astrophysicists make use of the elements as they investigate the cosmos. Yet, readers might wonder whether the

Neil deGrasse Tyson is an American astrophysicist, the director of the Hayden Planetarium at the American Museum of Natural History, host of the radio and television show StarTalk, *and a best-selling author of over a dozen books.*

chapters, on the whole, serve as a sample or actually represent all the key ideas one needs to know. Brief introductions in each chapter that explain how the concepts relate to one another would be useful.

Counterbalancing this weakness is Tyson's singular talent for luring the reader back in through his obvious delight in what he studies, not to mention his boundless energy and vivid imagination. His passion engages the reader when, for example, he describes what would happen if a human body visited intergalactic space, and when he offers a fabulous description of the Periodic Table "as a zoo of one-of-a-kind animals conceived by Dr. Seuss." How could scientists avoid thinking this way, he wonders, given that sodium is a "poisonous, reactive metal that you can cut with a butter knife, while pure chlorine is a smelly, deadly gas, yet when added together they make sodium chloride," also known as table salt? And while volatile and potentially dangerous alone, hydrogen and oxygen combine to make life-giving water. Passages like these make Tyson's love of science contagious. It becomes fascinating to learn that Jupiter is a "gravitational shield for Earth," and that Jupiter's moon Europa, which shows signs of liquid water, is a good candidate in the search for extraterrestrial signs of life. Tyson also captivates through his invocation of the senses, such as when he explains that despite the earth's seemingly formidable mountains and valleys, if some imaginary being had a giant finger that they could run across the earth's surface, it would feel "as smooth as a cue ball." Later in the book, readers learn what Tyson believes aliens would most likely see if they had the tools to observe Earth.

Especially fascinating are the many examples of scientific "revisions" of previous assertions as well as discussions of problems that remain to be solved. Tyson not only confirms that Pluto is no longer a planet but explains how scientists reached this conclusion. He reveals that scientists now know that going to the moon to retrieve lunar rocks is unnecessary because they have discovered that lunar meteorites can and do break through gravitational forces and land on Earth. Moreover, solving the problem of dark matter is perhaps more precarious than one might think. In part, through the discovery that dark matter exists, scientists believe the expansion of the universe will accelerate, which means that galaxies now visible in the night sky will eventually be indiscernible. This suggests that the expanding universe may have already made certain cosmic realities inaccessible, leading Tyson to express the following fear: "Behold my recurring nightmare: Are we, too, missing some basic pieces of the universe that once were? What part of the cosmic history book has been marked 'access denied?'" Such questions will compel the reader to think further about the balance that exists between hypotheses, knowledge gaps, empirical evidence, and what may appear to be scientific mistakes.

Reviews of *Astrophysics for People in a Hurry* were largely positive, as Tyson ultimately succeeds in his goal of igniting a spark in all types of readers to engage more with and appreciate a fascinating and significant topic. After all, as he emphasizes in the book, "The cosmic perspective comes from the frontiers of science, yet it is not solely the provenance of the scientists. It belongs to everyone." Critics commonly noted Tyson's ability to effectively blend humor and a more conversational tone with explanations of complex scientific concepts. While also praising the continued relevance of the book's topics, Josh Trapani wrote for *Washington Independent Review of Books*, "Tyson also has a knack for providing compelling tidbits that stick in your head and make concrete what might otherwise be hopelessly abstract." Commenting on the infectious nature of Tyson's passion for his subject that is palpable throughout the book, the reviewer for *Kirkus* called *Astrophysics for People in a Hurry* a "sublime introduction to some of the most exciting ideas in astrophysics that will leave readers wanting more." While some of the concepts covered may still be a bit difficult for some to grasp given the condensed format, overall the book serves as an intriguing foundation for developing further thoughts on and research into the compelling subject of the cosmos, which Tyson has explained in interviews as having been his ultimate mission in publishing the book.

Ashleigh Imus, PhD

Review Sources

Review of *Astrophysics for People in a Hurry*, by Neil deGrasse Tyson. *Kirkus*, 7 Mar. 2017, www.kirkusreviews.com/book-reviews/neil-degrasse-tyson/astrophysics-for-people-in-a-hurry/. Accessed 15 Feb. 2018.

Bethea, Charles. "What We're Reading This Week." Review of *Astrophysics for People in a Hurry*, by Neil deGrasse Tyson, et al. *The New Yorker*, 5 Dec. 2017, www.newyorker.com/culture/likes/what-were-reading-this-week-nomadland-astrophysics-for-people-in-a-hurry-the-corrections. Accessed 15 Feb. 2018.

Mason, Deborah. "*Astrophysics for People in a Hurry*: A Sprightly Overview of Space and Time." Review of *Astrophysics for People in a Hurry*, by Neil deGrasse Tyson. *BookPage*, May 2017, bookpage.com/reviews/21235-neil-degrasse-tyson-astrophysics-people-hurry#.WoXHfa6nFeM. Accessed 15 Feb. 2018.

Trapani, Josh. Review of *Astrophysics for People in a Hurry*, by Neil deGrasse Tyson. *Washington Independent Review of Books*, 12 May 2017, www.washingtonindependentreviewofbooks.com/index.php/bookreview/astrophysics-for-people-in-a-hurry. Accessed 15 Feb. 2018.

The Bear and the Nightingale

Author: Katherine Arden
Publisher: Del Rey (New York). 368 pp.
Type of work: Novel
Time: Fourteenth century
Locale: Northern Russia

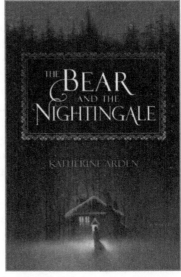

Courtesy of Del Rey

When Christianity and folk religion clash, leading to the awakening of an ancient evil, a young woman must choose between tradition and rebellion if she is to save her family and land.

Principal characters

VASILISA "VASYA" PETROVNA, a precocious
    child and rebellious woman
PYOTR VLADIMIROVICH, her father and lord
    of the region of Lesnaya Zemlya
ANNA IVANOVA, her stepmother
OLGA, her sister
SASHA, her brother
ALYOSHA, her brother
KOLYA, her brother
DUNYA, the children's nursemaid
KONSTANTIN NIKONOVICH, a Christian priest sent to Lesnaya Zemlya

Katherine Arden's first novel combines history with fantasy in the tale of an unexpected heroine whose bold attitude and behavior seem to be the only things standing between her world and the curse of the Bear, an enemy who is awakened when people begin to lose belief in the old folk religion.

Since the story is built around fantasy elements, it is not surprising that a folk story is central to the plot. The Russian folktale of the winter king, or frost demon, Morozko, is found throughout the novel. It is prominently featured in the opening pages, as the children of the nobleman Pyotr Vladimirovich gather around to hear their nursemaid, Dunya, tell the tale. The story tells of a man whose daughter was beautiful in every way. When the girl's stepmother becomes jealous of the girl, she orders her husband to abandon his daughter in the lethal cold of the Russian winter. He complies, but the girl is found by Morozko, who is impressed by the girl's polite endurance in the face of death, so he brings her home with gifts of riches. The girl's stepsister is sent to receive the same gift, but because of her selfish attitude, Morozko allows her to die. As the story ends, one of the children asks Dunya about the first daughter's fate and whether she married the winter king; Dunya replies, "What use does Winter have for a mortal maiden?" The novel then builds to the suggestion that Morozko does, indeed, need a mortal maiden.

Morozko appears in reality several times after this opening tale is told. For example, he briefly appears when six-year-old Vasya is lost in the forest and stumbles on a tree that shelters a mysterious one-eyed man, who awakens and beckons her. A stranger on a white horse saves her from the one-eyed man's pull, sending him back to sleep . As Vasya runs away, in a further foreshadowing clue, the man on the horse notes, "He is getting stronger." Later, Pyotr visits Moscow and meets a strange man who gives him a necklace for his youngest daughter. When Pyotr gives the necklace to Dunya to pass on to the child, Dunya recognizes it as a talisman and hides it for fear of its meaning. Morozko visits her dreams throughout the ensuing years until she is forced to acknowledge Vasya's ability to handle the talisman's power and passes it to the girl. This precedes the heroic actions Vasya later undertakes in an effort to save her home and her people. She is accompanied in these actions by a magical horse, who, in one form, is the nightingale of the title. Though Arden leaves the final chapter open-ended, Vasya will challenge Dunya's earlier expectation as the novel draws to a close.

The folktale element of the story is further explored in a thematic conflict that challenges the introduction of Christianity into the medieval Russian countryside. The idea of witchcraft is tied to Vasya even before she is born, as she is descended from a witch woman. The people of Lesnaya Zemlya believe in household spirts, whom Vasya can see and with whom she forms friendships. The presence of these spirits protects the region and the families. When Pyotr brings a new wife, Anna, to his home, she can also see the spirits—but rather than befriending them, as a zealous Christian she seeks out a priest to exorcise the "demons." The priest, Konstantin, a charismatic and handsome man, sways the attitudes of the local people, changing their beliefs and undermining the spirit protections that have been in place for centuries. His own faith is challenged when the Bear, an embodiment of fear and death awakened by the disruption, speaks to Konstantin, tricking him into believing that it is the voice of God he is hearing. The strength of Vasya's belief will be tested as she is called on to save her family and home.

The quality of characterization in the novel varies depending on the figure. Most of the characters are fairly one dimensional. Pyotr is the gruff but loving patriarch. He is crushed by the death of his first wife, the mother of his children, but he chooses to remarry to provide a mother figure for Vasya. Only at the end of the novel is Pyotr's true depth revealed. Anna, his new wife, has potential to be a well-developed character, but her constant sniveling over the household spirits she sees causes discord between her and the stepdaughter with whom she should be able to relate, as Vasya is the only other person who has the ability to see them. Anna spends her life worshipping the priest as much as God, and she falls as a result of her weakness. Pyotr's other children also hold hints of interesting character traits, but these traits are not developed either, leaving Vasya's siblings to serve primarily as stock characters. The two characters who are well developed are Konstantin and Vasya herself.

Konstantin is brought to the attention of Moscow's leadership when it is feared that he could "turn the people against the prince." His power lies in his "terrible beauty: old-gold hair and eyes like blue water. He was renowned throughout Muscovy for his piety, and despite his youth he had traveled far. . . . He read Greek and could argue obscure points of theology. Moreover he chanted with a voice like an angel, so that the people wept to hear him and lifted up their eyes to God." In an effort to dampen the priest's influence, the prince's advisors send Konstantin to Lesnaya Zemlya. Once there, he turns the people away from their traditions in an effort to turn them toward the God of Christianity. Anna dotes on the priest, clinging to him as she cringes away from the household spirits that she sees but does not understand. Konstantin uses his time to glorify himself as much as the God he claims to serve, seeming to pacify Anna without any real care for her soul. This character's development is complicated as he finds himself drawn to Vasya, desiring her in a very unpriestly way. His near obsession with the girl shows a depth of characterization that leads to unexpected choices that affect the outcome of the story.

Vasya, the central character, is the most developed. The novel's structure of three parts follows that of a bildungsroman, with Vasya's birth and early childhood in the first portion of the story. In this section, Vasya's powers are established as well as her rebellious personality. She is always bucking the expectations for girls, preferring outside work and play over sewing or cooking. The middle part of the book follows her teen years, including a short period when her father tries to find her a husband. She, somewhat surprisingly, goes along with her father's desire to marry her to a neighboring lord, but her true personality comes out when her nephew is endangered, and her suitor refuses to marry her. The final part of the novel establishes Vasya as the hero readers have been led to expect. Here, the action has come to a climax, and as Morozko points out, "Blood is one thing. The sight is another. But courage—that is rarest of all." Vasya's rebellion against expectations, her desire for power over her own destiny, and her courage in the face of adversity all add up to give her a depth of characterization that is missing in most of the other characters.

Katherine Arden graduated from Middlebury College in 2011. The Bear and the Nightingale is her first novel, and the first in a trilogy. It was followed later in 2017 by The Girl in the Tower.

Vasya's characterization leads to another thematic conflict. This happens as problems with traditional gender roles are revealed while Vasya is growing up and rejecting the expected behavior for a girl. The woman's place is established early, when six-year-old Vasya approaches her brother: "Aloysha quite liked Vasya, who was up for anything—nearly as good as a younger brother—but he was almost three years older and had to keep her in her place." Vasya continues to defy gender expectations throughout the novel, lamenting, "All my life . . . I have been told 'go' and 'come.' I am told how I will live, and I am told how I must die. I must be a man's servant and a mare for his pleasure, or I must hide myself behind walls and surrender my flesh to a cold, silent god. I would walk into the jaws of hell itself, if it were a path of my own choosing." Her final act of the story shows her strength of purpose in protesting her prescribed role.

The novel's critical reviews were primarily positive. The *Library Journal* reviewer called the book "a highly recommended exemplar of literary fantasy," while the *School Library Journal*'s reviewer claimed, "Arden's lyrical writing will draw teens in and refuse to let them go." In regard to the fantasy elements, *Kirkus* argued, "Arden has shaped a world that neatly straddles the seen and the unseen, where readers will hear echoes of stories from their childhood while recognizing the imagination that has transformed old material into something fresh." *Booklist*'s reviewer also praised the writing by calling the book a "beautifully written, auspicious first novel" that is "utterly bewitching." Finally, *Publishers Weekly* lauded the novel as a "beautifully written love letter to Russian folklore." Overall, fans of fantasy, folklore, and unconventional heroes will enjoy Arden's debut novel.

Theresa L. Stowell, PhD

Review Sources

Review of *The Bear and the Nightingale*, by Katherine Arden. *Kirkus*, 10 Oct. 2016, www.kirkusreviews.com/book-reviews/katherine-arden/the-bear-and-the-nightin-gale/. Accessed 8 Jan. 2018.

Review of *The Bear and the Nightingale*, by Katherine Arden. *Publishers Weekly*, 4 July 2016, www.publishersweekly.com/978-1-101-88593-2. Accessed 8 Jan. 2018.

Frostick, Cary. Review of *The Bear and the Nightingale*, by Katherine Arden. *School Library Journal*, 5 Apr. 2017, www.slj.com/2017/04/reviews/the-bear-and-the-nightingale-by-katherine-arden-slj-review/. Accessed 8 Jan. 2018.

Hoffert, Barbara. Review of *The Bear and the Nightingale*, by Katherine Arden. *Library Journal*, 28 Dec. 2016, reviews.libraryjournal.com/2016/12/in-the-bookroom/authors/spotlight-katherine-arden-libraryreads-author-january-2017/. Accessed 8 Jan. 2018.

Hunter, Sarah. Review of *The Bear and the Nightingale*, by Katherine Arden. *Booklist*, 15 Oct. 2016, www.booklistonline.com/The-Bear-and-the-Nightingale-Katherine-Arden/pid=8169490. Accessed 8 Jan. 2018.

Zipp, Yvonne. Review of *The Bear and the Nightingale*, by Katherine Arden. *The Christian Science Monitor*, 29 Jan. 2017, www.publishersweekly.com/978-1-101-88593-2. Accessed 8 Jan. 2018.

Behave
The Biology of Humans at Our Best and Worst

Author: Robert M. Sapolsky (b. 1957)
Publisher: Penguin Press (New York). Illustrated. 800 pp.
Type of work: Psychology, science

In Behave: The Biology of Humans at Our Best and Worst, *Robert M. Sapolsky explores the enormously complicated features and traits of the human brain, the center of all complex responses and behaviors.*

Principal personages
ROBERT SAPOLSKY, the author and narrator
SUSAN FISKE, a social psychologist at Princeton University
JONATHAN DAVID HAIDT, a social psychologist at New York University
WILLIAM DONALD HAMILTON, an evolutionary biologist formerly at Oxford University, now deceased
LAWRENCE KEELEY, a professor of archaeology at the University of Illinois

BEHAVE

THE BIOLOGY *of* HUMANS *at* OUR BEST *and* WORST

ROBERT M. SAPOLSKY

Courtesy of Penguin Press

Robert M. Sapolsky's book *Behave: The Biology of Humans at Our Best and Worst* has been very highly praised by reviewers, and it is easy to see why. It deals with perhaps the most complicated and most important structure known to exist: the human brain. Sapolsky tries to explain, in language that general readers will be able to comprehend, just how the brain is the center of everything humans think, feel, and do. He wants to show not only how the brain is responsible for the traits that make people most uniquely human, but also how it links humans to the most primitive, least evolved forms of life. He explains the brain's three-part structure and shows how all three structures, or layers, interact in extraordinarily complicated ways, with the cortex—"the newest part of the brain," he notes—sitting literally on top of the rest of it, like the very thin but crucially important bark of a tree (the root meaning of the word "cortex").

Aware that readers might find his topic intimidating, Sapolsky does his best to write in a clear, often comical, deliberately witty style. He is prone to colloquial turns of phrase—sometimes awkwardly so, as in the very first pages, when he reveals that humans' potential for violence "scares the crap" out of him. A few sentences later, he confesses that one of his own personality traits makes him "a pain in the butt"; on the next page, he writes that a rooster can give "a sexually solicitive gesture that is hot by chicken standards"; later still, commenting on some biological function, he asks, "Petty impressive, huh?" Many readers may find such phrasing entertaining; others may find it a bit cloying and overly cute, as if Sapolsky is trying too hard to enliven an already intriguing subject rather than letting it be interesting in and of itself. Most probably, the glibness on display here is just a personality trait—appealing in the classroom but potentially distracting in the pages of an eight-hundred-page book. Still, tastes vary, and this sort of writing obviously appeals to many, particularly to the ever-clever Sapolsky.

Another rhetorical device that readers may find distracting, and one that Sapolsky seems especially fond of, is his tendency to start down a particular line of explanation and then abruptly stop, telling the reader that the issue he is discussing right now is far too complicated to continue exploring and promising that he will return to it in some later chapter. It is not hard to imagine why this strategy may have seemed necessary—after all, the matters Sapolsky discusses here are indeed incredibly complex—but for many readers, this device may prove frustrating and even annoying, especially since it is repeated so often. Again, this technique may work well in a lecture room, but in a long book it may irritate some readers. It would be hard, in fact, to think of another nonfiction work about a complex topic, written for nonspecialists, that uses this tactic so often, if at all. Once or twice or thrice it can be provocative; repeated over and over, it can seem, at least to some readers, tediously overdone.

Such quibbles aside, however, there is no denying that Sapolsky has chosen an inherently compelling topic. Which readers would not want to know why they think, feel, and act as they do—and, just as important, why other people are the way they are? Sapolsky shows how nature and nurture interact in often unpredictable ways, but the real meat of his book lies in its focus on the nature aspect—on the physical brain itself, with its convoluted shape and structure, its extraordinarily varied circuitry, and its vast array of chemicals and chemical processes. Anyone who reads *Behave* will come away with a renewed sense of just how intricate the brain is, both in structure and in function, and just how remarkably it works (or sometimes fails to work properly). Sapolsky amasses all the evidence necessary to show how much human brains have in common with the brains of the more "primitive" creatures from which humans evolved, and how any thought, feeling, or behavior humans experience or enact can be traced back to chemical processes that began just milliseconds earlier but that also, in a sense, stretch back billions and billions of years into the past.

Behave is punctuated by helpful drawings and diagrams that illustrate many of the points Sapolsky tries to make. It is divided into many sections and subsections, each clearly labeled, and most chapters end with lucid summaries of the key points made in each section. The studies and experiments that Sapolsky describes are almost always fascinating, and the anecdotes he uses to emphasize various points are frequently memorable. Readers learn in great detail about the many traits that are generally hardwired into human brains, as well as how much variability there can be from one brain (that is, one person) to another. Environments often dictate how brains function, but brains can also influence and even alter environments. Nothing is very simple in this text; in fact, part of its real merit is that it makes readers aware of just how complex they and others are.

When Sapolsky puts cuteness and crudeness aside and writes as one might expect a renowned scientist to do, he produces text such as the following, from the conclusion of chapter 3: "No brain operates in a vacuum, and over the course of seconds to minutes, the wealth of information streaming into the brain influences the likelihood of pro- or antisocial acts. . . . Moreover, the brain also constantly receives interoceptive information. And most important, much of these varied types of information is subliminal. Ultimately, the most important point of this chapter is that in the moments just before we decide upon some of our most consequential acts, we are less rational and autonomous decision makers than we like to think." And sometimes Sapolsky writes in ways that are memorable without seeming over the top, as when he reveals, "Your heart does roughly the same thing whether you are in a murderous rage or having an orgasm. Again, the opposite of love is not hate, it's indifference." In both of these passages, the language is generally clear and straightforward, with a minimum of technical jargon ("interoceptive" being the obvious exception).

Sapolsky explains scientific findings that often seem to confirm common sense, just as he often reports data that frequently challenge

Robert M. Sapolsky is an award-winning research professor of neurobiology at Stanford University. He is the author of seven books about biology, many of them, like Behave, *aimed at a popular readership. He was awarded a MacArthur Fellowship, the so-called genius grant, in 1987.*

usual assumptions, such as the assumption that a higher testosterone level results in greater aggression. He discusses the intricate effects that particular chemicals can have on and within the brain, and he shows how the brain itself can evolve in ways that might seem unexpected. Dog lovers, for example, may take particular interest in his explanation of why they are quite literally lovers of dogs: during the last fifty thousand years, both dogs and their owners have developed strong positive chemical reactions to each other, rooted in the hormones known as oxytocin and vasopressin. The more frequently dogs and their owners look at each other, the more these literally pleasing chemicals are released by the brain. And dogs who are given injections of these chemicals look even longer and more affectionately at their humans. "So," Sapolsky concludes, "a hormone that evolved for mother-infant bonding plays a role in this bizarre, unprecedented form of bonding between species."

Moments such as this—and they are plentiful throughout the book—make Sapolsky's text endlessly fascinating. He explains, for instance, that humans generally "love stress that is mild and transient and occurs in a benevolent context. The stressful menace of a roller-coaster ride is that it will make us queasy, not that it will decapitate us; it lasts for three minutes, not three days." The total absence of stress is hard to handle, because no stress at all "is aversively boring"; mild, transient stress enhances various brain functions, among them the release of dopamine. Humans not only "love that kind of stress" but in fact "clamor for it, pay to experience it. What do we call that optimal amount of stress? Being engaged, engrossed, and challenged. Being stimulated. Playing." But, Sapolsky notes, "as stress becomes more severe and prolonged, those good effects disappear (with, of course, dramatic individual differences as to where the transition from stress as stimulatory to overstimulatory occurs; one person's nightmare is another's hobby)."

Steven Poole, writing for the *Guardian*, described *Behave* as "a miraculous synthesis of scholarly domains, and at the same time laudably careful in its determination to point out at every step the limits of our knowledge"; in his review for the *Spectator*, Stuart Ritchie cautioned about one of the book's shortcomings—Sapolsky's reliance on social psychology studies of dubious rigor and replicability—but added that "there is plenty to enjoy and plenty to learn, as long as you remember to treat the social-psychology research with the distrust it deserves." *New York Times* reviewer Richard Wrangham called *Behave* "the textbook you will regret never having had in college" and concluded that it "offers a wild and mind-opening ride into a better understanding of just where our behavior comes from." As Sapolsky leads readers on a long journey down winding and convoluted paths, readers will be thankful not only for the trip itself but also for the intelligent, qualified, and lucid guide.

Robert C. Evans, PhD

Review Sources

Anderson, Alun. "To Understand Why We Behave the Way We Do, We Need to Zoom Out." Review of *Behave: The Biology of Humans at Our Best and Worst*, by Robert M. Sapolsky. *New Scientist*, 12 July 2017, www.newscientist.com/article/mg23531341-000-to-understand-why-we-behave-the-way-we-do-we-need-to-zoom-out. Accessed 1 Oct. 2017.

Poole, Steven. "*Behave* by Robert Sapolsky Review: Why Do We Do What We Do?" Review of *Behave: The Biology of Humans at Our Best and Worst*, by Robert M. Sapolsky. *The Guardian*, 9 June 2017, www.theguardian.com/books/2017/jun/09/behave-by-robert-sapolsky-review. Accessed 1 Oct. 2017.

Ritchie, Stuart. "Can Good and Bad Behaviour Be Explained by Biology?" Review of *Behave: The Biology of Humans at Our Best and Worst*, by Robert M. Sapolsky. *The Spectator*, 29 July 2017, www.spectator.co.uk/2017/07/can-good-and-bad-behaviour-be-explained-by-biology. Accessed 1 Oct. 2017.

Wrangham, Richard. "Insights into the Brain, in a Book You'll Wish You Had in College." Review of *Behave: The Biology of Humans at Our Best and Worst*, by Robert M. Sapolsky. *The New York Times*, 6 July 2017, www.nytimes.com/2017/07/06/books/review/behave-robert-m-sapolsky-.html. Accessed 1 Oct. 2017.

The Best We Could Do

Author: Thi Bui (b. 1975)
Publisher: Abrams ComicArts (New York). Illustrated. 336 pp.
Type of work: Graphic novel, memoir
Time: 1950s–present day
Locales: Vietnam, the United States

Thi Bui's graphic memoir, The Best We Could Do *explores both her family's immigration story and her own life as a mother.*

Principal personages
THI BUI, the author
MÁ, her mother
BỐ, her father

In her graphic memoir, *The Best We Could Do*, artist Thi Bui recounts her family's immigration story from a fresh perspective after becoming a mother. Thi Bui's motherhood complicates and deepens her view of her parents, who, in 1978, made the difficult and dangerous decision to flee Vietnam for the United States. Born months before the end of the Vietnam War, she was three years old at the time, but she remembers the arduous journey. The family traveled first by a wooden boat, which her father was unexpectedly called upon to captain. Thi Bui, her mother, siblings, and others hid in the darkened hull. Their experience places them among the famous "boat people," who fled Vietnam by sea during these years. Thi Bui's mother, Má, who was eight months pregnant, gave birth to her sixth child after the family docked at a refugee camp in Malaysia. From Malaysia, they traveled to Indiana and stayed with family, before settling in San Diego, California, where Thi Bui and her brother and sisters struggled to fit in as Americans.

Thi Bui also recounts the very different childhood experiences of her parents, who grew up in Vietnam in the 1950s. Her difficulty in obtaining this information becomes a part of the book, which depicts, on one page, a grown Thi Bui sitting at a table with her father as a child, gently coaxing him to speak. The book's arc is similarly fragmented, splicing past and present in unusual ways that are both visual and narrative. Thi Bui writes in the preface that the book, begun as an oral history project while she was in graduate school, took her nearly fifteen years to complete. This time for rumination is evident in the depth of her research and the profound, hard-won truths she uncovers about her own parents and families in general. *The Best We Could Do* is about refugees and the physical and emotional toll of immigration, but it is, at its core, a book about parents and children, and how these relationships, for better or worse, shape who people are.

Thi Bui trained as an arts educator, and as a graduate student at New York University, she compiled an oral history of her family punctuated by drawings and photographs. She wanted to explore that history further but worried that her initial project was too academic. Inspired by classic graphic novels such as Art Spiegelman's *Maus* (1986), about the author's father, a Holocaust survivor, and Marjane Satrapi's *Persepolis* (2000–2001), about the author's coming-of-age during the Islamic Revolution in Iran, Thi Bui set out to make her family history into a comic. She had never drawn comics before, and she recalls producing her first clumsy pages in 2005. Over the course of the next ten years, she became a comic artist while creating this book. One working title was "Refugee Reflex," a self-developed concept she explores in the book, but as she wrote and drew, working simultaneously as a schoolteacher at an alternative public high school for immigrants in Oakland, California, her own life continued to unfold. She had become a mother, and she began caring for her aging parents. These milestones changed the way she thought about family, and by extension, her book. In 2011, she writes, "I realized that the book was about parents and children, and it became *The Best We Could Do.*" It was published in early 2017, the same year she illustrated the children's book *A Different Pond*, by Bao Phi.

The book begins in the thick of Thi Bui's own difficult labor in 2005. The process is depicted in a gruesome array of surgical instruments and needles, and doctors speaking babble. Thi Bui wants to refuse drugs but is too exhausted to intervene in the emergency plan the doctors have undertaken. Má is in the waiting room, too nervous to take part. After giving birth, there is more confusion. Why won't her baby boy eat? Why is the diaper sticking to his skin—is that normal? However, immediate concerns soon give way to a striking realization: "Family is now something I have created," she writes, "and not just something I was born into." She illustrates the pain and exhaustion of childbirth to convey the surprise of discovering that what comes after, a child's life, is much harder.

In the book, the birth of Thi Bui's son leads her to consider her own upbringing. *The Best We Could Do* moves intuitively, toggling between past and present, sometimes in a single frame. The second chapter—"Rewind, Reverse"—begins with Thi Bui moving to New York for college. She recalls the terse response she received from her mother after admitting that she was moving in with her boyfriend. Thi Bui's older sister, Bích, had not been so lucky. When Má discovered that Bích had a boyfriend (by reading her diary), the fallout was devastating. Bích ran away from home, and Má attempted suicide. It is significant, though not entirely clear why, that Thi Bui begins with this disturbing episode, one that she writes still makes her angry though all parties have since reconciled. "I have figured out, more or less, how to raise my little family," she writes, "but it's being both a parent and a child, without acting like a child, that eludes me."

One of the most remarkable things about *The Best We Could Do* is Thi Bui's candor. Her airing of dirty laundry, so to speak, is made all the more immediate—and her family members made all the more vulnerable—by her drawings, which are revealing in their simplicity. In his review of the book for *Vulture*, Abraham Riesman wrote that Thi Bui's "minimalism packs an emotional wallop." He went on to make an illuminating reference to cartoonist and cartoon theorist Scott McCloud, who devised a concept called "masking," which describes how a lack of detail in a drawing can often be more emotionally affecting to a reader than a drawing with more detail. To paraphrase McCloud, a detailed drawing of a face makes a comic reader an observer of the action on the page; a minimalist drawing of a face requires a comic reader to use their imagination. The reader thus participates in the character's actions and enters their emotional sphere.

A similar principle is at play in the traditional use of masks in theater. When the details of a face are obscured, viewers fill in the gaps with pieces of themselves. Fittingly, Thi Bui favors a sparse palette. Her figures, drawn in black ink, emerge from burnt orange wash as if out of the fog of the past. Additionally, when discussing her family's journey, she includes a page that combines drawings of anonymous refugees with the actual photographs of herself, her parents, and her sisters taken as they were being processed after reaching the refugee camp in Malaysia, which works effectively alongside her artwork to emphasize that this is a true story.

Thi Bui is propelled into her family history by an unexpected loneliness. After the birth of her son, she and her husband move to California to be closer to her parents. Her brother and sisters all live nearby. It should be an ideal situation, she writes, but her relationship with her parents is unexpectedly inert. "How did we get to such a lonely place?" she asks. "We live so close to each other and yet feel so far apart." To explore this issue and attempt to find an answer, she delves into her past. When Thi Bui was a young child, while Má was at work and her sisters were at school, she and her younger brother spent their days in a dark apartment in the care of their superstitious and troubled father, Bố, who told them frightening stories about demons and the neighbors across the street. Their memories from that period are colored by fear. Her reconstruction of her life at such a young age is built on tiny, ingenious details such as the blur of the car headlights as Bố drives the family home drunk and a favorite dream in which their apartment is filled with water and, unencumbered, she swims all the way through it. As an adult, she tries to understand why her father behaved this way. Did he not realize that he terrified his children? Growing up, she came to understand that his life was shaped by war. Unlike Má, the daughter of a civil servant, he knew extreme poverty and once nearly died hiding in an underground cavern while the French raided his village. Bố used to tell her that he had no parents, but when she figured out the right questions to ask about his past, she writes, "the stories poured forth with no beginning or end." Thi Bui explores her parents' stories in these short, evocative vignettes, depicting lives impeded by tragedy and destruction but also peppered with joy.

Thi Bui is a graphic artist and educator. The Best We Could Do, her first graphic memoir, was published in 2017. That same year, she illustrated a children's book titled A Different Pond, by Bao Phi.

The Best We Could Do was enthusiastically embraced by reviewers when it was published in 2017. Riesman noted its timely completion. For its deeply humane depiction of the immigrant experience, he deemed it "one of the first great works of socially relevant comics art of the Trump era." Other critics praised Thi Bui's ability to embrace the complexity of her family story. "In this mélange of comedy and tragedy, family love and brokenness, she finds beauty," a reviewer for *Publishers Weekly* wrote in the publication's starred review. *The Best We Could Do*, Laurie Hertzel of the Minneapolis *Star Tribune* wrote, describes Thi Bui's reckoning with her parents as people "who have endured unimaginable hardship and are doing the best they can. And yet the story is devoid of sentimentality." The graphic memoir even won an endorsement from Pulitzer Prize–winning author Việt Thanh Nguyễn, who described it as "a book to break your heart and heal it."

Molly Hagan

Review Sources

Review of *The Best We Could Do*, by Thi Bui. *Publishers Weekly*, 5 Dec. 2016, www.publishersweekly.com/978-1-4197-1877-9. Accessed 11 Jan. 2018.

Hertzel, Laurie. Review of *The Best We Could Do*, by Thi Bui. *Star Tribune* [Minneapolis, MN], 4 Sept. 2017, www.startribune.com/review-the-best-we-could-do-by-thi-bui/442500283. Accessed 11 Jan. 2018.

Kirby, Robert. Review of *The Best We Could Do*, by Thi Bui. *The Comics Journal*, 9 Mar. 2017, www.tcj.com/reviews/the-best-we-could-do. Accessed 11 Jan. 2018.

Riesman, Abraham. "Life as a Refugee Is Explored in the Stunning Comics Memoir *The Best We Could Do*." Review of *The Best We Could Do*, by Thi Bui. *Vulture*, 7 Mar. 2017, www.vulture.com/2017/03/thi-bui-best-we-could-do-refugee-comic.html. Accessed 11 Jan. 2018.

Between Them
Remembering My Parents

Author: Richard Ford (b. 1944)
Publisher: Ecco (New York). 192 pp.
Type of work: Memoir
Time: Early twentieth century to the present
Locale: American South

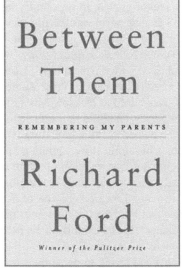

Richard Ford's two-part memoir Between Them: Remembering My Parents *considers the lives—both before and after his birth—of his deceased mother and father.*

Principal personages
RICHARD FORD, the author and narrator
PARKER, his father, a traveling salesman
EDNA, his mother, a homemaker

Pulitzer Prize–winning fiction author Richard Ford's new memoir, *Between Them: Remembering My Parents*, considers the lives of his parents, Parker and Edna Ford. Told in two parts, written thirty years apart, Ford's recount of his parents' life stories and his search to really understand them also reflect on his role "between them" as their only child. *Between Them* is a rumination loosely structured and peppered with rhetorical questions about his parents' unknowable thoughts and the life they shared before he was born. Ford explores this early period in their marriage, when his mother, Edna, accompanied his father, Parker, on his route as a traveling salesman. For years, the two young people lived in hotels across the American South in New Orleans, Memphis, Birmingham, Mobile, and Pensacola. Near the end of the book, Ford writes that he feels compelled to tell what he knows about his parents' lives if only to enter them into the historical record, so that they might live on in the book and in the memories of the people who read it.

The memoir is also colored by Ford's own age—in his early seventies, he is older than either of his parents were at their deaths—and his fascination with the passage of time and its effect on parental relationships. Remarking on his mother's alien upbringing in rural Arkansas in the early twentieth century, when much of the country was still frontier-like in character, Ford writes, "Our parents intimately link us, closeted as we are in our lives, to a thing we're not, forging a joined separateness and a useful mystery, so that even together with them we are also alone." Ford's depiction of his childhood and his relationship with his parents leaves much to be desired in terms of detail, but as a meditation on what it means to be the child of parents (Ford has no children of his own), it is a sharp, singular read.

Ford is a novelist and short-story writer best known for his series of novels about a character named Frank Bascombe, beginning with *The Sportswriter* in 1986. The book, about a sportswriter who throws himself into his work after the death of his son, is considered Ford's breakout novel, though he had published two other novels before it. The book's sequel, *Independence Day* (1995), revisits Frank, who is now working as a realtor in New Jersey and trying to repair his relationship with his younger teenage son. The novel was the first to win both the PEN/Faulkner Award for Fiction and the Pulitzer Prize in the same year. Ford is also a well-known short-story writer. His acclaimed collection *Rock Springs* was published in 1987. He is often characterized as a Southern writer in the mold of Nobel Prize–winning Mississippian William Faulkner (1897–1962) or Pulitzer Prize winner Eudora Welty (1909–2001), who, like Ford himself, was raised in Jackson, Mississippi. However, Ford's Bascombe novels are set in New Jersey, and Ford himself has lived all over the continental United States. He may not be a specifically regional writer, but his reserved, masculine prose and recurring themes of family strife conjure a kind of midcentury Americana. Ford comes from a specific postwar tradition of white male writers, but some critics have noted that he lacks the aggression and overt misogyny of some of his contemporaries.

In a *New York Times* review of *Between Them*, memoirist and writer Cheryl Strayed wrote that Ford applies the same "penetrating understanding of the nuances of human character" that he exhibits in his fiction to his nonfictional account of his parents. The character of Bascombe is a first-rate observer; so, too, is Ford, looking back on his parents and trying to parse their true selves. He notes in the afterword that the first section of the book, "Gone: Remembering My Father," was written in 2015, some fifty-five years after Parker Ford's premature death from a second heart attack in 1960, when Ford was sixteen years old. Parker was born to an Irish Presbyterian family in Arkansas. His father, Ford's grandfather, died by suicide after losing the family farm in 1916. His mother doted on him, her youngest son, and predictably hated Ford's mother, Edna.

Parker was shy and genial—"a man who liked to be happy," as Ford describes him. As a young man, he worked in a grocery store and then, sometime after marrying Ford's mother in 1928, began working as a traveling salesman peddling laundry starch. Parker and Edna's is a way of life difficult to imagine almost a hundred years later. The couple moved from town to town on company expense, jointly teaching young country homemakers how to starch their laundry in local tutorials. Parker and Edna longed for children, but none came until Ford, some fifteen years into their marriage, in 1944. While the family settled in Jackson, Parker continued to travel, and Ford recounts how his father's absences each workweek formed the rhythm of his young life. Memories of his father are an impressionist painting, a collage of weekends and holiday vacations. The family had recently bought a home in the suburbs when Parker unexpectedly died from a heart attack one weekend morning. (Parker had been in poor health since the 1950s.) Ford, who was a teenager at the time, describes the horrible scene, straddling his father's lifeless body and trying to administer CPR. Over fifty years later, the author shrewdly observes how his father's final absence shaped him, giving him a kind of morbid permission to become an independent adult.

The second section of *Between Them*, "My Mother, In Memory," was written shortly after Edna's death from cancer in 1981. Most of this section recounts her life after

Courtesy of Karen Robinson/eyevine/Redux

Richard Ford is a Pulitzer Prize–winning novelist and short-story writer. He is best known for his series about a character named Frank Bascombe, among them The Sportswriter *(1986) and* Independence Day *(1995).*

Parker's death, though Ford reiterates some tales from her early life, touched on in the first section. Born in poverty in the Ozarks, Edna's young life was shaped by her mother, who took up with a dashing young boxer-turned-hotelier when Edna was around twelve. (Thanks to that hotelier, Ford first went to college to study hotel management.) Ford's maternal grandmother sent his mother away to Catholic school only to pull her out again and put her to work at the hotel, introducing her to people not as a daughter but as a younger sister. Edna met and married Parker when she was seventeen. Intelligent and sharp-witted, she thrived as Parker's traveling partner, visiting new places and meeting new people. Ford wonders how much she missed that life after his birth relegated her to a single home in a single town.

After Parker's death, Ford writes that Edna "maintained, made an objective out of that," as she struggled to construct her identity as separate from her late husband. She took a succession of jobs and briefly dated a married man. Ford regretfully recalls inadvertently ruining one date with the man, whom he seems to have liked. Edna, to Ford's knowledge, never pursued another romantic relationship again. Ford and his mother made a pact after Parker's death; they would no longer be like mother and son but more like independent partners on the arduous journey of life. He moved away for college and married, living in places across the United States and Mexico. Edna, meanwhile, cared for her own elderly mother and lived out the rest of her life in Arkansas. Ford expresses harboring a great deal of regret from this period. He chastises himself for not paying more careful attention to his mother and her needs. His writing about her is subtly shaped by this anguish; he asserts that his mother was never truly happy after his father's death, suggesting some unknowable failure on his part.

Between Them was well reviewed by critics who seem to have enjoyed engaging with Ford's unconventional dual portrait, the structure of which cleverly serves as a physical representation of the themes and stories explored in his work. The memoir, not so much a page-turner as it is slow burning, invites more reflection than its length might immediately suggest. "This is not a book that runs on the steam of what-happens-next, but rather on the contemplative, inquisitive force of Ford's longing to finally *see* his parents," Strayed wrote. "There's a vulnerability that I've not observed in Ford's work before, a tender surrender to the search." A reviewer for *Kirkus* echoed Strayed's analysis, observing, not derisively, that the book "seems to have been written more for Ford . . . than for his readers." The memoir becomes a portrait of the author painstakingly collecting fragments of memory to piece together a picture of his parents as he knew (and did not know) them. Novelist William Giraldi, who reviewed the book for the *Washington Post*, made Ford's own childlessness a central part of his analysis. This may seem unfair, but Giraldi, who wrote that Ford once professed to "hate" children, offered an important lens through which to view the book. How much of one's understanding about parents is shaped by being one? A few lines in the book are worthy of further explanation that Ford does not offer. He characterizes his relationship with his parents as the only proper way to relate to a child—at a loving distance. In describing his own life, Ford seems to deeply value his independence, and sometimes it is difficult to tell how much he is projecting his own desires onto his parents. The frustrating answer to that question, Ford would likely respond, is that one can never know.

Molly Hagan

Review Sources

Review of *Between Them: Remembering My Parents*, by Richard Ford. *Kirkus*, 7 Mar. 2017, www.kirkusreviews.com/book-reviews/richard-ford/between-them. Accessed 8 Jan. 2018.

Review of *Between Them: Remembering My Parents*, by Richard Ford. *Publishers Weekly*, 20 Feb. 2017, www.publishersweekly.com/978-0-06-266188-3. Accessed 8 Jan. 2018.

Giraldi, William. Review of *Between Them: Remembering My Parents*, by Richard Ford. *The Washington Post*, 1 May 2017, www.washingtonpost.com/entertainment/books/richard-fords-new-memoir-between-them-remembering-my-parents/2017/04/28/72adedda-2c2f-11e7-be51-b3fc6ff7faee_story.html?utm_term=.804e41688131. Accessed 8 Jan. 2018.

Strayed, Cheryl. "Cheryl Strayed on Richard Ford's Masterly Memoir of His Parents." Review of *Between Them: Remembering My Parents*, by Richard Ford. *The New York Times*, 1 May 2017, www.nytimes.com/2017/05/01/books/review/richard-ford-between-them.html. Accessed 8 Jan. 2018.

Tsouderos, Trine. Review of *Between Them: Remembering My Parents*, by Richard Ford. *Chicago Tribune*, 2 May 2017, www.chicagotribune.com/lifestyles/books/sc-between-them-richard-ford-books-0503-20170501-story.html. Accessed 8 Jan. 2018.

Black Edge
Inside Information, Dirty Money, and the Quest to Bring Down the Most Wanted Man on Wall Street

Author: Sheelah Kolhatkar
Publisher: Random House (New York). 368 pp.
Type of work: Biography, economics, law
Time: 1956–2016
Locales: New York, Connecticut

In Black Edge: Inside Information, Dirty Money, and the Quest to Bring Down the Most Wanted Man on Wall Street, *Sheelah Kolhatkar chronicles the rise of the hedge-fund firm SAC Capital Advisors and its founder, Steven A. Cohen, and documents law enforcement's extended investigation into allegations of insider trading within the firm.*

NEW YORK TIMES BESTSELLER

BLACK EDGE

Inside Information, Dirty Money, and the Quest to Bring Down the Most Wanted Man on Wall Street

SHEELAH KOLHATKAR

Courtesy of Random House

Principal personages

STEVEN A. COHEN, the founder of SAC Capital Advisors
PATRICIA FINKE, his first wife
ALEXANDRA GARCIA, his second wife
MATHEW MARTOMA, a portfolio manager in SAC's CR Intrinsic unit
SIDNEY GILMAN, a neurologist at the University of Michigan's medical school
B. J. KANG, an FBI agent
DAVID MAKOL, an FBI agent
SANJAY WADHWA, assistant regional director for enforcement at the New York office of the Securities and Exchange Commission (SEC)
PREET BHARARA, US attorney for the Southern District of New York

Beginning in 2007, a global financial crisis left a devastating mark on the United States, prompting a wave of foreclosed homes, shuttered businesses, and failing financial institutions. At the time, however, not all financial firms in the United States were struggling. In July 2008, during the depths of the recession, the hedge-fund firm SAC Capital Advisors, headed by veteran Wall Street trader Steven A. Cohen, made an unusual and profitable series of stock trades. After holding large numbers of shares in the pharmaceutical companies Elan and Wyeth for some time, the firm abruptly reversed its strategy for those companies, selling off its holdings. Even more surprising to onlookers, Cohen himself shorted more than four million shares of Elan stock—that is, he made a potentially risky trade based on a bet that the stock's price would go down. Just over a week later, disappointing drug trial results sent the prices of Elan's and Wyeth's stocks down, and Cohen and SAC made millions of dollars despite the slumping economy. It was a fortunate move on SAC's part—and a suspicious one.

Drawing the attention of government agencies such as the Securities and Exchange Commission (SEC) and the Federal Bureau of Investigation (FBI), the Elan and Wyeth trades, plus other unusually lucky stock bets, sparked what would become an extensive investigation into insider trading within the firm, energetically chronicled and meticulously documented in *Black Edge: Inside Information, Dirty Money, and the Quest to Bring Down the Most Wanted Man on Wall Street*. The first book by *New Yorker* writer and finance journalist Sheelah Kolhatkar, *Black Edge* follows the investigation from its beginnings, tracing the FBI and SEC's attempts not only to determine whether SAC traders broke the law but also to prove the guilt of Cohen himself. As a former hedge-fund analyst, Kolhatkar is well suited to telling the story of SAC and the federal investigation of the firm, providing an inside glimpse of hedge funds' inner workings and financial dealings little understood by finance outsiders.

Kolhatkar begins *Black Edge* by delving into Cohen's early life and career, a knowledge of which, the book suggests, sheds significant light on Cohen's later actions and motivations. Born in 1956, Cohen grew up in a large middle-class family on New York's Long Island and spent his high school and college years winning poker games played against his wealthier classmates. After graduating from the University of Pennsylvania's prestigious Wharton School, he took a position at the brokerage firm Gruntal & Co., where he remained for more than a decade. During his early years in the volatile and competitive world of stock trading, Cohen thrived and made millions of dollars. He also became embroiled in his first insider-trading investigation after the SEC, the federal agency responsible for overseeing the trading of securities, noticed that Cohen and individuals close to him had invested in shares of the company RCA prior to the public announcement of its takeover by General Electric. Kolhatkar reports that Cohen's first wife, Patricia, later claimed that Cohen had received advance notice of the takeover from a former classmate and suggests that Cohen had traded based on that information. However, he was never charged with a crime. In 1992, more than five years after that investigation, Cohen launched his own firm, SAC Capital Advisors; over the subsequent years, it became known as one of the most successful hedge-fund firms in the United States.

Throughout *Black Edge*, Kolhatkar presents Cohen as a trader whose intense competitive drive filtered down to his employees at SAC and created a notoriously high-pressure, results-oriented environment. Indeed, Kolhatkar's depiction of SAC makes it easy to understand why employees of the firm might seek out and make trades based on the titular "black edge"—that is, information about a company, such as earnings reports or the results of prescription drug trials, that is not known to the public and gives the holder an advantage over other traders. According to Kolhatkar, who draws from interviews with relevant sources as well as court transcripts and related documents, that is precisely what Cohen and SAC did, perhaps most notably in the summer of 2008 when SAC liquidated its shares of Elan and Wyeth stock. She writes that prior to the 2008 trades, an SAC employee named Mathew Martoma, a portfolio manager in the firm's CR Intrinsic unit, made contact with Dr. Sidney Gilman, a neurologist who served as chair of a drug trial's safety monitoring committee. The drug in question was the Alzheimer's medication bapineuzumab, which was being jointly developed by Elan and Wyeth. As Kolhatkar documents, Martoma received information about the trial results prior to their public unveiling and advised his superiors at SAC—including Cohen, Kolhatkar alleges—to sell the shares and thus lock in the firm's profit and avoid losing money when the price fell. Although perhaps the most profitable, the Elan and Wyeth incident was not the only case of alleged insider trading that took place at SAC: Kolhatkar additionally recounts an incident in which an SAC employee learned ahead of time that the computer company Dell would be releasing lower earnings numbers than expected and passed that information on to his superiors. The inside information made its way to Cohen, who ultimately sold his five hundred thousand shares of the stock two days before Dell's disappointing earnings announcement caused its stock price to fall by nearly 14 percent.

While recounting the events taking place at SAC, Kolhatkar likewise chronicles the government's investigation of the firm, which took place on multiple fronts over many years and involved numerous parties, including FBI agents B. J. Kang and David Makol, SEC assistant regional director for enforcement Sanjay Wadhwa, and US attorney for the Southern District of New York Preet Bharara. Presenting memorable accounts of FBI agents tracking down hedge-fund employees at their gyms and grocery stores, convincing current and former SAC associates to turn on their friends and colleagues, and using wiretapping techniques reminiscent of those seen in films, *Black Edge* resembles a true-crime narrative at times as Kolhatkar traces the complex investigation down multiple twisting paths—and at times to dead ends. While she notes that several SAC employees were ultimately arrested, including Martoma, she reveals that the FBI investigators were unable to achieve their goal of securing Martoma's cooperation and, with it, testimony regarding Cohen's personal knowledge of and involvement in the insider trading suspected to be occurring at SAC. Although multiple SAC employees were charged with breaking the law, and the company paid substantial civil penalties, Kolhatkar notes that Cohen himself emerged from the investigation largely unscathed. In light of that revelation, the book's conclusion may seem unfulfilling to some readers, not because of any weakness in the narrative itself but because of the nature of the justice system and—as Kolhatkar might argue—the socioeconomic privilege that protects billionaires from the legal consequences of their actions.

Sheelah Kolhatkar is a staff writer for the New Yorker *and a former correspondent and features editor for* Bloomberg Businessweek. *Prior to beginning her career in journalism, she worked as a risk arbitrage analyst for two New York hedge funds.*

Throughout *Black Edge*, Kolhatkar presents a lively, engaging, and detailed narrative that sheds light on practices and individuals little discussed outside of the finance industry. Her explanations of the concepts crucial to the insider-trading investigation—such as edge and short selling—are clear and accessible, and she also helps readers make sense of the many parties involved by including a "Cast of Characters" following the book's main text. In addition to detailing the rise of Cohen and SAC and the investigation of both the firm and its founder, Kolhatkar includes a variety of information that is both relevant to the subject at hand and intriguing enough that readers may be inspired to research further. Among such topics is the practice of using companies such as the Gerson Lehrman Group, a consulting firm that Kolhatkar describes as a matchmaker of sorts, to connect interested investors with individuals affiliated with publicly traded companies. Although discussions between investors and such individuals ostensibly involve publicly available information only, Kolhatkar notes that in some cases—such as the interactions between Martoma and Gilman—connections facilitated through "matchmaking" companies were used to obtain inside information. Kolhatkar further notes that the participants were paid handsomely, writing that Gilman received $1,000 per half-hour conversation arranged via the Gerson Lehrman Group. Although her discussion of the ties between the medical and pharmaceutical research industries and the investment industry is limited, it adds an enlightening and concerning dimension to the book in addition to providing an explanation for how SAC's Elan and Wyeth trades took place.

Upon its publication in early 2017, *Black Edge* received a largely positive response from critics, including both reviewers writing for general audiences and those from financially oriented publications. Critics praised Kolhatkar's handling of both the book's central argument and narrative itself, with Jennifer Senior for the *New York Times* describing Kolhatkar's argument as "convincing" and Richard Poplak for the *Globe and Mail* describing *Black Edge* as "thrillerish" in tone and "[John] Grisham-esque" in style. Reviewers also called attention to Kolhatkar's success in writing a book that, although concerned with a specific series of events and relatively limited in scope, ultimately sheds light on the broader topic of the global financial crisis and the financial practices and institutions that contributed to it.

Although *Black Edge* was largely praised, it received criticism in some areas. The reviewer for *Kirkus Reviews* deemed it "formulaic but still intriguing," while Poplak noted that *Black Edge* critiques illegal practices taking place in the finance industry but does not challenge capitalism itself. In a review for the website *Observer*, attorney and former SAC trader Andrew Beresin took issue with the overall thesis of the book, arguing that it does not adequately explore the possibilities that SAC traders may have only used inside information to confirm their legitimate analyses and that Cohen was unaware of the actions of his employees. Despite such critiques, however, *Black Edge* was well received overall and is widely regarded as a strong addition to the body of work on the finance industry and financial crime in the early twenty-first century.

Joy Crelin

Review Sources

Beresin, Andrew. "Former SAC Trader on What Steve Cohen Bio *Black Edge* Doesn't Explore." Review of *Black Edge: Inside Information, Dirty Money, and the Quest to Bring Down the Most Wanted Man on Wall Street*, by Sheelah Kolhatkar. *Observer*, New York Observer, 13 Feb. 2017, observer.com/2017/02/sac-capital-book-black-edge-steve-cohen-review/. Accessed 30 Sept. 2017.

Review of *Black Edge: Inside Information, Dirty Money, and the Quest to Bring Down the Most Wanted Man on Wall Street*, by Sheelah Kolhatkar. *Kirkus Reviews*, 15 Dec. 2016, p. 118. *Academic Search Complete*, search.ebscohost.com/login.aspx?direct=true&db=a9h&AN=122749143&site=ehost-live. Accessed 30 Sept. 2017.

Burton, Katherine. "The Failed Quest to Bring Down Wall Street's Most Wanted Man." Review of *Black Edge: Inside Information, Dirty Money, and the Quest to Bring Down the Most Wanted Man on Wall Street*, by Sheelah Kolhatkar. *Bloomberg Businessweek*, 25 Jan. 2017, www.bloomberg.com/news/articles/2017-01-25/the-failed-quest-to-bring-down-wall-street-s-most-wanted-man. Accessed 30 Sept. 2017.

McClintick, David. "Outwitting the FBI and the SEC." Review of *Black Edge: Inside Information, Dirty Money, and the Quest to Bring Down the Most Wanted Man on Wall Street*, by Sheelah Kolhatkar. *The Wall Street Journal*, 9 Feb. 2017, www.wsj.com/articles/outwitting-the-fbi-and-the-sec-1486511759. Accessed 30 Sept. 2017.

Poplak, Richard. "Sheelah Kolhatkar's *Black Edge*, Reviewed: One of the Best Books about the 2008 Financial Meltdown." Review of *Black Edge: Inside Information, Dirty Money, and the Quest to Bring Down the Most Wanted Man on Wall Street*, by Sheelah Kolhatkar. *The Globe and Mail*, 24 Feb. 2017, www.theglobeandmail.com/arts/books-and-media/book-reviews/sheelah-kolhatkars-black-edge-reviewed-one-of-best-books-about-the-2008-financial-meltdown/article34127594/. Accessed 30 Sept. 2017.

Senior, Jennifer. "Review: *Black Edge*, an Account of a Hedge Fund Magnate and Insider Trading." Review of *Black Edge: Inside Information, Dirty Money, and the Quest to Bring Down the Most Wanted Man on Wall Street*, by Sheelah Kolhatkar. *The New York Times*, 1 Feb. 2017, www.nytimes.com/2017/02/01/books/review-black-edge-an-account-of-a-hedge-fund-magnate-and-insider-trading.html. Accessed 30 Sept. 2017.

Blitzed
Drugs in the Third Reich

Author: Norman Ohler (b. 1970)
First published: *Der totale Rausch: Drogen im Dritten Reich*, 2015, in Germany
Translated: from the German by Shaun Whiteside
Publisher: Houghton Mifflin Harcourt (Boston). 304 pp.
Type of work: History
Time: 1930s to 1945
Locale: Germany

Courtesy of Houghton Mifflin Harcourt

In Blitzed: Drugs in the Third Reich, *German journalist and novelist Norman Ohler presents a startling picture of a Nazi Germany powered in part by drugs. German soldiers helped maintain a killing pace during the Blitzkrieg bombing campaign in France in 1940 by taking officially sanctioned methamphetamines, and Adolf Hitler himself became increasingly dependent on dangerous injections of combined cocaine and opioids. Ohler's groundbreaking book sheds new light on the depravity of the Third Reich.*

Principal personages
ADOLF HITLER, dictator of Nazi Germany
THEODOR MORELL, his personal physician
FRITZ HAUSCHILD, the inventor of the methamphetamine Pervitin
OTTO F. RANKE, director of the Research Institute of Defense Physiology
HELLMUTH HEYE, an admiral in the German navy

The literature on the twelve years of National Socialist, or Nazi, rule in Germany is enormous. The evil wrought by Adolf Hitler and his minions was so profound and far-reaching that it has compelled exhaustive reexaminations in the more than seven decades since the Third Reich was bloodily crushed by invading armies. Such obsessive attention is justified by the need to warn future generations about the malign threats posed by totalitarianism and racial ideologies. While necessary and wholesome, the endless reinterpretation of the Nazi period seems to preclude any original discoveries by modern researchers. What can anyone say about one of the most studied phenomena in human history that is genuinely new? In *Blitzed: Drugs in the Third Reich*, Norman Ohler manages the seemingly impossible: writing a book about Nazi Germany that is truly surprising. The Nazi "Superman"—supposedly a physical paragon born of superior racial characteristics and clean living, celebrated as such in propaganda as Leni Riefenstahl's *Olympia* (1938)—was in fact doped on methamphetamines.

Norman Ohler is not a professional historian, but a German journalist and the author of several novels. The genesis of *Blitzed* lay in a conversation he had with a disc jockey friend who combined an interest in Nazi history with a taste for drugs. This friend had access to a stash of Nazi-era Pervitin tablets from an East German pharmacy; the ancient methamphetamines were still potent, and the resulting high delighted the deejay. Impressed by this story, Ohler began researching for what he intended to be novel on drug use in the Third Reich. As he dug deeper, he realized that he had discovered a story that transcended a few hipsters seeking kicks in the shadow of the swastika, and his prospective novel metamorphosed into a meticulously researched history that sheds fascinating light on the chemical underside of Nazi Germany.

In some ways, the fact that Nazi-era Germans had an affinity for drugs is unsurprising. Germany was a pioneer in the development of pharmaceuticals. In 1804, Friedrich Wilhelm Sertürner, a pharmaceutical assistant living in Paderborn, became the first person to extract morphine from the opium poppy plant; in 1827, Heinrich Emanuel Merck, the owner of a pharmacy in Darmstadt, began manufacturing and selling high-quality alkaloids for medicine and research, marking the birth of the mighty German pharmaceutical industry. In 1897, Felix Hoffmann, a chemist working for the Bayer pharmaceutical company, then headquartered in Elberfeld, developed a pain reliever that the company later sold under the trade name Aspirin; he also synthesized a form of morphine, trademarked by Bayer under the name Heroin, that the company initially sold as a cough suppressant and purportedly nonaddictive opiate. By the early twentieth century, Germany was the world leader in the production of pharmaceuticals, and the German university system produced a stream of brilliant chemists who kept advancing the creation of new drugs. German pharmaceutical companies were renowned for the purity and excellence of their products.

Norman Ohler is a journalist and the author of four novels: Die Quotenmaschine *(The quota machine, 1995),* Mitte *(Center, 2001),* Stadt des Goldes *(2002; Ponte City, 2003), and* Die Gleichung des Lebens *(The Equation of Life, 2017). He also cowrote the screenplay for Wim Wenders's 2008 film* Palermo Shooting.

After World War I, the German pharmaceutical industry continued to thrive. In 1925, a number of manufacturers combined to form IG Farben, a giant firm that became a major force in the chemical and pharmaceutical business. German drug companies prospered by supplying stimulants to a defeated nation that desperately needed them, but they had no access to natural mood lifters produced in colonies overseas. In the unmoored moral atmosphere of the Weimar Republic, large numbers of despondent Germans turned to pharmaceuticals to ease postwar anxiety and depression. German companies dominated the international manufacture of morphine and heroin, and the companies Merck (founded by descendants of Heinrich Emanuel), Boehringer Ingelheim, and Knoll produced much of the world's cocaine. Illicit competitors stamped their bootleg cocaine with Merck labels because of the German company's unassailable reputation for quality. While most of these drugs were exported, a lot were sold at home. In the 1920s, Berlin pharmacies alone legally sold over 160 pounds of prescription morphine and heroin in a single year, and cocaine use was endemic. The divinely decadent cultural atmosphere memorably captured by Christopher Isherwood's book *The Berlin Stories* (1945) and the subsequent musical *Cabaret* (1966) was expressed in the lyrics of a contemporary German song: "No need for genuflecting; / The only way to Paradise / Is snorting and injecting!"

Not all Germans embraced the escape provided by these drugs. Critics on both ends of the political spectrum denounced this "pleasure culture"; German nationalists reviled drug use as a sinister form of "moral decay," and the fading bourgeoisie condemned it as "decadently Western." When the Nazis came to power early in 1933, they took a hard rhetorical line against drug use; as Ohler mordantly observes, "for them there could be only one legitimate form of inebriation: the swastika." They wanted Germans intoxicated on their aggressively racialist ideology, not chemical substances, and the grandiose ceremonies and spectacles they staged were designed to whip participants and the general populace into a sort of spiritual high. The Nazi regime launched a "war on drugs" in which drug use was stigmatized, and drug addicts could be imprisoned indefinitely and were prohibited from marrying to prevent them from infecting the German gene pool with their supposedly incurable "psychopathic personalities." Persistent drug offenders often ended up in concentration camps. Inevitably, the Nazis associated the drug problem with Judaism. For Nazi ideologues, drugs and Jews both posed comparable threats to German racial purity.

Despite this official hard line against it, drug use persisted in Germany, in some cases in high Nazi Party circles. The new masters of the nation could not eradicate old habits and needs overnight. The regime was also aware that war was in the offing and that landlocked and resource-poor Germany would need effective stimulants in the conflict to come. The 1936 Berlin Olympics introduced Germans to the American amphetamine Benzedrine, which was at the time a permissible performance-enhancing drug for athletes. This inspired Fritz Hauschild, head pharmacologist at the Temmler pharmaceutical company, to synthesize a methamphetamine that in 1937 was trademarked as Pervitin. This drug gave its user a powerful and pleasant kick that spurred self-confidence and activity and a euphoric sense of heightened alertness and energy that could last for twelve hours or more. Unfortunately, over time it wore down nerve cells, leading to depression and cognitive problems. No one at Temmler worried about long-term side effects as the company marketed Pervitin pills as a healthy stimulant that could do everything from pepping up tired workers to alleviating the symptoms of alcohol and drug withdrawal to overcoming sexual "frigidity" in women. Temmler made the drug widely available as an over-the-counter medication, easily recognizable in its orange-and-blue packaging. Pervitin became a sensation, and soon Germans in all walks of life were giving themselves a daily chemical lift. Pervitin-laced chocolates were sold to housewives to help them speed through their housework.

The military took notice. Otto Ranke, the director of the Research Institute of Defense Physiology, experimented with Pervitin as a means of boosting the performance of German soldiers in the field. He became an apostle for the methamphetamine as a military pick-me-up, touring the front in France while dispensing thousands of Pervitin tablets. German officers and men in the field needed no convincing; they already had discovered the advantages of the drug. One of Ohler's most striking and original claims is that methamphetamines helped German soldiers maintain the momentum of the devastating Blitzkrieg campaign in France in 1940, enabling them to put off periods of sleep and rest to press relentlessly forward. The British and French could not understand how the Germans could keep attacking with so few breaks; the Germans did it because many of their men were speeding on a chemically induced Teutonic fury. Back in Germany, Nazi health officials were becoming concerned about the widespread use of Pervitin. Restrictions were placed on its use and distribution by civilians, though it could still be readily obtained by prescription. The military disregarded these late-blooming scruples and placed orders for thirty-five million tablets.

Over the course of the war, German commanders looked for new chemical means of stimulating their troops to greater efforts, especially as the tide turned against the Reich. None persevered more than Admiral Hellmuth Heye, who wanted a means of sustaining the pilots of such desperate "miracle weapons" as "two-man U-boats, midget submarines and one-man torpedoes" that were proposed in the last year of the conflict. Aided by willing scientists, Heye sponsored experiments with drugs combining opiates, cocaine, and methamphetamine. Unfortunately for Heye, and for his subjects, these concoctions proved more dangerous to those taking them than to the enemy. Pharmacology could not win the war for Germany.

Another of Ohler's startling revelations is the extent to which Adolf Hitler himself succumbed to addictive drugs. The key figure here was Dr. Theodor Morell, who ran a showy medical practice on Berlin's fashionable Kurfürstendamm. Morell specialized in treating well-to-do patients who complained of feeling run-down with vitamin injections, sometimes jazzed up with steroids. Some of his patients who were well connected in the Nazi Party introduced him to the Führer. Upon seizing control of the German state in 1933, Hitler was a teetotaler and vegetarian, but despite these healthy habits he suffered from a range of ailments, including digestive problems and skin disorders. At first, Morell probably helped the dictator by prescribing a treatment that restored the bacteriological balance in his intestinal tract. But then he began a regimen of injecting Hitler with his popular mixtures of vitamins, glucose, and other substances. Hitler did not object to the frequent injections, as they seemed to mirror his own blunt and aggressive response to problems, and he became increasingly reliant on these dubious analeptics to get him through speeches and diplomatic negotiations.

Convinced that he was benefiting from energizing but anodyne substances, Hitler was becoming dependent on the needle. He would also become addicted to the increasingly dangerous substances that Morell was putting in his syringes. By 1941, with World War II hanging in the balance as German forces invaded the Soviet Union, Morell was frantically injecting his patient with an increasingly toxic brew of hormones and steroids. Even this was not enough; in 1943, with the war decisively turning against Germany, Hitler needed more to get through his days. Morell began dosing him with Eukodal, a potent opiate. Soon Hitler could not function without this drug, which Morell characteristically began mixing with other narcotics. It is arguable that Hitler's growing dissociation from political and military realities was at least in part the result of his drug addiction. As the Allied armies closed in on Germany, Morell lost his access to Eukodal, and Hitler's last months were haunted by withdrawal pains as well as the bitterness of defeat.

Ohler tells his compelling tale of government-sanctioned drug abuse with verve and skill. His book deepens his readers' understanding of Nazi Germany and World War II, while opening a new window into the evils unleashed by Adolf Hitler. *Blitzed* received generally positive reviews, mainly for Ohler's engaging narrative and his examination of a little-discussed aspect of Germany in the war, although some critics questioned the certainty with which he attributes certain tactical missteps to the Nazis' drug use. Dagmar Herzog, reviewing the book for the *New York Times*, praised Ohler for "the rich array of rare documents he mines and the archival images he reproduces" as well as for his "persuasive" character studies of Ranke and other such figures, but warned that "the larger conclusions Ohler draws are unsubstantiated" and that he "frequently identifies causation where there is only correlation." In a review for the *New York Review of Books*, Antony Beevor similarly noted that "Ohler is on less certain ground" with some of his interpretations of events, such as "when he ascribes Hitler's famous order to halt the tanks short of Dunkirk to Reichsmarschall Hermann Göring's morphine dependency," but concluded that while "Ohler's book may well irritate some historians" with its "flippant remarks and . . . chapter titles such as 'Sieg High!' and 'High Hitler,'" *Blitzed* remains, as biographer Ian Kershaw asserted, "'a serious piece of scholarship,' and one that is very well researched."

Daniel P. Murphy

Review Sources

Beevor, Antony. "The Very Drugged Nazis." Review of *Blitzed: Drugs in the Third Reich*, by Norman Ohler, translated by Shaun Whiteside. *The New York Review of Books*, 9 Mar. 2017, www.nybooks.com/articles/2017/03/09/blitzed-very-drugged-nazis. Accessed 22 Jan. 2018.

Review of *Blitzed: Drugs in the Third Reich*, by Norman Ohler, translated by Shaun Whiteside. *Kirkus Reviews*, 1 Feb. 2017. *Academic Search Complete*, search.ebscohost.com/login.aspx?direct=true&db=a9h&AN=121021851&site=ehost-live. Accessed 22 Jan. 2018.

Herzog, Dagmar. "Hitler's Little Helper: A History of Rampant Drug Use under the Nazis." Review of *Blitzed: Drugs in the Third Reich*, by Norman Ohler, translated by Shaun Whiteside. *The New York Times*, 27 Mar. 2017, www.nytimes.com/2017/03/27/books/review/blitzed-drugs-third-reich-norman-ohler.html. Accessed 22 Jan. 2018.

Pendle, George. "War on Drugs." Review of *Blitzed: Drugs in the Third Reich*, by Norman Ohler, translated by Shaun Whiteside. *Esquire*, Apr. 2017, pp. 40–42. *Academic Search Complete*, search.ebscohost.com/login.aspx?direct=true&db=a9h&AN=121514100&site=ehost-live. Accessed 22 Jan. 2018.

Rohlwing, Brett. Review of *Blitzed: Drugs in the Third Reich*, by Norman Ohler, translated by Shaun Whiteside. *Library Journal*, 15 Mar. 2017, pp. 127–28. *Academic Search Complete*, search.ebscohost.com/login.aspx?direct=true&db=a9h&AN=121964510&site=ehost-live. Accessed 22 Jan. 2018.

The Blood of Emmett Till

Author: Timothy B. Tyson (b. 1959)
Publisher: Simon & Schuster (New York).
  304 pp.
Type of work: History
Time: 1954 to the present
Locale: Primarily Money, Mississippi

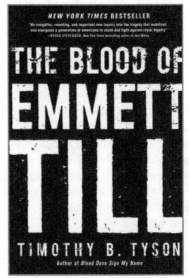

Courtesy of Simon and Schuster

The Blood of Emmett Till *provides an account of the murder of Emmett Till, a black fourteen-year-old who was killed near Money, Mississippi, after he allegedly insulted a white woman. Timothy B. Tyson examines the case itself but also its immediate background and its ongoing legacy.*

Principal personages
EMMETT TILL, a fourteen-year-old African
    American who was murdered in rural Mississippi
CAROLYN BRYANT, the white woman whom he had allegedly insulted or assaulted
MAMIE TILL BRADLEY, his mother
ROY BRYANT, Bryant's husband and owner of the store where the incident between
    Bryant and Till allegedly happened; he was tried for Till's murder
J. W. "BIG" MILAM, Roy Bryant's older half brother; he was tried for Till's murder
MOSES WRIGHT, Till's granduncle, a preacher and farmer whom Till was visiting
CURTIS M. SWANGO, the judge who presided over the trial of Bryant and Milam
HENRY CLARENCE "H. C." STRIDER, the sheriff of Tallahatchie County, Mississippi,
    who claimed jurisdiction over the Till murder case

The racially motivated murder of an African American man in the South, even in the 1950s, sadly was not a rare occurrence. As Timothy B. Tyson argues in this book, the murder of Emmett Till in rural Mississippi in August 1954 was different, however, because it prompted a national outcry and greatly affected the nascent civil rights movement. Just a few days after the men who were charged with Till's murder were acquitted, Rosa Parks refused to give up her seat on a bus to a white man, as the segregation laws in Montgomery, Alabama, required. Parks later reportedly told Rev. Jesse Jackson that when she took this action, she was thinking of Emmett Till.

Tyson has written widely on the history of the civil rights movement, but he was given a unique opportunity that makes this a remarkable book. In 2004, Tyson had published a book about a 1970 hate crime in Oxford, North Carolina. That book, *Blood Done Sign My Name*, told of the murder of Henry Marrow, a twenty-three-year-old African American veteran. Tyson lived in Oxford at that time, and the men accused of killing Marrow were family members of a friend. Tyson's father, a white United

Methodist minister, openly condemned the murder of Marrow, and backlash against his outspokenness resulted in the Tyson family leaving Oxford. The Marrow case, though much later, bore striking similarities to that of Emmett Till. In both cases, a young African American man was accused of making sexually charged comments about a white woman, and in both cases, an all-white jury found the white men accused of the murder to be not guilty.

A few years after publishing *Blood Done Sign My Name*, in 2008 Tyson received a call from a woman who had read the book and wanted to express her appreciation of it. She also said she had given the book to her mother-in-law, who had read it and wanted to talk to Tyson. The woman's mother-in-law was the former Carolyn Bryant, the woman whom Emmett Till was accused of molesting or offending, depending upon which version of events one accepted. Bryant had never given any extensive interviews about the case, and then, more than fifty years later, she was willing to talk to Tyson. Bryant's memories, and her admission that she could not remember some details of the incident that led to Till's death, are rich sources that Tyson uses effectively in this book.

The bulk of this book deals with Till's murder, the investigation into it, and the resulting trial. But Tyson also puts the events surrounding Till's death into a broader context—the general state of race relations in the South in that era and the widely held beliefs, especially in rural Mississippi, that whites were superior and that all African Americans should show deference to all whites. Just three months before Till was killed, the US Supreme Court had handed down its decision in *Brown v. Board of Education*, ordering the desegregation of schools throughout the nation. Many Southern whites became paranoid about the potential ramifications of integrating the schools, which they believed would lead to interracial

> *Historian Timothy B. Tyson teaches at the Duke Divinity School and is a senior research scholar at the Center for Documentary Studies at Duke University. His previous books include* Radio Free Dixie: Robert F. Williams and the Roots of Black Power *(2001) and* Blood Done Sign My Name *(2004).*

dating, mixed marriages, and miscegenation, and were looking for ways to defend their long-standing way of life.

Emmett Till's family participated in the Great Migration from the rural South to the North that occurred during and after World War I. His mother's family had moved to Argo, Illinois, just outside of Chicago, in 1924. Many African Americans living in Argo referred to it as Little Mississippi, because so many people from Mississippi lived in the town. The memories that Argo's African Americans had about life in Mississippi included the awareness of the strength of white supremacist thinking there and Mississippi's sordid record of lynchings. Tyson notes that "Mississippi outstripped the rest of the nation in virtually every measure of lynching." Mamie Till Bradley, Emmett's mother, recalled a story from her childhood about the cruel mistreatment of a young African American girl and reflected, "Was this a true story? I don't know. But I do know this: Somewhere between the fact we know and the anxiety we feel is the reality we live." Compounding the situation in rural Mississippi, many African American families lived as tenant farmers on farms owned by white men. Getting "out of line," according to the whites' expectations in that time and place, or speaking out too boldly about civil rights like voting, could lead to eviction, in which case the black family would lose both its livelihood and its housing.

But the Chicago connections were also an important part of both the background and the later developments in the Till case. Till was a fourteen-year-old boy who had grown up in Argo and Chicago and gone to summer with his granduncle Moses Wright, a farmer and preacher, near Money, Mississippi. Till had been told how he was expected to behave when interacting with white people in Mississippi, but he had no experience living in the kind of racially charged environment he was in that summer. In the aftermath of Till's murder, African American churches, labor unions, civil rights organizations, and African American newspapers such as the *Chicago Defender* led the way in making the case a tragedy that the rest of the nation could not ignore.

The incident that led to Till's murder happened in a small country store in Money on Wednesday, August 24, 1955. Wright's sons Maurice and Simeon had borrowed his car and driven to Bryant's Grocery and Meat Market in Money, also bringing Emmett Till, Till's cousin Wheeler Parker Jr., and neighbors Pete Parker, Ruthie Mae Crawford, and Roosevelt Crawford. While most of the group waited on the store's front porch, Till went inside, where twenty-one-year-old Carolyn Bryant was working. What happened inside still is not clear. When her husband, Roy, was on trial for killing Till, Bryant testified that Till had grabbed her waist and threatened her. But when she talked to Tyson more than fifty years later, she said that this did not happen. She claimed she could not remember exactly what happened but said that Till did not physically accost her. After Till left the store and Bryant went for a gun in the car, Till wolf-whistled at her. Regardless, Till made some comment that offended her, because as Tyson records, when Roy Bryant and his half brother J. W. Milam invaded Moses Wright's home early Sunday to kidnap Till, they said they were after "the one that done the talking up at Money," making no mention of any physical assault.

Although witnesses may have been intimidated, Wright testified to Bryant and Milam kidnapping the young man and evidence tied them to the place where the murder had happened. Till had been beaten, then shot, and his body tied to a large industrial iron fan and thrown into the Tallahatchie River. It was widely believed that other men may have been involved, but Bryant and Milam were the only ones ever charged with any crime in connection with the case.

Tyson notes that initially many whites in Mississippi spoke critically about the murder. Newspapers in Mississippi's major cities condemned the killing and worried about the image such acts presented to the world about the state. But as so much criticism from outside was heaped upon the state, the feelings of white Mississippians began to harden. Journalists and civil rights activists who visited Sumner, Mississippi, where the trial was held, were struck by the near-universal expression of two opinions: it was generally assumed that Bryant and Milam were guilty, but also that they would be acquitted. Outsiders present at the trial believed that the judge, Curtis M. Swango, did everything he could to see that the trial was conducted properly. But the result was just as many had predicted: the all-white jury deliberated for an hour before returning a verdict of not guilty.

A significant part of Tyson's book deals with the aftermath of the murder and the trial, both in the immediate period of the fall of 1954 through today. Mamie Till Bradley was determined to keep the murder of her son before the eyes of the public; against the advice of the mortician who prepared Till's body for burial, she insisted that the casket be open at the funeral, so that people could see what had been done to her son. In Chicago and other northern cities, the African American community and press called attention to the injustices involved. Rallies throughout the country, supported by civil rights leaders such as Thurgood Marshall as well as labor unions with significant African American membership, made the case into a national and even international cause. The US State Department eventually acknowledged that the injustices committed against African Americans in the South hurt the nation's image in dealing with other nations, especially emerging nations in Africa and Asia. Tyson argues convincingly that awareness of Till's fate—and of the failure to hold anyone accountable— galvanized the rising civil rights movement and still resonates with those protesting racial injustice. He notes that in 2014, for example, after a grand jury in Ferguson, Missouri, decided not to indict a police officer for the fatal shooting of Michael Brown, an unarmed African American teenager, crowds demonstrating in front of the White House chanted, "How many black kids will you kill? Michael Brown, Emmett Till!"

Critics have generally welcomed Tyson's book, although some reviewers noted that some earlier studies go into even greater depth in the case. But Tyson had two things at his disposal that earlier writers did not: his interview with Carolyn Bryant (then known as Carolyn Donham), including her admission that some of her trial testimony was untrue, and a copy of the trial transcript, which for some time was believed lost. Tyson writes with conviction and with passion. Some readers might feel uncomfortable with Tyson's argument that injustices such as those typified by the Till case are not as far in the past as they might wish to believe, but his evidence is worthy of consideration. This is a valuable book that brilliantly illustrates the complexities of race relations in the United States both in the 1950s and today.

Mark S. Joy, PhD

Review Sources

Review of *The Blood of Emmett Till*, by Timothy B. Tyson. *Publishers Weekly*, 24 Oct. 2016, p. 68.

Newkirk, Vann R., II. "How the Blood of Emmett Till Still Stains America Today." Review of *The Blood of Emmett Till*, by Timothy B. Tyson. *The Atlantic*, 16 Feb. 2017, www.theatlantic.com/entertainment/archive/2017/02/how-the-blood-of-emmett-till-still-stains-america-today/516891. Accessed 3 Oct. 2017.

Parham, Jason. "Emmett Till's Murder: What Really Happened That Day in the Store?" Review of *The Blood of Emmett Till*, by Timothy B. Tyson. *The New York Times*, 27 Jan. 2017, www.nytimes.com/2017/01/27/books/review/blood-of-emmett-till-timothy-b-tyson.html. Accessed 3 Oct. 2017.

Blue on Blue
An Insider's Story of Good Cops Catching Bad Cops

Authors: Charles Campisi and Gordon Dillow
Publisher: Scribner (New York). 368 pp.
Type of work: Memoir, history
Time: 1973–2014
Locale: New York City, New York

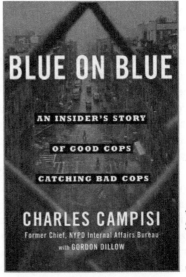

BLUE ON BLUE

AN INSIDER'S STORY

OF GOOD COPS

CATCHING BAD COPS

CHARLES CAMPISI

Former Chief, NYPD Internal Affairs Bureau
with GORDON DILLOW

Courtesy of Scribner

Part memoir, part history, Charles Campisi's
Blue on Blue: An Insider's Story of Good
Cops Catching Bad Cops *provides a treasure
trove of New York City cop lore and constitutes a valuable source of information from
an authority on law-enforcement efforts to
reduce police corruption and misconduct.*

Principal personages

CHARLES CAMPISI, a former New York Po-
lice Department (NYPD) officer of more than forty years and chief of the Internal
Affairs Bureau (IAB) from 1996 until he retired in 2014
RAY KELLY, the first NYPD commissioner to serve nonconsecutive terms (1992–94
and 2002–13)
HOWARD SAFIR, NYPD commissioner from 1996 to 2000
ABE BEAME, mayor from 1974 to 1977
ED KOCH, a law-and-order politician who served as mayor from 1978 to 1989
DAVID DINKINS, mayor from 1990 to 1993
RUDY GIULIANI, mayor from 1994 to 2001
MICHAEL BLOOMBERG, mayor from 2002 to 2013
BILL DE BLASIO, mayor from 2014 to present
BILL BRATTON, the second NYPD commissioner to serve nonconsecutive terms
(1994–96 and 2014–16)
JACK MAPLE, a New York City Transit police officer and author who transformed the
NYPD via computer analysis of statistics (CompStat) as deputy commissioner
from 1996 to 2001

Charles Campisi's *Blue on Blue* opens with a sequence that could appear in a television crime drama. A group of undercover police officers, disguised in plainclothes,
are watching a suspect. They follow the wily subject in nondescript vehicles as he
drives from his Bronx home to a known crack house in Washington Heights. The target
comes out with a duffle bag full of crack to ferry to southern distribution points. The
undercovers follow the target onto the turnpike before having uniformed cops pull
him over. The driver exits, holding up his NYPD shield. Yes, he really is a policeman,

a dirty cop who has been caught trafficking drugs. His career in law enforcement is over, and his new career as prison inmate will soon begin. His exposure as a crook and his capture has been effected because of the professional investigation of the Internal Affairs Bureau (IAB), the arm of the police department charged with clamping down on corruption and misconduct within the ranks.

IAB was under Campisi's command from 1996 to 2014. Before he reached that pinnacle, however, Campisi began as an ordinary cop. He wanted to join the NYPD from childhood, growing up near the Eighty-Third Precinct in Brooklyn. At age eighteen, he took the NYPD written and health examinations and submitted to a background check before the trainee program was cut and he enrolled at Long Island University–Brooklyn. In late 1973, at age twenty-one, he was selected as a recruit and entered the Police Academy, where the motto inspires potential officers to "Enter to learn, go forth to serve."

And learn he did. Campisi provides a close-up of the rigorous education that recruits must endure. The six-month training period focuses on four areas. "Law" covers state and city criminal and civil codes, incorporating lectures on integrity and honesty with warnings about corruption—such as accepting bribes and gratuities, or resorting to extortion—which can lead to dismissal, disgrace, loss of benefits, and possible imprisonment. "Police science" delves into department procedures and regulations. "Social science" covers human psychology and race relations, two important subjects in a city as large and diverse as New York. "Physical science" encompasses fitness training, firearms safety and practice, baton tactics, basic self-defense, takedown methods, handcuffing techniques, and first aid.

Campisi graduated from the academy in March 1974, during an era of high crime in New York City. In 1973 NYPD officers killed 58 people and wounded another 118; 7 cops were killed; and nearly 1,700 homicides and violent crimes took place. As a new officer, Campisi inherited shield 791, a badge with a lengthy history. He had to purchase his own guns (NYPD cops are required to be armed both on and off duty). During his entire career, Campisi, like most police officers, never fired a gun at another person while on the job. His virtuous character is illuminated by two dramatized incidents: in one, he prevented a fellow officer from shooting a fleeing burglar in the back; in the second, he refused to accept a free cup of coffee in a restaurant.

Campisi's first assignment was with the Manhattan Traffic Area Scooter Task Force, during which time he wrote tickets for traffic infractions. He afterward transferred to the Seventy-Third Precinct (also known as Fort Zinderneuf, after the French Foreign Legion outpost in *Beau Geste*), covering the high-crime Brownsville and Ocean Hill neighborhoods of Brooklyn. When Campisi arrived, Brownsville featured abandoned apartment blocks, burned-out and boarded-up buildings, and streets lined with stripped cars.

In mid-1975 Campisi and some five thousand other officers were laid off. During twenty-two months of diminished police presence, New York City descended into rampant crime, businesses fleeing and uncollected garbage mounting, which collectively depressed tourism, a longtime source of revenue. The downward slide began to reverse with the 1977 election of law-and-order candidate Ed Koch as mayor. Campisi was rehired and returned to the Seventy-Third Precinct just in time for the infamous blackout of July 13, 1977, a span of twenty-five hours without electricity that spawned lootings, riots, fires, and thousands of arrests in Brooklyn and the Bronx.

Campisi, electing to become a supervising officer (rather than a detective-investigator, a position that never achieves command), took the sergeant's exam in 1978. He waited out a NYPD freeze on promotions by teaching law at the Police Academy and advanced to the rank of sergeant in 1982. Assigned to Manhattan Traffic, he rose to lieutenant, then captain and commanding officer in 1985, in charge of managing traffic, VIP events, parades, and protests. By 1989, he commanded the Sixth Precinct, in the low-crime areas of Greenwich Village and West Village. About two years later, he headed the civilian-liaison NYPD Cadet Corps while teaching police science at John Jay College of Criminal Justice, where he had earned his master's degree.

In 1993 Campisi was assigned to a two-year stint as head of the Corruption Prevention and Analysis Unit for the Internal Affairs Bureau. Though initially reluctant—IAB is universally hated by rank-and-file police officers, who call them "the rat squad" for their dedication to investigating fellow cops—Campisi accepted the post and found his niche.

Corruption and misconduct, the author reminds readers, have been factors since the creation of the NYPD in 1845. Payoffs, bribes, extortion, and excessive force all undermine police authority. Furthermore, wrongdoing perpetuates a love-hate relationship with public and media, who perceive badge-wearers as necessary to maintain law and order but whose power permits individuals to do evil with impunity. Campisi notes that when corruption in the NYPD becomes widespread and obvious—typically about every twenty years—reformers demand changes. He refers to such past anticorruption efforts as the Lexow Committee (1894), Curran Committee (1912), Hofstadter Committee (1931), Helfand Commission (1951), Knapp Commission (1970–72), and Mollen Commission (1992). The Knapp Commission resulted in the creation of the Internal Affairs Division (IAD) to investigate cases of corruption and misconduct. The Mollen Commission replaced the poorly funded, understaffed, secretive IAD with the Internal Affairs Bureau (IAB), a separate entity equal to the Detective Bureau, Organized Crime Bureau, and other units of the NYPD. The IAB is charged with examining all allegations against the police. The bureau's ultimate purpose is not just to expose and prosecute crooked cops, but also to protect innocent officers from unjust accusations.

A journalist for over three decades, Gordon Dillow previously coauthored Where the Money Is: True Tales from the Bank Robbery Capital of the World *(2003),* Uppity: My Untold Story about the Games People Play *(2011), and* Trauma Red: The Making of a Surgeon in War and in America's Cities *(2014).*

Campisi, rising to IAB chief in 1996, built the organization into the world's largest police department operation specializing in internal corruption and misconduct investigations. In the twenty-first century, the IAB employs about 750 investigators equipped with high-tech devices to record, follow, and document illegal activities of suspects, often revealed in "integrity tests," or sting operations. He also helped remove the stigma of working for IAB by selecting candidates at random from across the

NYPD and assigning them to two-year terms with the bureau. To break down the Blue Wall of Silence (the philosophy of never informing on fellow officers), he instituted the PRIDE line, where cops can anonymously lodge complaints or report suspicious activities.

To illustrate the effectiveness of the IAB, Campisi provides case histories of controversial incidents that occurred during his watch as head of the bureau. One of these concerned Abner Louima, who was sodomized in 1997 with a broken broom handle while in police custody; Louima received millions of dollars in damages in a civil lawsuit, and two officers received extensive prison terms. Another case involved African immigrant Amadou Diallo, who, in 1999, was shot to death by four white cops as he reached for his wallet; a racially mixed jury ruled it a tragic accident and the officers were acquitted.

As might be expected of a career law-enforcement agent, Campisi comes across in

Courtesy of Cyberdiligence

A member of the New York Police Department from 1973 until 2014, Charles Campisi rose from police officer to chief of the Internal Affairs Bureau. He held the latter post for over seventeen years, the longest in New York City history. Blue on Blue is his first book.

Blue on Blue as conservative, opinionated, and somewhat self-righteous. Yet he also seems truthful and conscientious, as willing to expose departmental failures as to extol triumphs. He does not hide his hostility toward lawyers, politicians he perceives as soft on crime, and activists who question police behavior. And although stop-and-frisk was conducted in a racially discriminatory, and thus unconstitutional, manner, Campisi still supports the practice as a crime-fighting tool.

Nonetheless, as chief of IAB, Campisi achieved an unsurpassed reputation for integrity, which kept him at his post through several changes in city and departmental administrations. In the end, Campisi—now a respected police consultant—can claim partial responsibility for New York City's resurgence. In 2013, the year before Campisi retired, there were 335 homicides, a historic low, and no officers died in the line of duty. By working effectively to control police corruption and misconduct, he seems to have eliminated the twenty-year cycle of police reform. Campisi's contributions—primarily through setting a sterling example of what a police officer should be—have arguably made the NYPD a better place to work and New York City a better place to live.

Jack Ewing

Review Sources

Altschuler, Glenn C. "Campisi's 'Blue on Blue': Good Cops and Bad, from One Who Knows." Review of *Blue on Blue: An Insider's Story of Good Cops Catching Bad Cops*, by Charles Campisi with Gordon Dillow. *Philadelphia Inquirer*, 12 May 2017, www.philly.com/philly/entertainment/20170514_Campisi_s__Blue_ on_Blue___Good_cops_and_bad__from_one_who_knows.html. Accessed 13 Nov. 2015.

Barry, Michael Thomas. Review of *Blue on Blue: An Insider's Story of Good Cops Catching Bad Cops*, by Charles Campisi with Gordon Dillow. *New York Journal of Books*, 6 Feb. 2017, www.nyjournalofbooks.com/book-review/blue-on-blue. Accessed 13 Nov. 2017.

Review of *Blue on Blue: An Insider's Story of Good Cops Catching Bad Cops*, by Charles Campisi with Gordon Dillow. *Kirkus Reviews*, 1 Nov. 2016, p. 1. *Literary Reference Center Plus*, search.ebscohost.com/login.aspx?direct=true&db=lkh&A N=119153720&site=lrc-plus. Accessed 21 Nov. 2017.

Kosner, Edward. "The King of the Rat Squad." Review of *Blue on Blue: An Insider's Story of Good Cops Catching Bad Cops*, by Charles Campisi with Gordon Dillow. *The Wall Street Journal*, 8 Feb. 2017, www.wsj.com/articles/the-king-of-the-rat-squad-1486597201. Accessed 13 Nov. 2017.

Leavitt, Leonard. "Blue on Blue: More Actual Than Alternative Facts." Review of *Blue on Blue: An Insider's Story of Good Cops Catching Bad Cops*, by Charles Campisi with Gordon Dillow. *NYPD Confidential*, 6 Feb. 2017, nypdconfidential. com/columns/2017/170206.html. Accessed 13 Nov. 2017.

A Book of American Martyrs

Author: Joyce Carol Oates (b. 1938)
Publisher: Ecco (New York). 752 pp.
Type of work: Novel
Time: 1999–2012
Locales: Ohio; Michigan; New York City, New York; Indiana; West Virginia

In A Book of American Martyrs, *Joyce Carol Oates examines a volatile, divisive issue. She dramatizes the aftereffects of a violent confrontation between a fundamentalist antiabortion activist and a sympathetic doctor dedicated to the pro-choice cause, and humanizes those whose lives are forever changed by events beyond their control.*

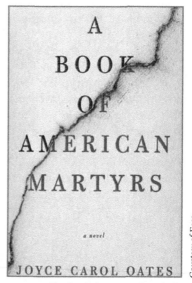

Courtesy of Ecco

Principal characters

LUTHER AMOS DUNPHY, carpenter-roofer, aspiring evangelical minister, and antiabortion activist
EDNA MAE REISER DUNPHY, his wife, mother of their five children
DAWN DUNPHY, their eldest daughter
AUGUSTUS "GUS" VOORHEES, doctor, abortion clinic chief, and pro-choice activist
JENNA MATHESON VOORHEES, a lawyer, Gus's widow, and mother of their children
DARREN VOORHEES, the Voorhees's son and eldest child
NAOMI ANNE VOORHEES, the Voorhees's daughter
MELISSA VOORHEES, the Voorhees's adopted daughter
REV. DENNIS KUHN, minister at the Dunphys' evangelical church
MADELENA "LENA" KEIN, Gus's estranged birth mother, a professor at New York University
KARL KINCH, Lena's disabled son
MAJOR TIMOTHY BARRON, a veteran, Gus's escort

A Book of American Martyrs is launched by a shocking act. One morning in late 1999, thirty-nine-year-old roofer-carpenter Luther Dunphy is lurking outside the Broome County Women's Center in Muskegee Falls, a fictional rural community in Ohio. When a minivan containing two men arrives, Luther charges forward and without hesitation blasts the two arrivals with a Mossberg twelve-gauge double-barrel shotgun. Afterward, he puts down the weapon, kneels in surrender, and waits calmly to be taken into custody beside the bleeding bodies of the two men he has killed: Dr. Augustus "Gus" Voorhees, an abortion provider, and his volunteer escort, retired US Army Major Timothy Barron.

Courtesy of Dustin Cohen

Joyce Carol Oates is one of America's most prolific and best-known authors. Since 1963, she has published more than fifty novels, numerous collections of short stories and poetry, plus novellas, young-adult and children's fiction, plays, and essays. Oates has won numerous honors, including the National Medal of Humanities, several O. Henry Awards, multiple Pushcart Prizes, a National Book Award, and several Pulitzer Prize nominations.

Following the opening salvo, the novel presents a profile of Luther Dunphy. Told from Luther's first-person perspective (he is the first of several narrators made unreliable by mental illness, extreme emotional distress, drugs, or other causes), the section headlined "Soldier of God" gives highlights of Luther's life from the age of twelve. Readers learn of his hardscrabble upbringing, his early years as a school bully, and his career as a teenaged sexual abuser—which is suddenly brought to a halt when a victim, Felice Sipper, stabs him several times with a jackknife as he is assaulting her. After Luther drops out of high school, he meets his future wife, Edna Mae Reiser, who eventually leads him into joining an evangelical sect, the St. Paul Missionary Church of Jesus, where they are subsequently married. The fundamentalist beliefs—the church is opposed to carbonated beverages, tobacco, chewing gum, artificial sweeteners, gambling, television, contraception, socialism, communism, atheism, homosexuality, and most of all, abortion—slowly seep into Luther's soul, thanks to fiery sermons from Rev. Dennis Kuhn. Luther feels called to become a preacher.

Though unqualified and unimaginative, he is accepted as a part-time theology student at the Toledo School of Ministry. Though he backslides for a time, drinking at local bars and consorting with prostitutes, he manages to earn a diploma. He fathers several children with Edna Mae: Luke, Dawn, Noah, and Anita. His youngest daughter, Daphne, afflicted with Down's syndrome, is killed at age three in an automobile crash that severely injures Luther. He becomes a lay minister, as well as an antiabortion activist with the Army of God and Operation Rescue. Inspired by the acts of others who have murdered abortion doctors, Luther one day picks up his shotgun and heads out to make a memorable gesture for the pro-life cause. He knows in advance he could become a martyr—like the Protestants of England and Scotland he read about in John Foxe's *A Book of Martyrs* (1563), who died while opposing the Catholic Church—because Ohio is a capital punishment state.

The narrative then shifts to the story of Dr. Gus Voorhees, Luther's main target. Readers are only acquainted with Gus through the impressions of others, primarily his daughter, Naomi, who becomes obsessed with collecting and archiving every possible scrap of information about her late father. The evidence she gathers—including clippings, photos, interviews, and personal memories of family members and acquaintances—reveals an individual as flawed in his own way as his killer. During his career as a respected activist for women's causes, including work as an abortion provider, Gus often put his family at risk. The Voorhees had to move frequently to avoid threats from fanatics. During the final two years of his life, Gus was an absentee father, working in Ohio while his family lived in Michigan. Like Luther, Gus realized he could end up dead, a martyr like other abortion providers before him, and despite that knowledge, pursued his work anyway. Oates suggests that both Luther and Gus, in pursuing their respective martyrdoms, were essentially suicidal.

In addition to the topic of abortion, *A Book of American Martyrs* deals with other significant issues that roil public opinion in the United States. The morality of capital punishment, for example, is extensively examined as it relates to Luther and the preferred method of death-dealing, lethal injection, which has come under scrutiny in the twenty-first century because of several botched executions. The stances of political conservatives and liberals are also explored, and both are found wanting.

One of Oates's strongest arguments is that fanaticism, whether for good or ill, is destructive. The author illuminates this point by showing how the violent interaction between Luther and Gus adversely affects their respective families, making them all unwitting, unwilling martyrs. Edna Mae Dunphy, after her husband's arrest, and during his trials and incarceration, for a time descends further into a twilight existence punctuated with doses of OxyContin. Her eldest daughter, Dawn, is suffused with suppressed rage after becoming the butt of cruel schoolyard taunts about her father, who is in jail. Worse, a group of bullying boys stalk, capture, and sexually assault her. Dawn gains revenge by seeking out her assailants and attacking them with a hammer. Expelled from school for her behavior, she works at menial jobs and channels her anger by training to become a boxer. Turning pro, she fights under the nickname "D.D. Dunphy, the Hammer of Jesus." When Dawn becomes successful enough to earn money as a boxer, she sends some of her earnings home to help her family. Edna Mae refuses to touch the cash, however, considering it a handout from Satan.

The Voorhees family is likewise shattered by the loss of Gus. Gus's widow, Jenna, who had put her own career as a lawyer on hold for the sake of her husband, has a mental breakdown. She ultimately leaves her children with their grandparents in Michigan and flees to Vermont to resume her occupation, maintaining only sporadic contact with her children thereafter. Gus's children, Darren and Naomi, suffer as objects of scorn throughout high school. Unmotivated in college, both of them become dropouts. Darren heads to the Pacific Northwest to become a graphic novelist, dealing with dark, morbid subjects, particularly lethal injection. Naomi continues to assemble her Gus Voorhees archive, living aimlessly until she is invited to visit Madalena "Lena" Kein, Gus's birth mother who nearly aborted him and then abandoned him when he was eight years old.

Over a ten-day stay, Naomi and Lena go on frequent excursions around the city. Naomi is introduced to many exciting people—writers, filmmakers, critics, and artists. She and Lena begin to bond. Toward the end of her visit, Naomi meets the brilliant but repellent poet and composer Karl Kinch. Karl, who has multiple sclerosis, HIV, and other physical problems, and is confined to a wheelchair, is taken with Naomi. As the women leave, Lena confesses that Karl is her son, and thus Naomi's half uncle. Naomi is the first person in the family to be entrusted with this secret. She is refreshed by her encounter with Lena and Karl and energized by New York's fast pace. She returns with new purpose to her initial objective: documenting the life of her lost father. As part of this goal, she vows to seek reconciliation, to interact with Dawn, the most prominent living member of the Dunphy family, in order to rid herself of the hatred she has harbored toward the innocent children of the man who murdered Gus.

A massive doorstop of a book—remarkably, Oates prefers to write first drafts of her works in longhand—and one of the perennially best-selling author's longest novels, *A Book of American Martyrs* nonetheless remains compelling throughout. This can be credited to Oates's ability to develop unique characters with credible voices and then set them into motion in plots that develop organically, generating conflict and suspense.

Martyrs revisits familiar Oates territory. A family saga in the fashion of *We Were the Mulvaneys* (1996) or *The Falls* (2004), it also touches on social stratification like that illustrated in *Carthage* (2014). The novel also tackles contemporary issues in the manner of *Do with Me What You Will* (1973) or *The Sacrifice* (2015). There is a strong religious undertone, as in *Son of the Morning* (1978), and there is sexual tension and mayhem of the type that drives such novels as *The Assassins: A Book of Hours* (1975) and *American Appetites* (1989). By deftly blending such diverse thematic elements, Oates has created in *A Book of American Martyrs* one of the most complex and nuanced novels she has produced in her long and distinguished career.

Jack Ewing

Review Sources

Charles, Ron. "Joyce Carol Oates's New Novel Arrives Splattered with our Country's Hot Blood." Review of *A Book of American Martyrs*, by Joyce Carol Oates. *The Washington Post*, 31 Jan. 2017, www.washingtonpost.com/entertainment/ books/joyce-carol-oates-wades-into-the-abortion-debate-giving-voice-to-both-sides/2017/01/30/d63d1250-e49e-11e6-ba11-63c4b4fb5a63_story.html. Accessed 29 Nov. 2017.

Franklin, Ruth. "A Deep American Horror Exposed." Review of *A Book of American Martyrs*, by Joyce Carol Oates. *The New York Review of Books*, 23 Mar. 2017, www.nybooks.com/articles/2017/03/23/joyce-carol-oates-american-martyrs-horror-exposed/. Accessed 29 Nov. 2017.

Mathis, Ayana. "Joyce Carol Oates's Novel Plumbs the Depths of America's Abortion War." Review of *A Book of American Martyrs*, by Joyce Carol Oates. *The New York Times*, 16 Feb. 2017, www.nytimes.com/2017/02/16/books/review/ book-of-american-martyrs-joyce-carol-oates.html. Accessed 29 Nov. 2017.

Scherstuhl, Alan. "It's Not Joyce Carol Oates Who Splashes Blood on Us. It's America." Review of *A Book of American Martyrs*, by Joyce Carol Oates. *Chicago Review of Books*, 13 Feb. 2017, chireviewofbooks.com/2017/02/13/its-not-joyce-carol-oates-who-splashes-blood-on-us-its-america/. Accessed 29 Nov. 2017.

Wagner, Erica. "*A Book of American Martyrs* by Joyce Carol Oates Review—Gripping Fiction." Review of *A Book of American Martyrs*, by Joyce Carol Oates. *The Guardian*, 20 Sept. 2017, www.theguardian.com/books/2017/jun/11/a-book-of-american-martyrs-joyce-carol-oates-review. Accessed 29 Nov. 2017.

The Book That Changed America
How Darwin's Theory of Evolution Ignited a Nation

Author: Randall Fuller (b. 1963)
Publisher: Viking (New York). Illustrated. 304 pp.
Type of work: History
Time: 1859–61
Locale: Concord, Massachusetts

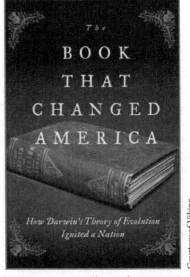

In The Book That Changed America: How Darwin's Theory of Evolution Ignited a Nation, *author Randall Fuller traces the relationship between the reception of Charles Darwin's 1859 book* On the Origin of Species *and the abolitionist movement in the United States. Fuller situates the reception of the text in the intellectual circle of Ralph Waldo Emerson, Henry David Thoreau, and the Alcott family, emphasizing its widespread and deeply felt influence on the development of the American intellectual community.*

Courtesy of Viking

Principal personages

AMOS BRONSON ALCOTT, a school superintendent and social reformer
LOUISA MAY ALCOTT, his daughter, an author best known for her novel Little Women
CHARLES LORING BRACE, a radical social theorist and advocate for disadvantaged youth
JOHN BROWN, a radical abolitionist
CHARLES DARWIN, a British scientist and the author of On the Origin of Species
RALPH WALDO EMERSON, a transcendentalist philosopher and abolitionist
ASA GRAY, a scientist and professor at Harvard University
FRANKLIN BENJAMIN SANBORN, a Concord schoolmaster, radical thinker, and supporter of John Brown
HENRY DAVID THOREAU, a transcendentalist philosopher and abolitionist

Two events coincide at the opening of *The Book That Changed America*, by Randall Fuller: the execution of John Brown in December 1859 and the arrival in Concord, Massachusetts, of the first copy of Charles Darwin's *On the Origin of Species*, published in November of the same year. Gathered for a modest New Year's celebration, several members of the intellectual community of Concord pore over a single copy of the book while they share their abolitionist ideals and mourn Brown's execution. Fuller interprets this gathering of friends as the point from which Darwin's ideas began to inform those of the American abolitionist movement.

The thinkers at the heart of this text—Charles Loring Brace, Asa Gray, Franklin

Benjamin Sanborn, and Henry David Thoreau—each had different professional interests, but they were bound together by their abolitionist tendencies and their radical intellectualism. Gray, a Harvard University scientist, was the closest to Darwin in his professional expertise. *The Book That Changed America* traces Gray's influence in guiding the successful reception of Darwin's science by an American audience. Sanborn, lesser known to modern readers, was a dynamic intellectual figure and a radically experimental educator, as well as a passionate supporter of Brown's cause. Thoreau, already the famed author of *Walden; or, Life in the Woods* (1854), linked the transcendentalist community of Concord with the scientific realities of Darwin's manuscript as he sought to integrate his own close study of nature with the ideas introduced by Darwin. Slavery itself is distant from the narratives of this book, and from the realities of life in Concord. Instead, Fuller's text demonstrates the intersection of scientific and philosophical thinking that brought the intellectual community of this town into the abolitionist fray.

The Book That Changed America follows a roughly chronological format within a tight interval of time, extending from New Year's Day in 1860 through the beginning of 1861. The most obvious significance of this interval is its correspondence to the outbreak of the Civil War in the United States, but it also corresponds with the arrival of Darwin's *Origin of Species* in the United States. Though the two events would seem to be unrelated, Fuller seeks to clarify that there was a close relationship between the reception of the manuscript and the development of more articulate, radical, and scientific opposition to slavery in the final months before the onset of war. Clearly, the historical threads with which Fuller's book is entangled extend before and after these months. This is addressed overtly in early and concluding chapters of the book, some of which engage with Darwin's scientific life before and during his composition of the *Origin of Species* and others of which trace the book's central figures after the conclusion of the Civil War.

Although centered on a single text, a small community, and a limited interval of time, *The Book That Changed America* nevertheless weaves a complex, transatlantic narrative. In it, a small group of Concord intellectuals enter into relationships with an international community of other intellectuals, largely via correspondence, sometimes with the opportunity to establish in-person friendships. Ideas about race, evolution, and the interrelationship of living beings are explored in a context that permits the synthesis of local observation and notations culled from far-flung international travel. In some ways, the intellectual and literary community of Concord is more the focus of this book than is Darwin's *Origin of Species*, which is the thematic glue that allows Fuller to interweave his specific narrative about these figures.

Perhaps the greatest interest of Fuller's study lies in the text's focus on the common influence of Darwin on Concord's intellectual community. The personages introduced within Fuller's text are familiar historical characters, several of them well known outside of academic circles. Within this book, they are reintroduced in a different light through their common engagement in science. At times, this connection is forced or speculative, built on a line or two in a journal entry or other scant documentary evidence of the figure's engagement with Darwin. At other times, as is the case with Gray and Thoreau, the intellectual focus on Darwin is sustained and amply evident. Fuller traces individual copies of Darwin's book and engages with marginalia in the texts or from other archival sources, such as the notebooks of Thoreau that capture his deep reading of the manuscript. Such engagement with archival sources allows Fuller to bring the minds of these individuals to life and to create a dynamic sense of the historical period. Since the individual figures under consideration in this book are generally well known and have been the subjects of extensive and individualized study, another strength of this book lies in its integration of their stories over these years, which brings the dynamics of Concord's tight-knit international and social community into clear focus.

A key dramatic tension of the book focuses on Sanborn's monetary support for Brown's rebellion and the concern that he will face "justice" for this action. While Sanborn provided Brown with financial support, he was not the only figure in Concord to support the radical abolitionist's cause; Thoreau offered a speech in support of Brown's memory, and others in the community welcomed Brown's widow and children to town. Sanborn's anxiety is realized late one night, when a group of Southerners with a warrant for his arrest attempt to kidnap him in the middle of the night. Fuller recounts a riotous street brawl in which Sanborn fought off his would-be captors and the people of Concord came to his defense, ultimately providing him with both physical and legal protection from his assailants. Later in the night, Thoreau himself would stand guard at Sanborn's home to ensure that no additional kidnappers would succeed that night. Here, gentle transcendentalists and heady philosophers are converted into local vigilantes, aggressively standing up to federal systems of justice that they deemed unjust and supporting all measures necessary to cleanse their country of slavery.

In its distance from the American South and its lack of African American figures, *The Book That Changed America* shifts the focus of Civil War history. None of the principal figures in the text are politicians or soldiers. Instead, their focuses on science, philosophy, and pedagogy emphasize the deep intellectual roots of the abolitionist movement. Fuller is aware of a chief criticism that can be leveled at the main figures of his text—that for intellectuals at a great physical remove from slave territories, the abolition of slavery was an intellectual, philosophical, and moral concern, but it was not highly personal other than in their abhorrence toward living in a nation that found slavery conscionable—and he addresses this criticism, though without much further exploration. Following the abolition of slavery and the subsequent Union victory, Sanborn and others in his circle concerned themselves no further with the dynamics of racial equality.

Fuller makes several important interventions in modern readers' historical understanding of the significance of Darwin and his influence on the specific intellectuals at the heart of this book. Perhaps most significant, as Eric Foner observed in his review for the *New York Times*, is Fuller's alignment of Darwin with abolitionists and social progressives rather than with "social Darwinism," which would see society's most unfortunate figures as inherently incapable of survival and thus unworthy of social support. "Unlike later social Darwinists," Foner wrote, "[the Concord intellectuals] interpreted evolution to mean that progress was decreed by nature. Disadvantaged people, black as well as white, were no more fixed in their condition than other forms of life in a continuously improving world." Also significant is Fuller's revelation that scientific thought of the period, in part through the mediation of Gray in his role as a reviewer for the *American Journal of Science* and an essayist for the *Atlantic*, found a way to reconcile Darwin's science with Christian faith. Although Darwin himself was less willing to envision a Christian explanation for his theory of evolution, Fuller recounts how Gray adapted

Randall Fuller is the Chapman Professor of English at the University of Tulsa. His previous books include Emerson's Ghosts: Literature, Politics, and the Making of Americanists *(2007) and* From Battlefields Rising: How the Civil War Transformed American Literature *(2011). His research has been supported by grants from the Guggenheim Foundation and the National Endowment for the Humanities. From* Battlefields Rising *earned him the Phi Beta Kappa Society's 2011 Christian Gauss Award for best literary scholarship or criticism.*

Darwin's scientific observations sufficiently to allow his readership to understand how they could be both people of faith and enthusiastic supporters of Darwin's revelations. Finally, in his intimate knowledge of the writings and archives of Thoreau, Emerson, and the Alcotts, Fuller is able to find the influence of Darwin in unexpected places that shed new light on these significant intellectuals. Here, Fuller's focus on Thoreau is particularly significant, leading him to close analysis of the study on which Thoreau was working at the time of his death—a consideration of local natural history strongly influenced by his reflections on the scientific observations of Darwin.

Reviewers generally praised Fuller's work while registering reservations about its limited scope. Megan Garber, writing for the *Atlantic*, praised Fuller as "an excellent writer, with an eye for irony and a unique ability to inject suspense into a story that is, at its core, about the mercurial nature of chromosomes," but qualified this with her assessment that "the book is also, in some ways, as limited as it is sprawling. It focuses on the intellectual elites—and on their pettiness, and their idealism, their humanity. As for the broader 'America,' though—its everyday denizens, among them wide swathes of people who were not yet afforded the dignity of citizenry—Fuller offers less detail." Foner, meanwhile, described Fuller as "a lively, engaging writer, with an eye for fascinating details," but added that his "rather grandiose title promises more than a study of a few New England intellectuals can reasonably deliver"; he also took issue with the lack of representation of African American perspectives, noting that "writers for the black press . . . cited *On the Origin of Species* as proof of mankind's 'progressive development,' which would lead inevitably to the abolition of slavery. They saw the Civil War as the nation's own evolutionary struggle for existence. Surely, they too form part of the American response to Darwin."

The Book That Changed America is convincing in its premise that Darwin's *Origin of Species* had a profound influence on a small group of intellectuals' perceptions of slavery and commitment to the abolitionist movement. Fuller's book does not enter into the heart of intellectual debates about Civil War history and politics, but it does provide a focused and engaging analysis of intellectual and scientific currents on the precipice of war. In its analysis of a significant, close-knit Massachusetts intellectual community, Fuller's book allows readers to gain a deeper understanding of how contemporary understandings of race and human evolution were transformed through engagement with the science of Darwin—and also how these intellectual developments transformed individual figures' engagement with the most pressing social and political concerns of their historical moment.

Julia A Sienkewicz

Review Sources

Abrams, Roger I. Review of *The Book That Changed America: How Darwin's Theory of Evolution Ignited a Nation*, by Randall Fuller. *New York Journal of Books*, 23 Jan. 2017, www.nyjournalofbooks.com/book-review/book-changed. Accessed 27 Nov. 2017.

Foner, Eric. "Evolutionary Wars: How Darwin's Masterwork Shook Up America." Review of *The Book That Changed America: How Darwin's Theory of Evolution Ignited a Nation*, by Randall Fuller. *The New York Times*, 20 Jan. 2017, www.nytimes.com/2017/01/20/books/review/book-that-changed-america-darwin-randall-fuller.html. Accessed 27 Nov. 2017.

Garber, Megan. "The Book That Bettered America." Review of *The Book That Changed America: How Darwin's Theory of Evolution Ignited a Nation*, by Randall Fuller. *The Atlantic*, 27 Jan. 2017, www.theatlantic.com/entertainment/archive/2017/01/the-book-that-changed-america-review/514517/. Accessed 27 Nov. 2017.

Smith, Wendy. "Tracing Ripples of Darwin's Book in 19th Century America." Review of *The Book That Changed America: How Darwin's Theory of Evolution Ignited a Nation*, by Randall Fuller. *The Boston Globe*, 27 Jan. 2017, www.bostonglobe.com/arts/books/2017/01/26/tracing-ripples-darwin-book-century-america/sxlNGcP12zhFB91Lo8hmJM/story.html. Accessed 27 Nov. 2017.

Borne

Author: Jeff VanderMeer (b. 1968)
Publisher: Farrar, Straus and Giroux (New York). 336 pp.
Type of work: Novel
Time: The near future
Locale: A ruined city of unknown location

In the desolate landscape of a derelict me-tropolis, a handful of ragged humans in a battle for survival scavenge for food while dodging bioengineered monsters created by a now-defunct firm known as the Company. Amid the rubble, a young woman finds and nurtures a creature she calls Borne, which looks like a plant, acts like an animal, and strives to become human.

Courtesy of Macmillan

Principal characters

RACHEL, a young woman who was born on an unnamed island, became a refugee with her parents when she was six, and later came alone to the city where she now dwells

WICK, Rachel's companion and lover, a slender, sickly scientist and a former Company employee, who created a new drug consisting of memory-altering beetles

BORNE, a mass of purplish-greenish matter Rachel finds, which grows and changes over time, becoming able to communicate

MORD, a voracious killing machine with formidable teeth and claws bioengineered by the Company, shaped like an enormous bear and capable of flying

THE MAGICIAN, a female rival of Wick with dark hair, bronze skin, and a facial scar; she is a former employee of the Company now living in a derelict observatory

Borne opens on a bleak, seemingly hopeless scene of widespread devastation. The novel's resourceful young narrator, Rachel, is out on her daily quest: touring a shattered, nameless city in search of food or other items that can be salvaged and repurposed. In an introductory section, "What I Found and How I Found It," Rachel describes the main antagonist of the story. This is Mord, a gigantic flying bear, once a human who was bioengineered into his present form by the Company, a failed corporate enterprise. The Company's bizarre biotech experiments have run amok across the terrain, which is now a wasteland of polluted water sources, toxic fumes, and tumbledown buildings where scattered survivors fight among themselves and with roaming creatures—such as Mord proxies, bloodthirsty bands of vicious, normal-sized, golden-colored bears—just to stay alive. On this excursion, Rachel bravely tracks Mord during his depredations, because she knows useful things become trapped in his fur. When

Mord falls asleep, she ascends his huge body, looking for salvageable debris. She finds a fist-sized, unidentifiable blob of matter that smells like the sea, reminding her of her youth. She retrieves the object to take home to the Balcony Cliffs, a derelict apartment building overgrown with vegetation and riddled with booby traps to foil intruders. Rachel lives there in uneasy alliance with her occasional lover, Wick, a former Company scientist who, among other things, makes and sells beetles that, when inserted into a user's ear, eliminate unpleasant memories or create new memories.

Normally, Rachel would have presented her find, which she names Borne to commemorate the process of carrying it home, to Wick to dissect and reuse in his laboratory beside a former basement swimming pool where he mixes up concoctions. But this time—despite Wick's concerns that her discovery might be a bomb or a beacon that could give away their location—she wants to keep the find for herself. Rachel is fascinated by Borne's ability to change colors and shape: the creature, initially a ball, soon assumes the form of a vase.

At first, Rachel thinks Borne is a plant. However, it moves when it is not being watched and does not like direct sunlight, so she decides it must be an animal. Believing it to be sentient, she talks to Borne and comes to care for it. The creature, which quickly grows in size, seems to eat anything, creates a variety of aromas, and produces no waste. Rachel becomes increasingly fond of Borne after a traumatic incident in which a group of bioengineered children follow her home, vandalizing her residence and torturing her. As she wakes from unconsciousness to find Wick, returned from selling his products, treating her wounds, she learns that Borne has grown again. Borne talks to her in the voice of one of the vicious children, and she assumes that the creature protected her by killing and absorbing her attackers.

In flashbacks, readers learn more about the backgrounds of Wick and Rachel, which helps explain their personalities and reveal their characters. Wick went to work for the Company soon after it arrived in the city, when the Company appeared beneficial for providing employment in a declining local economy. However, the Company simply extracted all the resources in the area before withdrawing and left ruin in its wake in the form of creations that ravaged the land. Wick lost his position after creating an air-breathing, land-based fish with a human face, which is rumored to haunt leftover Company holding ponds. Wick, working on a cure for his own mysterious illness, still possesses plans and technical specifications for various other Company projects that were never developed.

Rachel, on the other hand, grew up elsewhere. Her father, a politician, and her mother, a pediatrician, lived on an island in an archipelago when she was born. Rising sea waters swallowed the island, so Rachel and her family became refugees when she was six years old, moving from country to country. She came to the city alone, in her early twenties, before connecting with Wick.

As Borne continues to grow, it exhibits more unique abilities: able to change shape and color at will, it develops many different eyes and tentacles. Rachel, recovering from her ordeal with the children, decides Borne is male and treats him as a mother would treat her child. She shows him pictures from books, teaches him to read, plays hide-and-seek, and answers his many questions about the universe and the meaning of life. By the end of the first part of the three-part narrative, Borne has learned to walk, has developed a face, and has formed definite opinions.

Once Rachel is well enough to return to scavenging, Borne wants to go outside with her, but Rachel forbids it and locks Borne in a room. As she slinks through abandoned neighborhoods, looking for useful items to salvage, she sees movement: it is Borne, disguised as an old-time wizard as depicted in a picture book. He had no problem escaping from the locked room because he made himself as thin as a sheet of paper and slid under the door. On other excursions with Rachel, Borne playfully shifts shape numerous times, now a giant fly, now a lizard, now a rock, now a cowboy from the Old West. During one trip outside, they are stalked by a large group of feral bioengineered children but are saved when a pack of Mord proxies attack and kill the children. When the proxies turn their attention to Rachel and Borne and chase them onto the roof of an abandoned factory, Borne protects her by assuming the shape of a rock with Rachel inside his body, maintaining the position even when the proxies bite and wound him.

Jeff VanderMeer has published ten collections of stories and ten novels since 1989. A fifteen-time nominee for the World Fantasy Award (winning in 2000, 2003, and 2012), he has also won a 2013 British Science Fiction Association Award, a 2013 Locus Award, and a 2014 Nebula Award.

Eventually, like a child grown up, the maturing Borne moves out of Balcony Cliffs, but he maintains contact with Rachel and Wick. Borne's leaving is necessary, because the creature has begun assuming the shapes of both Rachel and Wick, forcing them to adopt passwords to be certain one or the other is not really Borne in disguise.

Rachel and Wick ultimately come into conflict with the Magician, who wants to take over their residence. The young couple is forced to take refuge elsewhere for their own safety. Dodging marauding Mord proxies, scavenging humans, and other predatory biotech creations, they trek together across the putrid terrain to the destroyed and abandoned Company buildings in an attempt to find materials necessary to make medicine to keep Wick alive. Descending into the bowels of the enormous corporate complex, they uncover secrets revealing the truth about their own existence. In the meantime, Borne, grown enormous and powerful, prepares to face off in a final, cataclysmic confrontation with Mord.

A blend of speculative fiction, fantasy, adventure, and apocalyptic literature, *Borne*, like other VanderMeer novels—particularly the books of the award-winning Southern Reach trilogy: *Annihilation*, *Authority*, and *Acceptance* (all 2014)—is bursting at the seams with enough ideas for several novels. The shadowy Company, apparently responsible for the destruction of the city in which the action unfolds, is seen only through the results of its work and would therefore seem to be a worthy subject for further fictional examination. While such Company creations as a gigantic flying bear might conceivably have military applications, it is hard to reconcile the operating philosophy or to discern the practical applications behind other Company projects, such as a human-faced, air-breathing fish.

Many different threads are interwoven throughout *Borne*: the definition of humanity, the responsibility of humans to communicate with and live in harmony with nonhuman species, the strength of maternal and survival instincts, the hope that endures in human hearts in the midst of the most desperate conditions. Underscoring one theme in the novel—the difference between what *could* be created and what *should* be created in a genetic engineering lab—is the contrast between the freelance inventions of two former Company employees, Wick and the Magician.

Wick's biotech creations are mostly benevolent, harmless, or defensive. He has embedded fireflies in the ceilings of rooms to provide light. His beetles remove painful memories from troubled minds. He has engineered worms and insects to act as diagnostic devices to aid healing. He has created minnows that when consumed release a burst of alcohol, and neuro-spiders to temporarily disrupt an attacker's nervous system. The Magician's work, however, is mostly malevolent, as demonstrated by encounters with the young humans she has bioengineered. Once innocent children, the Magician's creations have become cruel killing machines, lethal weapons. One has eye sockets containing wasps' eyes for compound vision, one sports grafted claws, and others have poisonous fangs, beetle-like carapaces, scales, and wings. Such modifications have made the children inhuman and, thanks to VanderMeer's skill in manipulating emotions, the reader, perhaps normally sympathetic toward young children, becomes indifferent about their fate.

Jack Ewing

Review Sources

Dimock, Wai Chee. "There's No Escape from Contamination above the Toxic Sea." Review of *Borne*, by Jeff VanderMeer. *The New York Times*, 5 May 2017, www.nytimes.com/2017/05/05/books/review/borne-jeff-vandermeer.html. Accessed 7 Sept. 2017.

Hand, Elizabeth. "Jeff Vandermeer's New Dystopian Novel 'Borne' Is Lyrical and Harrowing." Review of *Borne*, by Jeff VanderMeer. *Los Angeles Times*, 27 Apr. 2017, www.latimes.com/books/jacketcopy/la-ca-jc-borne-vandermeer-20170413-story.html. Accessed 7 Sept. 2017.

Miller, Laura. "Jeff VanderMeer Amends the Apocalypse." Review of *Borne*, by Jeff VanderMeer. *The New Yorker*, 24 Apr. 2017, www.newyorker.com/magazine/2017/04/24/jeff-vandermeer-amends-the-apocalypse. Accessed 7 Sept. 2017.

Mukherjee, Neel. "After the Biotech Apocalypse." Review of *Borne*, by Jeff VanderMeer. *The Guardian*, 16 June 2017, www.theguardian.com/books/2017/jun/15/borne-by-jeff-vandermeer-review. Accessed 7 Sept. 2017.

Shawl, Nisi. "'Borne' Is the Latest Dazzling Novel from New Weird Author Jeff VanderMeer." *The Washington Post*, 27 Apr. 2017, www.washingtonpost.com/entertainment/books/borne-is-the-latest-dazzling-novel-from-new-weird-author-jeff-vandermeer/2017/04/27/b8c647f6-2b74-11e7-b605-33413c691853_story.html. Accessed 7 Sept. 2017.

Wiersma, Robert J. "Borne to Be Great: Jeff VanderMeer's New Novel Is Much More Than a Familiar Dystopian Tale." *National Post*, 24 Apr. 2017, nationalpost. com/entertainment/books/book-reviews/borne-to-be-great-jeff-vandermeers-new-novel-is-much-more-than-a-familiar-dystopian-tale/wcm/4e83e15e-7ca3-4999-93d4-bcc99150219b. Accessed 7 Sept. 2017.

The Brain Defense
Murder in Manhattan and the Dawn of Neuroscience in America's Courtrooms

Author: Kevin Davis
Publisher: Penguin Press (New York). 336 pp.
Type of work: History
Time: 1991 to present

In The Brain Defense, *Kevin Davis presents an illuminating study of the ways in which modern neuroscience is becoming a contested tool in American jurisprudence. He focuses on the bellwether case of Herbert Weinstein, whose brutal murder of his wife was attributed by his defense to the effects of a brain tumor. Davis evenhandedly explores the debate over whether brain injuries negate free will and personal responsibility in criminal cases.*

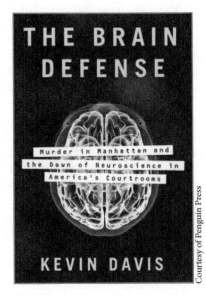

Courtesy of Penguin Press

Principal personages
HERBERT WEINSTEIN, a New York businessman
JONI WEINSTEIN, his daughter
DIARMUID WHITE, his lawyer
DR. NORMAN RELKIN, a neurologist
ZACHARY WEISS, an assistant New York district attorney
DAVID ALONSO, a construction manager

Kevin Davis is a journalist and an assistant managing editor of the American Bar Association's *ABA Journal*. Even before going to work for the American Bar Association (ABA), Davis had written two books on the American criminal justice system. His third, *The Brain Defense*, investigates an emerging frontier in American jurisprudence: the use of neuroscience by criminal defense attorneys to explain and extenuate the crimes of their clients. The application of modern discoveries about the brain to the legal system raises profound scientific and moral questions. It also presents very practical problems for a judicial process rooted in a centuries-old tradition of common law and trial by jury.

Davis builds his discussion of these issues around a case that looms large in the literature of neuroscience and the law. On January 7, 1991, a woman's body plummeted to the ground from a window in her twelfth-story apartment. The initial assumption when the police were called was that the woman had been a suicide, but investigators noticed a man behaving strangely in the apartment building lobby. He had scratch marks on his face. It was quickly determined that he was a sixty-five-year-old former advertising man named Herbert Weinstein, and the deceased woman was his wife, Barbara Weinstein. After some initial attempts at obfuscation, Weinstein confessed to killing his spouse. They had quarreled when Barbara, Weinstein's second wife, criticized his son. In their sudden altercation, Barbara scratched his face, and Weinstein found himself choking her, he believed to death. To cover up his crime, Weinstein tipped his wife's body out the window, hoping that it would appear that she had killed herself. A disquieting question that was raised later was whether Barbara Weinstein was in fact dead when her husband dropped her to the pavement outside their apartment.

On the face of it, the Weinstein murder seemed an open and shut case. Weinstein had confessed, providing a motive for his murderous action. But the investigation of Barbara Weinstein's death remained disquieting because Weinstein appeared such an unlikely perpetrator of a brutal killing. He had never been in trouble with the law. Friends and family were all stunned at such an act by a man whom they had all known as unfailingly affable and good-natured. In fact, Weinstein's prior life had been characterized by a notable evenness of temper, even a sense of detachment that impressed observers. He seemed to be the last man to fall prey to a fit of berserk rage. When Diarmuid White, Weinstein's defense attorney, first met his client, he was struck by the man's curiously dispassionate reaction to his predicament. It was this strange calm that prompted White to ask him to undergo medical and psychiatric evaluation; the lawyer wondered if Weinstein was mentally unbalanced. A psychiatric examination revealed nothing; Weinstein seemed completely normal. It was a magnetic resonance imaging (MRI) test that produced a great surprise. The MRI disclosed a growth the size of an orange in the left temporal lobe of Weinstein's brain, the part of the cerebrum that governs judgment and impulse control. Diarmuid White began organizing a defense that argued that Weinstein killed his wife in a moment of temporary insanity, brought on by the tumor pressing on the left lobe of his brain. In doing so, White would help pioneer the use of neuroscience in criminal law.

Davis notes that the effects of brain injuries on human personality have long been recognized. An early and well-documented instance of this is the story of Phineas Gage. In 1848, Gage was working with a crew clearing ground for a railroad in Vermont when a premature explosion sent a metal rod through his head. To the surprise of his coworkers, Gage survived this devastating blow. A local doctor, John Martyn Harlow, treated Gage and kept records of his case. Gage recuperated from his injuries and went back to work. But the Gage who returned to his occupation was a changed man, his personality radically different. A once sober and conscientious railroad foreman became unreliable, profane, and antisocial. As his contemporaries noted, Gage "was no longer Gage." The case of Phineas Gage helped speed recognition that damage to certain parts of the brain could affect behavior. Over time, this understanding raised questions about the criminal culpability of criminals with severe brain injuries.

A criminal's mental state is important because in the western legal tradition, intent has long been crucial when weighing degrees of guilt. The ancient Greeks and Romans accepted insanity as a mitigating factor in sentencing malefactors. Ever since, western jurisprudence has held that defendants judged *non compos mentis*, or "without mastery of mind," are not criminally responsible for their actions. The problem for jurists since the eighteenth century has been defining insanity, an elusive concept, especially when trying to determine if a person comprehends the distinction between right and wrong. There have been highly publicized instances of a successful insanity defense. John Hinckley Jr., who attempted to assassinate President Ronald Reagan in 1981, was eventually determined to suffer from schizophrenia and was confined for many years in a mental hospital rather than a prison. Despite this, defendants plead insanity in less than 1 percent of criminal cases, and in most instances they are convicted anyway. Appealing to a brain injury offers a variation on the insanity defense, reinforced by the physical specificity of scientifically observable damage. The great question remains, does this damage, like insanity, relieve an offender of guilt?

© Penguin Press (HC) 2017

Kevin Davis is a journalist and assistant managing editor of the ABA Journal. *He is also the author of* The Wrong Man *(1996) and* Defending the Damned *(2007).*

While the Weinstein case serves as the structural armature of his book, Davis makes fascinating digressions into topics such as post-traumatic stress disorder (PTSD) in veterans, chronic traumatic encephalopathy (CTE) in athletes, the "young brain" defense in cases of underage suspects, and the "broken brain" appeal in death penalty cases. All of these illuminate the ways in which modern neuroscience is increasing our knowledge of the potentially deleterious impact of brain injuries on human behavior. They also illustrate the limits of this knowledge in explaining particular actions. Davis discusses the well-known case of Charles Whitman. On August 1, 1966, Whitman murdered his mother and his wife. He then drove to the campus of the University of Texas, entered the Texas Clock Tower with a small arsenal of weapons, and killed three people. Stationing himself on the tower's observation platform, he shot and killed eleven more people and wounded thirty-one others before being dispatched by police. Whitman left behind a note in which he described a change in his personality and complained of incessant headaches. He asked that his brain be autopsied to see if there was a physical explanation for his actions. Medical examiners did, in fact, find a small, pecan-sized tumor near the thalamus, which regulates sleep and relays sensory information, and the amygdala, which helps control emotions and behavior. Members of Whitman's family seized on the tumor to explain his murderous rampage, and argued that he had been driven insane by this growth in his brain. The examining pathologist rejected this conclusion. A later Texas state commission of inquiry suggested that the tumor might have played a role in precipitating Whitman's murder spree, but could not definitively establish a causal connection between the two. As investigators discovered, Whitman's violent outburst was in some ways overdetermined. He was an angry young man who hated his father and felt rejected by his mother. He abused amphetamines, hit his wife, and was attracted to guns. Whitman's unhappy life might well have ended in a bloody climax regardless of the tumor in his brain.

Davis demonstrates the complexity of these issues with the contrasting story of David Alonso. Unlike Whitman, Alonso was a well-adjusted forty-eight-year-old man. He worked as a construction project manager, was married, and had a twenty-four-year-old daughter who lived at home. In June 2012 Alonso tripped and fell down the stairs in his house, hitting the base of his skull. He fell into a coma that lasted for hours. When he awoke, he was disoriented. The doctors at the hospital saw no reason to keep him under observation and sent him home. There Alonso began acting strangely. His balance was off, causing him to repeatedly stumble. He warned his wife and daughter that someone was coming to kill the family. Five days after his accident, Alonso attacked his wife and daughter with a five-pound metal dumbbell. Both were seriously injured. When police arrived, they found Alonso striking his own head with the dumbbell. The whole Alonso family was hospitalized in critical condition. It took months for the Alonsos to recuperate from their injuries. David Alonso presented a puzzle to the authorities: he had always been a law-abiding and peaceable man, but he had violently assaulted his family and himself. Alonso's wife and daughter were convinced that the attack was the result of damage to his brain sustained when he had his fall. Prosecutors ultimately came to agree, and in a plea deal, Alonso was judged not guilty by reason of insanity. After many months in a mental hospital, Alonso returned home. He remained horrified by what he had done and was deeply troubled that an injury to his brain could compel him to such savage actions.

The contrasting examples of Charles Whitman and David Alonso indicate the challenges facing the legal system when dealing with evidence of brain damage. Incontrovertibly, trauma to the brain can affect behavior and in some cases lead to violence. On the other hand, many neuroscientists argue that brain damage does not necessarily deprive individuals of control over their actions, or force them to commit criminal offenses. They note the also incontrovertible reality that most people with brain damage do not kill people. Neuroscience has not yet resolved age-old debates about sanity, insanity, determinism, and free will. All these questions were raised by the Weinstein case, as defense attorney White and prosecutor Zachary Weiss wrestled with the significance of neuroscientific evidence, establishing important precedents for the future.

To the end, Herbert Weinstein remained an enigma. What caused the genial businessman to kill his wife? Did his brain tumor explain, or at least mitigate, his crime? Davis does not try to force easy answers on his readers. He does argue that neuroscience will play an increasingly important role in criminal cases; its promise in helping lawyers, judges, and juries understand the actions of accused felons cannot be ignored. A better appreciation of the effects of a damaged brain may not relieve a criminal from responsibility for his or her actions, but it can offer the possibility of evaluating the defendant's culpability more effectively and compassionately. Davis's book is a stimulating and lucid survey of a dramatic development in American jurisprudence.

Daniel P. Murphy

Review Sources

Carr, Caleb. "Did His Mind Make Him Do It? How Neuroscience Entered the
    Courtroom." Review of *The Brain Defense: Murder in Manhattan and the Dawn
    of Neuroscience in America's Courtrooms*, by Kevin Davis. *The New York Times*,
    9 Mar. 2017, www.nytimes.com/2017/03/09/books/review/brain-defense-kevin-
    davis.html. Accessed 19 Oct. 2017.

Review of *The Brain Defense: Murder in Manhattan and the Dawn of Neuroscience
    in America's Courtrooms*, by Kevin Davis. *Kirkus Reviews*, 31 Oct. 2016, www.
    kirkusreviews.com/book-reviews/kevin-davis/the-brain-defense. Accessed 19
    Oct. 2017.

Review of *The Brain Defense: Murder in Manhattan and the Dawn of Neuroscience
    in America's Courtrooms*, by Kevin Davis. *Publishers Weekly*, 19 Dec. 2016,
    www.publishersweekly.com/978-1-59420-633-7. Accessed 19 Oct. 2017.

Maxwell, Lynne. Review of *The Brain Defense: Murder in Manhattan and the Dawn
    of Neuroscience in America's Courtrooms*, by Kevin Davis. *Library Journal*, 1
    Jan. 2017, p. 114.

Rosen, Jonathan. "My Mind Made Me Do It." Review of *The Brain Defense: Murder
    in Manhattan and the Dawn of Neuroscience in America's Courtrooms*, by Kevin
    Davis. *The Wall Street Journal*, 6 Mar. 2017, www.wsj.com/articles/my-mind-
    made-me-do-it-1488751572. Accessed 19 Oct. 2017.

Breathless

Author: Beverly Jenkins (b. 1951)
Publisher: Avon Books (New York). 384 pp.
Type of work: Novel
Time: 1870–86
Locales: Santa Catalina Mountains, Arizona
Territory

Portia Carmichael is determined to remain single and to open her own business, but when an old family friend arrives, her plans are challenged by an unexpected attraction to Kent Randolph. As the two get to know each other, they face challenges that could undermine their growing relationship.

Principal characters
PORTIA CARMICHAEL, an accountant and
hotel manager in her late twenties
REGAN CARMICHAEL, her sister
EDDY CARMICHAEL FONTAINE, her aunt
RHINE FONTAINE, her uncle
KENT RANDOLPH, a ranch hand and family friend
OLIVER RANDOLPH, Kent's father, a doctor
EDWARD SALT, a con artist
CORINNE, her estranged mother

Beverly Jenkins has authored over forty romance books. Her focus on African American characters has made her popular in the romance genre. *Breathless* is the second book in the Old West series, which began with *Forbidden* (2016), the story of Rhine and Eddy Fontaine's relationship. The third installment, *Tempest*, which is slated to release early in 2018, will follow Regan Carmichael and her romantic experiences. Jenkins has won the 2017 Romance Writers of America Nora Roberts Lifetime Achievement Award and the 2016 Romantic Times Reviewers' Choice Award for historical romance. She has also been recognized by the National Association for the Advancement of Colored People (NAACP) with a nomination for the Image Award in Literature.

Jenkins is known for making connections between her novels, allowing fans of her books to revisit characters and locations from book to book, and as *Breathless* is the second book in the series, Portia Carmichael is not a completely new character. True to Jenkins's habit, Portia and a few other characters were also briefly introduced in an earlier novel. While Uncle Rhine was introduced in *Through the Storm* (1998), Portia and her sister, Regan, were minor characters in *Forbidden*, which established their close relationship with their aunt Eddy.

Romance is, of course, the main driving force in the novel. Portia is introduced as an intelligent, independent twenty-seven-year-old woman who manages her uncle's hotel in the Arizona territory. She has a degree from Oberlin College as well as professional experience at respectable institutions, so her ability to do what would have been considered a man's job is never in doubt. Early in the book, she establishes her desire to remain single and open her own bookkeeping business. Readers are told "although the twenty-five-year-old Regan longed for love and children, Portia, two years older, wanted neither. Being the manager of the family's successful hotel was more than enough to make Portia's life complete." This, along with comments like "numbers won't keep you warm at night, sister mine," and "one of these days Cupid's going to hit you with an arrow right between the eyes," foreshadows the inevitable outcome of Portia's downfall. From Kent Randolph's greeting of "Hello, Duchess," Portia's heart clearly is not quite as hard as she pretends. The fact that the two had known each other years earlier adds a credibility to the immediate attraction despite her earlier claims. Kent's encouragement of Portia's independence and desire to open her own business just adds to his attractiveness.

The fast-moving plot follows the expected path of a formula romance, but the introduction of romantic rivals and family complications keep it from becoming too predictable. As an attractive African American woman who holds a powerful position in a wealthy uncle's business venture, it is not surprising that Portia has a variety of suitors. James Cordell, the son of the local minister, is the most pleasant of these men, but his shy personality is no match for Portia. Edward Salt is an aggressive newcomer who is certainly more interested in Rhine's money than in Portia, and Winston Jakes is a guest at the hotel who is easily turned away when Portia reveals her parentage. Portia has no interest in any of these men, especially after Kent steals her attention. Kent is not free of romantic prospects either. Elvenna Gordon, a widow, is another hotel guest who makes no bones about her attraction to the cowboy, and when Kent's father and stepmother come to visit, they bring an extended family member with the idea of pairing her up with him. Another area of conflict is found in family relationships. Though Portia is close with her sister, aunt, and uncle, she has not seen her mother, Corinne, since she was a child, so when she has a quick run in with Corinne while in San Francisco, difficult emotions arise. Kent's parental relationships are troubled as well. His father, Oliver, is critical of Kent's choice to be a cowboy rather than a doctor, so an unexpected visit from Oliver throws Kent's emotions into turmoil as well.

Most romance novels do not lack sex scenes, and this book is no different. As Portia and Kent's interest in each other blossoms, the sexual heat kicks up. Jenkins provides an amusing start by letting Portia believe that kissing Kent will temper her wild attraction to him, and the cowboy is certainly open to being her test subject. Once the two have shared a first kiss, the sexual tension steps up, however, and before long, Kent has tempted Portia into removing her shirt for his touch. Though there is certainly sexual tension before Portia capitulates to marriage, once the two are legally bound, the scenes become longer and much more detailed.

Alongside the novel's entertainment, Jenkins introduces more serious topics. One of these is classism. Several side characters show a remarkable lack of tact in expressing their opinions of physical laborers, a point that regularly offends Portia. Further, though Portia's education and professional work after earning her degree impress on one level, some characters find the story of her parentage much less acceptable because Corinne was a prostitute.

Jenkins also uses the novel to teach readers some nineteenth-century history, with a focus on African American experiences after the Civil War through the end of the century. The novel begins with a prologue that takes place after the end of *Forbidden*. It is 1870, and Eddy frantically wakes twelve-year-old Portia and ten-year-old Regan. They flee their home as a "crowd of men carrying torches surrounded the house," and when the children ask why their house has been set afire, Eddy answers, "They're angry because Uncle Rhine pretended to be White." Though they have escaped, Portia fears that

Courtesy of Sandra Vander Schaaf

Beverly Jenkins is an award-winning author of over forty books, as well as a number of short stories and novellas. Her critically acclaimed romance novels focus on African American characters.

her uncle will be lynched. The novel then jumps forward fifteen years, and the Arizona territory seems friendlier to African Americans than Nevada did. The family has a healthy social life with the neighbors and run a successful hotel that caters to a diversity of guests from the United States and abroad. At the end of the novel, in a letter to her readers, Jenkins reveals, "The Fontaine Hotel is loosely based on the Mountain View Hotel founded in Oracle, Arizona, in 1895 by Annie Box Neal and her husband William 'Curly' Neal, who were both of African-American and Native-American descent." Famous figures of color are also mentioned throughout the story. Frederick Douglass and Frances Ellen Watkins Harper, the abolitionists and writers, are referenced at a few points, and Geronimo also makes an appearance. Geronimo's sister, Lozen, a respected Apache warrior, is identified for her strength, pointing to the ability of women in leadership roles. The novel also explores women's issues of the time, illustrated through Portia's desire to remain unmarried, her college degree, her professional experience (including her management position at the hotel), and her interest in the women's suffrage movement. Elizabeth Cady Stanton's name is dropped in a brief discussion of African American women's right to vote, as the feminist leader's racism threatened to stand in the way of all women's ability to make their voices heard. Jenkins builds this threat into the plot as the women's group that Portia, Regan, and Eddy belong to discuss the widely debated issue: "More and more women of the race were jumping on the bandwagon even as some White women were doing their best to keep their darker sisters away from their conventions. In response the Colored women were sponsoring their own conferences and the gathering being held in San Francisco would be one."

Sexual assault is also touched on at several points in the story. Kent remembers the way twelve-year-old Portia reacted to his presence in the past. Her constant shying away from and distrust of men imply that she had been exposed to sexual advances from her mother's customers before she moved to live with her aunt and uncle. Later in the novel, one of the men who has been trying to get her to marry him physically threatens her as well. His choice of a public venue for his initial attack ends up being foolish, as Portia not only stands up for herself but defends her virtue in an amusing way. Portia defends herself at the end of the novel as well when the same man kidnaps her, and she takes revenge for the fear he has caused.

Though critical attention for this specific novel has been limited, it has been positive. Amy Alessio's review for *Booklist*, for example, lauded the novel's treatment of social justice issues: "Jenkins cleverly layers this captivating love story with subtle observations about race and women's rights" and compares the author to Lorraine Heath. The *Kirkus* reviewer added appreciation of Jenkins's characterizations with, "Her writing is both sexy and smart, and her characters come to life as real people the reader will want to know better. A thrilling and enjoyable read."

Jenkins's development of African American characters living in a challenging historical period provides stories that will appeal to a broad audience. Her skillful integration of problematic themes of those times will enlighten.

Theresa L. Stowell, PhD

Review Sources

Alessio, Amy. Review of *Breathless*, by Beverly Jenkins. *Booklist*, 1 Dec. 2016, pp. 35–36. *Literary Reference Center Plus*, search.ebscohost.com/login.aspx?direct=true&db=lkh&AN=119890871&site=lrc-plus. Accessed 23 Feb. 2018.

French, Asha, and Latoya Cross. "Love Fearlessly." Review of *Breathless*, by Beverly Jenkins, et al. *Ebony*, Feb. 2017, p. 36. *Academic Search Complete*, search.ebscohost.com/login.aspx?direct=true&db=brd&AN=120434434&site=ehost-live. Accessed 23 Feb. 2018.

Review of *Breathless*, by Beverly Jenkins. *Kirkus Reviews*, 1 Nov. 2016, p. 1. *Literary Reference Center Plus*, search.ebscohost.com/login.aspx?direct=true&db=lkh&AN=119153864&site=lrc-plus. Accessed 23 Feb. 2018.

The Bright Hour
A Memoir of Living and Dying

Author: Nina Riggs (1977–2017)
Publisher: Simon & Schuster (New York).
   320 pp.
Type of work: Memoir
Time: 2015–17
Locale: Greensboro, North Carolina

Nina Riggs wrote The Bright Hour: A Memoir of Living and Dying *as she struggled with the repercussions of a cancer diagnosis that would eventually take her life. In this memoir, she shares the everyday moments that people often take for granted as well as the difficulties of living with and through a terminal illness.*

Courtesy of Simon and Schuster

Principal personages

NINA RIGGS, the author, a woman with terminal cancer
JOHN DUBERSTEIN, her husband
FREDDY, their older son
BENNY, their younger son
TITA, her best friend
GINNY, her friend who also has terminal cancer

In Nina Riggs's book *The Bright Hour: A Memoir of Living and Dying*, the phrase "one small spot" becomes a mantra in a number of ways. Its obvious meaning is relevant to the medical diagnosis of breast cancer that began Riggs's journey: these were the words given to her by the technician, and later by the doctors. They were also the refrain that she and her husband repeated to keep perspective as she went through the chemotherapy and other treatments for that initial diagnosis.

In a larger context, the phrase serves as a reminder to appreciate the small moments in one's life. Riggs begins her memoir with a prologue in which she and her husband teach their younger son, Benny, how to ride a bike. This is a brief snippet of her life, but it is an important milestone for Benny. Later, she recalls when her mother called years earlier to reveal her own cancer diagnosis (multiple myeloma), and that Riggs was nursing her older son, then a newborn, at the time. She relays the moment when she and her husband met, and her phone conversations with a friend who also suffered from cancer.

The Bright Hour does not recount Riggs's whole life; instead, it is a collection of brief essays and snippets, primarily focused on the limited time period following her cancer diagnosis. Though they are loosely chronological, organized around the four stages of the disease, the various vignettes often provide unexpected and untimed glimpses into the author's childhood, young-adult years, and early marriage. The everyday realities of those earlier memories that she took for granted serve to remind both the author and her readers that simple, seemingly inconsequential moments are integral to the formation of a person's life. At the same time, the challenges of the cancer diagnosis, the treatments, and the constant pain and illness occasionally overcome Riggs as she plows through her present, attempting to appreciate the little details, such as her six-year-old asking if she knows what his three favorite ungulates are. Her daily thoughts are clouded by concerns over a future that she knows will not include her, and she worries about how her sons will turn out and whether her husband will want to marry again after she is gone.

Though the book could have become a maudlin depiction of death, Riggs was careful to imbue it with humor, even if the humor is often dark. For instance, she and Ginny, a friend who has the same form of terminal cancer, jokingly talk of a line of preprinted thank-you cards dedicated to the people who want to express sympathy for them and other terminal patients but do not know how, and so offer flowers and prayer and casseroles in lieu of real comfort. The cards would feature snarky messages such as "Thank you for the taco casserole. It worked even better than my stool softeners" and "Thoughts and prayers are great, but Ativan and pot are better" instead of poetry. The two women also joke about their bodies and the medical advice they receive that often seems so obvious that it becomes ridiculous. When Riggs is told that she needs a second form of birth control before she starts on a trial medication, for example, she laughs over the idea that abstinence is not enough. When Ginny says, "I basically have a tap in my back now. I'm never having sex again," Riggs points out, "I bet there is a whole subculture for people who are into that. Medical equipment fetishes. You just need to search the Internet and find them"—to which Ginny responds, "Do you really think I haven't done that already?" Riggs's husband's patience and loving kindness are also evidenced in his attempts to make her smile at the awful ridiculousness of their situation, and their sons bring light into the story just by being themselves, two silly little boys who know that their mother is ill but do not truly comprehend the depth of her illness.

Another thread of humor revolves around the cane that Riggs relies on as her cancer progresses and breaks down her ability to walk unassisted. One of the people at the hospital tapes the word "FAITH" to the curve of the cane, and Riggs, who is not completely sure of her belief in life after death or other religious views, points out the irony after her sons begin calling the cane Faith as if it needs a name (resulting in questions such as "Did you lose Faith again?"). She points out the multiplied meanings in a simple reflection: "Some days I don't need Faith, my crutch, at all—and others I depend on her heavily. I live on fentanyl, oxycodone, ibuprofen—but Faith is what keeps me moving forward."

Throughout her memoir, Riggs also explores the different ways people look at the moments of everyday existence. For instance, she tells a childhood story about being stranded on the side of the road with her father. Even as an adult, this memory holds adventurous tones of a special time spent huddled in the cab of an old pickup truck and listening to her father sing along to Stevie Wonder. When her older son, Freddy, says that he misses the closeness of a period she spent caring for him while he was in the hospital being diagnosed with diabetes, she realizes that a child's point of view may vary greatly from the parental one. While Freddy longs for the cuddles and attention she showered on him in that hospital bed, she remembers the fear and sadness over his diagnosis.

Riggs does not focus only on her own medical issues; she introduces the problems experienced by other people in her life as well. In addition to her mother, previously diagnosed with cancer, the disease touched several members of her father's family as well. She relates the experiences of her mother's final months and her grief over her mother's death, spending quite a bit of time describing her mother's physical breakdown, the preparation for the funeral, and the days after the loss. She also talks quite a bit to and about Ginny, whose identical diagnosis gives the two friends a shared insight that holds up both of them throughout their struggles. Though Riggs's cancer is the major empha-sis, her husband's type 1 diabetes was another health issue in their home, and she grieved when that diagnosis was also given to their son Freddy.

The great-great-great-granddaughter of Ralph Waldo Emerson, Nina Riggs was a poet, author, and blogger who held an MFA in poetry and taught for nearly a decade in the creative writing program at the University of North Carolina at Chapel Hill. Her poetry collection, Lucky, Lucky, *was published in 2009. She died as a result of breast cancer on February 26, 2017.*

Relationships are explored throughout Riggs's journey. Her and her husband's friends Adam and Melissa and her best friend, Tita, are also included throughout the memoir. Adam and Melissa, Riggs reports, "are close enough friends of ours that we have considered them possible guardians of our children." Tita is the friend who car-ries much of the burden of taking Riggs to her medical treatments and scans. Tita's husband, Drew, is also mentioned, as he was in a car accident during a Christmas break when Riggs was hospitalized for a tumor on her back. Riggs carried the burden of knowing that, as she puts it, her "situation is complicit" in the distraction that caused the accident.

In addition to carrying the weight of her cancer's effects on the adults in her life, Riggs clearly displays her concerns for her sons throughout the memoir. As an adult child of a terminal cancer patient, she understood the fear and the grief of a parent's illness. As a mother herself, she struggled with knowing how to help her young chil-dren. "I keep a running list on my phone of the things I'm worried no one will teach my kids: table manners, how to play Scrabble without getting in a fight, long divi-sion, how to pack light, how to find the orange juice in the refrigerator," she writes. She and Ginny plot long-term parenting strategies for the care of their children after their deaths. Though these do include serious notes—at one point Ginny becomes obsessed with purchasing clothes for her children as they grow; at another, Riggs spends hours searching for the perfect sofa to leave for her family—there are some lighter thoughts as well. Ginny proposes leaving video lectures for her children, and both women consider writing emails that their loved ones can share after their deaths.

Ginny's irreverent lessons about sex amuse Riggs, who observes, "The idea of parenting a teenage daughter from the grave sounds worse than terminal cancer." The thought of leaving Freddy and Benny is one of the most difficult points for Riggs, and she grieves at the knowledge that their future will not hold the kinds of memories she wants to leave for them.

On another path of the memoir, Riggs shares reflections on her great-great-great-grandfather Ralph Waldo Emerson's philosophies and how they fit her own experiences. Her interest in literature and poetry seems an inherited trait, and she finds poetry in much of what she goes through. She provides one story about a man dressed in a fox suit sitting in a hospital waiting area. This man wrote poems for the patients coming through, and though the poetry was not of stellar literary quality, Riggs points out that he created a memorable moment for her and her husband to hold onto. She also finds poetry in their lawyer's words, analyzing the differences between "will" and "shall" in the language of her medical desires. Literary references to Emerson's philosophies appear throughout the book. In addition to her ancestor's wisdom, she pulls from Michel de Montaigne, a sixteenth-century French philosopher, and snippets from his life are sprinkled liberally throughout the book.

The book ends with a chapter that shows Riggs on a good day spent with her children, a "bright hour" that she never wants to end. This is followed by an acknowledgements section written by John Duberstein, Riggs's husband. He relates the last days of her life as he offers appreciation for those who helped her complete her memoir.

The Bright Hour was widely praised by critics. The reviewer for *Kirkus Reviews* observed that Riggs "writes with a seamless flow and an honest, heartfelt tone" and described the book as "a luminous, heartbreaking symphony of wit, wisdom, pain, parenting, and perseverance against insurmountable odds." *Booklist* reviewer Stacy Shaw was more reserved, praising Riggs's writing but warning that readers may find "the gallows humor that helps her cope . . . off-putting in its depth of darkness" and that "this brutally honest depiction of terminal illness is not for the faint of heart, but will be appreciated for its raw honesty." Bette-Lee Fox, in her review for *Library Journal*, disagreed, writing, "Whether confronting disease or not, everyone should read this beautifully crafted book, as it imbues life and loved ones with a particularly transcendent glow."

Theresa L. Stowell, PhD

Review Sources

Review of *The Bright Hour: A Memoir of Living and Dying*, by Nina Riggs. *Kirkus Reviews*, 1 May 2017, p. 77. *Academic Search Complete*, search.ebscohost.com/login.aspx?direct=true&db=a9h&AN=124546867&site=ehost-live. Accessed 1 Nov. 2017.

Review of *The Bright Hour: A Memoir of Living and Dying*, by Nina Riggs. *Publishers Weekly*, 24 Apr. 2017, p. 85. *Academic Search Complete*, search.ebscohost.com/login.aspx?direct=true&db=a9h&AN=122683219&site=ehost-live. Accessed 1 Nov. 2017.

Fox, Bette-Lee. Review of *The Bright Hour: A Memoir of Living and Dying*, by Nina Riggs. *Library Journal*, 1 Apr. 2017, pp. 103–4. *Academic Search Complete*, search.ebscohost.com/login.aspx?direct=true&db=a9h&AN=122230165&site=ehost-live. Accessed 1 Nov. 2017.

Shaw, Stacy. Review of *The Bright Hour: A Memoir of Living and Dying*, by Nina Riggs. *Booklist*, 15 Apr. 2017, p. 9. *Academic Search Complete*, search.ebscohost.com/login.aspx?direct=true&db=a9h&AN=122582840&site=ehost-live. Accessed 1 Nov. 2017.

Cannibalism
A Perfectly Natural History

Author: Bill Schutt (b. 1955)
Publisher: Algonquin Books of Chapel Hill
(Chapel Hill, NC). Illustrated. 352 pp.
Type of work: Natural history, anthropology, science
Locales: Locations all over the world

Having previously published a nonfiction book about creatures that feed on blood, zoologist and biology professor Bill Schutt next examines the phenomenon of animals—from insects to humans—that consume their own kind. Filled with interesting facts, helpful illustrations, and characteristic humor, Cannibalism: A Perfectly Natural History *provides a wealth of information about a largely understudied and misunderstood topic in the science world.*

Courtesy of Algonquin Books of Chapel Hill

Principal personages

DAVID PFENNIG, a biology professor
LAUREL FOX, an ecologist, one of the first to approach the study of cannibalism scientifically
GARY POLIS, an ecologist and scorpion expert who observed examples of invertebrate cannibalism
WILLIAM ARENS, an American anthropologist who argued that little evidence exists to support the historical practice of ritual cannibalism
JEROME WHITFIELD, an American anthropologist and scholar of ritual cannibalism
REAY TANNAHILL, a British historian who wrote and published the first academic study of cannibalism for the general public
ED GEIN, a twentieth-century American serial killer
JEFFREY DAHMER, a twentieth-century American serial killer

One of the main messages of *Cannibalism: A Perfectly Natural History* (provocatively titled *Eat Me: A Natural and Unnatural History* for overseas distribution) is that the practice of consuming one's own species, typically considered culturally taboo, is not a particularly rare or necessarily random phenomenon across the animal kingdom. Author Bill Schutt illustrates this concept with numerous examples of the ingenious ways in which a wide array of creatures—from amphibians such as spadefoot toad tadpoles to arachnids such as the black lace-weaver spider, and from fish such as the sand tiger shark to various mammals, including rabbits—have incorporated cannibalism into their behavior and way of life. At the same time, he explores cannibalism in human history, providing a deeper analysis of the role of the practice outside of the realms of serial killers or struggles for survival.

In chapters with clever headings such as "Animal the Cannibal" and "Go On, Eat the Kids," Schutt, supported by both field research with other biologists and gleanings from writings on the subject, enumerates reasons why cannibalism is often routinely included in animal behavior and lists rules that separate survivors from victims. For example, immature offspring—eggs, larvae, infants—are typically more vulnerable than adults of the species, and the nutrition they furnish allows other newborns to grow quickly and avoid being eaten. Furthermore, among many animals, especially invertebrates, the young or immature are consumed—a practice termed "filial cannibalism"—because they are not distinctive enough to be recognized as belonging to the same species. Cannibalism is more prevalent in times of hunger, scarcity, or overcrowding; such consumption serves a real purpose, in keeping with the pragmatic natural world, where nothing goes to waste. Eating litter runts and malformed, dead, or dying offspring eliminates potential infection, avoids drawing flies, and cancels the smell of death that might attract scavengers or predators. From general characteristics, *Cannibalism* then proceeds to specific examples of evolved behavior. Readers learn that cannibalism is not always inevitable among praying mantises or black widow spiders, and that the practice is more common among species where sexual dimorphism (including differences in body size, coloration, and features such as horns and crests) is prevalent.

The latter two-thirds of the book considers human cannibalism, from the distant past to the twentieth century, when such notorious criminal cannibals as Ed Gein, Jeffrey Dahmer, and Andrei Chikatilo operated. Evidence from ancient history suggests that Neanderthals, extinct relatives (possibly a subspecies) of modern *Homo sapiens*, may have consumed their own kind; excavations in several locations have uncovered caches of human bones with cut marks, tooth marks, and other signs of processing for food. However, there is no conclusive evidence as to whether such behavior was related strictly to survival or if it formed part of some burial practice ritual.

In a chapter titled "Eating People Is Bad," Schutt moves the narration forward by many millennia to a time when the morality of cannibalism and the taboo against the practice among humans—originally known as anthropophagy, from the Greek root words for "man" and "eating"—were first incorporated into literature. Homer's *Odyssey*, written around the eighth century BCE, contains a vivid passage in which the cyclops Polyphemus consumes several of Odysseus's men, much to the repugnance of the Greek hero. Other ancient Greek writers, such as the poet Hesiod and the historian Herodotus, as well as Romans such as the poet Ovid and the philosopher-dramatist Seneca, reinforced negative sentiments about cannibalism in their work. More modern writers, including William Shakespeare), Charles Perrault, and Daniel Defoe, as well as the psychoanalyst Sigmund Freud, each added in unique ways to the societal condemnation of cannibalism.

Historical events further increased the proscription. During Christopher Columbus's second voyage to the New World in 1493, he was greeted by a fierce indigenous

Bill Schutt is a professor of biology at Long Island University–Post and a zoological research associate at the American Museum of Natural History. His first nonfiction book was Dark Banquet: Blood and the Curious Lives of Blood-Feeding Creatures *(2008). He has also written two eco-thrillers in collaboration with J. R. Finch,* Hell's Gate *(2016) and* The Himalayan Codex *(2017).*

tribe called the Caribs (a mispronunciation of their name as "Canib" is proposed by several scholars to be the origin of "cannibal"). The Caribs were said to eat their captives, which justified to European minds their subsequent conquest; the conquistadors were aided in their efforts by the Catholic Church, which in 1510 decreed cannibalism a sin. Schutt also notes that, ironically, the Catholic Church itself promoted what has been viewed by some as a form of cannibalism through the doctrine of transubstantiation, in which worshippers are invited to consume the blood and body of Christ through the drinking of wine and eating of bread when taking communion. Adding further complexity to the issue of humanity's relationship with cannibalism, Schutt also details that many Europeans from the Renaissance into the twentieth century practiced what he refers to as medicinal cannibalism: the consumption of human blood, pulverized bones and organs, and the fragmented remains of mummified corpses as supposed remedies for a variety of ailments.

Despite such contradictions, cannibalism served as a major excuse over succeeding centuries for the subjugation of tens of millions of indigenous peoples in the Caribbean, and in the rest of the Americas, via outright murder, slavery, and the accidental or purposeful introduction of lethal diseases such as smallpox and influenza, to which the inhabitants had no immunity. Schutt's research illustrates that there may have been a factual basis for some of the rumors of cannibalism that the conquerors used to justify their conquests; the Aztecs and Incas, for example, were witnessed making human sacrifices that may have been misconstrued as a preliminary to feasting on the bodies of the dead. Anthropologists have since discovered evidence of ritualized cannibalism among various groups, particularly the practice of mortuary cannibalism (the consumption of small pieces of vanquished enemies or deceased family members in the belief that their favored traits would be passed along), which is well documented in Fiji, the Solomon Islands, Papua New Guinea, and elsewhere, including parts of North and South America.

As Schutt notes, one of the few types of cannibalism that scientists can agree has existed throughout recorded history is survival cannibalism. The Bible tells of the practice during the long sieges of Samaria and Jerusalem, when starving people, after consuming everything else, ate the dead. Likewise, cannibalism occurred often throughout the long history of China, especially in times of famine or following natural disasters. The modern era has its own examples of people resorting to cannibalism at moments of desperation. One incident cited is that of the American ship *Peggy*, which became becalmed at sea in 1765, forcing sailors to draw straws to determine who should be sacrificed so their shipmates could survive. The Donner party of the mid-nineteenth century, which consisted of settlers bound for California, became snowbound in the Sierra Nevada and had to resort to eating the dead. During World War II and the German siege of Leningrad in the Soviet Union, in which at least eight hundred thousand people perished between 1941 and 1944, desperate citizens ate the last crumbs of food, then ate zoo animals and pets, and finally dined on the bodies of the dead, though the practice was officially forbidden—some two thousand people were arrested and several were executed on the spot when caught eating human corpses. In 1972, following a plane crash in the Andes mountains, those who survived the impact remained alive for the weeks before their rescue by consuming the bodies of those who died. To fully immerse himself in his subject, author Schutt, in a chapter titled "Placenta Helper," describes how he also participated in a type of cannibalism, sharing in the contemporary trend among women of consuming their own cooked placentas following the birth of a child.

Though *Cannibalism* gets bogged down a bit at the end by detailed discussion of the transmission via cannibalism of kuru, a disease once common among the Fore people of Papua New Guinea, and its relationship to the similar bovine spongiform encephalopathy (also known as mad cow disease), the book is an overall informative and entertaining read. Schutt's work includes lore about this long-standing taboo, but overall he remains focused on discussing these examples from anthropological, evolutionary, and biological angles. In this way, *Cannibalism* serves as a significant contribution toward greater knowledge and understanding of the practice. Schutt notes in the prologue that in writing the book, he adopted "a hard line on sensationalism by highlighting and differentiating between physical evidence, ethno-history, unfounded information, and horse feathers"; in the end, he leaves readers wondering whether cannibalism might lose its iniquitous nature if the future, like the past, continues to be periodically plagued by drought and famine and the insatiable hunger of starving people. *Cannibalism*, which includes supplementary illustrations by well-regarded scientific artist Patricia J. Wynne, largely received critical praise, with reviewers particularly noting the level of research involved.

Jack Ewing

Review Sources

Review of *Cannibalism: A Perfectly Natural History*, by Bill Schutt. *Kirkus Reviews*, 15 Dec. 2016, p. 131. *Academic Search Complete*, search.ebscohost.com/login. aspx?direct=true&db=a9h&AN=122749171&site=ehost-live. Accessed 21 Sept. 2017.

Review of *Cannibalism: A Perfectly Natural History*, by Bill Schutt. *Publishers Weekly*, 24 Oct. 2016, p. 65. *Academic Search Complete*, search.ebscohost.com/ login.aspx?direct=true&db=a9h&AN=119017640&site=ehost-live. Accessed 21 Sept. 2017.

Copeland, Libby. Review of *Cannibalism: A Perfectly Natural History*, by Bill Schutt. *Slate*, 9 Jan. 2017, www.slate.com/articles/arts/books/2017/01/bill_schutt_s_cannibalism_reviewed.html. Accessed 21 Sept. 2017.

Montgomery, Sy. "Pass the Fava Beans: A New Book on Cannibalism Says It's Not as Rare as We Once Thought." Review of *Cannibalism: A Perfectly Natural History*, by Bill Schutt. *The New York Times*, 31 Jan. 2017, www.nytimes.com/2017/01/31/books/review/cannibalism-bill-schutt.html. Accessed Sept. 21 2017.

The Color of Law
A Forgotten History of How Our Government Segregated America

Author: Richard Rothstein
Publisher: Liveright (New York). 368 pp.
Type of work: Sociology, history, current affairs
Time: Primarily mid-twentieth century
Locale: United States

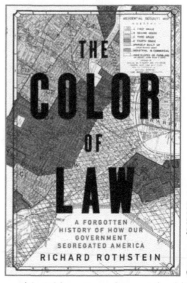

Courtesy of W.W. Norton

Noted scholar Richard Rothstein provides an exhaustively researched look at the official and unofficial governmental policies that led to a long history of highly segregated housing in the United States and argues that because these policies were both official and unconstitutional, the government has a responsibility to make things right today.

The United States is a highly segregated nation, with African American and white citizens living, for the most part, in different neighborhoods and towns, and whites generally reaping the benefits of more affluent and desirable dwellings. Many people have different ideas about why this pattern of segregation developed the way it did. Some might choose to either blame African Americans for their own plight or suggest that they prefer to live by themselves in segregated communities; others might argue that a history of racist decision-making and policies is to blame for the current state of housing, although the question of who made those decisions and policies is one that is often debated. In the common imagination, it is generally the actions of private individuals—banks that refused to loan to African Americans, white neighbors who protested the integration of their neighborhoods—that were to blame. In his heavily researched book *The Color of Law: A Forgotten History of How Our Government Segregated America*, Richard Rothstein argues convincingly that, in fact, it was official governmental action that ensured the segregation of the country.

Beginning with a discussion of constitutional law, Rothstein suggests that a governmental policy of segregation violates the Fifth, Thirteenth, and Fourteenth Amendments. Although he acknowledges that the Thirteenth Amendment, which abolished slavery, might not seem a logical choice as a tool of enforcement, he demonstrates that it does apply, since it also bars the "badges and incidents of slavery," of which segregated housing is an example. He then takes readers briefly through nineteenth- and early twentieth-century legislation and legal rulings to lay the groundwork for his discussion of governmental manipulation.

The Color of Law focuses primarily on the mid-twentieth century, which is when, Rothstein argues, the government did the most to enforce segregation. Following the passage of the Fair Housing Act as part of the Civil Rights Act of 1968, it became increasingly difficult for federal, state, and local governments to pursue official policies of segregated housing; before that time, however, the various levels of government did all they could to keep whites and African Americans separate, and the results are still being felt today. Segregated housing was by no means inevitable, but following Reconstruction, when the post–Civil War government pulled its troops out of the South, racist legislators sought to restrict African Americans to isolated communities in which they could be controlled and rendered inferior. These efforts redoubled as the twentieth century rolled on, and as several Supreme Court decisions made it harder for different levels of government to explicitly discriminate, officials devised more and more devious means to maintain a policy of segregation.

The fact that these governmental bodies were primarily responsible for the segregation of the United States is one that Rothstein insists on throughout, and proving this fact stands as *The Color of Law*'s most significant achievement. As Rothstein explains early on, if segregation were "a product not of state action but of private choices," as Supreme Court chief justice John Roberts asserted in a 2007 majority opinion for the Court, then the government would not be obliged to offer restitution to afflicted African American families. But if, as Rothstein argues in his book, "African Americans were unconstitutionally denied the means and the right to integration in middle-class neighborhoods, and . . . this denial was state-sponsored, [then] the nation is obligated to remedy it." This insistence is the book's chief political maneuver, and it is a powerful one.

The book proceeds by focusing, chapter by chapter, on different governmental policies and tactics aimed at maintaining segregation, along the way exploding common misconceptions that many readers may hold about private versus public segregation. For example, many people are aware of the redlining policies that banks employed throughout the twentieth century to avoid giving loans to people buying houses in predominantly African American areas. But as Rothstein explains, this was not a decision simply made by banks in their capacity as private lenders. It was, rather, a New Deal program, the Home Owners' Loan Corporation (HOLC), that began the process of color-coding maps by racial demographics. HOLC's function was to help out homeowners who were about to default on their mortgages by buying up those mortgages and then offering the homeowners new ones at far more favorable terms. To determine who to help, the agency drew up maps, noting which races lived in which areas. Although it would occasionally help people living in African American neighborhoods, it set the precedent that other governmental agencies and banks would soon make standard.

When, in 1934, the government created the Federal Housing Administration (FHA), that institution soon adopted HOLC's strategy of mapping neighborhoods. But the FHA took things further. Since its function was to guarantee bank mortgages, it wanted to ensure that it would only guarantee low-risk investments. This, of course, meant that the FHA refused to guarantee loans not only in black neighborhoods, but also in mixed neighborhoods and even in white neighborhoods that were near to black neighborhoods. As the agency's first official underwriting manual baldly stated in 1935, "If a neighborhood is to retain stability it is necessary that properties shall continue to be occupied by the same social and racial classes. A change in social or racial occupancy generally leads to instability and a reduction in values." Because banks would not offer mortgages at reasonably affordable terms to borrowers not insured by the FHA, African Americans were largely unable to buy houses, and this, in conjunction with other racist governmental policies, meant they were often confined to cramped urban quarters where they remained renters and were unable to gain sufficient equity to achieve better economic conditions. Although it remains possible that banks would be hesitant to offer even FHA-backed loans to African American borrowers, Rothstein definitively proves that it was governmental institutions—HOLC, the FHA, later the Veterans Administration (VA, now the Department of Veterans Affairs)—that were responsible for keeping African Americans from widespread homeownership.

Even when African Americans were able to buy homes, Rothstein shows, it was often only in lower-income, predominantly African American neighborhoods, where their properties were unlikely to appreciate nearly as much as houses in white suburban communities. When the first preplanned suburban tracts, such as Levittown in Long Island, were being created, these developments were insured by government-backed loans before the ground was even broken—but they were only insured on the understanding that they would be exclusively for white tenants, even as African American laborers such as Robert Mereday, a working-class man who settled in nearby Hempstead, helped build them.

Courtesy of Judy Licht Photography

Mereday is one of several people whom Rothstein profiles at length in his book, bringing a human face to a story that is otherwise largely a sometimes-dry discussion of official governmental policy. The figure that features most prominently is Frank Stevenson, a man whose story begins the book and whose legacy closes it. Stevenson was

Richard Rothstein is a fellow of the Haas Institute at the University of California–Berkeley, a research associate at the Economic Policy Institute, and a fellow at the Thurgood Marshall Institute of the NAACP Legal Defense and Educational Fund. He is the author or coauthor of numerous books.

an African American man who, during World War II, took a job building ships in the Bay Area town of Richmond, California. He settled in Richmond, where he still lives, after moving there from Louisiana, where he was born. Although he was forced to live in inferior segregated housing, he was able to establish a life in Richmond that would have been impossible if he had stayed in the South. Unfortunately, the plant soon moved south to Milpitas, California, in the Santa Clara Valley. Stevenson wanted to relocate to one of the new subdivisions being built near the plant, but they were whites-only, so he could not. There were no apartments in Milpitas, so he could not even rent in the area. He had to make a long daily commute from Richmond, which became increasingly African American as white residents fled for better opportunities, resulting in property values failing to rise as they would have in white neighborhoods. Although Stevenson bought a home in 1970, he was unable to gain the kind of equity available to people living in subdivisions.

To drive home the injustices inflicted on Stevenson and others like him, the victims of official racist governmental policy, Rothstein ends his book by considering the lost opportunities suffered by the former shipyard worker. The last chapter is devoted to solutions, although, as with many books that aim to diagnose the ills of society, the fixes it offers are not particularly convincing. But the chapter is boosted by its final section, in which Rothstein returns to the Stevenson family. He takes readers through the subsequent generations, children and grandchildren, and shows how their lives shook out: growing up in segregated Richmond, going to segregated schools, and being denied the opportunities of their white counterparts. After listing the modest occupations that Stevenson's grandchildren have taken up—nurse assistants, security guards, clerical workers—Rothstein bemoans what might have been for this family had they lived in an unsegregated United States. "What might have become of these Stevenson grandchildren," he writes, "if their parents had grown up and attended school in an integrated Milpitas, not in a *de jure* segregated Richmond? . . . How different might the lives of the Stevenson grandchildren have been were it not for the federal government's unconstitutional determination to segregate their grandparents, and their parents as well?"

These are the hard questions that Rothstein asks throughout his book, a book that takes as its starting point a history of constitutional violation on the part of the government and then goes on both to prove these violations and to show their human cost. Although few would deny the racism inherent in American history, many people like to think that it belongs safely to that past and has no effect on modern-day life. Rothstein shows that, contrary to this belief, the legacies of entrenched American racism continue to shape the country today, in part by continuing to hold back African Americans from achieving true equality. Only by acknowledging not only the racist housing policies of the past, but also the facts that these policies were dictated officially by the government and that their effects continue to loom large in the present, can Americans hope to move on from that past. It will not be easy, Rothstein acknowledges, but the knowledge that his book brings offers an important first step toward bringing about a more just future.

Andrew Schenker, MLIS

Review Sources

Cohen, Rachel M. "Discrimination Is Not De Facto." Review of *The Color of Law: A Forgotten History of How Our Government Segregated America*, by Richard Rothstein. *Slate*, 5 May 2017, www.slate.com/articles/news_and_politics/jurisprudence/2017/05/richard_rothstein_s_the_color_of_law_reviewed.html. Accessed 22 Jan. 2018.

Kahlenberg, Richard D. "Why Segregated Neighborhoods Persist." Review of *The Color of Law: A Forgotten History of How Our Government Segregated America*, by Richard Rothstein. *Washington Monthly*, June–Aug. 2017, washingtonmonthly.com/magazine/junejulyaugust-2017/why-segregated-neighborhoods-persist/. Accessed 22 Jan. 2018.

Oshinsky, David. "A Powerful, Disturbing History of Residential Segregation in America." Review of *The Color of Law: A Forgotten History of How Our Government Segregated America*, by Richard Rothstein. *The New York Times*, 20 June 2017, www.nytimes.com/2017/06/20/books/review/richard-rothstein-color-of-law-forgotten-history.html. Accessed 22 Jan. 2018.

The Cooking Gene
A Journey through African American Culinary History in the Old South

Author: Michael W. Twitty (b. 1977)
Publisher: Amistad (New York). Illustrated. 464 pp.
Type of work: Memoir, history
Time: Seventeenth century to the present
Locales: Washington, DC; American South

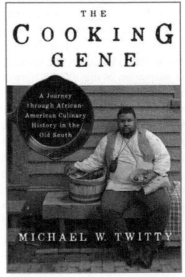

The Cooking Gene *excavates the history of African American foodways from the earliest eras of slavery in the American South to the present day. The book fuses the genres of history and autobiography to trace the intertwined stories of food, culture, and bloodlines in the South.*

Principal personages

MICHAEL TWITTY, author and narrator
B. J. DENNIS, a Charleston, South Carolina, chef with whom he discusses cooking and race relations
VINCENT HENDERSON, a second-generation chef in Mobile, Alabama, who introduces him to Creole cuisine in the state
ELOISE BOOKER, his paternal grandmother, who introduced him to food consumption habits derived from slavery
KEITH DOAR, a Jewish descendent of a South Carolina plantation family
KEVIN MITCHELL, a South Carolinian chef who shares research about enslaved cooks with Twitty
LEAH CHASE, a New Orleans chef who welcomes Twitty into her Creole kitchen
MILDRED COVERT, a cookbook author who introduces Twitty to the Jewish traditions of New Orleans cuisine
NIC BUTLER, a historian at Charleston County Public Library who deepens Twitty's understanding of the slave trade in Charleston
PATRICIA "PAT" ANITA TOWNSEND, Twitty's mother, from whom he gained his earliest passion for cooking
TED LEE, a culinary figure known for the Lee Bros. cookbooks and catalog; one of Twitty's guides at a South Carolina rice plantation
TONI CARRIER, a genealogist who works with Twitty to trace his family tree
WILLIAM LEE TWITTY, Twitty's father, who introduces him to many aspects of southern culture through family trips to Virginia

In this well-received debut book, *The Cooking Gene*, Michael W. Twitty offers an account of the African American experience interpreted through foodways and family heredity. While the book could be most simply categorized as "culinary history," this term undersells its breadth and significance. Twitty interweaves elements of memoir, African American studies, historical reenactment, social history, and cultural critique into the text. Across the manuscript, he traces the history of his family through centuries of slavery, interweaving this reconstructive history into larger narratives about southern foodways and history. *The Cooking Gene* identifies the African origins for many of the most distinctive dishes of the American South and traces the distribution and adaptation of these foods across cultural groups and environments in the United States. Perhaps most significantly, the book constructs an intertwined and interdependent history of the black, white, and indigenous populations of the South. Without sweetening his discussions of the brutal treatment of enslaved people and the permanent damage that slavery caused to the African American community, Twitty suggests a route forward that acknowledges the intermingled blood and heritage of the region. In his accounting, southern heritage requires acknowledging white blood in black veins and black blood in white bodies. By tracing foodways alongside bloodlines, Twitty looks toward a complex and bodily reinterpretation of the American South.

Twitty has made an innovative career as a historic food interpreter and writer. At historical sites throughout the South, he has offered live cooking performances in order to introduce audiences to the historic foodways of the region. Twitty grew up just within the borders of the South in Washington, DC. He could trace his family heritage to western Virginia, South Carolina, and Alabama. As a child, he was fed heritage African American foods of the South and watched his grandmother prepare and consume traditional survival foods from the years of slavery and Reconstruction. He is quick to add, though, that he did not enjoy these reminders of his heritage as a child; indeed, he confesses, as a small child, he "hated soul food and [he] didn't really like being black." Indeed, the family's southern origins were not celebrated—rather, they seemed most closely associated with a past from which the family felt fortunate to have escaped. Instead, multicultural influences were dominant forces in his family gatherings, with traditional southern foods like pigs' feet and chitlins being guilty, almost hidden, pleasures of the older generation. This book is, in part, an account of a multiyear travel and research project, in which Twitty traveled in the South in order to trace sites with connections to his family's history and to become more deeply acquainted with regions and historic agricultural techniques tied to historic livestock and traditional crops like sorghum, rice, and cotton. Reckoning with the ghosts of his family's past and seeking out the traces of his ancestry are the central motivations of the text. This organization around Twitty's own family heritage gives the book intimacy and depth, as do his rich descriptions of the southern landscape and its people. His text explores the full life cycle of foods and the ways in which rituals of raising, harvesting, and preparing foods shaped the region. With similar tenacity, *The Cooking Gene* lays out Twitty's pursuit of his family heritage, across written documents, oral history, and the data of his own DNA.

As a self-described African American culinary history, *The Cooking Gene* is the result of Twitty's realization that in searching for the African American past, "the food is in many cases all we have." If contemporary struggles of African American communities are sometimes crystalized around discussions of food deserts and the malnutrition that results from pervasive fast-food consumption, historic foodways can initiate "larger conversations about individual and group survival," an agenda that speaks to Twitty's consistently constructive and forward-looking approach to his material. Thus, while *The Cooking Gene* seeks to introduce its readers to the interdependent nature of race in the American South, it foregrounds a task of seeking hereditary repair and uplift for the African American community. Unlike other ethnic groups, African Americans have experienced the systematic and nearly complete suppression of their ancestry. To search for this history is to "take a completely shattered vessel and piece it together, knowing that some pieces will never be recovered." By turning to the role of food in the history of the South, Twitty is able to interpret food as an active agent, or as he puts it, "the exercise of specific histories, not just the result." In the pursuit of these histories, he explains, "Our ancestry is not an afterthought; it is both our raison d'être and our mise en place, it is action and reaction."

A final thread in Twitty's text is its somewhat surprising focus on Jewish history. A convert to Judaism, Twitty has also sought to reconstruct the influence of Jewish cuisine on southern food. In the process, he has pursued the complex relationship of the Jewish and African American communities in the South. Twitty is not the first to identify a Jewish strain in southern cooking—he pays tribute to Mildred Covert and others in this regard—but he offers an engaging account of the merging of African and Jewish cuisines in Alabama and Louisiana. *The Cooking Gene* also reckons, to some degree, with Jewish ownership of slaves, as well as the strategic silence of the Jewish community in Birmingham, Alabama, during the years of greatest violence during the civil rights movement.

Most chapters of the book conclude with recipes, some gleaned from Twitty's family, others that are historical recipes that he has helped to reconstruct for the modern chef. Intended to pay tribute to the historic foodways of the African American community, most of these are relatively simple recipes, though a few include ingredients that are relatively rare in the modern kitchen. They range from haunting recipes that re-create the traumatic foods of slavery—such as "Trough Mush" (fed, by means of an animal trough, to enslaved children) and "Hoecake" (the common food for farm laborers)—to feast-worthy specialties like "Sorghum Brined Chicken." A few poignant recipes are also included as part of Twitty's reckoning with his mother's death during the process of writing the book. Here "Macaroni and Cheese the Way My Mother Made It" and "Funeral Potato Salad" both mark his mother's death, but also help to emphasize Twitty's point about the deep-rooted intermixing of white and black America, at least from the perspective of culinary history.

While the discussions of food are certainly Twitty's strong point, the book is also valuable in its tracing of his family's story. His accounts of his own childhood in Washington, DC, are engaging. His openness about his conversion to Judaism and the family tensions over his homosexuality are surely valuable pieces within his wide-ranging exploration of African American culture. Tracing each element of Twitty's family tree becomes one of the motivating mysteries of reading the text. It is unsurprising, though powerful, when he digs into the meaning of his roots in Ghana and Sierra Leone in terms of the culinary histories of his ancestors. Equally intriguing, though, is his pursuit of the white strains that constitute nearly a third of his genetic makeup. He confronts the realities of rape and sexual violence on the lives of enslaved people (which he also closely associates with plantation kitchens), but he also discovers a female European ancestor who may have immigrated as an indentured servant and had a relationship with

Michael W. Twitty is a culinary historian, Judaic studies professor, and writer who has been recognized for his blog, Afroculinaria, *which traces African American historic foodways. He has a fellowship at the Southern Foodways Alliance and is the inaugural Revolutionary in Residence at the Colonial Williamsburg Foundation. The Cooking Gene is his first book.*

an African American man. Twitty openly admits that some steps of this history into his family's eighteenth-century origins are guesswork and reconstructive. Nevertheless, his account is a valuable reminder of the diversity of heritage common within the African American community.

Although written for a popular audience, *The Cooking Gene* is informed by extensive historical research and engagement with scholarly literature. Throughout the text, readers will encounter Twitty's adept application not only of culinary history research, but also a broad range of cultural, social, scientific, and historical literature. The book offers an original contribution to these disciplines, reflecting Twitty's innovative methodology of producing living food history. His research in this book is personal, autobiographical, and physical, but it also offers contributions and interventions in the metanarratives concerning, especially, southern history and slavery. He builds on the work of historical sites like Colonial Williamsburg and introduces knowledge gained from conversations with archivists and local genealogists, not solely from the academic literature. The result is an engaging writing style that integrates quoted dialogue and recounts Twitty's surprises and realizations on the road to tracing his family's history. The downside of this conversational approach is that citations are minimal, and by his own admission, Twitty does not necessarily feel limited to statements that can be proven through historical evidence. In seeking to trace the untraceable, Twitty is willing to step beyond the accepted boundaries of academic history to attain a more fulfilling connection with the past. As such, his text is closer to a historical reenactment than it is, strictly, to the discipline of history.

The Cooking Gene is a valuable contribution to the ongoing cultural reckoning with both the history of slavery and the rising fame of southern cuisine.

Julia A. Sienkewicz

Review Sources

"Dinner in Black and White: Cooking in the American South; Two New Books Tackle Race and American History around the Table." Review of *The Cooking Gene: A Journey through African American Culinary History in the Old South*, by Michael W. Twitty, and *The Potlikker Papers: A Food History of the Modern South*, by John Edge. *The Economist*, 27 July 2017, www.economist.com/news/books-and-arts/21725549-two-new-books-tackle-race-and-american-history-around-table-cooking-american. Accessed 11 Feb. 2018.

Norton, James. "*The Cooking Gene* Views the African-American Experience through Its Food." Review of *The Cooking Gene: A Journey through African American Culinary History in the Old South*, by Michael W. Twitty. *The Christian Science Monitor*, 2 Aug. 2017, www.csmonitor.com/Books/Book-Reviews/2017/0802/The-Cooking-Gene-views-the-African-American-experience-through-its-food. Accessed 11 Feb. 2018.

Watman, Max. "Hearty Helpings from Three Culinary Histories." Review of *The Cooking Gene: A Journey through African American Culinary History in the Old South*, by Michael W. Twitty, et al. *The New York Times*, 21 July 2017, www.nytimes.com/2017/07/21/books/review/culinary-history-3-southern-cookbooks.html. Accessed 11 Feb. 2018.

The Dark Flood Rises

Author: Margaret Drabble (b. 1939)
Publisher: Farrar, Straus, and Giroux (New York). 336 pp.
Type of work: Novel
Time: Present day
Locales: England; the Canary Islands

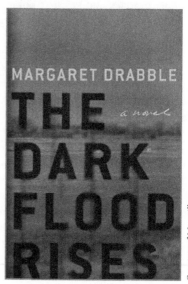

Courtesy of Macmillan

Drabble explores the varied issues of aging in this character study about several people who are moving into the golden years of their lives.

Principal characters

FRANCESCA "FRAN" STUBBS, a woman who inspects housing for the elderly
TERESA QUINN, her childhood friend
JO DRUMMOND, her best friend
CLAUDE STUBBS, her ex-husband
CHRISTOPHER STUBBS, her son
POPPET STUBBS, her daughter
BENNETT CARPENTER, a historian and writer
IVOR WALTERS, Bennett's partner and caretaker

The Dark Flood Rises is unabashedly about the experience of aging. A character study more than a plot driven book, Margaret Drabble's twentieth novel boldly confronts what life might mean to people in their later years. As the major characters' stories of their current experiences are told through third person limited narration, Drabble introduces a variety of thematic issues which are often, but not always, connected to growing old. And like much of Drabble's work, the perspective of women is first and foremost in the narrative.

The novel focuses on the internal lives of a group of people who are connected in some way to central protagonist Francesca "Fran" Stubbs, who is the first and most developed of the narrators. From the first page of the book, readers learn that Fran is old enough to be considered "old," and is dealing with the inevitable physical changes that come with age. However, she is not one to let these changes slow her down. In her seventies, Fran could be retired, peacefully enjoying a life of leisure, but she continues to work. Her job, ironically, takes her on trips all over England to inspect housing for the elderly, so she is continually confronted with her own mortality. This is not completely frightening for Fran, however, as it is revealed that she is quite self-aware and has long been interested in the idea of heroic or tragic ends.

Though Fran is the main character, the one whose internal conflicts are most clearly developed, a wide variety of other characters are also presented. Many of these are

Fran's peers, who are going through their own unique experiences of aging, including her ex-husband, Claude Stubbs; her friends Jo Drummond and Teresa Quinn; and the expatriate historian Bennett Carpenter. Others are of a different generation, but no less caught up in the passing of time. These include Fran's children, Christopher Stubbs and Poppet Stubbs, but also Ivor, Bennett's younger but still late-middle-aged lover and caregiver.

As the story follows these individuals, a number of topics and thematic ideas are introduced. The somewhat humdrum existence of Fran and others in England is compared with the sunny, touristy environment of Lanzarote in the Canary Islands, where Bennett has retired with Ivor and where Christopher connects with them. This duality of setting also allows the novel to explore the subject of immigrants from North Africa to the Canary Islands, an issue that affects the perspective of certain characters. Christopher's partner, Sara, had begun a film about the plight of these immigrants, and after her unexpected death Christopher continues to be concerned with the issue. His stay with Bennett and Ivor in the Canaries gives him time to reflect on the work Sara started, and his current lack of direction gives him the ability to pursue her study. By making connections between seemingly disparate topics such as homeless migrants and housing challenges for the elderly, Drabble keeps attention on universal human concerns, providing meaning even when the plot takes a back seat to character.

Health is another primary focus of the novel. For example, Teresa, Fran's childhood friend, is dying of mesothelioma. Yet her terminal illness does not stop her from conducting herself gracefully, and even inspires an exploration into the way different personalities deal with religious questions about life after death. Claude, meanwhile, is mostly bedridden because of heart problems. His corpulence in combination with the cardiac weakness leaves him reliant on the care of others, including Fran and a visiting nurse. Bennett suffers a fall, a common threat to older adults, and his hospitalization brings a lessening of his mental acuity, suggesting dementia. Similar issues are also frequently addressed by Fran as she visits elderly care facilities for her job. Drabble presents physical concerns as another inevitable part of aging, but again something that can be faced with a variety of actions and mindsets.

Secondary only to the aging process is death as the primary thematic note in the book. Throughout her portraits of her characters, Drabble explores the ways people die, especially older people but also younger adults. The deaths occur both as mentions of minor characters and as deeply felt direct blows to Fran's world, reinforcing the universality of loss. The circumstances also vary, from expected to surprising and from peaceful to terrible. For example, the death of the comparatively young Sara is an abrupt, shocking tragedy, while Teresa's death is assumed well in advance. It is the death of another one of her friends, however, that perhaps provokes the most reflection from Fran. She is torn over the fact that the loss was totally unexpected, but also occurred in essentially the most peaceful way possible. Confronted with "the burden of living," Fran has to consciously choose to keep moving on.

Planning for the future is a concern for people of any age, and *The Dark Flood Rises* shows how it impacts people differently—and often contradictorily. Fran is aware and appreciative of the fact that she is still independent, but also understands the

Margaret Drabble is an award-winning novelist, critic, and biographer. Appointed a Dame Commander of the Order of the British Empire (DBE), she has been recognized for her lifetime achievements in literature with the Golden PEN award and as a member of the Royal Society of Literature.

physical decline she is undergoing. Despite her firsthand knowledge of the perils that unsuitable housing can provide to the elderly, she lives in a run-down apartment because it is convenient and cheap. Meanwhile, her relationships are shaping her future as well, particularly her reconnections with Claude and Teresa.

The relationship between Bennett and Ivor also illustrates how personal connections and aging affect one's outlook. Bennett has always financially supported the couple and been the more outgoing personality. As he begins to decline in health and mental acuity, Ivor struggles with his own prospects. He has difficulty conceiving of life on his own, and all the responsibility that entails. As an unmarried couple, he and Bennett lack a binding legal connection, adding a unique layer of uncertainty about final arrangements to Ivor's future. Drabble weaves this status into her portrayal in an engaging way, showing what life might look like for a partner who feels powerless despite a lifelong commitment.

The novel presents relationships as essential to life, even as they invite complications (not least due to aging) and eventually bring on the pain of loss. Friendships, marriage, partnerships, parenting, divorce, and ultimately death are all introduced as the characters work through what life throws at them. Drabble is particularly skillful in her depiction of the similarities and differences in female friendships through the years: Fran and Teresa are childhood friends who grew apart but reconnected years later, while Fran and Jo grew close as young wives with small children and have remained friends even as their lives changed in different ways.

Romantic relationships are also portrayed as things that change with age. Fran and Claude's marriage, divorce, and subsequent relationship is the starkest example of this always unique process. Despite the failure of their short marriage, the two are reconciled and Fran finds herself bringing meals to the incapacitated Claude. Needing to feel useful, Fran gets as much out of this new arrangement as Claude does, despite the odd circumstances. The family dynamic is further explored through Fran's relationships with her children, which are somewhat distant. Other relationships are also explored, with minor figures providing extra links between key characters.

Since the novel is primarily character driven, the plot is limited. There is little sense of overall rising action or climax since the individual characters' experiences are the focus. In fact, there are no clear chapter breaks. In some ways, this lack of defined action reflects the aging process—also symbolized by the rising flood of the title—which often meanders slowly through periods of lessened activity. This does not mean that there are not crisis moments for some of the characters, but it does mean that contemplation takes precedence over excitement. Critics were generally receptive to this tone, noting that for some readers the novel may be depressing and slow, but for others, especially those who can identify closely with Fran, it is a successful, even meditative work. Many reviewers noted that the elements of humor help to counterbalance the otherwise melancholy subject matter.

Widely received as a strong literary work from an accomplished novelist, *The Dark Flood Rises* acknowledges that death is the natural conclusion to life, but suggests it is not always a climactic event. And even death is not fully an end, as others go on living. Most lives unfold slowly and mundanely, with relative longevity and a final period of decline as the new normal. Yet all lives are punctuated by occasional abrupt endings. Abrupt endings, in fact, are used to conclude the novel, as Drabble wraps up the stories with a succinct epilogue. She provides brief closure to most of the lives she has introduced throughout the previous pages—a decision that some may find off-putting.

Like the flood waters that can insidiously take over a countryside, aging and death can sneak up on a person, stealing physical and mental health, altering or ending relationships, and changing the way a person experiences everything. Drabble depicts this slow movement realistically and sympathetically, making for compelling reading.

Theresa L. Stowell, PhD

Review Sources

Review of *The Dark Flood Rises*, by Margaret Drabble. *Kirkus Reviews*, 7 Nov. 2016, www.kirkusreviews.com/book-reviews/margaret-drabble/the-dark-flood-rises/. Accessed 1 Nov. 2017.

Love, Barbara. Review of *The Dark Flood Rises*, by Margaret Drabble. *Library Journal*, 15 Dec. 16, pp. 82.

Miner, Valerie. "The Journey Into the Unknown." Review of *The Dark Flood Rises*, by Margaret Drabble. *Women's Review of Books*, Sept./Oct. 2017, pp. 24–25. *Literary Reference Center*, search.ebscohost.com/login.aspx?direct=true&db=lfh&AN=125411202&site=eds-live. Accessed 1 Nov. 2017.

Ozick, Cynthia. "Death and Disaster Stalk the Characters in Margaret Drabble's New Novel." Review of *The Dark Flood Rises*, by Margaret Drabble. *The New York Times*, 14 Feb. 2017, www.nytimes.com/2017/02/14/books/review/dark-flood-rises-margaret-drabble-.html. Accessed 1 Nov. 2017.

Seaman, Donna. "Review of *The Dark Flood Rises*." *Booklist*, 1 Jan. 2017, pp. 34.

Dear Fahrenheit 451
Love and Heartbreak in the Stacks

Author: Annie Spence
Publisher: Flatiron Books (New York). 256 pp.
Type of work: Letters
Time: Present day

Annie Spence presents a series of letters she has written to the books she has encountered during her years as a librarian. Often funny or sarcastic, sometimes worshipful, the book talks to and about her favorite, and least favorite, tomes.

Courtesy of Macmillan

Principal personages
ANNIE SPENCE, author and librarian
JEFFREY EUGENIDES, author of *The Virgin Suicides*
AUDREY NIFFENEGGER, author of *The Time Traveler's Wife*
CORMAC MCCARTHY, author of *Blood Meridian*
DAVID SEDARIS, essayist and short-story writer
STEPHENIE MEYER, author of the *Twilight* series
E. L. JAMES, author of the *Fifty Shades* series

Librarian Annie Spence's debut book, *Dear Fahrenheit 451: Love and Heartbreak in the Stacks*, starts with an introduction that prepares readers for Spence's letter-writing format that then dominates the rest of the piece. In this opening letter, Spence tells readers that she is symbolic of their own librarians, explaining that she intimately knows something about each personality type who enters the library. Even more than the patrons, though, she assures readers that she knows the books, and she knows them so well that she converses with them. *Dear Fahrenheit 451* shares some of those conversations and initiates its own dialogue with its readers as "it wants you to connect to it, to laugh with it, and to walk away with a whole new list of other books that you can't wait to get involved with." The rest of the book is then broken into two sections: part one is "Books—The Letters" and part two is "Special Subjects—Library Employees—Assistance to Readers." Furthering the library connection, each section opens with the image of an old-fashioned card-catalog card against a black background. These cards contain fun and pertinent quotes that prepare readers for the content of each section.

The first section includes Spence's letters to the books, authors, and bookshelves she has encountered during her years as a librarian. These notes, averaging two to four pages each, talk directly to the best and worst of the books many avid readers will recognize, enjoy, or even hate. Though most letters address the books themselves, Spence also comments on her own life, the people to whom she recommends the books, and broader societal issues. Her tone is often hilarious, sometimes sarcastic, occasionally worshipful, and her opinions stand out clearly, even when she knows there might be disagreement with her assessment. Though some letters speak to specific tomes, such as Donna Tartt's *The Goldfinch* (2013) or Jeffrey Eugenides's *The Virgin Suicides* (1993), others address genres, like science fiction, paranormal romance, nonfiction, and realistic fiction, and some letters consider subgenres or specific series, such as "Celebrity Autobiographies" or "The Harlequin Romance Spinner Rack." Her knowledge of books crosses audience boundaries as well, touching on children's books and young-adult pieces alongside reading that appeals to adults. There is, however, no truly logical reason for the order of the books she presents. She jumps from pieces she loves to pieces she wants to break up with, from adult fiction to children's books. Each letter follows the same format, with a heading that indicates the book type or subject matter, the author, and a few defining phrases. For instance, in the second letter, she lists "FICTION—Tolstoy, Leo" followed in list form with "—Classic Russian Literature," "—The Bachelor," and "—Choices." She then addresses the author, book, or genre directly, as in "Dear *Anna Karenina*," and ends with a closing "Goodbye, Annie" (or something similar that recaps the opinion presented).

Annie Spence is a librarian who has worked at the Newberry Library in Chicago, Illinois, and other libraries in the Midwest. Dear Fahrenheit 451: Love and Heartbreak in the Stacks *is her first book.*

One of the most noticeable elements of Spence's book is the humor. Readers will find themselves laughing and cringing along with her as she introduces books that need to be "weeded" from the library's collection or her own collection, in what she dubs "book breakups." Her first letter, to Tartt's *The Goldfinch*, is not a true breakup; it is more of a relocation based on the physical condition of the book. Since this long volume has become "cracked" and ragged, Spence promises it that she will add it to her own personal bookshelf, where "no one but you and I will ever see the duct tape holding you together or the DISCARD stamp on your title page." In some cases, as with Nicholas Sparks's novel *Dear John* (2006), she is not quite as gentle, and her mockery of the pedestrian writing will amuse sophisticated readers. She tells the book, "In the prologue you say, 'Our story has three parts: a beginning, a middle, and an end.' No sh——, *John*. That's how that works. Give me something I've never heard." She is even less patient with E. L. James's *Grey: Fifty Shades of Grey as Told by Christian* (2015), lamenting when she is asked where to find it or if she has read it: "It makes me want to shake readers and scream: YOU'RE SURROUNDED BY GREAT LITERATURE AND THIS SH—— ISN'T EVEN THAT DIRTY!" Meanwhile, she is horrified that she has "to explain to a little old lady who only reads Karen Kingsbury novels what erotica is and watch her pretend to put it back and then pick it up again when I'm pretending not to look. You made me say 'erotica' to an old lady, *Grey*! I'm going to hate you forever for that." Her breakup with this book asks for revenge: "I hope someone drops you in the bubble bath they are sitting in when they read you."

Poorly written romance is not the only reason Spence tells some books that they need to move on. Relevance is another major reason. When chatting with Barbara Williams's *Cornzapoppin'! Popcorn Recipes and Party Ideas for All Occasions* (1976), Spence points out that some of the recipes, though original, might not precisely do what they suggest. The "'Beefy Popcorn Alternate for Dieting Dads,'" for instance, offers "throwing a stick of butter and a jar of beef jerky on top of a bowl of . . . you guessed it: popcorn," in a less than appetizing or healthy option. Her real reason for passing this book into the sale pile is its 1976 publication date. Bob Schwartz's *The One Hour Orgasm: A New Approach to Achieving Maximum Sexual Pleasure* (1992) is the climactic choice for part one of Spence's book. She assures the book that its lack of circulation in a several-year period is not the reason for its dismissal. It is "because your pages suggest that patrons bring you along with two large mirrors and a tub of Vaseline into a space 'warm enough for you to be nude for about one hour.' That's just not the kind of environment we like to encourage library readers to venture into with material that other people will subsequently touch."

Spence addresses tomes for varied audiences while also broaching societal themes. Her children's book selections are recognizable, allowing many readers to relate to both the good and the bad of not only the books themselves but of parenting and adulthood. Shel Silverstein's *The Giving Tree* (1964), for example, is often a favorite, but Spence points out some faults with its logic: "This tree you talk about keeps giving and giving and GIVING and you say she's happy, but I don't know. The little boy brands her with his initials, takes everything she has, and leaves. And she's happy about it? The End? Maybe it was just the sleepless nights or the hormones, but WTF?" She also challenges her own son's one-time favorite: "You're only six pages long, but you take a half hour to read because you point out all your parts. Your wheels and windshields and mudflaps. All that sh——. . . . Have you ever heard of a narrative arc? Just one time I'd like to open you and see an actual driver in one of your trucks. What's his name? What's his home life like? How high is his cholesterol? Nope. Not *My Truck Book*." In contrast to these less than stellar reactions, she does laud several children's books. *Frog and Toad Storybook Treasury* (2014), by Arnold Lobel, is a favorite that "bring[s] such joy into my life. Something about you makes me want to ignore all of my adult responsibilities and sit around having tea and cake, waiting for the mail to come. . . . For all his worrying, Toad is living the dream. And actually, when I think about it, so am I." She also argues that *Yertle the Turtle and Other Stories* by Dr. Seuss is still relevant even though "since your release in 1950, you may have assumed fascism was dead, but you need only look around this lot of tyrant tots and their proud parents to see that not everyone absorbed your line about all creatures being free." If the parents on the playground unite, Spence assures readers, they can use *Yertle*'s ideas to start a revolution. Other audience concerns include feminism (see *Women of the Street: Making It on Wall Street—The World's Toughest Business* (1997)), sexuality (see *Coming Out Straight: Understanding and Healing Homosexuality* (2000) and *Cult of the Born-Again Virgin: How Single Women Can Reclaim Their Sexual Power* (1999)), dieting (see *Better Homes and Gardens Dieting for One* (1984)), and changing perceptions (see *The Time Traveler's Wife* (2003) or *Forever* (1975)).

Spence's own favorite and least favorite books stand out throughout *Dear Fahrenheit 451*. Eugenides's *The Virgin Suicides* is addressed at least three times, the first letter opening with "Congratulations on your fifteenth consecutive year as my favorite book." Audrey Niffenegger's *The Time Traveler's Wife* also earns multiple mentions because of its timelessness. Spence writes "I knew that I loved you, but I didn't remember the reasons," but after picking the book up again, she says, "I fell in love all over." She tells Ray Bradbury's *Fahrenheit 451* (1951), "Don't ever change. And stay here with us, always. . . . If we ever get to a point when you're not included in the core of a book collection, we're all f——ed." In contrast, she bluntly tells Cormac McCarthy's *Blood Meridian* (1985), which she offered to her husband as a distraction so she could finish her own book, "I'm less than charmed with the philosophical theory you're advancing that 'humans are still awful and selfish; we've just come up with ways to f—— each other up without scalping.'" One potential criticism of the book is Spence's graphic language. She is not afraid to swear, and expletives appear regularly enough that some readers might be offended.

The second half of the book provides a different perspective on reading. Instead of telling the books what she thinks of them, she addresses readers, offering helpful tips for finding time to read, choosing what to read, and making other people enjoy reading as well. These guidelines are interspersed through Spence's conversational tone and contain tidbits from her own life, allowing the reader to feel as if they are talking to a librarian face-to-face rather than just reading a book.

Theresa L. Stowell, PhD

Review Sources

Bachowski, Donna. Review of *Dear Fahrenheit 451: Love and Heartbreak in the Stacks*, by Annie Spence. *Library Journal*, Jan. 2018, p. 55. *Literary Reference Center Plus*, search.ebscohost.com/login.aspx?direct=true&db=lkh&AN=127046 203&site=lrc-plus. Accessed 23 Jan. 2018.

Bostrom, Annie. Review of *Dear Fahrenheit 451: Love and Heartbreak in the Stacks*, by Annie Spence. *Booklist*, Aug. 2017, p. 13. *Literary Reference Center Plus*, search.ebscohost.com/login.aspx?direct=true&db=lkh&AN=124626935&sit e=lrc-plus. Accessed 23 Jan. 2018.

Review of *Dear Fahrenheit 451: Love and Heartbreak in the Stacks*, by Annie Spence. *Kirkus Reviews*, 15 July 2017, p. 40. *Literary Reference Center Plus*, search.ebscohost.com/login.aspx?direct=true&db=lkh&AN=124081389&site=l rc-plus. Accessed 23 Jan. 2018.

Dear Ijeawele, or A Feminist Manifesto in Fifteen Suggestions

Author: Chimamanda Ngozi Adichie (b. 1977)
Publisher: Alfred A. Knopf (New York). 80 pp.
Type of work: Letters, essays
Time: Present day
Locales: Nigeria, United States

Responding to a friend who has asked how to raise her daughter as a feminist, Chimamanda Ngozi Adichie writes a letter, which becomes a manifesto, outlining her suggestions.

Principal personages
CHIMAMANDA NGOZI ADICHIE, respondent and narrator
IJEAWELE, her friend, a new mother and recipient of the letter

Chimamanda Ngozi Adichie

Dear Ijeawele, or A Feminist Manifesto in Fifteen Suggestions

Courtesy of Knopf

Chimamanda Ngozi Adichie's best-selling *Dear Ijeawele, or A Feminist Manifesto in Fifteen Suggestions* is a tour de force. That claim might surprise some readers, given the book's mere eighty pages. Yet those pages are packed with insight from a writer who has successfully bridged the worlds of serious literature and pop culture and emerged as a leading voice of modern feminism. Prior to publishing *Dear Ijeawele,* Adichie had already achieved success as a novelist and through her TED Talk "We Should All Be Feminists," which was sampled in a song by the pop sensation Beyoncé in 2013 and then published as a book in 2014. This previous media attention no doubt boosted *Dear Ijeawele*'s commercial success, but that attention proves to be more than justified, as the book displays a rhetorical mastery making it worthy of its best-seller status.

This slim volume started out as a letter responding to a friend who wrote Adichie asking for advice on how to raise her daughter as a feminist. Some time later, in October 2016, Adichie posted her response on the social media site Facebook, where it began attracting significant attention. She subsequently developed the piece for publication as a book, making a few edits and adding an introduction explaining how it came about. Crucially, though, the book retains the original epistolary form—written as a letter—which, along with other rhetorical techniques, makes it so effective.

In championing feminism, Adichie backs a movement that has struggled to gain widespread acceptance both in the United States and her native Nigeria. Although women have worked steadily for greater access to education and positions of economic, social, and political power, progress has been slow in many ways. Relatively few women hold political office compared to men, and no woman has served as US president even as other nations have had female leaders. Significant pay gaps between men and women still exist. Policy issues such as the lack of universal paid family leave and affordable daycare contribute to these gaps, but resistance to feminism and even outright sexism also exist.

In part, the problem has been one of perception. Many people perceive feminism as either unnecessary, because they believe that women have already achieved equality, or as a threat, because opponents have cast feminists as angry man-haters rather than as people who simply want equal rights for women. The triumph of *Dear Ijeawele* is Adichie's ability to counter these negative perceptions through deceptively simple rhetorical strategies. Much of what Adichie advises is familiar, and not only to feminists. Many people who reject the label "feminist" can nonetheless accept the basic ideas put forth in the book as the fifteen suggestions of the title. These include that women should not have to apologize for working outside the home (part of the first suggestion), the importance of reading (fifth suggestion), that girls should not be criticized or shamed for their appearance (tenth suggestion), that girls should not be taught that their sexuality and bodies are shameful (twelfth suggestion), and that girls should be taught to respect diversity (fifteenth suggestion).

Many of the book's other points represent longstanding feminist ideas that have still not gained widespread acceptance. Some of these are highlighted through anecdotes, such as a reference to a newspaper story in Lagos, Nigeria, to make the point that a female mechanic should simply be called a mechanic, not a "lady mechanic." Others are presented from a broader sociological view, such as the concept that the "ideal" of chivalry rests on a widespread belief in the weakness of women. They often include clear, simple ideas on how to improve things, such as the suggestion that the title "Ms." is preferable to "Mrs." because the former de-emphasizes a woman's marital status as the key marker of her identity.

Such points are not new, but Adichie gives them freshness through form. The book's epistolary address represents a classic form that was once common. By writing directly to a friend, Adichie immediately personalizes her messages. She is writing to an individual seeking advice, not lecturing "the public" or some hazy notion of an audience. And the fact that the book emerged from an actual response validates the address as genuine rather than merely a rhetorical trick.

This form, in fact, together with Adichie's prowess as a writer, enables her to quickly win readers over. In the added introduction, she immediately invokes humility, confessing that upon receiving her friend's request for advice for raising a feminist daughter, "my first thought was that I did not know." She then proceeds to subtly build her authority by explaining how her friend may have perceived her as an expert on feminism because she had spoken publicly about it. Her brief note that she had experience as a babysitter, caring for younger relatives, and simply observing and thinking further reinforces her humble credibility. Additionally, Adichie states that having a daughter herself since writing the original letter has given her a new perspective, but she still stands behind her suggestions. While not everyone speaks publicly about feminism, the dominant message here is that feminism is for ordinary women.

Adichie begins the letter itself by honoring her friend—"what a magnificent thing you have done, bringing a human being into the world"—creating intimacy with both her recipient and readers. The ordinary immediately becomes real and meaningful. To fulfill this promise, Adichie's strategy is to offer practical advice, rather than laying out feminist theories or detailing the current problems roiling feminist debates. Her friend has asked, in effect, how to be a feminist mother, and Adichie delivers. While admitting there is no all-encompassing formula for feminism, she first offers two tools that can help in any situation. The first is the unconditional premise "I matter equally." The second is the question "Can you reverse X and get the same results?" For example, if a man can be forgiven for infidelity, could his wife expect the same treatment? The idea is that the answer to questions like these should inform a feminist woman's decisions.

Chimamanda Ngozi Adichie is the author of award-winning novels including Americanah *(2013) and* Half of a Yellow Sun *(2006) as well as her influential TED Talk published as the 2014 book* We Should All Be Feminists. *She received a MacArthur Fellowship in 2008.*

Courtesy of Wani Olatunde

From these tenets follow Adichie's fifteen suggestions, which, although offering much that is not new, are deeply valuable. Indeed, by revisiting ideas that either were never fully accepted or were once accepted but have lost ground, this manifesto serves to remind readers that culture moves in waves and circles, not a straight line. She protests the way that children's clothes and toys are rigidly gendered, with pink dresses and dolls dominating "girl" aisles in stores, and trucks and pants defining "boy" territory. She points out that feminism does not mean abandoning femininity. And she urgently insists that female sexuality is not taboo or shameful. In many cases, Adichie makes her case strongly and succinctly. For example, in explaining power structures she writes, "Our world is full of men and women who do not like powerful women." Such direct, simple statements are not groundbreaking, but they are effective reminders and pieces of advice.

Occasionally, Adichie offers new or unexpected revelations. She confesses to feeling lonely in her anger about sexism, because although she has no trouble finding peers who acknowledge racism as a fact of life, she is repeatedly asked by members of her community to "prove" the existence of sexism. While many people perceive marriage as a life achievement, Adichie rejects the idea that girls and women should think this way, because men often do not. She cautions that such an imbalance in values sets people up for unequal marriages in which women feel compelled to sacrifice more because they have been trained to value the institution disproportionately. She also cautions Ijeawele to beware of "Feminism Lite," which she defines as "conditional female equality." Adichie recommends teaching children about oppression, but warns against automatically attributing "saintliness" to the oppressed. The idea that women are somehow special or morally better than men can actually contribute to sexism, as it implies that women need special protection. Here, she also tackles internalized sexism, the fact that many women in the world dislike other women, which, she says, further validates her suggestion and reveals the extent of the world's misogyny.

Adichie's feminism reflects intersectionality, the idea that people experience oppressive forces such as racism, sexism, and classism not in isolation but as these forces intersect with one another. She addresses this in several ways. Besides her brief comparison of how she experiences racism and sexism, she touches on black pride in urging that parents should stop making the care and styling of black girls' hair synonymous with pain. She decries the ubiquity of whiteness held up as the ideal and recommends that Ijeawele actively counter it, for example, by teaching her daughter about notable African women. She also acknowledges, in her suggestion regarding romance, that she is herself using heterosexuality as the norm, which will not be the case for every girl or woman. Adichie's suggestions occasionally reference the Igbo culture to which her friend belongs, but overall the book is striking for the universality of its content. This is part of the book's power, as most of the issues that African women such as Ijeawele struggle with are the same or similar to those faced by women around the globe.

If Adichie is sensitive to the reality of intersectional feminism, she nonetheless avoids thorny issues that have become central to feminism in the twenty-first century. These include the ongoing struggle over abortion rights and the issue of the rights, experience, and status of transgender women. In some ways, this avoidance can make her manifesto seem overly cautious at times, as some reviewers noted. On the other hand, it can be forgiven due to her focus on how to raise a girl in a relentlessly sexist world. Most critics praised *Dear Ijeawele* as whole, comparing it favorably to her acclaimed fiction, while acknowledging the great challenge it faces in taking on such a broad and contested subject.

Adichie's warmth and frankness act as a tonic to the dangers she describes, and the book's conclusion again displays her rhetorical brilliance. Here, she mobilizes humor and apparent humility when she apologizes to Ijeawele for going on so long—or, rather, appears to: "Do you have a headache after reading all this? Sorry. Next time don't ask me how to raise your daughter feminist." This sly "sorry-not-sorry" move, invoking and swiftly rejecting the tired female apology, is emblematic of Adichie's skill in this book. She seems to be "just" offering advice to a friend. In fact, she is doing what very few advocates of women's rights have managed to do: launching feminism into mainstream culture in the twenty-first century.

Ashleigh Imus, PhD

Review Sources

Greenberg, Zoe. "Chimamanda Ngozi Adichie's Blueprint for Feminism." Review of *Dear Ijeawele, or A Feminist Manifesto in Fifteen Suggestions*, by Chimamanda Ngozi Adichie. *The New York Times*, 15 Mar. 2017, www.nytimes.com/2017/03/15/books/chimamanda-ngozi-adiche-dear-ijeawele.html. Accessed 16 Feb. 2018.

Hadley, Tessa. "*Dear Ijeawele* by Chimamanda Ngozi Adichie Review—a Feminist Manifesto." Review of *Dear Ijeawele, or A Feminist Manifesto in Fifteen Suggestions*, by Chimamanda Ngozi Adichie. *The Guardian*, 4 May 2017, www.theguardian.com/books/2017/may/04/dear-ijeawele-or-a-feminist-maniesto-in-fifteen-suggestions. Accessed 16 Feb. 2018.

Krug, Nora. "Women, Stop Worrying about Being Liked—Chimamanda Ngozi Adichie's Advice for Living Boldly." Review of *Dear Ijeawele, or A Feminist Manifesto in Fifteen Suggestions*, by Chimamanda Ngozi Adichie. *The Washington Post*, 8 Mar. 2017, www.washingtonpost.com/entertainment/books/women-stop-worrying-about-being-liked--chimamanda-ngozi-adichies-advice-for-living-boldly/2017/03/08/a411379e-fec4-11e6-99b4-9e613afeb09f_story.html?utm_term=.ca2de885f6a6. Accessed 16 Feb. 2018.

The Death and Life of the Great Lakes

Author: Dan Egan (b. 1967)
Publisher: W. W. Norton & Company (New York). Illustrated. 384 pp.
Type of work: Environment, natural history
Time: Prehistory–present
Locales: Great Lakes; Ontario, Canada; New York; Pennsylvania; Ohio; Indiana; Michigan; Chicago, Illinois and environs; Wisconsin; Minnesota; Lake Mead, Nevada

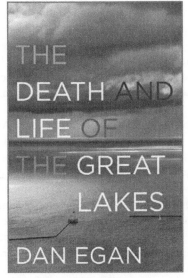

Courtesy of W.W. Norton

In The Death and Life of the Great Lakes, environmental journalist Dan Egan traces the history of the Great Lakes, the world's largest reservoir of freshwater, from their origin during the last ice age to the present. Egan demonstrates how, through ignorance and greed, humans brought a once-pristine resource to the brink of disaster.

Principal personages

JEAN NICOLET, a French explorer, the first European to see Lake Michigan and to land in the present state of Wisconsin

JACQUES CARTIER, an explorer who claimed present-day Canada for France and mapped the St. Lawrence River

FATHER JACQUES MARQUETTE, a Jesuit missionary who mapped the Mississippi River

DEWITT CLINTON, a New York politician who promoted building of the Erie Canal

ALDO LEOPOLD, an influential American naturalist and author

VERNON APPLEGATE, a sea lamprey specialist

HOWARD TANNER, a Great Lakes fisheries biologist and salmon specialist

DAVID LODGE, an ecologist, evolutionary biologist, and leading invasive species expert

JAKE VANDER ZANDEN, director of the Center for Limnology at the University of Wisconsin, Madison

GENERAL JOHN PEABODY, deputy commander of civil and emergency operations of the US Army Corps of Engineers

The Death and Life of the Great Lakes gives readers a brief historical and geographical lesson to underscore a complex modern problem. At some unknown point in the distant past—the process began as long ago as two million years and ended as recently as ten thousand years ago—the miles-thick glaciers of the last ice age began to loosen their grip upon the land. As they retreated in North America, the weighty, frozen masses gouged deep troughs near the center of the continent. Over time, these depressions filled with glacial meltwater, rainwater, and runoff from surrounding waterways to form an interconnected system of bodies of freshwater that came to be called the Great Lakes. Stretching around a thousand miles east to west and encompassing over 94,000 square miles of surface area, Lakes Ontario, Erie, Huron, Michigan, and Superior grew to comprise the world's largest freshwater system, containing one-fifth of Earth's surface freshwater. The four uppermost lakes are about six hundred feet above sea level, stepped slightly from west to east, so outflows move eastward. Eventually the enormous volume of combined waters roar over Niagara Falls into Lake Ontario, which is significantly lower than the other Great Lakes, and ultimately empty into the St. Lawrence River to be carried to the Atlantic Ocean.

For most of their existence, the Great Lakes were a precious, ecologically pure natural resource, where native fish thrived. The lakes and forests that grew up around them afforded shelter and sustenance for a variety of plant and animal life, which in turn provided nutrition over millennia for indigenous hunter-gatherer inhabitants. Those conditions prevailed for several hundred years following the arrival of Europeans on the continent in the sixteenth century.

Settlers' expansion westward from the eastern coast of North America began testing the freshwater system. Early European explorers sailing down the St. Lawrence River had to lift their boats (portage) out of the water to avoid rapids near modern-day Montreal, Quebec. Once past Niagara, such explorers reached the other Great Lakes and new settlements began to spring up along their shores. Attempts to improve and accelerate the water-borne journey from east to west began in the late seventeenth century with the building of lock-and-canal systems that gave access to the fertile interior of the continent. These efforts culminated in the 1820s with the completion of the United States' Erie Canal between Albany and Buffalo, New York (opened 1825), and Canada's Welland Canal between Lakes Erie and Ontario (opened 1829). Both canals were periodically widened, deepened, and improved with additional locks to accommodate larger boats and hoist heavier cargoes up the several hundred feet of elevation to allow delivery of supplies to the new settlements of the Great Lakes.

In the mid-1950s, a plan was devised to duplicate the success of the Suez and Panama Canals and to make global ports of landlocked cities like Chicago, Cleveland, Detroit, Duluth, and Toronto. This resulted in a major joint US-Canadian project, the St. Lawrence Seaway, which was completed in 1959. The Seaway exhibited several built-in restrictions from the beginning that caused the project to be less successful than envisioned, such as three-month shutdowns in winter, narrow chokepoints requiring superior navigation skills, and insufficient lock length to handle oversized bulk and container ships—all limitations that caused revenues to shrink by the early 1980s. The biggest concern, however, was the discovery that the Seaway escalated the invasion of foreign sea life into the Great Lakes, which over the course of time devastated commercial and recreational fishing industries.

According to Egan, the invasions probably began during the late 1890s, after a major expansion of the Welland Canal. First to arrive were ancient predators, sea lampreys. These bloodsuckers migrated from the Atlantic Ocean, spread throughout the Great Lakes to feed upon lake trout and other native species, and by 1960 reduced

A Milwaukee Journal Sentinel *reporter since 2003, Dan Egan is also Brico Fund Senior Water Policy Fellow in Great Lakes Journalism at the University of Wisconsin–Milwaukee School of Freshwater Sciences. Twice nominated for the Pulitzer Prize, he has received several journalism awards.* The Death and Life of the Great Lakes *is his first book.*

100-million-pound harvests of whitefish and lake trout to less than 25,000 pounds and zero, respectively. The infestation prompted the widespread scientific pursuit of a viable method of eliminating the lampreys. By the mid-1960s a poison effective enough to keep the lamprey population a manageable level was developed.

By then, new inhabitants to the Great Lakes were drawing attention. The next invader was the ocean-dwelling, freshwater-spawning river herring, also known as the alewife. Too small, at a half-foot long, to become prey for lampreys, the prolific alewife in a half-century spread across the five lakes, feasted on the young of native species, and by the mid-1960s came to dominate in Lakes Huron and Ontario. They also tended to die off in great, stinking masses. In 1967, it was estimated that as many as 6 to 20 billion alewives had died all at once in Lake Michigan, costing more than $100 million to clean up. Research revealed that the alewife was physically unsuited for the territory they had come to control: they were not a true freshwater species, suffered from iodine deficiency, and succumbed to large temperature swings. To speed their demise, Pacific salmon were introduced to all the Great Lakes in the late 1960s to feed upon the alewives. The introduction spurred a salmon fishing craze and a related economic spurt due to the newcomer's size (up to 100 pounds for chinook salmon), speed, and fighting ability. The boom lasted until the early 1990s, then went bust: too many salmon were breeding, and they were starving because there were too few alewives for them to feed on. The alewives themselves were starving because something was depleting the phytoplankton, a vital building block of the food chain.

Researchers discovered a whole realm of potentially destructive, non-native sea life in certain areas of the Great Lakes: humpbacked peaclams, burrowing worms, spiny water fleas, flatworms, crustaceans, algae, and other visitors typically found in European or Asian waters. The foreign invaders had not swum to America; they had been unwittingly smuggled in. The problems originated in ballast, weight added low in seagoing vessels to lend stability. In olden days, ballast was provided by sand, rocks, bricks, or metal bars. In modern times, seawater provides the necessary weight. Unfortunately, pumping tons of water into a ship's hold also brings with it whatever biological samples are found locally. When ships arriving from overseas via the St. Lawrence Seaway to the Great Lakes offload their cargoes, they typically dump their ballast water, and with it, the non-native species they have brought along for the ride.

Some of the most prolific new invaders, discovered in in the Great Lakes in the late 1980s, were the quagga and zebra mussels, mollusks native to the Black and Caspian Seas. Nuisance species, the mussels exude a strong adhesive that allows them to attach to almost anything. When they cluster at the mouths of water intake pipes, they block the vital flow of water to human consumers. Worse, they filter nutrients, such as phytoplankton, from the lakes. Such filtering makes the water clear, but strips it of nutrients that other species need to live and initiates a vicious cycle. Increased water clarity promotes growth of seaweed that upon decomposition supports colonies of bacteria; the bacteria are ingested by the mussels, which are in turn consumed by the only fish capable of cracking their shells to eat them, the invasive round goby; the poisoned gobies subsequently fall prey to many species of birds, which are often killed by the poison. Though measures of varying effectiveness—flushing, disinfectants, chlorine, ozone, ultraviolet light—were instituted by the Environmental Protection Agency in efforts to prevent future invasions via water used as ballast, it was too little, too late.

Today, zebra and quagga mussels are found in all the Great Lakes and dominate in Lake Michigan. They have since spread—the hardy mussels can survive for a considerable time out of water—by hitchhiking on pleasure boats—as far west as Lake Mead, Nevada, and are considered a threat to native fish in other bodies of water in the Pacific Northwest. The mollusks were just two of the twenty-seven exotic species discovered between 1990 and 2008, joining at least 186 other non-native organisms that live in the Great Lakes and keep scientists busy inventing methods to combat the invaders.

The Death and Life of the Great Lakes is a cautionary tale illustrating the dangers of tampering, either accidentally or purposefully, with nature. The book adds a new chapter to the continuing saga of human-induced, resource-harming catastrophes that includes the poisonous cane toads hopping all over northeastern Australia, the giant African snails ravaging Hawaii, and the Burmese pythons infesting the Florida Everglades. The informative, well-researched story is backed by interviews with leading scientists, concerned citizens, governmental authorities, commercial fisheries specialists, and other experts from around the world. Mostly, *Death and Life* is told with quiet passion by Egan, who has specialized in reporting on the Great Lakes since 2003 and who, through his straightforward prose, makes the reader care about the future of one of the greatest natural sources in North America.

Jack Ewing

Review Sources

Egan, Dan. "New Book on 'Death and Life' of Great Lakes." Interview by Great Lakes Today. *PRX*, 2017, beta.prx.org/stories/201059. Accessed 9 Jan. 2017.

Elder, Jane. Review of *The Death and Life of the Great Lakes*, by Dan Egan. *Wisconsin Academy of Science, Arts & Letters Magazine*, Summer 2017, www.wisconsinacademy.org/magazine/summer-2017/book-review/death-and-life-great-lakes-dan-egan. Accessed 18 Dec. 2017.

Henry, Tom. Review of *The Death and Life of the Great Lakes*, by Dan Egan. *SEJ BookShelf*, Society of Environmental Journalists, 7 Nov. 2017, www.sej.org/publications/bookshelf/death-and-life-great-lakes. Accessed 18 Dec. 2017.

Holland, Eva. "Dan Egan's 'The Death and Life of the Great Lakes,' Reviewed: Troubled Waters." Review of *The Death and Life of the Great Lakes*, by Dan Egan. *The Globe and Mail*, 14 Apr. 2017, www.theglobeandmail.com/arts/books-and-media/book-reviews/dan-egans-the-death-and-life-of-the-great-lakes-reviewed-troubled-waters/article34263664/. Accessed 18 Dec. 2017.

Nies, Jim. "Dan Egan's 'The Death and Life of the Great Lakes' Reviewed." Review of *The Death and Life of the Great Lakes*, by Dan Egan. *The Mantoulin Expositor*, 5 Apr 2017, www.manitoulin.ca/2017/04/05/dan-egans-death-life-great-lakes-reviewed/. Accessed 18 Dec. 2017.

Scheffler, Ian. Review of *The Death and Life of the Great Lakes*, by Dan Egan. *Columbia Magazine*, Summer 2017, magazine.columbia.edu/reviews/summer-2017/"-death-and-life-great-lakes". Accessed 18 Dec. 2017.

138

Difficult Women

Author: Roxane Gay (b. 1974)
Publisher: Grove Press (New York). 272 pp.
Type of work: Short fiction
Time: Present day and future
Locales: Various locations in the United States

Courtesy of Grove Atlantic

In this collection of short stories, Roxane Gay imagines the lives of diverse women, focusing on their romantic relationships and challenging popular notions of certain women as "difficult."

The stories in Roxane Gay's *Difficult Women* glimmer with gorgeous prose and craft, demonstrating both her razor-sharp intellect as a social commentator and her skill and inventiveness as a writer. However, the collection also includes less-developed pieces and a few shorter sketches that might have been better left out. The book focuses centrally on what it means to be a "difficult" woman. Some readers have defined Gay's difficult women simply in terms of their active sexual agency and refusal to subordinate their desires to the men in their lives or to society in general. More interesting readings recognize Gay's complex understanding of the inextricable link between "difficult" and "difficulty," as the women in these stories are not simply wild and hungry but often emerge conflicted, even damaged, from deeply troubled personal histories. As the author Megan Mayhew Bergman pointed out in her review of Gay's book for the *Washington Post*, sex, abuse, and the resulting trauma course "like a current through the collection." Gay's varied treatment of these themes, which is deeply informed by the women's race, age, and social class, results in many stories of profound insight as well as some others that can seem superficial, strained, or unfinished.

It would be easy to fault Gay for indulging in static sketches rather than consistently creating fully realized characters based on their life histories and circumstances. Some of the collection's shorter pieces are simply underdeveloped, such as "Open Marriage," in which a wife and husband briefly consider finding other partners, and "A Pat," in which a woman brings a stranger back to her apartment for a meal. Both of these vignettes suggest rich potential for the characters they introduce, but they seem like the beginnings of stories and fail to be as compelling as the collection's longer and more complex stories; they simply need more time and development.

Other sketches, such as the piece bearing the collection's title, invoke stereotypes in an effort to dismantle them. Not really a narrative, "Difficult Women" consists of descriptive text organized through a series of headings and subheads, such as "Loose

Women" ("Who a Loose Woman Looks Up To," "How a Loose Woman Sits at the Bar," and so forth) and "Frigid Women" ("How She Got That Way," "What a Frigid Woman Wears"). The accompanying descriptions gesture at individual histories that ostensibly aim to dismantle or challenge common stereotypes and snap judgments of women. A loose woman, for example, is portrayed (in one brief paragraph) as never looking up to her mother because her mother was intimidated and possibly abused by her father.

Stereotypes, in fact, are not uncommon in this collection, but it would be a mistake to overlook the complexity with which Gay sometimes deploys them. Several of her stories mobilize stereotypes to show the ongoing impacts of racism, sexism, and child abuse. In the first story, "I Will Follow You," two sisters grapple with the trauma of having been kidnapped as young girls and sexually abused by a pedophile. The story reveals the sisters' heartbreaking, desperate closeness that results from their abuse and how ultimately they can never really escape their attacker, in physical and psychological terms, even as they find support in one another.

In "La Negra Blanca," Gay powerfully challenges readers to witness the ways in which racism, classism, and sexism interact and overlap. The protagonist, Sarah, is of mixed-race heritage and works as a stripper to put herself through college. One of her wealthy customers, William Livingston III, comes from a family of men who lust after black women but who feel ashamed of their desires. Livingston recalls leering at his family's black housekeepers with his father. Gay renders the modern vestiges of the racial history of the United States, showing how Livingston, who clearly is meant to stand in for a whole class of men, is driven by deep envy, desire, yet revulsion of African American culture and people. Livingston channels his monstrous sense of entitlement through sexist rap music and his belief that Sarah is an object to purchase. Sarah, too, internalizes the sexism and classism of her work, catching herself in stripper dance moves at home and, ultimately, blaming herself when Livingston follows her home and brutally rapes her, refusing to go to the police, and calling the rape an "occupational hazard." Gay offers a few brief details about Sarah, such as her attendance at college and her love for a server at a nearby diner, that humanize her and universalize her story; Sarah could be any young woman doing what she feels she must do to get herself through college. After Livingston rapes Sarah, he "settles into the leather of his BMW and is instantly comforted by German engineering" and then vomits on the drive home. Just as Sarah cannot imagine a world in which suffering violence is not inevitable, Livingston cannot imagine one in which his terrible, mundane dominance does not rule.

These characters perhaps serve as "everyman" types in part to show how oppression reduces people to its basest claims. This strategy may account for some of the stories' occasional clichéd language and strained dialogue, which some reviewers have singled out for criticism. More controversial is that Gay portrays some women's trauma as leading them to find pleasure in being hurt. Here, the message seems to be that oppression does its work in part by forcing victims to internalize it in order to survive. In some stories, Gay presents women who seek out abuse as a way to heal, as in "Break All the Way Down." In this story a mother, after the death of her toddler, leaves

her husband and deliberately finds a boyfriend who beats her—destructive behavior
that she uses to navigate her grief and ultimately return home to her husband. Stories
like these have led some reviewers to disap-
prove of what appears to be an affirmation
of abusive sex, including Sandra Newman,
who wrote in a review for the *Guardian* that
Gay "is in danger of suggesting that women
can find abuse both cathartic and sexually
satisfying." On the other hand, Bergman
defended this approach, writing, "Gay excels in her allowance for human complexity.
Trauma gives way to unusual pleasure, and
healing might be found through more pain or
submission."

*Roxane Gay is the author of the multi-
genre collection* Ayiti *(2011), the novel*
An Untamed State *(2014), the essay collection* Bad Feminist *(2014), and a memoir titled* Hunger *(2017). She has also
written for Marvel Comics. Her awards
include the PEN Center USA Freedom to
Write Award.*

Not all of the stories reflect this controversy. "North Country" recounts a different
kind of suffering, offering a moving portrait
of Kate, an African American engineer who
moves to an overwhelmingly white small
town in northern Michigan and falls in love
with a white man named Magnus, a mysteri-
ous lumberjack who lives in a trailer. In her academic job, Kate must negotiate a lonely
world in which her well-meaning but clueless white colleagues and acquaintances
continually stereotype and alienate her, as they assume repeatedly, for example, that
she must be from Detroit. More crucially, Kate must negotiate her past: as a graduate
student she had an affair with a professor and became pregnant, which resulted in a
stillborn child, only to have the professor betray her with a frivolous affair. Gay offers
a deep, beautiful account of whether and how Kate will risk crossing the boundaries
of culture, race, and class and overcome her crippling grief to allow herself to love
Magnus.

Some of the best stories, ones in which Gay succeeds in showing how characters
develop rather than merely react to difficult circumstances, appear near the end of the
collection and invoke fantastic worlds. In "The Sacrifice of Darkness," Gay merges
myth with the short-story form to explore how her characters negotiate betrayal, exclusion, and the rage that inevitably results. Similarly, in "Noble Things," Gay imagines
a terrible future for the United States in which a "New Civil War" occurs. This time,
the South wins and actually secedes, leaving the former United States divided by a
border fence along the Mason-Dixon line, Florida a colony of Cuba, and the Republic
of Texas "soon to be annexed by Mexico." The consequences of the war tear a family
apart, as a couple decides to send their son to his maternal grandparents in the North—
a slap in the face to the boy's paternal relatives, a long line of generals and soldiers
loyal to the old and new South. Separated from their son for more than a year, the boy's

parents must decide whether to stay or go. That decision ultimately demands that they take an honest measure of their courage, loyalty, and integrity: to each other, their son, their parents, their heritage and respective cultures.

A key feature of the women in these stories is that all of their difficulties arise from their interpersonal relationships. In a way, this makes sense, given that the measure of a person's "difficulty" is usually understood in social terms. Yet women too often are valued only in terms of their relationship to others, as wives, mothers, sisters, friends, or lovers. These stories never imagine that a woman's difficulty might be rooted, for example, in her own intellectual or spiritual life.

Still, the unevenness of this volume is itself interesting, as Gay allows readers to see examples of some of her finest work along with pieces that do not work so well. The collection is not a finished masterpiece. It shows its seams, and there is something satisfying about that. This is not the sort of small satisfaction that readers might take in knowing that Gay has underachieved, because she has not; it is the satisfaction of a simultaneous vision that is as instructive as it is wonderful. Gay unabashedly showcases a final work as a work in progress. In a sense, this approach is in line with Gay's philosophy in her New York Times Best Seller *Bad Feminist* (2014), a collection of essays in which she argues that women need not be perfect practitioners of feminist ideals in order to identify as feminists. *Difficult Women* enacts an artistic and literary version of that philosophy. Revealing that every story need not be a masterpiece, Gay proves her chops as a deeply gifted writer of fiction as well as an astute social commentator.

Ashleigh Imus, PhD

Review Sources

Bergman, Megan Mayhew. "Roxane Gay's Powerful New Story Collection, *Difficult Women*." Review of *Difficult Women*, by Roxane Gay. *The Washington Post*, 3 Jan. 2017, www.washingtonpost.com/entertainment/books/roxane-gays-powerful-new-story-collection-difficult-women/2017/01/03/ad937ee4-d1e7-11e6-945a-76f69a399dd5_story.html. Accessed 8 Sept. 2017.

James, Anna. "Roxane Gay's New Book *Difficult Women* Proves Her Power." Review of *Difficult Women*, by Roxane Gay. *Los Angeles Times*, 12 Jan. 2017, www.latimes.com/books/jacketcopy/la-ca-jc-roxane-gay-20170112-story.html. Accessed 23 Aug. 2017.

Newman, Sandra. "Bold Feminist Stories." Review of *Difficult Women*, by Roxane Gay. *The Guardian*, 10 Feb. 2017, www.theguardian.com/books/2017/feb/10/difficult-women-by-roxane-gay-review. Accessed 23 Aug. 2017.

Sieff, Gemma. "No Shrinking Violets: A Short Story Collection from Roxane Gay." Review of *Difficult Women*, by Roxane Gay. *The New York Times*, 3 Jan. 2017, www.nytimes.com/2017/01/03/books/review/roxane-gay-difficult-women.html. Accessed 23 Aug. 2017.

Don't Call Us Dead

Author: Danez Smith
Publisher: Graywolf Press (Minneapolis, MN). 104 pp.
Type of work: Poetry

Don't Call Us Dead, poet Danez Smith's second book of verse, features a collection diverse in attitudes, tones, and subject matter, although its main emphases are on the experiences of black people in general and black "boys" in particular.

Courtesy of Graywolf Press

A finalist for a 2017 National Book Award, *Don't Call Us Dead* is the second book of poetry by Danez Smith, an African American writer who identifies as queer and goes by the pronouns "they" and "them." Smith's work exhibits a high level of both talent and political engagement. Their ear for sound and eye for imagery are already evident in the book's very first lines, in a poem alliteratively titled "summer, somewhere":

> somewhere, a sun. below, boys brown
> as rye play the dozens & ball, jump
>
> in the air & stay there. boys become new
> moons, gum-dark on all sides, beg bruise
>
> -blue water to fly, at least tide, at least
> spit back a father or two. i won't get started.

These stanzas exemplify many of the skills evident on practically every page of *Don't Call Us Dead*, including an abrupt opening that immediately situates readers in a specific (but also deliberately generic) place; heavy emphasis on alliteration; relatively simple, clear, straightforward diction; colloquial allusions that often summon up aspects of everyday African American life; effective use of enjambment; strong stress on verbs; clever internal rhymes; subtle use of assonance; alternating sentence lengths; and stretches of difficult language. What, for instance, does "gum-dark" mean? What should readers make of "beg bruise / -blue water to fly, at least tide"? All the diction in the lines that precede and follow these phrases is absolutely lucid, but readers are offered a few mysterious words to puzzle over. For the most part, however, Smith writes in ways that make this book's poems immediately accessible, and the texts' consistently memorable sound effects make them as intriguing to the inner ear as they

Courtesy of David Hong

Poet Danez Smith's first book, [insert] *Boy (2014), won the Lambda Literary Award for Gay Poetry. Smith has also won a fellowship from the National Endowment for the Arts as well as the Kay Tufts Discoveries Award.*

would obviously sound if read aloud.

In "summer, somewhere," as in many of his poems, Smith's focus is on young black men, and their status as the victims of racial violence, or of racism in general. (They are also often presented as the subjects of the poet's erotic gaze.) Politically, the book is fully engaged in the progressive project of trying to communicate the lived experience of people from racially and sexually marginalized communities to a largely deaf society; this in itself does not make the book original. However, Smith has subtle surprises in store for readers in practically every line: the pleasures of reading this book derive not from being told how to feel or think but rather from watching (and listening to) a talented poet at work. Consider, for example, the lines that follow the ones just quoted:

> history is what it is. it knows what it did.
> bad dog, bad blood. bad day to be a boy

Here again all of Smith's characteristic traits are evident, but some others have also been added, especially sudden juxtaposition of brief sentences, jamming together short phrases, and lots of repetition of all sorts (an especially prominent feature of many of Smith's poems). Even someone who did not know English could enjoy hearing poems like this one read aloud: Smith's works almost always have chant-like rhythms and a talent for hypnotic alliteration, assonance, and anaphora that make them quite literally musical. They often make their political points without sounding preachy or propagandistic, and in this respect they are much more satisfying, simply as *poems*, than, say, many of the lyrics to be found in Claudia Rankine's award-winning volume *Citizen* (2014), with which Smith's book can often be compared (but more often contrasted). Smith, by focusing so much and so often on the brown boys whose experiences *Don't Call Us Dead* both celebrates and laments, achieves a winning distance and objectivity. In their poems, Smith's eyes are usually trained on others, rather than inward, and although the book suggests many autobiographical experiences, Smith themself does not come across as the poems' main concern.

Although Smith has a real talent for using couplets, the sheer diversity of form this book displays is itself impressive. Sometimes the poems are long, but sometimes they are strikingly brief, as in this lyric that is embedded in a longer series of related texts:

dear badge number

what did i do wrong?
be born? be black? meet you?

For many readers, the sound of these lines will be as interesting as the meaning, especially the sounds of that last line. The very brevity of the lyric (and of its brief component phrases) gives it added impact. Within a few pages, however, Smith shifts to a long prose poem called "dear white america"—a massive, eye-catching block of black text that (perhaps symbolically) fills an entire white page and begins as follows:

i've left earth in search of darker places, a solar system revolving too near a black hole, i've left in search of a new God. i do not trust the God you have given us. my grandmother's hallelujah is only outdone by the fear she nurses every time the blood-fat summer swallows another child who used to sing in the choir. take your God back.

This poem offers some memorable language, as in that passing reference to a "blood-fat summer," as well as a compelling shape. This text is then immediately followed by a poem consisting of seven five-line stanzas followed by a single half-phrase set off by itself. (Smith is especially good at ending poems emphatically.) That poem, in turn, is succeeded by one that somewhat resembles a curtailed sonnet, and then the volume turns back to couplets, only to be followed by a poem whose shape seems chaotic, which is then succeeded by a very brief prose poem. Smith, in short, likes to experiment with forms, and the forms almost always help stress the meanings. Rather than seeming arbitrarily chosen, the shapes seem tightly tied to the themes. Sometimes the shapes can seem wittily inventive, as in a brief poem titled "O nigga O." Even more striking is the typography in the poem "litany with blood all over," in which the phrases "my blood" and "his blood" spill all over the pages in random, chaotic profusion, becoming ever-darker as the eye moves down the page.

Equally inventive, and often highly imaginative, is the imagery of Smith's poems. One lyric—part of a series titled "seroconversion"—reads as follows:

there was a boy made of bad teeth & a boy made of
stale bread & together they were a hot mouth
making mush out of yeasty stones & in the end the
one made of bad teeth walked away broken jawed,
sick with hunger & the one made of stale bread
walked away half of himself, his softness proved a
lie & what remains left for unparticular birds.

What, exactly, does any of this mean? One cannot be entirely sure, but the sheer originality and ingenuity of the phrasing command attention. Often in their poems, Smith seems to be inhabiting their own, somewhat surrealistic world, but just as often they are inhabiting physical and psychological territory that seems very familiar. In either case, however, Smith manages to make the real *sound* real and the bizarre seem convincing.

Whether the topic is white racism, black boys, police brutality, life in ghettos, enduring AIDS, or any of a number of other recurring subjects, Smith almost always manages to sound, in various ways, authentic, as if they know whereof they speak. Smith has mastered a whole range of attitudes and tones, as in the mixture of real anguish and bizarre humor in this brief text:

> i told him what
> happened to my body
>
> but all he could hear
> was light falling
> between my legs
>
> next time a man comes
> over, i'll cut the veins
> out of my arms, arrange them
>
> like cooked linguine
> on the kitchen table
>
> in the shape of a boy's face
> & *say here's what happened*

What *did* happen, exactly? One cannot be sure, but whatever Smith says, they say it with conviction. There is no hemming or hawing. There is, instead, the voice of one who knows precisely what they mean, even if that meaning is sometimes less than obvious to readers. Again, the very sounds of Smith's varied voices, rather than the poems' paraphraseable content, are usually the traits that often make the lyrics stick inside one's head.

As in the poem just quoted, Smith's texts often end in ways that catch readers off guard. In this as in practically every other way (except in some of their themes), Smith is winningly unpredictable. There is often a sense of suspense involved in reading their works; one never quite knows what will happen next. About the only thing readers can be sure of is that Smith will typically clinch the whole performance in the final line, as in the following poem, with its emphatic gaps in spacing:

> in our blood
>
>
> men hold each other

like they'll never let go

& then they let go

If one had to situate Smith among other prominent American poets, the first name that might come to mind would probably be e. e. cummings (1894–1962). Both cummings and Smith share a preference for lower-case spelling, idiosyncratic forms, the unexpected, and the sheer joy of playing with shapes, words, and sounds. One also thinks of William Carlos Williams (1883–1963) and Langston Hughes (1902–67) and, further back, of Emily Dickinson (1830–86). All three of those poets drew on the full resources of vernacular speech and distinctively inventive forms. All three also, like Smith, wrote in ways that have come to seem wholly their own. In other words, Smith is in the grand tradition of American originals. In fact, in some of this poet's longer-lined poems, even Walt Whitman (1819–92) or Carl Sandburg (1878–1967) come to mind. And, of course, Smith, like Whitman—perhaps even more than Whitman—seems obsessed with male bodies, male bonding, male sex, and male love. The word "boys" certainly seems the word most present and urgent in the minds of Smith's speakers. Smith is, arguably, one of the more important of the recent queer poets, and Smith has the liberty to write, as Whitman and others could not, not only as openly queer but as gender nonconforming. Ultimately, Smith has written a book they can be proud of—a book likely to win them much attention and many admirers.

Robert C. Evans, PhD

Review Sources
Chiasson, Dan. "Danez Smith's Ecstatic Body Language." Review of *Don't Call Us Dead*, by Danez Smith. *The New Yorker*, 2 Oct. 2017, www.newyorker.com/magazine/2017/10/02/danez-smiths-ecstatic-body-language. Accessed 29 Dec. 2017.

Review of *Don't Call Us Dead*, by Danez Smith. *Publishers Weekly*, 17 July 2017, www.publishersweekly.com/978-1-55597-785-6. Accessed 29 Dec. 2017.

Farmer, Jonathan. "'i've never been so alive': On *Don't Call Us Dead* by Danez Smith." *Kenyon Review*, Oct. 2017, www.kenyonreview.org/reviews/dont-call-us-dead-by-danez-smith-738439/. Accessed 29 Dec. 2017.

Smith, August. "*Don't Call Us Dead*: Poetry Like a Phoenix." Review of *Don't Call Us Dead*, by Danez Smith. *BookPage*, 5 Sept. 2017, bookpage.com/reviews/21770-danez-smith-dont-call-us-dead#.Wkb0Kt-nGUk. Accessed 29 Dec. 2017.

Dorothy Day
The World Will Be Saved by Beauty: An Intimate Portrait of My Grandmother

Author: Kate Hennessy (b. 1960)
Publisher: Scribner (New York). 384 pp.
Type of work: Biography
Time: 1920 to the present
Locales: New York City, various other locations

Dorothy Day, one of the founders of the Catholic Worker movement, was one of the most prominent Roman Catholic activists and laypeople of the twentieth century. This biography by her youngest granddaughter offers a rare view of family connections and Day's personal life.

Courtesy of Scribner

Principal personages
DOROTHY DAY, Catholic activist, writer, and
    cofounder of the Catholic Worker movement and the Catholic Worker newspaper
CATHERINE ANN "KATE" HENNESSY, her granddaughter
TAMAR BATTERHAM HENNESSY, her only child, Kate's mother
DAVID HENNESSY, her son-in-law, Kate's father
FORSTER BATTERHAM, her lover and Tamar's father
ARISTIDE PIERRE "PETER" MAURIN, her friend and fellow cofounder of the Catholic
    Worker movement and the Catholic Worker newspaper
STANLEY VISHNEWSKI, her close friend, a worker with the Catholic Worker movement

Kate Hennessy, the youngest grandchild of Dorothy Day, grew up knowing that many perceived her famous and controversial grandmother as a model of holiness and spirituality. But she also knew that her mother, Day's only child, Tamar Batterham Hennessy, had a complex and sometimes troubled relationship with this woman who many saw as a living saint. A major theme that runs through *Dorothy Day: The World Will Be Saved by Beauty*, Kate Hennessy's biography of Day, is how Hennessy reckons with these two perceptions of her grandmother. In the preface, she writes that her intention in writing this book was not only to describe the life of her grandmother, but also to tie the stories of Day's life and Tamar's life together, and admits that the project for her "is nothing less than a quest to find out who I am through [Day] and through Tamar."

As Hennessey wrote about her grandmother and their family, she also found that the institution Day helped found, the Catholic Worker movement, loomed so large in the family's history that it was like a member of the family. Many of the people associated with the *Catholic Worker* newspaper that Day also started, and the hospitality houses run by the movement, are also portrayed as family members. Hennessy writes of her extended family: the household of John Day, Dorothy's father, and to a lesser extent the family of Dorothy's mother, Grace Satterlee Day. Hennessy's own mother's rocky marriage to her father, David Hennessy, and the lives of her siblings from this marriage also figure prominently in the story.

Hennessy begins the biography when Day was twenty years old. Day had been raised in a nominally Protestant family, and as a young adult in 1918, she led a bohemian life before her conversion to Roman Catholicism. She wanted to be a writer, but her father, who had been a journalist, discouraged her from pursuing a career in that field. Day moved to New York City, and worked for a variety of activist newspapers, earning little money and living in a series of apartments that often lacked central heat or running water. Her life intersected with a variety of writers, intellectuals, and other characters living in New York City in the post–World War I era, perhaps most notably the playwright Eugene O'Neill, with whom she had a long platonic relationship.

Day had several lovers as a young woman working in New York City. An unplanned pregnancy in 1919 led to her having an abortion, after which, suffering from grief and depression, she attempted suicide twice. On a rebound from a failed earlier relationship, she married Berkeley Tobey, a wealthy man from a prominent Boston family. But she soon realized the marriage was a mistake, and they divorced the following year. In 1925, Day met William Forster Batterham, and they soon fell in love. They shared many interests, such as an interest in literature and nature, but they were fundamentally different in many ways, especially as Day moved toward a deeper spiritual life.

Tamar Batterham was born to Day and Batterham in the spring of 1926. Day wanted to marry Batterham, but he was fundamentally opposed to the institution of marriage, and Day's spiritual quest drove the two of them apart. Neither Day nor Batterham wished to live hypocritically; Day refused to deny her spiritual impulses, and Batterham refused to pretend to have a faith that he did not have. They separated and had little contact for many years, although Batterham remained involved in Tamar's life.

The birth of Day's daughter intensified her spiritual longings, and she had Tamar baptized in the Roman Catholic Church before she became a member herself. As Hennessy puts it, her grandmother hungered for "mystery, sacrament, and symbolism." Day converted into the Roman Catholic Church and was baptized in 1927. In spring 1933, she met the French activist and farmer Peter Maurin in New York City; together, they founded the Catholic Worker movement and the *Catholic Worker* newspaper, which would become Day's life work. Eventually, in accordance with the charitable principles of the movement, houses of hospitality were established, as were farming communities where people could return to an agrarian lifestyle.

As Day was a busy single mother and leader of a growing activist religious movement, Tamar spent some time in convent schools, but her education was often interrupted by travels with her mother. Day was not fully committed to the idea of formal higher education; she believed that her life experiences living among the poor and marching in union picket lines and antiwar marches had prepared her for the work of a journalist better than any school could have. She also learned on the job as she worked

Courtesy of Gary Jones

Kate Hennessy has written for numerous travel magazines, and her work was included in the 2002 edition of the Best American Travel Writing *anthology. With photographer Vivian Cherry, she published Dorothy Day and the Catholic Worker:* The Miracle of Our Continuance *(2016), which includes excerpts from Day's writings and commentary by Hennessy.*

for a series of newspapers and interacted with established writers such as O'Neill. Because of her own experience, she never encouraged Tamar to pursue higher education, which caused Tamar to believe that Day did not think she was intelligent to enough go to college—a perception that led to trouble in the relationship between mother and daughter.

Tamar met David Hennessy at a Catholic Worker farm in Easton, Pennsylvania. He was from an urban background but had been drawn to the farm by articles he had read in the *Catholic Worker*. Hennessy, a devout Catholic, married Tamar in 1944. They were both attracted to the back-to-the-land movement and the idea of Catholic families raising children on small farms. Together they had nine children, the author being the youngest. The family lived on a succession of small farms that never prospered. David was eventually hospitalized for psychological treatment due to his drinking, and the marriage ended, though they did not divorce. Tamar later told Kate that she realized "within weeks of the wedding" that the marriage had been a mistake. Despite her strong Catholic convictions about the sanctity of marriage, Day once said to Tamar, sometime after her marriage to David had ended, that she was surprised Tamar had been able to endure it as long as she did. To Tamar, this revelation helped begin a rapprochement with her mother.

There was a sharp edge to Day that sometimes put people off. Hennessy recalls that she once asked her mother if her grandmother was a saint, and Tamar refused to answer. For a time, Day's spirituality turned toward a somewhat hard-edged asceticism; perhaps, Hennessey suggests, because of the influence of Father John Hugo, who led retreats that emphasized mortification and self-denial. Tamar believed the influence of Father Hugo had a negative impact on her mother, and many Roman Catholic leaders looked upon Hugo's teachings with suspicion. Hennessy's view on the retreat was that it was "about afflicting the comfortable, but it could also, in its rigor . . . afflict the afflicted." Hennessey relates how Day's public persona seemed to become more serious and even dour under Hugo's influence, and she gave up colorful clothing to dress more "religiously." Stanley Vishnewski, who came to the Catholic Worker house in New York when he was seventeen and spent most of the rest of his life working there, came to be a good friend of Day's, but he was aware that she could be a hard person with whom to live and work. In the 1930s, the nationwide Catholic Action campaign adopted the slogan "The love of Christ drives me on," but Vishnewski expressed it differently saying, "The fear of Dorothy Day drives us on." He also would occasionally remark, even in Day's hearing, "There are the saints and the martyrs. The martyrs are the ones who live with the saints."

Cardinal John O'Connor of New York City began the process of having Day considered for canonization in 2000. When Pope Francis I spoke to the US Congress in 2015, he mentioned Day along with the Trappist monk Thomas Merton, Martin Luther King Jr., and Abraham Lincoln as moral exemplars. Even if official canonization never comes, Hennessy fears that the public's perception of her grandmother as a saint makes it more difficult for people to understand Dorothy Day as a person.

Hennessy's book was warmly welcomed by reviewers and by the general reading public. Day was a hero to many religious people with a concern for social justice, and they welcome this intimate account of her life—although, as Peter Steinfels noted in a review for the journal *Commonweal*, "there are things in this book that could jar anyone still inhabiting the traditional world of hagiography." Tamar Hennessy donated many of Day's papers to research archives, such as the Catholic Worker collection at Marquette University, but she wrote virtually nothing about her mother herself and gave few interviews, although she was always interested in what people wrote about Day. Kate Hennessy's conversations with her mother about Day are, in many ways, the heart of this book, and they are what makes it so uniquely worthwhile.

Mark S. Joy, PhD

Review Sources

Lewis, Peter. "*Dorothy Day*, Portrayed by Her Granddaughter, Is a Hero but Not a Saint." Review of *Dorothy Day: The Day Will Be Saved by Beauty; An Intimate Portrait of My Grandmother*, by Kate Hennessy. *The Christian Science Monitor*, 23 Jan. 2017, www.csmonitor.com/Books/Book-Reviews/2017/0123/Dorothy-Day-portrayed-by-her-granddaughter-is-a-hero-but-not-a-saint. Accessed 3 Oct. 2017.

Parker, James. "A Saint for Difficult People." Review of *Dorothy Day: The Day Will Be Saved by Beauty; An Intimate Portrait of My Grandmother*, by Kate Hennessy. *The Atlantic*, Mar. 2017, www.theatlantic.com/magazine/archive/2017/03/a-saint-for-difficult-people/513821/. Accessed 3 Oct. 2017.

Roberts, Sam. "Houses of the Holy, and of the Working Class." Review of *Dorothy Day: The World Will Be Saved by Beauty; An Intimate Portrait of My Grandmother*, by Kate Hennessey, and *Rockaway Before and After*, by Jennifer Callahan. *The New York Times*, 27 Jan. 2017, www.nytimes.com/2017/01/27/nyregion/dorothy-day-hurricane-sandy-rockaway.html. Accessed 3 Oct. 2017.

Steinfels, Peter. Review of *Dorothy Day: The World Will Be Saved by Beauty; An Intimate Portrait of My Grandmother*, by Kate Hennessey. *Commonweal*, 22 Feb. 2017, www.commonwealmagazine.org/dorothy-day. Accessed 3 Oct. 2017.

Down Among the Sticks and Bones

Author: Seanan McGuire (b. 1978)
Publisher: Tor.com (New York). 192 pp.
Type of work: Novel
Time: Present day
Locale: The Moors (fantasy world)

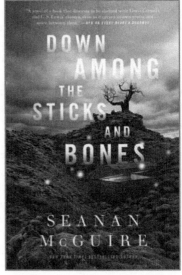

Courtesy of Tor Books

When Chester and Serena Wolcott have twin girls, they each choose a child to favor. This leads to confusion for the twins, so when a mysterious set of steps appear in the attic of their house, the girls follow the steps to a fantasy world where their differences are emphasized even further.

Principal characters

JACQUELINE WOLCOTT, a.k.a. Jack, the older twin
JILLIAN WOLCOTT, a.k.a. Jill, the younger twin
CHESTER WOLCOTT, their father
SERENA WOLCOTT, their mother
LOUISE "GEMMA LOU" WOLCOTT, their grandmother
DR. BLEAK, Jack's master, a scientist
THE MASTER, Jill's master, a vampire
ALEXIS CHOPPER, Jack's romantic interest

Seanan McGuire, who also publishes under the name Mira Grant, writes novel-length books along with a variety of short fiction pieces, poems, and nonfiction essays. Many of her stories involve details of reinterpreted fairy tales with unique folkloric twists and often dark themes. Her books include an adult urban fantasy series featuring the protagonist October Daye, and the Incryptid series about monsters, or *cryptids*. McGuire also has penned two other series that are specifically geared toward young adult readers: the Velveteen series, which takes place in a universe of superheroes, and the Indexing series that mixes fairy tale archetypes with more realistic details of setting and character.

Down Among the Sticks and Bones is the standalone prequel to *Every Heart a Doorway*, which was published in 2016 and won the Nebula Award for Best Novella from the Science Fiction and Fantasy Writers of America in the year of its publication. Both books are part of McGuire's Wayward Children series. The set also includes *Beneath the Sugar Sky*, slated for publication in January 2018. These novels are primarily written for the young adult audience, but appeal to adult readers as well.

The Wayward Children series, including *Down Among the Sticks and Bones*, is set in a variety of worlds, including a contemporary reality where children and teens often find themselves presented with the opportunity to escape the pressures of their lives when a mysterious door appears, offering them the chance to explore a new world. The background of these doors is explained in *Every Heart a Doorway*, the first published book in the series. This novel features Nancy, a girl who has recently returned from her trip into the Halls of the Dead. Nancy's desire to return to that world frightens her parents, so when they find Eleanor West's Home for Wayward Children, they quickly pack their daughter up and leave her in Miss West's capable hands. Miss West and her boarding school, however, are not what they seem. The school is a place where both the students and Miss West herself have been transported back through portals from magical realms. Miss West's desire is to protect them, so they can learn to adapt to real life or, for a lucky few, return to their fantasy worlds. Though Nancy is the main character of *Every Heart a Doorway*, she soon befriends Jack and Jill Wolcott, and these twins become a central part of Nancy's life. When people at the school start to die in violent ways, Nancy and her new friends set out to find the murderer, only to discover that the twins are at the center of the mystery.

Down Among the Sticks and Bones takes readers backward in time to explain what happened to Jack and Jill before they arrived at Miss West's school. This book begins before their conception with an introduction to their future parents, Chester and Serena Wolcott, and lays the groundwork for why they chose to have children. The Wolcotts' reasons for starting a family are misguided at best and they soon require the help of Chester's mother, Gemma Lou, to help raise the twins.

The book is structured in four parts and the tone of the writing, as well as the section titles, allude to motifs of fairy tales and pay homage to childhood rhymes. Part 1, entitled titled "Jack and Jill Live Up the Hill," establishes the twins' home life in the real world with Chester, Serena, and Gemma Lou. Part 2, titled "Jill and Jack into the Black," begins the twins' adventure when through the portal in the attic. In part 3—"Jack and Jill with Time to Kill"—focuses on the girls' experiences in the Moors, the fantastic world they arrive in after their disappearance in the attic. Part 4, "Jill and Jack Will Not Come Back," shows Jack taking responsibility for her sister's safety by returning to their parents' home.

Within each section, McGuire plays on the Jack and Jill nursery rhyme, titling chapters in a way that foreshadows the events, offers a sense of irony, or reminds readers of the childhood rhyme. The first chapter, "The Dangerous Allure of Other People's Children", points to the poor motivation behind Chester and Serena's choice to become parents. Irony can be seen in the titles of both chapter 2, "Practically Perfect in Virtually No Ways", and chapter 12, "Everything You Never Wanted." In the second part of the book, the opening chapter foreshadows the fantasy element by referring to a variation of a nursery rhyme: "To Market, To Market, To Buy a Fat Hen." Another nursery rhyme connection from the "Jack and Jill" rhyme can be found in chapter 7, titled "To Fetch a Pail of Water."

One of the major themes in the novel is choice. Poor choices are illustrated primarily by the girls' parents, who have children despite an innate selfishness that blocks their ability to nurture or parent the girls. In an effort to bolster their own reputations, Chester and Serena mold the girls into perfect little automatons who do only what is

Courtesy of Beckett Gladney

Seanan McGuire is an award-winning fantasy writer with several series to her credit. One of her most prestigious recognitions is that she was nominated for five Hugo Awards in 2013. She also writes under the pen name of Mira Grant.

expected, even when those expectations are challenged by each girl. The parents' inability to understand their children's needs is established early in the novel when the reader learns, "The thought that babies would become children, and children would become *people*, never occurred to them." When the girls turn five, Chester and Serena make another questionable choice by sending away their grandmother, who has been caring for the girls since they were babies. Gemma Lou departs despite knowing "she was going to leave those precious children in the hands of people who had never taken the time to learn anything about them beyond the most narrow, superficial things."

The poor choices made by Chester and Serena make the twins' choice to escape easier. The idea of an exit from their lives, even at twelve years old, is attractive because they have not been able to choose anything up to this point. Once on the Moors, the girls are forced to make a variety of choices which will affect the rest of their lives. As they wander the new world, choosing the Moors over the sea or the mountains, they experience free will. Their fate is further determined when a mysterious man takes them into his home, and the girls are forced to choose who will stay with the Master of the castle and who will go with Dr. Bleak, the mad scientist of the Moors.

Other themes in the novel include characters discovering self-identity and navigating changing interpersonal relationships. Jack has been raised to be her mother's favored child, garbed in fancy dresses and prevented from getting dirty or playing rambunctiously. Jill, on the other hand, has been chosen by her father to replace the male child that he wanted, so she is encouraged in rough, loud play. Jacqueline is the brave one who provides Jill with a support structure, while Jill is less adventurous than she seems. Their parents never fully understand this about the girls, and the girls sense it. This lack of emotional connection leads to the twins escaping through the portal. It is suggested that this lack of understanding of the girls' personalities by their parents also undermines the relationships that could have given the girls happiness or stability. The parents' neglect of the twins begins when Gemma Lou leaves them when they are five, allowing the twins to find "final, irrefutable proof that adults, in the end were not and never to be trusted." The girls' own relationship with each other is also damaged, and by the time they are twelve, "They are not twins who have been taught the importance of cleaving to each other, and the cracks between them are already beginning to show. It will not be long before they are separated." Thus, it is easier for them to part ways when they choose between the Master and Dr. Bleak.

One further relationship that is important to the novel is the one that Jack forms with a girl from one of the families who lives in the Master's realm. At seventeen, Jack falls into the first loving relationship in her life, and "When Alexis kisses her for the first time, out behind the windmill, Jack realizes that she and Jill have one thing in common: she never, never wants to go back to the world she came from. Not when she could have this world, with its lightning and its blue-eyed, beautiful girls, instead."

Critical reviews of the novel are primarily positive. Ala Rusa-Codes argues that the book is "Insightful, harrowing, and wickedly funny, it will enthrall readers." Another reviewer for *Library Journal* writes, "Beautifully crafted and smartly written, this fairy-tale novella is everything that speculative fiction readers look for: fantastical worlds, diverse characters, and prose that hits home with its emotional truths." The book's author and format are also lauded by a *Booklist* reviewer: "She taps into the horror and romance of classic fairy tales while weaving an extraordinarily modern and wise allegory of girlhood. Exquisitely well crafted, this is the rare companion novel that can stand alone." A *Publishers Weekly* reviewer calls the book "bittersweet" and "heartbreaking."

Still, some readers may be frustrated with the lack of character development. Even as main characters, the girls do not gain much depth despite their changing roles and adventures in the Moors. An additional issue might be the lack of detail about the hidden world in which they find themselves. Some of this detail is provided in *Every Heart a Doorway*, so despite this book being a standalone work, a reading of the earlier book will clarify some questions about the fairy tale framing as well as the characters themselves.

Theresa L. Stowell, PhD

Review Sources

Chadwick, Kristi. Review of *Down Among the Sticks and Bones*, by Seanan Mc-Guire. *Library Journal*, vol. 142, no. 7, 2017, pp. 63–5. *Literary Reference Center Plus*, search.ebscohost.com/login.aspx?direct=true&db=lkh&AN=122467613&site=lrc-plus. Accessed 2 Dec. 2017.

Howerton, Erin Downey. Review of *Down Among the Sticks and Bones*, by Seanan McGuire. *Booklist*, 1 May 2017, vol. 113, no. 17, 2017, pp. 62–3. *Book Review Digest Plus*, search.ebscohost.com/login.aspx?direct=true&db=brd&AN=122995785&site=ehost-live&scope=site. Accessed 2 Dec. 2017.

Review of *Down Among the Sticks and Bones*, by Seanan McGuire. *Publishers Weekly*, vol. 113, no. 17, 2017, pp. 62–63. www.publishersweekly.com/978-0-7653-9203-9. Accessed 2 Dec. 2017.

Rusa-Codes, Ala. Review of *Down Among the Sticks and Bones*, by Seanan Mc-Guire. *Library Journal*, vol. 142, no. 10, 2017, p. 98. *Book Review Digest Plus*, search.ebscohost.com?direct=true&db=brd&AN=123352637&site=ehost-live. Accessed 2 Dec. 2017.

The Dry

Author: Jane Harper (b. ca. 1980)
Publisher: Flatiron Books (New York). 326 pp.
Type of work: Novel
Time: Present day
Locale: Kiewarra, Australia

When Aaron Falk's childhood friend Luke Hadler dies, Aaron is called home by a cryptic message from Luke's father. Within hours, Aaron is drawn into an investigation which will plunge him into the past and bring unexpected complications to light.

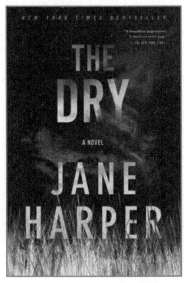

Courtesy of Macmillan

Principal characters
LUKE HADLER, a sheep farmer
AARON FALK, his childhood friend, a federal investigator
ELLIE DEACON, his childhood friend
GRETCHEN SHONER, his former girlfriend
GREG RACO, police sergeant in Kiewarra
SCOTT WHITLAM, Kiewarra's school principal
GERRY AND BARB HADLER, his parents
KAREN AND BILLY HADLER, his wife and son
MAL DEACON, Ellie's father
GRANT DOW, Ellie's cousin

When Aaron Falk, a federal investigator in Australia, is called back to his hometown of Kiewarra for the funeral of his former best friend Luke Hadler, he finds himself in the midst of a murder investigation. Evidence suggests that Luke killed his wife and son before turning his gun on himself, but Luke's mother cannot accept this as the truth, so she asks Aaron to investigate Luke's financials to see if a debt collector might have been out for revenge. As Aaron walks through Luke's home, the murder scene, with police sergeant Greg Raco, he learns that several strange clues suggest that Luke may have been innocent. First, the bullets were not Luke's usual brand. Second, Billy's room was searched before the boy was found and shot—an odd action for a father who knew his son. Third, Luke's thirteen-month-old daughter was left alive; Raco wonders if this is because she is too young to give evidence or identify the killer. Further, Luke's fingerprints on the murder weapon are suspiciously clear, not smudged as one would expect.

As Aaron becomes embroiled in the accusations against his old friend, the past haunts him, and he wonders how much he really knew about Luke Hadler. The earlier death of another friend, Ellie Deacon, becomes central to the new investigation as well. Whether Ellie's death was a murder or a suicide is still unknown, and Aaron and his father were blamed for the death at the time. Now that he has returned to Kiewarra, Aaron is pulled into a double investigation of the deaths of Ellie and Luke, which reveals secrets that rock the small farming town.

The Dry, Harper's debut novel, was given the Australian Book Industry Award in 2017 for Book of the Year and Fiction Book of the Year. It was also named the Indie Book Awards Book of the Year and Indie Debut Fiction Book of the Year for 2017. Other recognition come from the Ned Kelly Awards, where it was named Best First Fiction for 2017; the Sisters in Crime Australia 2017 Davitt Awards, where it was named Best Adult Crime Novel Readers' Choice; the Wheeler Centre, who gave it the 2015 Victorian Premier's Literary Award for Unpublished Manuscript; and the UK Crime Writers' Association, which gave the book the Gold Digger Award.

Critical reception of the novel was largely positive, particularly praising the unpredictable and intricate plot. The *Booklist* review, for instance, called it a "page-turner with a shocker of an ending" and compared Harper's writing to that of James Lee Burke, Robert Crais, Arthur Upfield, and Nancy Pickard. *Kirkus Reviews* lauded it as "a nail-biting thriller" and says "Harper plots this novel with laser precision." *Publishers Weekly* praised it as "a suspenseful tale of sound and fury as riveting as it is horrific." Janet Maslin's *New York Times* reviews suggests that the novel is "Sherlockian" in its development of a plot that includes a "constant recovery of forgotten facts and little clues" while it "skips along on frequent changes of focus." Some reviews were more critical, however; Wilda Williams, for *Library Journal*, wrote that the book had "slow, tedious pacing; poor character development; [and a] lack of suspense or surprise."

One of the novel's main thematic ideas revolves around secrets; Kiewarra contains many undisclosed confidences that trouble Aaron. One of the most important secrets is from the past: Aaron and Luke's alibis for the night of Ellie's death. Though Aaron had been out fishing by himself, Luke came to him after Ellie's body had been discovered and told him to say they were together. This protected Aaron from prosecution, but it also protected Luke. Now, Luke's father reveals that he knew the boys were lying, and that he had seen Luke coming from the river area where Ellie was found on the night she died. He also reveals that someone else saw Luke, but that other person has also kept quiet in the years since Ellie's death. Another secret comes out as Aaron reunites with Gretchen, Luke's high school girlfriend. Now a single mother with a five-year-old son, Gretchen welcomes Aaron back to town with open arms. However, while having dinner at her home one night, Aaron stumbles across the true identity of her son's father, a fact that ultimately tears their renewed friendship apart. Other secrets lead to the revelation of an unexpected suspect in the Hadler family's deaths.

A second issue explored in the novel is trust. When the word "Falk" was found on a piece of paper in Ellie Deacon's room, Aaron's father and Aaron himself became the main suspects in her death. Ellie's father and cousin focused on the Falk men despite a lack of real evidence suggesting their involvement in the case. After the Falks were harassed to the point that they feared for their lives, they fled town. Aaron's father, however, did not trust that his son was innocent, and their relationship was forever stained

Jane Harper has worked as a journalist in both England and Australia. She holds a degree from the University of Kent, Canterbury, where she studied English and History. The Dry *is her first novel.*

by the shadow of that distrust. In the years following Ellie's death, Aaron and Luke met several times, and each time Aaron brought up the topic of where Luke had really been that night, Luke merely repeated the alibi he came up with years before. His refusal to reveal his whereabouts to Aaron keeps the men from returning to their earlier ease with each other. The lack of trust, tied up with the community's terrible secrets, links together the flashbacks Harper introduces throughout the novel.

The mystery is enhanced with just enough glimpses into the past to make readers question the veracity of the suspicions surrounding the Hadler family's deaths. For instance, though Aaron does not want to believe that his friend would have become so desperate as to kill his own wife and child, he does remember childhood instances that suggest Luke's capability to do so. Luke's own father's fear that the man was capable of murder-suicide further suggests a darkness that could have led to such an outcome. Ellie's unsolved death when she, Aaron, and Luke were sixteen adds another layer of uncertainty. Aaron's own innocence in Ellie's death, despite the town's conviction that he was involved, is one of the reasons he continues to search for answers, but his tunnel vision about the earlier death may undermine his ability to solve the more recent ones. As the story unfolds, readers are thrust into the past through the memories of varied characters, including Luke Hadler himself. Harper's skillful integration of memory with present day action keeps readers wondering what the outcome will reveal.

Aaron's homecoming is fraught with persecution from people who are still convinced that he killed Ellie, but he is also reminded of good times and he meets newer community members who could easily become friends. Greg Raco, the police detective who doubts Luke's guilt, encourages Falk to investigate at his side. McMurdo, Aaron's temporary landlord, also befriends him, and Scott Whitlam, the school's new principal, seems sympathetic as well. Each of these characters plays a surprising role in helping Aaron solve the murders of Ellie and the Hadlers.

As Aaron has experienced since Ellie's death at sixteen, taking responsibility for one's actions is often less popular than blaming someone else. Mal Deacon, Ellie's father, blames everyone for his daughter's death, but he does not accept that his abuse of the girl drove her away. The townspeople jumped on Aaron and his father as responsible for Ellie's death, refusing to accept that there was no real proof. Grant Dow, Ellie's cousin, holds Aaron responsible because Aaron's last name was on a piece of paper in Ellie's room, but he refuses to see that what seems to be his own name on a piece of paper in Karen Hadler's room might point to him as a suspect in the Hadlers' deaths. Even Gretchen, Luke's high school girlfriend and one of the only people in town who is sympathetic to Aaron, refuses to acknowledge that her silence when Ellie died had long-lasting repercussions. Most frighteningly, the irresponsible actions of a weak person led to a truly evil act that had lifelong consequences for too many in Kiewarra and beyond.

The book's title refers to the drought that has plagued Kiewarra for two years. The effects of this weather issue lead some to believe that Luke had lost hope financially and acted out as a result. It has, more importantly, plunged the whole area into economic downfall that leads to raised tempers and suspicions. Not only has the lack of water limited farming opportunities, but the threat of fire and the horrific damage that it could bring hangs over the heads of everyone who has remained in the unfriendly town.

Jane Harper's success with this debut piece suggests that she will be a strong voice in the canon of mystery novels. Fans of this book will look forward to the potential of a film version, which has been discussed with the author, and to Harper's second novel *Force of Nature*, also starring Aaron Falk, set to release in 2017–18.

Theresa L. Stowell, PhD

Review Sources

Maslin, Janet. "'The Dry,' a Page-Turner of a Mystery Set in a Parched Australia." Review of *The Dry*, by Jane Harper. *The New York Times*, 9 Jan. 2017, www.nytimes.com/2017/01/09/books/review-dry-jane-harper.html. Accessed 22 Nov. 2017.

Murphy, Jane. Review of *The Dry*, by Jane Harper. *Booklist*, vol. 113, no. 5, 2016, pp. 30–31. *Book Review Digest Plus*, search.ebscohost.com?direct=true&db=brd&AN=119163072&site=ehost-live. Accessed 22 Nov. 2017.

Review of *The Dry*, by Jane Harper. *Kirkus Reviews*, vol. 86, no. 20, 2017, p. 5. *Book Review Digest Plus*, search.ebscohost.com?direct=true&db=brd&AN=118735668&site=ehost-live. Accessed 22 Nov. 2017.

Review of *The Dry*, by Jane Harper. *Publishers Weekly*, vol. 263, no. 28, 2016, p. 45. *Book Review Digest Plus*, search.ebscohost.com?direct=true&db=brd&AN=1167 69426&site=ehost-live. Accessed 22 Nov. 2017.

Williams, Wilda. Review of *The Dry*, by Jane Harper. *Library Journal*, vol. 141, no. 19, 2016, p. 83. *Education Full Text*, search.ebscohost.com?direct=true&db=eft&AN=119492599&site=ehost-live. Accessed 22 Nov. 2017.

Enduring Vietnam
An American Generation and Its War

Author: James Wright (b. 1939)
Publisher: Thomas Dunne Books (New York). 464 pp.
Type of work: History
Time: 1945–2016
Locales: United States, Vietnam

In Enduring Vietnam, *James Wright chronicles the history of the Vietnam War and the generation it most affected, the baby boomers. Within this framework, Wright focuses on the experiences of Americans who fought, served, and died in Vietnam, giving a voice to service members who have largely been unheard.*

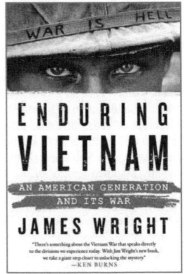

Courtesy of Macmillan

Spanning two decades and five US presidential administrations, the Vietnam War, which began in November 1955 and ended with the fall of Saigon (now Ho Chi Minh City) to the North Vietnamese Army (NVA) in April 1975, is widely regarded in the United States as a national failure. Fought during a highly turbulent period in American history, the war was marked by an unsettling tableau of feelings and emotions that sparked ceaseless debates about its point and purpose. Many assumptions and judgments have since been made about the bitter conflict, which came to be known in Vietnam as the American War, but most generally agree that US involvement in the war was a grave mistake—one that ultimately cost 58,220 American lives.

For that reason, the war in Vietnam continues to hover over the United States like a dark cloud. In the years since its conclusion, just the word "Vietnam" has become sufficient to signify the war, almost universally in a pejorative sense. Unlike previous military contests, Vietnam was a war without clear-cut objectives and was largely characterized by small-scale ambushes and firefights; consequently, it was devoid of dramatic campaigns and traditional front lines, and was ultimately overshadowed by the controversy it engendered. Few popular heroes emerged from the war, the success of which, during military combat operations, was measured in terms of body counts and kill ratios. Many Vietnam veterans, upon returning to their native soil, disappeared into anonymity as they tried to make the difficult adjustment to civilian life.

In *Enduring Vietnam: An American Generation and Its War*, author James Wright helps give these veterans their human faces, bringing them into the foreground of a complex Shakespearean tragedy that played out on the world stage. A comprehensive and clearly written history of the Vietnam War, Wright's book provides an intimate portrait of the more than 2.5 million US military personnel who served, most of whom grew up in post–World War II America as part of the generation known as the baby boomers. Wright focuses primarily on the five to six hundred thousand ground combat troops—or, as he terms them, "war fighters"—whose experience of the war was far removed from those who challenged it back home. Drawing on more than 160 interviews, in addition to a wide array of primary and secondary sources, he puts to rest many of the negative stereotypes that marred their service.

To provide context, Wright offers an in-depth overview of the political and historical factors that led to US involvement in the war. Early chapters of the book chronicle Vietnam's emergence in the 1950s and 1960s as a pivotal chess piece in the fight against Communism. In 1954, after Vietnamese Communist leader Ho Chi Minh's Viet Minh forces defeated the French, the country was divided into northern and southern zones; Ho Chi Minh became president of North Vietnam, which was established as a socialist state, and Ngo Dinh Diem, a devout Catholic and staunch anti-Communist, eventually assumed control of the south. In the ensuing decade, the United States, under successive presidents Dwight D. Eisenhower, John F. Kennedy, and Lyndon B. Johnson, sent billions of dollars in economic and military support to South Vietnam as part of its efforts to halt the spread of Communism in the region.

Throughout *Enduring Vietnam*, Wright illustrates how this geopolitical maneuvering shaped the social and cultural environment of the baby boomer generation. Coming of age in the early days of television and rock-and-roll music, baby boomers grew up in an America that was characterized by optimism and prosperity. It was also the era of the Cold War, however, and the looming threat of Communism was never far from the American consciousness. The possibility of a nuclear showdown between the United States and the Soviet Union further exacerbated people's fears.

By the time the 1960s began, baby boomers were well versed in duck-and-cover drills and the anti-Communist domino theory and had been instilled with a sense of duty and responsibility to their country. Deeply affected by President Kennedy's 1961 inaugural address, many young American men and women joined the US military with idealized notions of a free and democratic South Vietnam. But by the end of 1963, both Kennedy and South Vietnamese leader Ngo Dinh Diem had been assassinated, and by 1965, the US position in Vietnam under President Johnson had shifted from an advisory role to a full combat role. US ground combat soldiers gradually came to the troubling realization that Vietnam was a war much different from their parents'—one fought against an elusive enemy amid hostile natives in unknown terrain.

Wright addresses perceived political miscalculations, ambiguous military objectives and tactics, and the debates they spawned, but he does not dwell on them. Instead, he focuses his attention to the experiences of ground combat soldiers, whose central preoccupation was survival. This driving human instinct was never more palpable than on Dong Ap Bia, a menacing 3,074-foot mountain in Vietnam's western A Shau Valley, in May 1969, a watershed period of the war on which Wright concentrates heavily. That month, Dong Ap Bia served as the site for a brutal eleven-day battle between units of the US Army's 101st Airborne Division and the NVA. The battle for Dong Ap Bia, which eventually came to be known to Americans as Hamburger Hill for the way it mercilessly ground up combatants, resulted in more than one hundred US casualties. Though US forces ultimately succeeded in taking the hill, they abandoned it about a week later after it was determined that the land was of little strategic value. The NVA reoccupied the hill one month later, prompting a firestorm of criticism back in the United States.

For Wright, the battle of Hamburger Hill represents a microcosm of the futility of the American War in Vietnam. It would become one of the best-known battles of the war, but it too failed, like other sustained, large-scale combat operations in Vietnam, to generate the kind of attention and positive publicity associated with major battles in other wars. No flag was raised atop Hamburger Hill to signify victory, as was done at Iwo Jima in World War II. Participants in the battle were treated not as heroes but as afterthoughts, overshadowed by the protests and criticism that surrounded it. Wright notes that the fighting occurred immediately prior to President Richard Nixon publicly announcing in early June that the United States was no longer seeking military victory in Vietnam and that US troop levels would be drawn down.

Despite these proclamations, little changed on the ground in Vietnam during this time. Wright notes that May 1969, ironically, marked the highest US troop levels of the entire war—some 540,000 men and women. Casualties suffered on Hamburger Hill represented only a small fraction of the casualties suffered in the scores of other small-scale battles that were concurrently being waged throughout Vietnam. Most battles went unreported by the American news media, which instead updated the public by way of aggregate death tolls. By this time, more than 40 percent of the US soldiers being killed in the war were draftees, with a median age of twenty-one.

Through his interviews with veterans of these battles and with family members of those who died in them, Wright brings a deep-focus lens to their experience, which was defined by routine and terror. With the skill of a novelist, he transports the reader to the battlefield with vivid firsthand recollections, the most harrowing of which appear in chapters 6 and 7 of the book, titled "The American War in Vietnam" and "Getting Out of This Place," respectively. Among them are the stories of a marine who, during his first daytime patrol as a radio operator, witnessed his point man vaporize in front of him "like a mushroom going straight up in the sky"; a soldier who had never forgotten the overwhelming, ever-present "salty, ocean" smell of blood; and a chaplain who, while helping medics after an ambush, cared for a still-living soldier who had "part of his brain hanging out."

Bearing witness to the horrors of war was part of ground combat soldiers' everyday existence in Vietnam, but so were acts of heroism. Though acknowledging the absence of iconic military figures such as Sergeant Alvin York (of World War I) and Lieutenant Audie Murphy (of World War II), Wright asserts that Vietnam produced "as many heroes as any other war." Throughout the book, he recognizes individual acts of bravery and sacrifice, which were often committed, more than anything else, out of necessity in order to survive. Most importantly, he points out that soldiers gave little thought to the politics of the time and to the heated debates that surrounded the war, instead focusing on their obligations to their brothers-in-arms. And while growing racial tensions between white and black Americans also carried over to the war, combat situations, Wright notes, tended to ease those tensions.

In his introduction, Wright, who served in the US Marines for three years before entering a career in academia, writes that *Enduring Vietnam* is a follow-up to his 2012 book *Those Who Have Borne the Battle: A History of America's Wars and Those Who Fought Them*, which examines the experiences of American war veterans. Unlike veterans of

James Wright is president emeritus and Eleazar Wheelock Professor of History emeritus of Dartmouth College. He has authored or edited eight books, most notably Those Who Have Borne the Battle: A History of America's Wars and Those Who Fought Them *(2012).*

other wars, many Vietnam veterans encountered hostility from Americans upon their return home. Labeled "baby killers" and drug addicts, some were spit on by antiwar protestors, or even beaten. Nonviolent hostility was equally disturbing, as many veterans were discriminated against in their everyday lives, from having banks refuse to cash their government checks to being turned away at job interviews.

While these are by no means new revelations, Wright acknowledges that the treatment of returning Vietnam veterans was just as tragic as the war they fought in. Still, he does not gloss over disturbing aspects of the war itself, detailing some of the war's worst atrocities—particularly the My Lai massacre of March 1968, in which US soldiers killed hundreds of innocent Vietnamese civilians. He condemns the military's handling of Lieutenant William Calley, the leader of the massacre, who ultimately served less than four years of house arrest before receiving a commutation from President Nixon, and laments the fact that Calley remains among the most recognizable names from the Vietnam War.

Yet Wright also challenges arguments made by other Vietnam historians, among them Nick Turse, that the killing of civilians at My Lai was characteristic of US soldiers' behavior during the war. Though recognizing that My Lai was not an isolated occurrence, he argues that incidents like it, as well as instances of other criminal acts such as fragging and drug use, were far less common than stereotypes suggest. Wright backs up these arguments, as he does throughout *Enduring Vietnam*, with firsthand stories and pertinent statistics gathered from a bevy of surveys and polls.

The tone of Wright's book nevertheless remains evenhanded, and he succeeds in giving readers a strong sense of what it was like for US ground combat soldiers who endured the treacherous terrain of Vietnam. Wright skillfully avoids getting lost in controversies and debates surrounding the war, instead honoring those who served and died in it and those who still struggle with its aftereffects, which have included everything from post-traumatic stress disorder to Agent Orange–related diseases.

Enduring Vietnam was well received by critics. The reviewer for *Publishers Weekly* called the book a "well-researched and readable work," while Mark Levine, writing for *Booklist*, proclaimed it "among the most powerful and heartbreaking" of the "hundreds of books written about the Vietnam War." The book is undeniably an important contribution to the literature and will serve as a good starting point for readers looking to gain a thorough understanding of the Vietnam War and its lasting impact on the baby boomer generation. Wright admirably achieves his intentions of portraying Vietnam veterans not as villains but as American heroes.

Chris Cullen

Review Sources

Review of *Enduring Vietnam: An American Generation and Its War*, by James Wright. *Publishers Weekly*, 9 Jan. 2017, p. 53. *Literary Reference Center Plus*, search.ebscohost.com/login.aspx?direct=true&db=lkh&AN=120625773&site=1 rc-plus. Accessed 26 Jan. 2018.

Helicher, Karl. Review of *Enduring Vietnam: An American Generation and Its War*, by James Wright. *Library Journal*, 1 Jan. 2017, pp. 113–14. *Literary Reference Center Plus*, search.ebscohost.com/login.aspx?direct=true&db=lkh&AN=120745 474&site=lrc-plus. Accessed 26 Jan. 2018.

Levine, Mark. Review of *Enduring Vietnam: An American Generation and Its War*, by James Wright. *Booklist*, 1–15 Jan. 2017, p. 32. *Literary Reference Center Plus*, search.ebscohost.com/login.aspx?direct=true&db=lkh&AN=120651757&site=1 rc-plus. Accessed 26 Jan. 2018.

Ernest Hemingway

Author: Mary V. Dearborn
Publisher: Alfred A. Knopf (New York).
752 pp.
Type of work: Biography
Time: 1899–1961
Locales: Illinois; Italy; Paris, France; Spain;
Key West, Florida; Cuba; Idaho

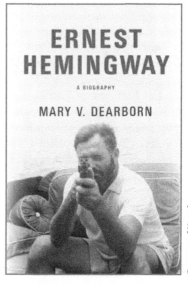

Courtesy of Knopf

*Noted biographer Mary V. Dearborn offers
a detailed account of the life of Nobel Prize–
winning author Ernest Hemingway, detailing his relationships with family, friends, and
professional associates. The biography also
analyzes the factors that led to the development of his larger-than-life persona and,
eventually, to his suicide.*

Principal personages
ERNEST MILLER HEMINGWAY, a novelist, short-story writer, and essayist
GRACE HALL HEMINGWAY, his mother
HADLEY RICHARDSON, his first wife
PAULINE PFEIFFER, his second wife
MARTHA GELLHORN, his third wife, a journalist
MARY WELSH, his fourth wife, a journalist

Mary V. Dearborn's *Ernest Hemingway* joins an already crowded field of biographies
of the Nobel-winning writer. It is not unusual that Hemingway has drawn so much attention. While many writers avoid the limelight, letting their work speak for them, he
sought out publicity, making himself as much the subject of popular publications as his
fiction and nonfiction were. The immediate popularity of his first major novel, *The Sun
Also Rises* (1926), thrust him into the international spotlight and he never relinquished
center stage. Gossip columnists covered his romantic escapades—he married four
times and was rumored to have had several affairs—while newspaper and magazine
writers followed his adventures on African safaris, his hunting and fishing expeditions
in the Gulf Coast region and the wilds of the American Northwest, and his activities
as a war correspondent during the Spanish Civil War and World War II. His suicide in
1961 was front-page news in national and international newspapers.

Even before Hemingway died, his life was scrutinized by academics and professional biographers whom he claimed to despise. He threatened to sue Philip Young if
he did not cease work on *Ernest Hemingway* (1952) and erected roadblocks to keep
Charles Fenton from completing *The Apprenticeship of Ernest Hemingway: The Early
Years* (1954). However, he seemed to tolerate Carlos Baker's critical work; therefore,

it was no surprise that, within months of Hemingway's death, his widow, Mary, selected Baker as Hemingway's official biographer.

Baker's biography, published in 1969, was a tome that attracted mixed reviews—heavy on fact, light on assessing Hemingway's character—but it set a standard for what followed. Michael Reynolds devoted his life to analyzing Hemingway's life and works, producing five volumes that are exhaustive, if not definitive. Peter Griffin attempted a similar study but gave up (or, as rumored, was prevented from finishing by the Hemingway estate) after publishing only two of five planned volumes. During the 1980s and 1990s, several blockbuster works revised the general view of Hemingway as "he-man par excellence": Jeffrey Meyers's *Hemingway* (1985), a rather acerbic assessment that makes Hemingway seem small and mean-spirited; Kenneth Lynn's *Hemingway* (1987), which stresses Hemingway's lifelong fascination with androgyny; and James Mellow's *Hemingway: A Life without Consequences* (1992), a more balanced portrait. More focused biographies—including those specifically chronicling Hemingway's activities during World War II or his adventures aboard his boat, the *Pilar*—provide evidence that his life continues to interest biographers and the reading public. When these biographies are added to the numerous memoirs by family, ex-wives, and associates, the number of books trying to explain "how it was" (a favorite Hemingway phrase) extends into the dozens.

Inevitably, Dearborn's biography will be judged against those of her predecessors. Given the many life studies already in print, the first question likely to be asked is: Why is another biography of Hemingway necessary? Dearborn provides one answer to the question by pointing out that she was drawn to write Hemingway's life story for a general readership because she was a woman who brought to her writing "no investment in the Hemingway legend," as she notes in the prologue of the book Dearborn, author of biographies of Henry Miller and Norman Mailer—two men often thought of as kindred spirits of Hemingway who, she also writes in *Earnest Hemingway*, "helped define American masculinity through both their lives and their fiction"—avoids any temptation to expound upon Hemingway's macho legend, presenting instead a thoughtful portrait that acknowledges Hemingway's significant accomplishments while laying out his considerable personal foibles.

Most biographers who write about literary figures are forced to make a choice between retelling the story of their subject's life or discussing the subject's work at length. Rarely does a biographer succeed in doing both. Among Hemingway biographies, Linda Wagner-Martin's *Ernest Hemingway: A Literary Life* (2007) is exceptional in its focus on Hemingway's work placed in the context of his life; however, this is a book for scholars and students, not the general public. Dearborn, on the other hand, is aiming at a wider audience, as suggested by the publicity campaign mounted by Knopf, her publisher, to promote the book. Hence, Dearborn concentrates on Hemingway's life, weaving in commentary about his fiction to give readers some sense of its reception and impact on his career.

Dearborn's book is long—perhaps the longest single-volume biography since Baker's. Like Baker, she is primarily interested in sorting out what really happened from the many myths Hemingway created about his experiences to bolster his own image as a macho adventure seeker. One of Dearborn's strengths is her ability to place Hemingway's life in the larger context of family and professional associations, and in relationship to world events. During his life, Hemingway met, and in some cases formed lasting relationships with, hundreds of notable men and women of the time. Dearborn offers sketches of Hemingway's on-again, off-again friendships with literary notables Ezra Pound, Gertrude Stein, Archibald MacLeish, F. Scott Fitzgerald, and John Dos Passos, as well as lesser-known figures (Robert McAlmon, Owen Wister, Max Eastman, and Wyndham Lewis, among others). She devotes attention to his many hunting and fishing companions, along with others whose paths crossed his during his four decades in the international spotlight. As Dearborn points out on more than one occasion, the greatest sin any of these friends could commit was to be kind to Hemingway and help him when he was in need. Seemingly incapable of being beholden to anyone, he consistently lashed out at those who did him favors, often revising (in his own mind, at least) events to convince others (and himself) that he was in some way wronged by their acts of kindness.

Another strength of this biography is Dearborn's discussion of Hemingway's relationship with the women in his life—probably the best assessment since Bernice Kert's *The Hemingway Women* (1983). Relying on materials in the Harry Ransom Center at the University of Texas at Austin, Dearborn revises the portrait of Hemingway's mother that Hemingway and many of his earlier biographers had created. Far from these descriptions of a domineering, prudish, self-centered shrew who humiliated and vilified her older son from the time he was a small child, Dearborn paints Grace Hemingway as a strong-willed but complex figure, trapped in a marriage to Hemingway's father that seemed constraining, if not stultifying. Grace's dealings with her son were sometimes harsh, but as Dearborn discovers in correspondence between the two, their strained relationship did not prevent Hemingway from maintaining contact or supporting his mother and his siblings after his father committed suicide. His relationships with his sisters are also scrutinized, and the motives for his hatred for his older sister Marcelline are analyzed with attention and balance.

Mary V. Dearborn is the author of biographies on Peggy Guggenheim, Louise Bryant, Norman Mailer, and Henry Miller.

The story of Hemingway's four marriages is told with the same critical attention, although Dearborn seems to be more sympathetic toward the women who became Mrs. Hemingway than to the four-time husband. Hadley Richardson, Hemingway's first wife, comes off as particularly long-suffering and saintly. Pauline Pfeiffer, the woman who devoted her life to pleasing her husband, only to have him leave her for writer and war correspondent Martha Gellhorn, is also drawn sympathetically. The tough, career-minded Gellhorn may have proven too much for Hemingway to stomach—he hated competition of any kind, Dearborn notes—and their marriage was the shortest of the four into which Hemingway entered.

In later life, Hemingway had numerous liaisons, several of them undoubtedly involving intimate relations. Dearborn points out the personal flaws in Hemingway's character that led him to be a serial philanderer. Once he found another woman with whom he wanted to spend his life, he was quick to invent reasons why his current wife was to blame for his unhappiness; in his mind, divorce and remarriage seemed not only right, but just.

Although Dearborn is interested principally in exploring Hemingway's life and character, she also offers some sense of his literary accomplishments. Generally, her critiques of individual works follow the now-accepted judgments about the Hemingway canon: the first two short-story collections are considered innovative and influential; *The Sun Also Rises* and *A Farewell to Arms* (1929) make important contributions to modern American literature; *Death in the Afternoon* (1932) and *Green Hills of Africa* (1935) are interesting and well written, but essentially literary anomalies; and *To Have and Have Not* (1937) is a great mistake (largely, Dearborn points out, because Hemingway was interested in other matters, particularly the Spanish Civil War, when he was finishing it). Her assessment of *For Whom the Bell Tolls* (1940) is noteworthy for her insightful comments on Hemingway's use of highly stylized language and individual set pieces: "The love story between Robert Jordan and the victimized Maria," she observes, "though it made the novel enormously popular at the time, does not hold up well today." Dearborn describes *The Old Man and the Sea* (1952), the work that seemed to signal a comeback for Hemingway two years after the 1950 debacle *Across the River and Into the Trees* (1950), as lacking "the ambition and passion" of earlier work.

While Dearborn's book is written for a popular audience, it is also of interest to scholars. Though they may find little new in the way of facts, Dearborn provides much to ponder in her assessment of Hemingway's career. Additionally, while *Ernest Hemingway* is not encumbered with footnotes embedded in the text, nearly 10 percent of the book is devoted to annotating the sources on which Dearborn relies for specific information. Unlike many authors of popular books, Dearborn is generous in crediting her predecessors, citing dozens of them by name in her text (rather than burying acknowledgments in her notes) so that the sources for many of her facts and assessments are clear to readers.

Because Hemingway has generated, and continues to generate, passionate responses from readers for more than eight decades—he is adored by many, vilified by many others—it may seem unusual to find a biographer attempting an evenhanded portrait. Dearborn argues that achieving a balanced assessment is important if Hemingway's place in literary history is to be understood correctly: "It does no good to read (or write) his biography anew if we simply shine up the legend," she says, "or if we reflexively debunk a literary legacy that has proved durably fascinating and inspiring for nearly a century." What is necessary, she argues persuasively, is "to understand what happened, in part because what was lost is incalculable."

Though it is unlikely that Dearborn's biography will supplant all of its predecessors, it is certain that it will be mandatory reading for Hemingway scholars and fans alike for decades.

Laurence W. Mazzeno

Review Sources

Adams, Matthew. "Ernest Hemingway: The Man behind the Cultivated Image of Hyper-Masculinity." Review of *Ernest Hemingway*, by Mary V. Dearborn *The Washington Post*, 17 May 2017, www.washingtonpost.com/entertainment/books/ ernest-hemingway-the-man-behind-the-cultivated-image-of-hyper-masculinity/2017/05/17/c54e1aae-3b04-11e7-8854-21f359183e8c_story.html?utm_term=. b1667cb77326. Accessed 21 Sept. 2017.

Reveal, Judith. Review of *Ernest Hemingway*, by Mary Dearborn. *New York Journal of Books*, www.nyjournalofbooks.com/book-review/ernest-hemingway-biography. Accessed 21 Sept. 2017.

Rollyson, Carl. Review of *Ernest Hemingway*, by Mary Dearborn. *SFGate*, 10 June 2017, www.sfgate.com/books/article/Ernest-Hemingway-A-Biography-by-Mary-V-11208103.php. Accessed 21 Sept. 2017.

Showalter, Elaine. "A Hemingway Tell-All Bares His Tall Tales." Review of *Ernest Hemingway*, by Mary V. Dearborn. *The New York Times*, 25 May 2017, www. nytimes.com/2017/05/25/books/review/ernest-hemingway-biography-mary-dearborn.html. Accessed 21 Sept. 2017.

The Evangelicals
The Struggle to Shape America

Author: Frances FitzGerald (b. 1940)
Publisher: Simon & Schuster (New York). 752 pp.
Type of work: History
Time: Mid-eighteenth century to the present
Locale: United States

Beginning with the Great Awakening in the mid-eighteenth century and ending with the 2016 presidential election, Frances Fitzgerald explores how Protestant evangelical Christians have influenced American culture, history, and politics.

Principal personages
JONATHAN EDWARDS, an eighteenth-century Calvinist preacher and theologian, a leader of the First Great Awakening
GEORGE WHITEFIELD, an eighteenth-century Anglican preacher, a leader of the First Great Awakening
J. FRANK NORRIS, a twentieth-century separatist Baptist preacher, early founder of megachurches
WILLIAM B. RILEY, a twentieth-century Baptist pastor and influential fundamentalist
BILLY GRAHAM, an evangelical Southern Baptist minister, televangelist, and one of the most influential preachers of the twentieth century
JERRY FALWELL, an independent Baptist pastor, televangelist, and founder of the conservative Moral Majority
PAT ROBERTSON, a former Southern Baptist minister, founder of the Christian Broadcasting Network, and 1988 presidential candidate
GEORGE W. BUSH, forty-third president of the United States and conservative Christian Republican
RALPH REED, conservative Republican activist and executive director of the Christian Coalition
JIM WALLIS, evangelical left-wing activist and founder of the progressive Sojourners magazine

When the 2016 election results were tabulated, Republican Donald J. Trump—a reality television star and "thrice-married libertine"—became the forty-fifth president of the United States. He defeated the Democratic former first lady, senator, and secretary of state Hillary Rodham Clinton. While ethnic and racial minorities tended to favor Clinton, eighty-one out of every hundred evangelical Christians cast their vote for Trump, despite his less than pious background. This high percentage was perhaps not unusual, however, given that 78 percent of evangelicals also chose Republican presidential candidates Ronald Reagan and George W. Bush. By and large, these statistics indicate that people who identify themselves as evangelical Protestants also champion "conservative" and "Republican" values and policies. Yet when the evangelical movement first began take shape in the nineteenth century, politics and religion were not so closely intertwined. In fact, pastors and their congregations believed in the separation of church and state referenced in the First Amendment to the United States Constitution. If that was the case then, how and why did evangelicals become a political force in the twentieth and twenty-first centuries?

In *The Evangelicals: The Struggle to Shape America*, Pulitzer Prize winner Frances FitzGerald attempts to answer this question as she traces the rise of conservative white Protestant influence in American secular life and politics. Her complex, authoritative, and enlightening study was long in the making. As far back as 1980, she visited Jerry Falwell's Thomas Road Baptist Church in Lynchburg, Virginia, which provided material for her *New Yorker* article "How the Christian Right Became a Political Force" (1981). Since then she has written other articles about the growing political influence of evangelicalism, including "Holy Toledo" (2006) and "The New Evangelicals" (2008), both of which also appeared in *The New Yorker*.

How does one define "evangelical"? FitzGerald explains that the term is a religious one derived from the Greek word *evangel*, which means "good news" or "the Gospel." In Matthew 28:16–20, Jesus issues the Great Commission, in which he calls his followers to preach the good news of God's kingdom. However, in the twentieth and twenty-first centuries, the definition of the word has taken on a different connotation. The contemporary perception of an "evangelical" is someone who believes in the inerrancy of the Bible, is "born again" in Christ, and espouses conservative religious, political, social, economic, and cultural views. But it was not always so.

In the first third her book, FitzGerald offers a survey of early evangelical movements, prominent leaders, and the theology that laid the foundation for modern evangelicalism. She begins by chronicling the First Great Awakening, which was a populist, anti-intellectual religious movement begun in the 1730s. Originally spearheaded by influential preachers such as Jonathan Edwards and George Whitefield, this sweeping spiritual revival was characterized by passionate emotional responses of the faithful, a heightened belief in the supernatural, and, eventually, a disengagement from established state-sanctioned denominations such as Congregationalism.

The Second Great Awakening, which started in the 1780s and ended in the mid-nineteenth century, gave birth to progressive social ideas and activism. Slavery was the dominant issue of the day, and many Northern evangelicals were abolitionists who understood the Bible to say that God created all people equal. On the other hand, Southern evangelicals pointed to Bible passages condoning slavery. Fitzgerald comments, "The southern defense of slavery extinguished the reformist zeal, affected evangelical theology, and made the South a closed society."

When the Civil War ended, the economic, intellectual, cultural, and religious divide between North and South did not. FitzGerald notes that Southern evangelicals viewed themselves as "the sacred community" and the North as "the world." Conservative evangelical Protestantism in both the North and South was divided yet again between the modernists—who focused on transforming the economic and social institutions to bring the kingdom of God to earth—and the traditionalists, who believed that the kingdom of God would be best served by taking the Bible as the literal Word of God and emphasizing individual conversions.

Some fundamentalists became disillusioned with established Protestant denominations such as the Baptists and Presbyterians and separated to form their own groups. FitzGerald paints vivid portraits of the colorful, and often controversial, men who led the separatist movement. For example, J. Frank Norris, a flamboyant Baptist preacher, was a fierce opponent of liberalism, evolution, and Communism. He protested what he viewed as the "modernist" leanings of the traditionally inclined Southern Baptist Convention and eventually separated from it. In the North, Norris's contemporary William B. Riley also opposed theological liberalism and founded the World Christian Fundamentals Association, Northwestern Bible and Missionary Training School, and the Anti-Evolution League of Minnesota. Neither man was concerned with political activism, however. Instead, they both focused on building "religious empires" to aid them in establishing God's kingdom on earth.

FitzGerald's survey of the various spiritual, social, and cultural factors that influenced the early days of evangelicalism lays a solid foundation for the main thrust of her study—the contemporary relationship between evangelical Protestantism and American politics. With the advent of Billy Graham's post–World War II ministry, the gap between religion and government began to close. Graham's revivals drew huge crowds, which created an effective platform for his fundamentalist message. Graham often preached against the atheistic principles of Communism, which dovetailed with the government's efforts to eradicate it. FitzGerald notes that President Dwight D. Eisenhower—not a religious man—stated, "Spiritual strength is the real source of America's power and greatness." Graham reinforced this view by claiming, "If you would be a loyal American, then become a loyal Christian." Graham's uncompromising position was divisive. Those who followed him and other fundamentalist preachers believed that personal conversion would change the world, while more progressive Protestants thought that social justice was the most effective way to address society's ills.

Journalist and historian Frances FitzGerald is the author of Fire in the Lake *(1972), winner of the Pulitzer Prize, National Book Award, and Bancroft Prize. She has also written several other books and numerous articles in such prominent publications as the* New Yorker *and the* Atlantic.

The political and social turmoil of the 1960s alarmed evangelicals, especially those living in the Bible Belt. They were determined that the "South would rise again" and "Christianize America." From the mid-1970s to the mid-1980s, the Christian Right dominated American politics. FitzGerald offers a compelling profile of its primary standard bearer, Jerry Falwell, the son of a bootlegger, who founded the Thomas Road Baptist Church in his hometown of Lynchburg, Virginia. In 1979, Falwell founded the Moral Majority, the largest lobbying group of evangelical Christians in the United States. They favored family, segregation, and prayer in public school, and opposed homosexuality, abortion, and secularism. At its height, the Moral Majority wielded tremendous power and helped elect Ronald Reagan to the presidency. However, by the end of Reagan's second term, the influence of the Moral Majority declined, and the group disbanded in 1989.

With the demise of the Moral Majority, televangelist Pat Robertson filled the void by founding the Christian Coalition. Fitzgerald calls him a "formidable political organizer" and "a serious and innovative entrepreneur." His Christian Broadcasting Network (CBN), home of the popular news-oriented talk show *The 700 Club*, used the latest media to extend the influence of religious broadcasting. Robertson's message of "peace, plenty, and freedom" appealed to millions of American citizens who felt economically deprived. FitzGerald observes that he saw no conflict between his religious and political interests and quotes him as saying, "I think the popular conception of the separation of church and state is one of the great fictions that have been foisted upon us by those who do not like religion." Because many of his views were considered extreme, he lost his bid to become the Republican Party's presidential nominee in 1988.

FitzGerald offers an extensive assessment of the relationship between the Christian Right and the George W. Bush presidency—more than one hundred pages. By the time Bush ran for office, the Christian Right had so integrated with the Republican Party that, in the words of one unnamed scholar quoted by FitzGerald, it had become "in part an interest group and in part a faction of the GOP." In contrast to Reagan, who was conservative but not religious, George W. Bush was a born-again Christian who openly acknowledged his faith. He had the backing of powerful right-wing evangelicals like James Dobson of the Focus on the Family media organization. His support for faith-based social programs, antiabortion legislation, same-sex marriage bans, and other conservative causes won him the loyalty of the Christian Right. However, after Bush failed to keep some of his campaign promises to conservatives, his popularity among Christian Right voters waned, and so did their power.

FitzGerald quotes Jim Wallis, a progressive evangelical and founder of the progressive *Sojourners* magazine, as noting, "Younger evangelicals who previously were committed to Religious Right organizations are defecting because they are as concerned with issues like global warming, poverty and the Iraq War as with saving unborn children." In her penultimate chapter, "The New Evangelicals," FitzGerald contrasts the concerns of the older Christian Right with the concerns of the millennial generation of evangelicals. Although many younger evangelicals still oppose abortion, they often support the LGBT community, embrace racial and ethnic diversity, and are concerned about social justice and environmental issues. For that reason, FitzGerald claims that the days of the old guard Christian Right are numbered.

Most critics have offered qualified praise for FitzGerald's monumental study. The *New York Times'* Alan Wolfe, the *New Republic's* Jeff Sharlet, and the *New York Review of Books'* Garry Wills found fault with her focus on white evangelicals to the exclusion of their African American counterparts. In the preface, FitzGerald anticipates this critique by noting that African American churches have a different history. Randall Balmer, writing for the *Christian Century*, critiqued FitzGerald's narrow focus on conservative evangelicalism at the expense of progressive evangelicalism, with its long historical and theological roots. Sharlet further contended that FitzGerald's discontinuous historical narrative fails to bridge the temporal gap between the 1980s and the rise of Trump adequately. Despite those flaws, *The Evangelicals* does provide a relatively in-depth view of evangelicalism in modern politics and its antecedents in US history.

Pegge Bochynski

Review Sources

Balmer, Randall. "Reading Evangelical History with One Eye Closed." Review of *The Evangelicals: The Struggle to Shape America*, by Frances FitzGerald. *The Christian Century*, 4 Apr. 2017, www.christiancentury.org/review/books/reading-evangelical-history-one-eye-closed. Accessed

Review of *The Evangelicals: The Struggle to Shape America*, by Frances FitzGerald. *Kirkus Reviews*, 6 Feb. 2017, www.kirkusreviews.com/book-reviews/frances-fitzgerald/evangelicals. Accessed

Sharlet, Jeff. "Pew Research." Review of *The Evangelicals: The Struggle to Shape America*, by Frances FitzGerald. *New Republic*, vol. 248, no. 6, 2017, pp. 50–55.

Wills, Garry. "Where Evangelicals Came From." Review of *The Evangelicals: The Struggle to Shape America*, by Frances FitzGerald. *The New York Review of Books*, vol. 64, no. 7, 2017, pp. 26–29.

Wolf, Alan. "With God on Their Side: How Evangelicals Entered American Politics." Review of *The Evangelicals: The Struggle to Shape America*, by Frances FitzGerald. *The New York Times*, 28 Mar. 2017, www.nytimes.com/2017/03/28/books/review/evangelicals-struggle-to-shape-america-frances-fitzgerald.html. Accessed 6 Feb. 2018.

Exit West

Author: Mohsin Hamid (b. 1971)
Publisher: Riverhead Books (New York).
240 pp.
Type of work: Novel
Time: Present day
Locales: A war-torn country; Greece; England; the United States

Mohsin Hamid's fourth novel, Exit West, *explores the psychological and emotional toll of displacement in a world where people are increasingly on the move.*

Principal characters
SAEED, a young man in a war-torn country
NADIA, a young woman in a war-torn country

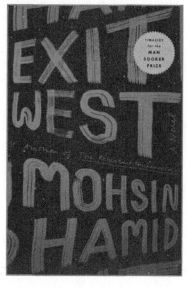

Courtesy of Riverhead Books

A large portion of Mohsin Hamid's fourth novel, *Exit West*, is set in an unnamed city in an unnamed, war-torn country. Shortly before the real breakout of war, Saeed and Nadia, the novel's dual protagonists, meet at a class on corporate branding. Saeed is reserved, thoughtful, and spiritual; he is drawn to Nadia, a nonbeliever who dresses in flowing black robes to fend off the unwanted advances of men. Saeed lives with his parents and prays twice a day. Nadia, unusually for an unmarried woman, lives alone and rides a trail bike to work. The two come together, first as friends and then as lovers, as their city falls to insurgency. For about half of Hamid's compact novel, Saeed and Nadia cling to their daily routines: they go to class and work, they meet for coffee, and they eat psychedelic mushrooms under the lemon tree on Nadia's tiny apartment balcony.

However, the violence slowly and inevitably closes in around them. At first, Hamid writes, the young people are aware of sporadic outbreaks of fighting on a cellular level. It exists as a feeling "in one's chest cavity as a subsonic vibration like those emitted by large loudspeakers at concerts." In scenes that effectively describe the atrocities of the war without becoming overly gruesome, Nadia's cousin is murdered, and later, so is Saeed's mother. Bombs fall across the city, and people are confined to their homes, which are frequently raided. A neighbor's throat is cut, and his blood stains the ceiling of Saeed's apartment. Amid this anarchy, rumors begin to circulate about the sudden and random appearance of magical doors that open to faraway countries such as Greece, England, and the United States.

While the typically emotionally and physically arduous journey itself to another place has been covered in a multitude of literature, the fictional device of the doors allows Hamid to focus intriguingly and thoroughly on a different part of the refugee

experience. Saeed and Nadia, who arrive first on the Greek island of Mykonos, struggle to make a new life together after having left everything they had ever known.
"It was said in those days that the passage was both like dying and like being born,"
Hamid writes. Saeed proves to be the less adaptable of the two. His distrust of others
and yearning for home becomes a sticking point in their relationship. Nadia, who had
always chafed against the conservative mores of her home country anyway, is eager
to embrace new things. Saeed, still grieving his parents, retreats further into prayer,
preferring to talk to god more than Nadia. The trauma of migration changes Saeed and
Nadia, revealing parts of themselves that the other never knew. *Exit West* is a story
about the refugee experience but also a story about the souring of young romance.
(Despite all they have been through, Saeed and Nadia are still at the beginning of their
lives.) Through Saeed and Nadia, a relatable and authentic couple attempting just to
live in the face of a dire situation that is beyond their control, Hamid pits the everyday
against the extraordinary, suggesting, as Sophie Gilbert wrote in her review for the *Atlantic*, "how familiar and persistent human existence is, even at the edge of dystopia."

As the novel progresses, Saeed and Nadia move again and again, but so too does
everyone else. In London, an influx of migrants spurs a citywide siege, with vigilante citizens fighting to "take back" Great Britain. California, meanwhile, experiences
something like a rebirth. The hardship and possibility of life there suggests the frontier
of the Old West. Hamid cleverly describes the United States as a land of constant
migration and occupation, with one group taking the land from another and so on. He
further suggests that migration, in the sweep of human history, is the natural order of
things and that perhaps, despite the violent upheaval, everything just might turn out
fine. Three-quarters into the book, nearly everyone in the world is fleeing where they
were born and migrating somewhere else. This is a prescient narrative choice, as *Exit
West*, Gilbert wrote, is "not putting a human face on refugees so much as putting a
refugee face on all of humankind."

Hamid's spare style approaches a parable in its detachment. He manages to communicate both tenderness for his characters—flaws and virtues are described in the
same reserved tone—and the banality of the horrors they experience. The death of
Saeed's mother, for instance, is couched in a long sentence that describes Nadia's
misgivings about moving in with Saeed. The death ultimately pushes Nadia to accept
the living arrangement, and Hamid manages to make this choice heartbreaking instead
of crass. In another scene, Saeed's father feels a pull of nostalgia watching teenage
boys play soccer in the street. Venturing closer to their game, he sees that they are not
kicking a ball but a human head. The mundane and the horrific are braided together in
Hamid's long, precise sentences, sweeping through time and space. Action featuring
Saeed and Nadia is punctuated by short vignettes featuring nameless people across the
globe. These people are connected to Saeed and Nadia by time alone. For instance,
just after the couple emerge from the haze of their mushroom trip, an old man in La
Jolla, California, talks with a young officer who is securing his property after another
door opens. Later, as Nadia barricades herself in her apartment, a man in the same
city guards a rooftop with a knife and a pistol. As the novel progresses, the vignettes
feature more prominently the moving in and out of doors. A love story, about two old

men who meet through an open door, makes for a tiny gem of a magical realist tale.

In the *New York Times*, renowned critic Michiko Kakutani compared the doors in *Exit West* to C. S. Lewis's classic children's fantasy *The Lion, the Witch and the Wardrobe* (1950), in which a magical wardrobe serves as a portal to another world. The doors are a contradictory image, part childlike fantasy and part dangerous quest. Shadowy, mysterious things, they show up without warning in people's homes and in doctors' offices. Word of their location spreads quickly. Migrants stream through, smugglers exact their payment for entry, and just as quickly as it opened, the door shuts. Then, another door appears in another place, and the cycle begins again.

To compare the arduous, often fatal journeys of real-world migrants—who set out in rubber boats across the Mediterranean and Aegean Seas, ride in pickup truck beds across the Sahara Desert, and hike through

Courtesy of Jillian Edelstein

Pakistani-born author Mohsin Hamid has written four novels: Moth Smoke *(2000),* The Reluctant Fundamentalist *(2007),* How to Get Filthy Rich in Rising Asia *(2013), and* Exit West *(2017), which was short-listed for the Man Booker Prize.*

rural Eastern Europe—to the opening of a door might sound strange or even reductive. Yet the simplicity of the image suggests a larger view of the mass migration underway all over the world. In another book from 2017, a nonfiction account titled *The New Odyssey*, author Patrick Kingsley chronicles the various routes by which migrants and refugees travel to Europe from the Middle East and Africa. Access to these passages requires money and a good bit of luck. For a time, migrants from all over pooled into Libya to reach Italy by boat—then the preferred destination became Greece. Passages are shaped by restriction and war. When one route closes, another, somewhere, opens. Like the people in *Exit West*, real-life migrants catapult themselves into the unknown, traveling until they are stopped or choose to stop, trying their best to sidestep harsh penalties and laborious aid processes.

Hamid, who grew up in Lahore, Pakistan, and California, published his first novel, *Moth Smoke*, in 2000. His second novel, *The Reluctant Fundamentalist* (2007), about a disillusioned Pakistani financial analyst living in the United States after the terrorist attacks of September 11, 2001, was made into a movie starring Riz Ahmed in 2013, the same year that his third novel, *How to Get Filthy Rich in Rising Asia*, was published. The latter, a hybrid self-help and coming-of-age story, is told in the second person and written in "prose so pure and purposeful it passes straight into the bloodstream," Parul Sehgal wrote for the *New York Times*. "It intoxicates." In each of his previous fiction works, Hamid has dealt creatively with significant current affairs.

Exit West (2017) continues this trend with its focus on refugees inspired by mass migration stemming from the ongoing conflict in Syria. It was short-listed for the Man Booker Prize and was named one of the *New York Times*'s ten best books of the year. Jia Tolentino of the *New Yorker* wrote that the book "feels immediately canonical, so firm and unerring is Hamid's understanding of our time and its most pressing questions." Kakutani was similarly impressed by Hamid's handle on the times. "By mixing the real and the surreal, and using old fairy-tale magic, Hamid has created a fictional universe that captures the global perils percolating beneath today's headlines, while at the same time painting an unnervingly dystopian portrait of what might lie down the road," she wrote. Additionally, reviewers argued that Hamid's strategic choice to leave Saeed and Nadia's home country ambiguous effectively makes their experiences universal to the reader. While *Exit West* largely received glowing reviews, criticism was aimed at the novel's pace, which seems to flag in the last third. The plot, so carefully sculpted at the beginning of the book, meanders toward a resolution.

Molly Hagan

Review Sources

Review of *Exit West*, by Mohsin Hamid. *Kirkus*, 6 Dec. 2016, www.kirkusreviews. com/book-reviews/mohsin-hamid/exit-west. Accessed 20 Nov. 2017.

Gilbert, Sophie. "*Exit West* and the Edge of Dystopia." Review of *Exit West*, by Mohsin Hamid. *The Atlantic*, 8 Mar. 2017, www.theatlantic.com/entertainment/ archive/2017/03/exit-west/518802. Accessed 20 Nov. 2017.

Kakutani, Michiko. "Review: In *Exit West*, Mohsin Hamid Mixes Global Trouble with a Bit of Magic." Review of *Exit West*, by Mohsin Hamid. *The New York Times*, 27 Feb. 2017, www.nytimes.com/2017/02/27/books/review-exit-west-mohsin-hamid.html. Accessed 20 Nov. 2017.

Motion, Andrew. "*Exit West* by Mohsin Hamid Review—Magic and Violence in Migrants' Tale." Review of *Exit West*, by Mohsin Hamid. *The Guardian*, 2 Mar. 2017, www.theguardian.com/books/2017/mar/02/exit-west-mohsin-hamid-review-andrew-motion-migrants. Accessed 20 Nov. 2017.

Tolentino, Jia. "A Novel about Refugees That Feels Instantly Canonical." Review of *Exit West*, by Mohsin Hamid. *The New Yorker*, 10 Mar. 2017, www.newyorker. com/culture/jia-tolentino/a-novel-about-refugees-that-feels-instantly-canonical. Accessed 20 Nov. 2017.

The Fact of a Body
A Murder and a Memoir

Author: Alexandria Marzano-Lesnevich (b. 1977)
Publisher: Flatiron Books (New York). 336 pp.
Type of work: Memoir, true crime
Time: 1964–2003
Locales: Louisiana, New Jersey, Massachusetts

Alternating memoir-like chapters about her own life with chapters telling the story of convicted child murderer Ricky Langley, Alexandria Marzano-Lesnevich uses the parallels between the two stories to investigate her own complex feelings about justice, abuse, and the ways in which people shape their lives into easily digestible narratives.

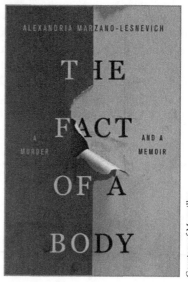

Courtesy of Macmillan

Principal personages

ALEXANDRIA MARZANO-LESNEVICH, the author, now a lawyer
RICKY LANGLEY, a child molester and murderer
JEREMY GUILLORY, a six-year-old boy
LORILEI GUILLORY, Jeremy's mother
BESSIE LANGLEY, Ricky's mother

Life is messy. It does not happen in neat orderly chunks, but rather it unfolds as a seemingly meaningless series of events. In order to understand what has happened in their lives, people inevitably shape these events into coherent narratives, telling stories to control the chaos. While just about everyone tends to create a narrative of their lives, this tendency is particularly acute in the case of the memoirist. A memoirist looks back at his or her own life and presents this randomness as a coherent story. In a similar way, the lawyer must take the mere facts of a case and shape them into a narrative that can help the jury make sense of reams of disordered testimony.

This need to bang stubborn reality into manageable forms is especially acute in the case of Alexandria Marzano-Lesnevich, a naturally curious woman who is both a lawyer and a memoirist. These two sides of her résumé are both on full display in her searching memoir–true crime hybrid *The Fact of a Body: A Murder and a Memoir*, in which, in alternating chapters, she details her own upbringing, her sexual abuse, and her early years as an idealistic young lawyer, alongside the reconstructed narrative of Ricky Langley, a pedophile and convicted child murderer whose case she came across during a summer internship while at law school.

The narrative begins in the prologue, in June 2003, when the young Marzano-Lesnevich has traveled to New Orleans for an internship with a law firm that specializes in representing people in death penalty cases, driven by her lifelong opposition to capital punishment. But when she is shown a videotape of the confession of Ricky Langley, one of the firm's clients, she is instinctively repulsed and, in that instant, finds her feelings about the death penalty becoming complicated. This, readers learn, is because Marzano-Lesnevich herself was molested by her grandfather for several years when she was a girl. As she watches the tape, her thoughts get confused: "I came here to help save the man on the screen. . . . But I look at the man on the screen, I feel my grandfather's hands on me, and I know. Despite what I've trained for, despite what I've come here to work for, despite what I believe. I want Ricky to die."

This reaction is one that Marzano-Lesnevich sets out to explore throughout the book. Because she is filled with a desire to understand, she delves much deeper into her own thought processes than her simple declaration of wanting Langley dead. The question of abuse (herself as victim, Langley as perpetrator) is only one of several threads linking the two narratives, and Marzano-Lesnevich is relentless in working out the implications of all the connections. One of the most haunting parallels is the existence of phantom siblings that both she and Langley have to come to terms with. In Marzano-Lesnevich's case, she has vague memories of having had a sister; her parents later tell her that she was one of three triplets and that she did have a sister who died in infancy (her brother, Andy, survived). Langley, meanwhile, finds out that his family was involved in a car crash before he was conceived and that he had a brother, Oscar, who was killed. He obsesses about his lost brother, so much so that Oscar becomes his imaginary friend and then begins taunting him, a delusion that will continue throughout his life. In a particularly stirring passage, Langley recounts that, when committing the central crime of the book, his strangulation of six-year-old Jeremy Guillory, he was being harassed by a vision of Oscar and thought that he was actually strangling his dead brother.

Marzano-Lesnevich's treatment of Langley, and of other figures involved in his story, is a particularly empathetic act of imagination and is remarkably fair-minded. Although she only met once, briefly, with Langley and never talked to many of the other figures, she draws on extensive research of court documents as well as her narrative powers in order to vividly recreate the story of the child murderer, his family, the victim, the victim's family, and the town of Iowa, Louisiana, where the crime took place. She shows particular understanding in her sympathetic treatment of Lorilei Guillory, the mother of the victim, who says she does not forgive Langley but nonetheless pleads with a jury that he not be executed. This complex figure and her story capture Marzano-Lesnevich's (and the reader's) imagination. As the author confesses, "When I began writing this story I thought it was because of the man on the tape. I thought it was because of Ricky. In him I saw my grandfather. I wanted to understand. But I think now I write because of Lorilei."

Marzano-Lesnevich's vivid re-creations of many scenes at which she was not personally present pose some interesting questions about her narrative concerns and about the methodology of the true-crime writer. She often attributes to her subjects thoughts that she could not know they are having and, by her own admission, changes some facts for smoother storytelling. Although these are techniques that all nonfiction writers use at times, here they contribute to the feeling that the author is stretching the truth a little too far for the sake of narrative. But this feeling itself becomes especially interesting when one considers that the whole book is, in the end, a meditation on the process of narrative making, a process that the narrator herself comes to distrust.

Alexandria Marzano-Lesnevich was the recipient of the 2010 Rona Jaffe Foundation Writers' Award for nonfiction and has received fellowships from the Mac-Dowell Colony, the Yaddo artists' community, and the National Endowment for the Arts, among other honors. She teaches at the GrubStreet creative writing center in Boston and is an adjunct lecturer in public policy at the John F. Kennedy School of Government at Harvard University. The Fact of a Body *is her first book.*

In the book's introduction, Marzano-Lesnevich details the legal concept known as proximate cause. Because events do not exist in a vacuum, but are related to other events in a long chain of causality, it can be difficult to determine exactly what event caused another event. If a person is hurt or suffers damages, it is the job of the jury to decide whether another person is at fault; because there are often many other possible events that may have caused a given injury, the lawyers attempt to show the "proximate cause" of the event in question, the one incident that is most responsible for the damages. It is an inexact science, a narrative fiction that is necessary to the proper functioning of the legal system. As Marzano-Lesnevich writes, "The idea of proximate cause is a solution. The job of the law is to figure out the source of the story, to assign responsibility. The proximate cause is the one the law says truly matters. The one that makes the story what it is."

Marzano-Lesnevich's project then becomes one of complicating this neat legal fiction and showing that life is far more complex than the stories we tell to make sense of it. If she goes into her investigation seeing Langley only as refracted through her grandfather, then she soon learns that there is far more to his story than that of a simple pedophile. Similarly, as a memoirist, she also learns that there are no simple solutions, and so, in presenting her own life, she teases out the varied implications of her abuse and her family's unsettling reaction to it. (They make sure it does not continue, but they do not acknowledge it, and they proceed as if nothing has happened.)

In the end, Marzano-Lesnevich comes to reject the fictions that allow this reductive understanding. "What I fell in love with about the law so many years ago was the way that in making a story, in making a neat narrative of events, it finds a beginning, and therefore cause," she writes. "But I didn't understand then that the law doesn't find the beginning any more than it finds the truth. It creates a story. That story has a beginning. That story simplifies, and we call it truth." In investigating the twin cases of her own life and Ricky Langley's, she performs a skillful high-wire act between adhering to narrative and questioning and complicating that narrative. If people do not impose any stories onto their lives, she understands, then all they are left with is a bunch of raw facts and events that become meaningless. But forcing these facts and events into the too-tight yoke of narrative simplifies the lives involved and creates a similar lack of understanding. At times, *The Fact of a Body* tries too hard to have it both ways, as when Marzano-Lesnevich imagines Langley's life a little too vividly, but for the most part she maintains a fine balance.

Because she is dealing with memory, re-creation, and conflicting accounts, Marzano-Lesnevich realizes she cannot pin down one definitive truth. "The feeling" of chasing Langley's story, she writes, "is like chasing a memory that slips from your mind just as soon as you start to grasp it. Sure, it's dangerous to read metaphor into life; sure, it smacks of a desire to read meaning into cold fact, but doesn't all of this? All the facts in this case slip away from me the minute I try to grasp them." Reading meaning into cold fact, then, may be the special province of the lawyer, the memoirist, and the true-crime writer, Marzano-Lesnevich's three professions on display, but that does not mean that it is always a productive way to get at the truth. Marzano-Lesnevich's achievement here is to complicate the ways that people look at their lives and the lives of others, acknowledging the need to shape these existences into narrative while still remaining productively skeptical about the possibility that the narrative will ever approach anything like an objective truth.

Andrew Schenker

Review Sources

Bolin, Alice. "One Mystery Will Solve Another: Alexandria Marzano-Lesnevich's *The Fact of a Body*." Review of *The Fact of a Body: A Murder and a Memoir*, by Alexandria Marzano-Lesnevich. *Los Angeles Review of Books*, 9 July 2017, lareviewofbooks.org/article/one-mystery-will-solve-another-alexandria-marzano-lesnevichs-the-fact-of-a-body/. Accessed 6 Sept. 2017.

Bosson, Julia. "Say Everything: *The Fact of a Body* by Alexandria Marzano-Lesnevich." Review of *The Fact of a Body: A Murder and a Memoir*, by Alexandria Marzano-Lesnevich. *The Rumpus*, 20 June 2017, therumpus.net/2017/06/the-fact-of-a-body-by-alexandria-marzano-lesnevich. Accessed 6 Sept. 2017.

Skidelsky, William. "*The Fact of a Body* Review: A Tale of Two Crimes." Review of *The Fact of a Body: A Murder and a Memoir*, by Alexandria Marzano-Lesnevich. *The Guardian*, 20 May 2017, www.theguardian.com/books/2017/may/20/fact-of-a-body-alexandria-marzano-lesenevich-ricky-langley-child-killer-review. Accessed 6 Sept. 2017.

Tuttle, Kate. "A Murder, a Memoir and the Secrets That Bind Them Together." Review of *The Fact of a Body: A Murder and a Memoir*, by Alexandria Marzano-Lesnevich. *Los Angeles Times*, 16 June 2017, www.latimes.com/books/jacket-copy/la-ca-jc-fact-of-a-body-20170616-story.html. Accessed 6 Sept. 2017.

Van der Leun, Justine. "At a Law Firm That Defended a Child Murderer, an Intern Recalls Her Own Childhood Abuse." Review of *The Fact of a Body: A Murder and a Memoir*, by Alexandria Marzano-Lesnevich. *The New York Times*, 21 July 2017, www.nytimes.com/2017/07/21/books/review/the-fact-of-a-body-memoir-alexandria-marzano-lesnevich.html. Accessed 6 Sept. 2017.

Five-Carat Soul

Author: James McBride (b. 1957)
Publisher: Riverhead Books (New York).
320 pp.
Type of work: Short fiction
Time: Nineteenth to twenty-first centuries
Locale: United States

McBride offers a diverse collection of short stories and novellas, often dealing with African Americans but also featuring characters of many different backgrounds in many different settings.

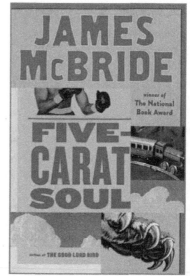

James McBride was already a notable writer and musician when he won a new level of attention and acclaim, as well as the National Book Award, for his stunning 2013 novel *The Good Lord Bird*. Many critics considered that work a true masterpiece of the finest kind—full of humor and horror, wit and pain, and propelled along by an unforgettable narrative voice that made each page seem like a revelation of a long-lost time and a genuinely complex human mind. The novel was often compared to Mark Twain's *Adventures of Huckleberry Finn*, not only because both have narrators who are naïve teenaged boys, but also through the use of phrasing that somehow seems both convincingly colloquial and instantly classic.

Five-Carat Soul, a collection of short stories and novellas, is McBride's first work of fiction since the triumph of *The Good Lord Bird*. And while the collection may not fully measure up to the standard set by the earlier novel, this is only to say what is true of many gifted writers: that their gifts appear only rarely in flawless form. Twain never wrote another book quite as perfect as *Huckleberry Finn*, and it remains to be seen if McBride will ever again achieve another work quite as impressive as *The Good Lord Bird*. In the meantime, though, the stories collected in *Five-Carat Soul* will impress many readers for many reasons. The individual works cover a wide range of subjects, characters, and settings, demonstrating McBride's skill in adapting his style into various perspectives while retaining a unique voice. Many of his trademark themes are present, including race, masculine identity, and American history.

McBride's gift for genuine literary inventiveness is on immediate display in the first paragraph of the book's very first story, a tale titled "The Under Graham Railroad Box Car Set." The story gets off to a vivid start as its narrator, who sells toys to collectors, lists all the different kinds of toys he sells. Early on, he recounts how in his youth he performed "in summer theater, best described as continually shouting 'Blow thou winter wind!' to retired New York garment workers who wouldn't know iambic pentameter from a pair of pliers." This type of quirky description is typical of

Courtesy of Chia Messina

James McBride is an acclaimed author of novels, memoirs, biographies, short fiction, and screenplays. His 1995 memoir The Color of Water *became a best seller and is considered a classic, while his 2013 novel* The Good Lord Bird *won the National Book Award. Also a successful tenor saxophonist, McBride received the National Humanities Medal in 2016.*

McBride at his creative best, and helps propel the story as the toy dealer struggles with the realization that the poor, deeply religious owner of an extremely valuable model train is trying to give it away for free. Elements of race and ethnicity (the dealer is Jewish, the train owner black), religion, and the legacy of slavery (the model train in question was made for Confederate general Robert E. Lee's son) underlie humorous dialogue, fusing thought-provoking questions with plain entertainment.

This collection's first story, like many others in the volume, ends with a surprise. Indeed, the stories so often conclude with something unexpected that readers may even begin to expect such twists, though they are well crafted. One of the most effective endings occurs in a tale title "Buck Boy," one of several interrelated stories about the hardluck African American teenagers in the Five-Carat Soul Bottom Bone Band. It exemplifies McBride at his best through a complexity of morality, tone, and style. In the story, a Chinese merchant named Mr. Woo shoots and kills a young African American man (the title character) who attempted to rob his store. Such a premise could easily lead to a wholly predictable plot and subtext, but McBride is willing to risk writing with a kind of unexpected honesty in describing the characters and developing the action. There is drama, but also the kind of witty humor that appears often throughout the book—the narrator, describing a rotund reverend, says, "I seen him undress at the pool one time, and it took me five minutes to see all of him." The realistic blending of tones makes the central figures come to life; as in much of his fiction, McBride seems interested in doing real justice to his characters rather than depicting them stereotypically. The final impact of the story speaks for itself, making a rich moral point that McBride has no need to spell out. It is easy to imagine "Buck Boy" becoming a widely reprinted anthology piece, ripe for student discussion from multiple angles.

"Buck Boy" is also much shorter than most of the other pieces in the collection, and McBride arguably works best on smaller canvases. In the more concise works, intriguing characters, fascinating plots, and, above all, striking phrasing all make a lasting impact partly because the stories develop and end as quickly as they do. Another example is the genuinely moving story "Father Abe." It focuses on a group of young black orphans living in Richmond, Virginia, in the very last days of the Civil War. As the orphans move through the streets of the ruined city on their way to and from meals, they provide daily entertainment to a group of hard-working African American soldiers doing back-breaking work under the hot Virginia sun. The soldiers look forward to watching the orphans pass by each day—especially the smallest child, nicknamed "Little Abe Lincoln." They tease Little Abe, a winningly innocent character who is desperate for a father, that he is the son of President Lincoln, which he takes to heart. Revealing the story's outcome would diminish its impact, but the tale manages to be moving without being sentimental. Each of the characters is memorably drawn, and McBride combines humor and poignancy in ways that many readers will find appealing.

By contrast, the longer stories in *Five-Carat Soul* can seem to lag or run out of energy. A story called "The Moaning Bench" comes close, at first, to recreating some of the magic of *The Good Lord Bird*, with almost every sentence leaving a memorable impression. A motley assemblage of characters suddenly find themselves sitting in hell while being grilled by a character named the Gatekeeper, who, it soon becomes clear, is Satan operating as a kind of insult comic who makes Don Rickles seem the soul of kindness. Both the premise of the story and the snappy dialogue are exceptionally inventive, but this work, like several others in the collection, goes on too long, eventually losing much of its striking impact. In this case, the tale begins to flounder when a boxer who sounds exactly like Muhammad Ali appears. At this point, McBride sounds as if he is transcribing someone else's words rather than creating his own.

"The Moaning Bench" ends, as several of these pieces do, with prose that rather bluntly spells out an already obvious moral. At times this somewhat old-fashioned tactic works, invoking fables or the earnest words of down-home preachers to create an interesting, if nostalgic, tone. In other places, however, it risks veering into sentimentality or detracts from the characters' realism. For example, in "The Moaning Bench," the symbolism of the tale's ending is clear enough without it being spelled out as directly as McBride eventually does. As in many of his other works, McBride embraces many Christian themes. While generally these add to the richness of the writing, there is also occasionally a didactic impulse that can distract, as opposed to the example of *The Good Lord Bird*, in which situations and characters were allowed to speak for themselves in immensely complicated ways. Especially in the context of other contemporary literature, the tendency to moralize may be jarring.

On the other hand, McBride's commitment as an unusually compassionate writer, one who lacks the cynicism that often passes for wit in literary fiction, can be refreshing. A good example comes in the form of the five pieces that make up the book's last entry, a novella titled "Mr. P and the Wind." Set in a zoo, these chapters show the inner lives of the animals there, who communicate telepathically with each other and eventually one human. McBride originally conceived the idea to help his nephews overcome their fear of the zoo, but it works as more than a children's story by including the author's trademark bold approach to deep themes and strong humor. Though such a fantasy may seem out of place among the more realistic stories that make up the rest of the book, its success is a testament to McBride's skill as a storyteller.

Reviews of *Five-Carat Soul* were almost uniformly positive, with critics lauding it as a highly successful first pass at short stories from an already multitalented writer.

Particular praise was given to McBride's deft characterization and his ability to both uplift and challenge the reader at the same time. In a review for *NPR*, for example, Michael Schaub wrote, "The characters in this book—human and otherwise—feel real and beautifully drawn, and their stories are bound to stay with readers for a very long time." Writing for the *New York Times*, Tayari Jones suggested that McBride practically invents "a new genre" through the "sweet nostalgia" he incorporates into most of the stories, mixing contemporary literary style with older forms. Some critics did note the occasional issue with pacing and the risk of sentimentality posed by the nostalgic tone, but the consensus was that the collection is a worthy effort from a proven artist.

While in the end *Five-Carat Soul* may not equal *The Good Lord Bird*, this is arguably because they are not directly comparable. As a collection of stories rather than a novel, the newer book necessarily takes a more varied approach, bringing together disparate elements under the strength of the author's creative vision. Rather than seek to surpass his earlier work, McBride has taken his diverse talents in yet another direction, illuminating many of his favorite themes from a multitude of new angles.

Robert C. Evans, PhD

Review Sources
Alexander, Donnell. "The Light in Black America: 'Five-Carat Soul' by James McBride." Review of *Five-Carat Soul*, by James McBride. *Los Angeles Review of Books*, 26 Sept. 2017, lareviewofbooks.org/article/the-light-in-black-america-five-carat-soul-by-james-mcbride/#!. Accessed 7 Dec. 2017.
Bentley, Rosalind. Review of *Five-Carat Soul*, by James McBride. *Star Tribune*, 22 Sept. 2017, www.startribune.com/review-five-carat-soul-stories-by-james-mcbride/446580683/. Accessed 7 Dec. 2017.
Jones, Tayari. "A Set of Brilliant Miniatures by the Author of 'The Good Lord Bird.'" Review of *Five-Carat Soul*, by James McBride. *The New York Times*, 23 Oct. 2017, www.nytimes.com/2017/10/23/books/review/james-mcbride-five-carat-soul-stories.html. Accessed 7 Dec. 2017.
Schaub, Michael. "James McBride's 'Five-Carat Soul' Is a Gem." Review of *Five-Carat Soul*, by James McBride. *National Public Radio*, 26 Sept. 2017, www.npr.org/2017/09/26/548665579/james-mcbride-s-five-carat-soul-is-a-gem. Accessed 7 Dec. 2017.

The Future Is History
How Totalitarianism Reclaimed Russia

Author: Masha Gessen (b. 1967)
Publisher: Riverhead Books (New York).
515 pp.
Type of work: Current affairs, history
Time: 1980s–2017
Locale: Russia

In The Future Is History, *Masha Gessen, a prolific Russian American journalist, provides a somber account of the degeneration of the post-Soviet Russian Federation into a dictatorship headed by Vladimir Putin. Instead of a traditional historical narrative, Gessen tells this story by tracing the lives of several individuals, some of them born in the 1980s, who lived through the tumult that followed the collapse of the Soviet Union.*

Courtesy of Riverhead Books

Principal personages

VLADIMIR PUTIN, President of the Russian Federation
MIKHAIL GORBACHEV, last leader of the Soviet Union
BORIS YELTSIN, first President of the Russian Federation
ALEXANDER YAKOVLEV, politician who encouraged reforms in the Soviet system
YURI LEVADA, sociologist who studied the effects of totalitarianism on Soviet citizens
BORIS NEMTSOV, political reformer and democratic activist in the post-Soviet era
SERYOZHA, the grandson of Alexander Yakovlev
ZHANNA, the daughter of Boris Nemtsov
MASHA, an organizer of opposition to Vladimir Putin
LYOSHA, an academic and gay activist
MARINA ARUTYUNYAN, a psychoanalyst
LEV GUDKOV, a student of Yuri Levada who continues his sociological analyses of
    the Russian people
ALEXANDER DUGIN, a nationalist theoretician who provides ideological support to
    the Putin regime

Masha Gessen's personal history prepared her well to write the story of the Vladimir Putin's consolidation of power in the post-Soviet Russian Federation. Born in Russia, she twice had to flee her homeland. In 1981, Gessen's Jewish family escaped Russian anti-Semitism by immigrating to the United States. Gessen returned a decade later as a journalist and covered the collapse of the Soviet Union. Unfortunately, over the next two decades she witnessed the failure of efforts to create a true democracy in Russia.

A critic of President Putin's political and social policies, she was forced to move to the United States in 2013. In many ways *The Future Is History* is her story as well as that of her country.

Gessen's approach to her account of the reemergence of the totalitarian temptation in Russia echoes the expansiveness and ambition of great Russian novelists such as Leo Tolstoy, Boris Pasternak, and Alexander Solzhenitsyn, both in page number and moral seriousness. She tells her tale on a grand scale, alternating between descriptions of important political developments and examination of the lives of people living through these events. Gessen chooses to frame her narrative around seven people whose varying stories capture important aspects of Russian political and social history from the break-up of the Soviet Union to the present. She looks at four individuals born in the 1980s who came of age in the period when it seemed briefly possible that democracy might come to Russia. These include two young men and two young women.

Born to privilege, Seryozha is the grandson of Alexander Yakovlev, a Soviet official who promoted Mikhail Gorbachev's policy of glasnost, or openness. Lyosha emerged from a much humbler background as the son of a provincial school official. Masha grew up with a single mother who became a budding small-scale entrepreneur in post-Communist Russia. Zhanna's father was the charismatic prodemocracy politician Boris Nemtsov. Gessen's other three protagonists are all intellectuals. Marina Arutyunyan studied psychology and became one of Russia's first psychoanalysts with credentials recognized in the West. Lev Gudkov is a sociologist who studied and collaborated with Yuri Levada, who became well known for analyzing the effects of totalitarianism on the Russian people. Alexander Dugin is a bit of an odd man out for Gessen. An autodidact, Dugin synthesized elements from communism, fascism, Orthodox Christianity, and a reflexive anti-Westernism into a virulent Russian nationalism. Dugin's ideas have proved increasingly influential in recent years and provided an ideological rationale for supporters of Putin's autocracy.

Gessen provides a clear-eyed and unsparing postmortem report on the descent of the Russian Federation into what she argues is essentially tyranny. In her view, Russian democracy was not assassinated by a cabal of high-placed conspirators—Putin is portrayed as the beneficiary of a resurgent totalitarian impulse, not its agent. The bitter truth, she argues, is that the whole nation was complicit in democracy's demise. History weighs heavily in Gessen's political autopsy. Arguably Russian democracy was doomed from the start because centuries of czarist despotism and seventy years of Soviet oppression left the nation unprepared for a path so radically different. At the end of 1991, Russians were presented with an opportunity to create an equitable and law-abiding society that respected human rights and gave citizens a meaningful voice in their governance. Unfortunately, the Russian people and the leaders they embraced were unable to meet this challenge.

Gessen addresses this theme early, with a discussion of Gorbachev's attempt to reform the Soviet system in the 1980s. Yakovlev, a government point man for this initiative, found it impossible to make serious headway because the Soviet officials charged with making changes resisted reforms that threatened their cherished prerogatives.

These bureaucrats could not adapt to the imperatives of market forces or adjust to a modicum of free expression.

That the apparatchiks of the Soviet regime could not accept new ways is unsurprising. More interesting is the reaction of ordinary Russians. Westerners might assume that they yearned for freedom, but Gessen takes pains to explain that the reality was more complicated. One of the effects of the 1917 Bolshevik Revolution and the subsequent repression of dissident opinions was to cut Russians off from currents of thought developing in the West and elsewhere. This extended beyond political and economic ideas. In the hermetically sealed intellectual atmosphere of the Soviet Union, where Marxism and Communist Party orthodoxy could not be challenged, the human sciences atrophied. There was no room for psychological or sociological exploration of Russian reality when objective class relations purportedly explained everything, and any research critical of the official party line could end a career or worse. As a result social science in-

Courtesy of Tanya Sazansky

Masha Gessen is a Russian American journalist. Her reporting has appeared in publications such as the New York Times, *the* New York Review of Books, *and the* New Yorker. *She is the author of several books, including* The Man Without a Face: The Unlikely Rise of Vladimir Putin *(2012) and* The Brother: The Road to an American Tragedy *(2015).*

evitably descended into propaganda. After more than two generations of Soviet rule, the Soviet people had little means to understand themselves.

This is why Gessen focuses on two people attempting to comprehend the Russian experience. Arutyunyan addressed the effects of the Soviet system on individuals, waging a long battle to gain training and accreditation in Western psychoanalysis. Gudkov worked to unravel the effects of totalitarianism on the mass of his fellow citizens. Gudkov was a protégé of Yuri Levada, a self-trained sociologist who dared to study the structures of Soviet society. In the late 1980s, as Gorbachev launched his unsuccessful attempt to salvage the Soviet Union, Levada hypothesized that a totalitarian social order required a particular type of citizen to remain stable. He argued that the resulting "Homo Sovieticus" was shaped into a subservient conformist who relied on state paternalism, but otherwise cultivated a defensive self-isolation. Homo Sovieticus stubbornly clung to a "hierarchical egalitarianism," enforcing a shared equality of misery amongst the masses while deferring to the governmental apparatus which guarded the narrow paths to advancement. Levada believed that Homo Sovieticus would disappear as the older generation raised under Communism passed away, and a new breed used to greater liberties took their place. Gudkov would join Levada in tracking this social transformation through a program of extensive polling.

At first events seemed to bear out the assumption that Russians were prepared to embrace radical change. In 1991, when Soviet hardliners attempted to depose Gorbachev and reverse his reforms, large crowds rallied around Boris Yeltsin as he defied this old guard. When the coup fizzled out, Yeltsin declared the end of the Soviet Union. The Russian Federation was born amid hopes that it would usher in a new era of liberty and democracy. But from the first the new order proved fragile. A chaotic reorganization of the economy left much of the nation's wealth in the hands of a few well-connected oligarchs. Economic hard times and disastrous inflation led to misery, insecurity, and a growing nostalgia for the predictability of the past. Yeltsin crushed a parliamentary revolt against his authority with tanks. He stumbled into a ruinous war with the breakaway republic of Chechnya. After briefly touting the democratic reformer Boris Nemtsov as his successor, Yeltsin instead promoted the career of Vladimir Putin, a former KGB officer adept at bureaucratic machinations.

Once elected president, Putin began solidifying his control over the government, aided at first by rising Russian oil revenues which engendered a period of prosperity in the first years of the new century. His personal popularity helped Putin crush opposition to his increasingly authoritarian rule. Carefully monitoring Russian public opinion through these tumultuous years, Gudkov and his colleagues were stunned to discover that Homo Sovieticus did not disappear as they had anticipated; instead the attitudes fostered during totalitarianism showed a resurgence in the early twenty-first century. The controversial Dugin flourished, attracting popular attention and winning official favor as he purveyed a fashionable rationale for the growing hostility to democracy.

Gessen's four younger subjects felt the sting of Russia's trajectory from totalitarianism to dictatorship. Seryozha lived for a time in Ukraine. Mindful of the family tradition of political reformism, he came home to Moscow to vote, only to discover that the election was a farce, with government candidates guaranteed victory. Lyosha became a university professor and gay activist. During the Putin years homosexuality was increasingly stigmatized, with gay people seen as a threat to the traditional family values championed by the authorities. Lyosha eventually moved to the United States and settled in New York City, finding work with a nonprofit focused on AIDS. Masha emerged as a vocal member of the prodemocracy opposition to Putin and associated with the protest band Pussy Riot. Though legally harassed by officials, she worked for an organization created by the exiled dissident businessman Mikhail Khodorkovsky. Zhanna worked as a journalist. Her father, Boris Nemtsov, remained an outspoken advocate for democracy and became one of the most prominent critics of President Putin. In 2015 Nemtsov was gunned down on a bridge within sight of the Kremlin. Zhanna moved to Bonn and worked for a German broadcasting company, doing interviews on a web-based program aimed at Russians.

Gessen's bleak account of the triumph of Homo Sovieticus over democracy holds out little hope for Russia. According to the author, the bitter truth is that Putin could never singlehandedly have engineered the revival of Russian autocracy. Gessen ends her main narrative with the Arutyunyan meditating on Sigmund Freud's theory of the death drive—she wonders if her country wants to destroy itself. Gessen's convincing study serves as a warning that such fears are well founded.

Critics responded positively to Gessen's sprawling analysis, with many citing it as a timely work in light of Russia's efforts to influence the 2016 US presidential election. Some reviewers, such as Francis Fukuyama for the *New York Times*, hesitated to label Russia fully totalitarian due to Putin's lack of a clear ideology. But most agreed Gessen provides considerable evidence that Russia is far from the path of democracy.

Daniel Murphy

Review Sources

Cottrell, Robert. "Russia's Gay Demons." Review of *The Future Is History: How Totalitarianism Reclaimed Russia*, by Masha Gessen. *The New York Review of Books,* 7 Dec. 2017, pp. 36–38.

Hayford, Elizabeth. Review of *The Future Is History: How Totalitarianism Reclaimed Russia*, by Masha Gessen. *Library Journal,* 1 Sept. 2017, pp. 133–34.

Freeman, Jay. Review of *The Future Is History: How Totalitarianism Reclaimed Russia*, by Masha Gessen. *Booklist,* Sept. 2017, p. 10.

Fukuyama, Francis. "The Spector of Homo Sovieticus: Masha Gessen Recounts the Experiences of Seven People Living in Post-Communist Russia." Review of *The Future Is History: How Totalitarianism Reclaimed Russia*, by Masha Gessen. *The New York Times Book Review,* 22 Oct. 2017, p. 17.

Review of *The Future Is History: How Totalitarianism Reclaimed Russia*, by Masha Gessen. *Publishers Weekly,* 28 Aug. 2017, p. 118.

Kotkin, Stephen. "Lamenting the Motherland." Review of *The Future Is History: How Totalitarianism Reclaimed Russia*, by Masha Gessen. *The Wall Street Journal,* 18 Oct. 2017, www.wsj.com/articles/review-lamenting-the-motherland-1508365046. Accessed 6 Feb. 2018.

Gather the Daughters

Author: Jennie Melamed
Publisher: Little, Brown (New York). 352 pp.
Type of work: Novel
Time: The near future
Locale: An unnamed island

Gather the Daughters *is a work of speculative fiction about a group of teenage girls who live on a dystopian island where misogyny reigns. It is American author Jennie Melamed's debut novel.*

Courtesy of Little, Brown Company

Principal characters

VANESSA, a teenage girl who is a voracious reader and whose father is a wanderer
CAITLIN, a shy teenage girl whose family is newer to the island and who is regularly beaten by her father
JANEY, a teenage girl who has been starving herself as an act of rebellion
AMANDA, a newly married teenage girl who is expecting a child

Author Jennie Melamed has said that her inspiration for her debut novel, *Gather the Daughters* (2017), has been many years in the making. As a psychiatric nurse who specializes in children's behavioral health, she has regularly worked with sexual abuse survivors. In addition to being heartbroken by the trauma that her patients endured by the very adults who were supposed to be their caretakers, she was shocked by the overwhelming number of survivors. The sexual abuse of girls and young women, it seemed, was far more prevalent than she previously thought.

Gather the Daughters takes an unfiltered look at this issue and aims to illustrate how quickly and easily a society can permit and excuse sexual abuse. A work of speculative fiction, it depicts a small, religious community inhabiting an unnamed island in what appears to be the near future. Descended largely from ten families, this community lives by the creed that the love between a father and daughter is sacred. Incest is encouraged as long as the daughters are prepubescent. Once they begin to menstruate, the young women are then forced to pick a husband, marry, and begin having babies. By the time they are in their late thirties and have teenage grandchildren of their own, the women are forced to drink lethal poison known as their "final draft." Ultimately, it is a culture that poses as pious and principled but in fact uses religion as a means of control to make women view their bodies as nothing more than vessels for male pleasure and reproduction.

Gather the Daughters is a work of feminist dystopian fiction that belongs in the canon with Margaret Atwood's *The Handmaid's Tale* (1985). Like Atwood, Melamed succeeds at taking the oppression women face in contemporary patriarchies and demonstrating what would happen if such oppression were taken one step further. In *The Handmaid's Tale*, this resulted in a fictional world where women are forced to marry autonomous men or become pregnancy surrogates. While extreme, the story is not entirely unbelievable, as it echoes the puritanical belief that the role of women should be that of an obedient wife and mother. In *Gather the Daughters*, Melamed accomplishes a similar feat by depicting a culture that accepts the sexual abuse of girls as normal. Although it may be difficult to accept that any group of people would ever allow incest and pedophilia, it is important to note that parts of Melamed's narrative are inspired by stories of real religious cults. And while mainstream society does not accept sexual abuse, it can be argued that it does not do enough to curb its occurrence, which ruins the lives of so many people.

A large part of what makes *Gather the Daughters* engaging is its unique literary style, structure, and tone. The book is written predominantly in the third-person, present tense point of view—a choice that amplifies its eeriness by seemingly suggesting that the story is taking place now. Its narrative is organized into multiple story lines, with each chapter following a different protagonist. Melamed's cast is composed exclusively of teenage girls, each navigating the island society's oppression in different ways. There is fourteen-year-old Amanda, who, after years of being abused by her father, is married to a young man whom she actually loves and is expecting a child. When she discovers that her baby is a girl, however, she becomes determined to move away from the island so that she can offer her child a better life. Meanwhile, the characters of Caitlin (a quieter girl who is especially harshly abused by her drunken father) and Vanessa (who is often reading the books that her father, a wanderer responsible for obtaining supplies from outside of the island, brings home) are still viewed as children by their community and subsequently have not been forced to become the property of men. Still, they dream of a bigger world and are fascinated by the stories they hear about the "wastelands" that exist outside of the island. Finally, there is Janey, a seventeen-year-old who rebels against cultural expectations by refusing to allow her father to touch her. In an effort to postpone marriage and children, she starves herself so that she cannot menstruate. By telling the story through more than one of these young, entrapped women facing the same doomed fate, Melamed creates a tone that is both dark and innocent.

The world-building of *Gather the Daughters* is highly impressive. The island's culture revolves around the worshipping of the residents' ancestors, the small group of men who founded the community after some unclear event in the "wastelands" caused them to migrate there. There are specific rules within the community, known as "shalt-nots," that everyone must obey. By describing the smallest of details that comprise her characters' everyday lives, Melamed ensures that the world feels fleshed out and real to the reader. For example, the mosquitoes are so bad in the summer that the adult men walk around covered in metallic netting. To get to the mysterious "wastelands," the community's wanderers must climb aboard boats captained by a tongueless ferryman. Most intriguing, however, are all of the rituals and ceremonies that take place on the island. Every summer, the children are allowed to run around outside without supervision. Free of clothes and the community's oppressive rules, these months become a utopia of joy and innocence. Once girls begin menstruating, however, they must undergo a "summer of fruition," wherein they have sexual relations with all of the single men in the community before choosing one to marry. Ultimately, the culture that Melamed has created for the island is otherworldly yet somehow intriguingly believable.

Gather the Daughters explores a number of different themes. Perhaps the most important of these is that of womanhood. It can be argued that one of Melamed's primary purposes in writing the novel is to examine what it means to be born female in an oppressively misogynistic society. Consequently, her young protagonists grapple with the idea that their purpose is to serve the needs of men. Eventually, they realize that they are capable and deserving of more and begin a resistance by tapping into the very strength, intelligence, and independence they were told their gender lacked. Another important theme is that of innocence. Despite the fact that most of her characters are put into sexual scenarios where they are treated as adults, Melamed strictly portrays them as children in their thoughts, feelings, and actions. As a result, it becomes painfully clear just what a valuable force innocence is and how wrong it is for adults rob children of it.

Jennie Melamed is a psychiatric nurse practitioner who specializes in working with traumatized children. Gather the Daughters *is her debut novel.*

More than anything, however, *Gather the Daughters* is a story of abuse and survival. Throughout the novel, Melamed succeeds in her mission to bring the issue of widespread sexual predation into focus. She illustrates how, even though abuse survivors find ways to cope with trauma, they have been irreparably harmed. Furthermore, she shines a light on patriarchies and how any culture that devalues women essentially enables issues such as sexual abuse to occur regularly and without consequence. While Melamed does not demonize all of the male characters of her book, she does demonstrate the dangers of complicity in allowing women to be treated as bodies rather than human beings. Significantly, *Gather the Daughters* is a book that contextualizes the distorted ideas and forces behind sexual abuse while celebrating the strength of survivors.

Reviews of *Gather the Daughters* have been mixed. A common complaint among many of the critics who did not enjoy the book is that it is unoriginal. In her *USA Today* review, literary critic Zlati Meyer attributed the commercial success of *Gather the Daughters* at least in part to the fact that it was published within months of the television adaptation of Atwood's *The Handmaid's Tale*. Meyer called Melamed's novel, "Derivative at best and a faded photocopy at worst." The influence of Atwood is undeniably present throughout *Gather the Daughters* and it is likely that fans of *The Handmaid's Tale* will feel as though they are in familiar narrative territory. This is especially true in the way that both novels depict religious communities where the primary purpose of women is to serve men. Despite this, however, *Gather the Daughters* still feels as though it is exploring an entirely different issue. Where Atwood focuses on the systematic oppression of adult women, Melamed takes on the effects of oppression on young, developing girls, and the subsequent story is quite different.

Another issue that critics have taken with *Gather the Daughters* is the way that it portrays widespread sexual abuse. For many, reading about a community that openly accepts incest and pedophilia is too pessimistic and disturbing. In her review for the *Independent*, Lucy Scholes wrote, "Melamed certainly doesn't revel in titillation, but I had to wonder whether adult human nature really is as perverse, cruel and blindly unquestioning as she seems to believe." It is true that, at times, reading a story about a place where most of the young protagonists have been continuously raped by the men in their families and community can be overwhelming. However, Melamed rarely provides details about the traumatic events that her characters endure at the hands of their fathers and other men but instead alludes to them in a matter-of-fact way. Still, the idea is disturbing and likely to alienate some readers.

Critics who claimed *Gather the Daughters* as one of the best books of the year have been quick to extol Melamed's skill in navigating complex, horrific social issues. *Kirkus Reviews* called her debut novel "fearsome, vivid, and raw." It is well-deserved praise; even those who are disturbed by the story cannot deny the fact that it is unapologetically bold and well written. This was also the sentiment of the reviewer for *Publishers Weekly*, who stated, "Melamed's prose is taut and precise. Her nuanced characters and honest examination of the crueler sides of human nature establish her as a formidable author." Ultimately, the novel will be enjoyed by many speculative fiction and feminist dystopian fans alike. With an important premise, imaginative setting, and relatable protagonists, *Gather the Daughters* proves to be an exceptional debut from an author who will hopefully continue to use fiction as a platform to address serious social and gender issues.

Emily Turner

Review Sources

Review of *Gather the Daughters*, by Jennie Melamed. *Kirkus*, 2 May 2017, www.kirkusreviews.com/book-reviews/jennie-melamed/gather-the-daughters/. Accessed 25 Jan. 2018.

Review of *Gather the Daughters*, by Jennie Melamed. *Publishers Weekly*, 22 May 2017, www.publishersweekly.com/978-0-316-46365-2. Accessed 25 Jan. 2018.

Heltzel, Ellen Emry. "*Gather the Daughters* Review: A Grim Outlook for Women in a Fictional Dystopian World." Review of *Gather the Daughters*, by Jennie Melamed. *The Seattle Times*, 24 July 2017, www.seattletimes.com/entertainment/books/gather-the-daughters-review-a-grim-outlook-for-women-in-a-fictional-dystopian/. Accessed 25 Jan. 2018.

Meyer, Zlati. "Debut novel *Daughters* Recycles *The Handmaid's Tale*." Review of *Gather the Daughters*, by Jennie Melamed. *USA Today*, 25 July 2017, www.usatoday.com/story/life/books/2017/07/25/debut-novel-daughters-recycles-handmaids-tale/493966001/. Accessed 25 Jan. 2018.

Scholes, Lucy. "*Gather the Daughters* by Jennie Melamed, Book Review: I Doubt
    It Will Become a Cult Classic." Review of *Gather the Daughters*, by Jennie
    Melamed. *Independent*, 26 July 2017, www.independent.co.uk/arts-entertainment/
    books/reviews/gather-the-daughters-jennie-melamed-the-handmaids-tale-
    a7860906.html. Accessed 25 Jan. 2018.

Ginny Moon

Author: Benjamin Ludwig
Publisher: Park Row Books (New York). 368 pp.
Type of work: Novel
Time: Present day
Locales: Various locations in the United States

Ginny Moon *is the story of an autistic teen who struggles with being understood as her adoptive parents prepare for the birth of a child.*

Principal characters
GINNY MOON, an autistic teen
GLORIA LEBLANC, her birth mother
BRIAN, her adoptive father
MAURA, her adoptive mother
WENDY, her newborn sister, Brian and Maura's baby
CRYSTAL WITH A C, her aunt, Gloria's sister
PATRICE, her counselor

This debut novel by Benjamin Ludwig approaches autism and the issues surrounding adoption from an autistic child's perspective. Narrated in the first person by the central character, autistic teen Ginny Moon, it is the story of a girl whose self-awareness is often underestimated. Ginny knows she is treated differently and that she has autism and developmental disabilities, and through her compelling point of view, Ludwig brings a fresh and engaging voice to her story. Though the idea of making a person with a developmental disability the narrator of a novel is not unique, Ludwig's focus on autism in combination with the issues of child abuse and adoption provides an original story that is, at turns, joyous, heartbreaking, and frustrating.

Family is one of the most important themes in Ginny's story. Just turning fourteen, she has been shuffled around numerous times since she was taken from the apartment of her birth mother, Gloria, when she was nine. Ginny has little confidence in the adults in her life. She tells readers, "Before I was adopted I tried to run away three times from my different Forever Homes but the police always found me and brought me back." Those homes did not provide the security that Ginny needed, so she attempted to leave. With Brian and Maura, the parents who adopt her and who are the novel's primary minor characters, Ginny experiences some security for the first time; she refers to the two as her Forever Mom and Forever Dad.

The emotional and physical abuse Ginny suffered in Gloria's care so affected her that she cannot stop worrying about those she feels are more vulnerable than she is. Shortly after the novel begins, the reader learns that Maura is pregnant, and she eventually gives birth to a baby named Wendy. The baby is one of those more vulnerable people Ginny worries about, and her Baby Doll is the other. The adults believe that when Ginny talks about her Baby Doll, she is speaking about a toy. The reader later learns, however, that Baby Doll is Ginny's younger sister, whom she took care of while living with Gloria. To curb Ginny's anxieties, a health teacher at her school gives her a robotic plastic baby doll to help her model appropriate care of a baby and prepare her for being a big sister to Wendy.

Ginny's attempts to return to Gloria to check on Baby Doll are the basis of much of the drama in the story. She is obsessed with Baby Doll because she fears that she is the only one who knows how to care for her and, if left with Gloria, she is sure that Baby Doll will be abused. Ginny reaches out to Gloria and plots her own kidnapping to get back to Baby Doll. Her obsession with Baby Doll is continually misperceived by the adults. Even her Aunt Crystal and Gloria, who both know that Baby Doll is a real child, ignore or misunderstand Ginny's anxiety about Baby Doll's welfare. It is only when Ginny's counselor, Patrice, learns the truth about Baby Doll that the girl's concern is acknowledged.

Throughout most of the book, the adults miss many subtle clues about Baby Doll. The fact that Ginny calls her aunt "Crystal with a C" and will not let anyone call her Crystal should imply the importance of names for Ginny, but even when the adults in her life realize that Baby Doll is a child, they do not make a connection to the child's name as "Krystal with a K." Ginny, unfortunately, also misses something significant regarding her younger sister. She understands that time has passed in her own life, but she does not comprehend that same change for Baby Doll, and her inability to see Baby Doll as a six-year-old child leads to significant confusion for her later in the book.

The abuse and neglect Ginny suffered when she lived with Gloria motivates most of Ginny's actions throughout the novel, especially those actions she knows are wrong. Gloria's boyfriend, Donald, also participated in abuse of the girl, and though it is never clearly confirmed, there are hints that he sexually abused Ginny. The story briefly introduces Ginny's birth father, Rick, whom she comes to appreciate, but her manipulation of him to help with her plan to return to Gloria and Baby Doll and his inability to comprehend the depth of abuse that Ginny experienced with Gloria end the relationship before it can develop into any form of true attachment.

Ginny's difficult background complicates her behavior throughout the book, leading to misunderstandings that almost tear apart her stable life with Brian and Maura. Her fear of Gloria is clearly revealed throughout the novel, and Gloria's temper creates fear in Maura, too, when Gloria unexpectedly visits Ginny at Brian and Maura's house. Ginny's obsessive worrying is based on her knowledge that "Gloria can't take care of my Baby Doll. They don't understand she gets mad and hits. . . . Gloria needs someone with her all the time or my Baby Doll will suffer serious abuse and neglect which is what happened to me."

Ginny's inability to completely understand what is happening in the world around her influences the poignancy and humor of the novel's narrative voice. Because she takes things literally, she often misses subtle differences in meaning. For instance, after Wendy's birth, Maura breastfeeds the baby. Ginny knows that babies need milk to survive because she had been told to give milk to her plastic doll, so when she insists that Wendy needs milk, she cannot comprehend that breast milk is better than the cow's milk from the carton. She tells Brian, "That isn't real milk. Real milk comes from the refrigerator."

What Ginny does understand, on the other hand, is numbers. She equates numbers and mathematics with order, and that provides comfort and helps her to cope. Certain numbers are symbolic for her, as well. Every morning, she eats nine grapes for breakfast. She goes to bed at nine o'clock every night, and a change from that routine causes her stress. The number nine is important because it is symbolic of the age when she was taken from Gloria's household. She also creates associations between abstract ideas such as her feelings in mathematical terms. Time is also structured around mathematical principals that she creates. The author reflects her connection to time in his organization of the novel, which is structured in chapters based on times of day, specific days of the week, and months. The story begins with the chapter headed "6:54 at Night, Tuesday, September 7th" and progresses through to "Exactly 4:35 in the Afternoon, Thursday, January 27th." This precision is reflective of Ginny's need to order her world.

Ginny Moon is Benjamin Ludwig's first full-length book. This book was inspired by his own family's fostering and adoption of an autistic teen and her preparation for the Special Olympics.

The way others perceive Ginny's ability to comprehend is the basis of much of the irony and pathos in the novel. At the beginning of the story, when she hides her plastic doll that is supposed to be training her to deal with a new baby in the house, Maura becomes frightened of the girl. This instance, in conjunction with Gloria's later visit, leads to Maura retreating from what had been a positive relationship with Ginny, and after Wendy's birth, Maura isolates Ginny from the baby. Ironically, Maura cannot comprehend that Ginny has more experience in taking care of a baby than she does.

As Ludwig has expressed in the press and on his website, he and his wife are also adoptive parents of an autistic child and his parenting experiences helped him create Ginny's particular voice and motivations. Therefore, he introduces a variety of other issues into her life that characterize some children on the autism spectrum, as well as challenges that occur for families in fostering and adoption. Ginny's agitation often shows itself in the form of excoriation. Early in the novel, Brian notices that Ginny has been picking at her skin. Brian's own health becomes another complication in the plot. With his stress over his newborn, Gloria's visits to their home, and Ginny's behavioral issues, his existing heart problem becomes more problematic. This health concern further challenges the stability in Ginny's Forever Home.

Details of Ginny's schooling are also woven into the story. Her education in Room Five introduces other children who have special needs as secondary characters. The focus on special needs is further emphasized when she goes to basketball practice in preparation for participation in the Special Olympics. What happens to an autistic child who manifests difficult behavior is addressed with the suggestion that Ginny may need to go to a boarding school where she cannot harm others. She dubs the school St. Genevieve's Facility for Girls Who Aren't Safe, and when she stands up for herself by saying she does not want to be sent away, an emotional barrier is broken, illustrating a desire for attachment to Brian and Maura that begins to turn her home life back in the positive direction it was headed before her behavioral issues.

The reviews of *Ginny Moon* were primarily positive. Deborah Donovan wrote for *Booklist*, "Ginny is remarkably engaging, and Ludwig has surrounded her with other strong characters, each of whom navigates her compulsive behavior and unpredictability in their own ways." The critic for *Kirkus Reviews* also commented on the strength of the narrative voice in the novel, while Beth E. Andersen, reviewing the book for *Library Journal*, claimed, "This stunning debut novel grabs readers by the heart and doesn't let go," and referred to Ginny as "one of the truest voices in modern literature." At the same time, other criticism found the abrupt nature of the narrative voice, marked by short sentences, too repetitive.

Theresa L. Stowell, PhD

Review Sources

Andersen, Beth E. Review of *Ginny Moon*, by Benjamin Ludwig. *Library Journal*, 15 Mar. 2017, p. 110.

Donovan, Deborah. Review of *Ginny Moon*, by Benjamin Ludwig. *Booklist*, 15 Mar. 2017, p. 18.

Review of *Ginny Moon*, by Benjamin Ludwig. *Kirkus Reviews*, 1 Mar. 2017, p. 223.

Review of *Ginny Moon*, by Benjamin Ludwig. *Publishers Weekly*, 6 Feb. 2017, p. 45.

Stuart, Jan. "Debut Novels for Armchair Olympians, Rom-Com Fans, and More." Review of *Ginny Moon*, by Benjamin Ludwig, et al. *The New York Times Book Review*, 16 June 2017, www.nytimes.com/2017/06/16/books/review/debut-novels-for-armchair-olympians-rom-com-fans.html. Accessed 8 Sept. 2017.

The Girl in Green

Author: Derek B. Miller (b. 1970)
First published: *The Girl in Green*, 2016, in Australia
Publisher: Houghton Mifflin Harcourt (Boston). 336 pp.
Type of work: Novel
Time: 1991, 2013
Locales: Iraq, Syria, England

A fierce indictment of warmakers and peace negotiators entangled in the complex politics of the Middle East, The Girl in Green *spans more than two decades of sectarian conflict. The taut, sometimes farcical narrative demonstrates both the ultimate senselessness of war, as well as the opportunity for personal redemption for individuals swept up in the chaos of battle.*

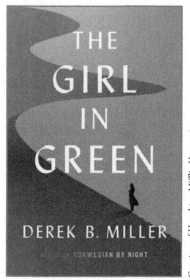

Courtesy of Houghton Mifflin Harcourt

Principal characters

ARWOOD HOBBES, a US soldier who served at a remote Iraqi outpost in 1991
THOMAS BENTON, a British war correspondent
MÄRTA STRÖM, a Swede who is project director for the United Nations High Commissioner for Refugees (UNHCR) in Iraqi Kurdistan
HERBERT "HERB" RESTON, an African American former US Special Forces sergeant who works with Märta
FRANÇOIS ARMAND, a.k.a. Tigger, a French North Atlantic Treaty Organization (NATO) observer who works with Märta
LOUISE BALLAN, Swiss-born head of the International Committee of the Red Cross in Iraq
JAMAL AL KHEDAIRY, a young Iraqi who drives for Märta
ADAR AL-KAYSI, a teenaged girl dressed in green, who survives a mortar attack
LIEUTENANT HARVEY MORGAN, Hobbes's commanding officer

The Girl in Green is structured like a classical three-act play. "Part I: An Early Spring: 1991" of the novel serves as the first act, in which the main characters, the setting, and the major conflict of the story are introduced. In Miller's work, this section is told in the third person, past tense. The story opens in mid-1991 following the ceasefire that ended Operation Desert Storm, the first Gulf War in Iraq. As the curtain rises, the focus is on a young US Army private, Arwood Hobbes, of Third Squadron, Second Cavalry Regiment. He is stationed at a remote outpost, a former oil refinery in the Iraqi desert about 150 miles from the Kuwaiti border, designated Checkpoint Zulu. Arwood, manning a sandbagged machine gun emplacement in view of the village of Samawah a mile away across the ceasefire line, is supremely bored. As he waits for something to happen, he is approached by Thomas Benton, a middle-aged London *Times* journalist embedded with Arwood's company. The two men talk about the current situation, agreeing that a civil war, with vicious fighting between the country's two main Islamic sects, the Sunnis and the Shiites, will probably soon begin.

To relieve the tedium of inaction, Benton offers to walk into Shiite-controlled Samawah to fetch ice cream. Soon after he reaches the town, Iraqi ground forces arrive. Iraqi Army helicopter gunships appear over Samawah; without warning they destroy a hospital with rockets and machine-gun a refugee camp. Refugees flee toward the American base, and the commander, Lieutenant Harvey Morgan, orders his men to take them in, tend to the wounded, and feed them, but he stresses they are not to fire back unless fired upon.

Arwood notices that Benton is not among the rescued townspeople and deserts his post to look for the journalist. In the village, Benton, though stunned by the suddenness of the attack, is unharmed. He begins working his way back toward the American base, along the way encountering a teenaged girl in a green dress sheltered behind a burning truck. Together, Benton and the girl move toward Checkpoint Zulu as Arwood arrives, and all three run toward the American lines. Just before they reach safety, however, they are surrounded by Iraqi troops. A mustachioed Iraqi colonel demands they leave the girl behind, but Arwood, defiant and feeling protective toward the girl, pulls out a pistol and threatens the Iraqi officer. Lieutenant Morgan appears, ordering Arwood to put his weapon away. As the trio attempts to cross the last hundred feet to the ceasefire line, the Iraqi colonel shoots the girl in the back, and she dies in Arwood's arms. The soldier wants to shoot the colonel in retaliation, but Benton stops him.

Upon entering Checkpoint Zulu, Morgan orders Benton off the base and then berates Arwood in front of the other soldiers for leaving his post. When he makes a disparaging remark about the dead girl, Arwood attacks Morgan and beats him severely. Though he receives a less-than-honorable discharge for deserting his post and for attacking a superior officer, Arwood escapes a court-martial, which would undoubtedly have resulted in prison time. There is a good reason why Arwood gets off lightly: a court-martial would result in bad press for the military. The international media covering the war is already highly critical, particularly as the US commander, General Norman Schwartzkopf, had permitted Iraqi helicopters to fly during the ceasefire. The resulting bloody suppression of rebellion against Iraqi president Saddam Hussein was already being blamed on the Americans.

After being dismissed, Benton leaves for north Iraq and joins civilians in taking refuge in the mountains after a Kurdish assault on Saddam Hussein fails. There, the disgraced Arwood arrives as part of a humanitarian relief effort. They encounter several other characters who will figure prominently in the rest of the story: Swedish United Nations refugee project manager Märta Ström (with whom Benton has a brief affair), African American US Special Forces sergeant Herb Reston, and a French NATO observer nicknamed Tigger. They are all witnesses to a botched American air drop of food to the refugee camp—some people are crushed by heavy pallets of supplies, and others are injured when a case of frozen whole chickens breaks open scatters like flying bowling balls. Arwood demonstrates his humanitarian concern by risking his life to rescue a frightened Kurdish boy from a minefield.

The second act, which traditionally encompasses the story's rising action, offering complications that build upon the initiating incident and the opportunity for character development, is titled "Part II: The Long,

An international affairs specialist, Derek B. Miller's first book was his dissertation, Media Pressure on Foreign Policy: The Evolving Theoretical Framework *(2007). His debut novel,* Norwegian by Night, *which was first published in Norway in 2010 and in the United States in 2013, won the John Creasy Dagger Award and other honors. His third novel,* American by Day, *is scheduled for release in 2018.*

Cold, Hard, and Dark of It." To differentiate this section from the preceding one, Part II (like Part III) is told in third person, present tense, which gives the events more immediacy and lends additional tension. Readers are informed that Part II occurs twenty-two years later, in 2013.

Thomas Benton, now in his early sixties, has returned to the Middle East on what he assumes will be his final assignment, shortly after finding his wife in bed with another man. Out of the blue, he has received a phone call in England from Arwood Hobbes, who tells him about a recent video showing a girl in a green dress visible just before a mortar explosion. Benton watches the video in question, and the girl does indeed resemble the teenager they tried to rescue in 1991. Benton, feeling responsible for what happened decades earlier, agrees to meet Arwood in Iraq. Arwood, now in his mid-forties, is still lean and fit and has acquired tattoos on his knuckles: "More" and "Less." The two men are reunited with Märta (she and Benton resume their affair), and with Herb and Tigger, who work with Märta and the International Refugee Support Group (IRSG). Arwood and Benton explain why they are there, to try to find the girl in green captured days earlier in the video and to rescue her if she is alive.

Märta takes Benton and Arwood to see Louise Ballan, the Swiss-born head of the local International Red Cross. Despite the long odds of being able to accomplish their objective, Benton and Arwood are allowed to pursue their mission, which will take them through a series of hostile territories occupied by various tribal and Islamic militias before they reach the spot where the girl in green was last seen. They are given headsets and call signs, detailed maps, phones, and a driver, Jamal, for the 1990s Toyota Corolla in which they will travel.

Though the intrepid travelers have been given specific instruction about when, where, and how they should check in, the headstrong Arwood asks Jamal to detour to a small village. While the others wait in the car, Arwood goes off alone for a time before returning. As they return to the main highway, Benton asks what he has done. Arwood tells him he tracked the Iraqi colonel who shot the original girl in green to this village and killed him. Benton frets that Arwood's rash act will cause the Iraqi military to hunt them; if they are caught they will be locked in an Iraqi prison beyond hope of rescue.

As they near their destination, Arwood orders another detour onto a dirt road. They find the remains of a humanitarian convoy and scattered bodies. In one ruined truck, they find the only survivor: the girl in green, named Adar, who has subsisted on rations over the four days since the mortar attack. They begin the trek back but their journey is interrupted by a terrorist attack during which Benton, Arwood, Adar, and Jamal are captured and spirited away to a secret hideout in the mountains.

The third act, in which the main story and its subplots are typically resolved, is titled "Part III: Other Than Honorable." In this final, exciting section are detailed the efforts of the captives to resist physical and psychological torture while their colleagues with the refugee groups and Red Cross frantically work to locate and extricate them before a planned military assault is carried out in the territory where they are thought to be held. Miller delivers a satisfying, if unexpected, conclusion to his novel which, by turns, gives readers a pulse-pounding thriller, a character study of individuals wracked with guilt for their inability to prevent incidents beyond their control, and a perceptive insight into the myriad problems involved when outsiders meddle in Middle Eastern complexities.

Jack Ewing

Review Sources

Ealy, Charles. "'The Girl in Green' Is a Smart Thriller out of the Wars in Iraq, and a Quest for Hope." Review of *The Girl in Green*, by Derek B. Miller. *Dallas News*, 5 Jan. 2017, www.dallasnews.com/arts/books/2017/01/05/girl-in-green-derek-b-miller-thriller-book-review. Accessed 18 Sept. 2017.

Hardy, Karen. "Derek B. Miller's *The Girl in Green* Makes Sense of the Middle East." *Sydney Morning Herald*, 12 Aug. 2016, www.smh.com.au/entertainment/books/derek-b-millers-the-girl-in-green-makes-sense-of-the-middle-east-20160714-gq5q4c.html. Accessed 18 Sept. 2017.

Harrison, Stephenie. "*The Girl in Green*: Taking a Risk for a Second Chance." Review of *The Girl in Green*, by Derek B. Miller. *Bookpage*, Jan. 2017, bookpage.com/reviews/20759-derek-b-miller-girl-green. Accessed 18 Sept. 2017.

Hartlaub, Joe. Review of *The Girl in Green*, by Derek B. Miller. *Book Reporter*, 6 Jan. 2017, www.bookreporter.com/reviews/the-girl-in-green. Accessed 18 Sept. 2017.

Kidd, James. "*Girl in Green*, Thriller Set in War-Torn Iraq, Leaves Indelible Mark." Review of *The Girl in Green*, by Derek B. Miller. *Post Magazine*, 25 Jul. 2017, www.scmp.com/magazines/post-magazine/books/article/1992814/book-review-girl-green-thriller-set-war-torn-iraq. Accessed 18 Sept. 2017.

Toohey, Elizabeth, "'The Girl in Green' Tells a Dark, Funny, Poetic Tale of the US in Iraq." Review of *The Girl in Green*, by Derek B. Miller. *Christian Science Monitor*, 16 Jan. 2017, www.csmonitor.com/Books/Book-Reviews/2017/0116/The-Girl-in-Green-tells-a-dark-funny-poetic-tale-of-the-US-in-Iraq. Accessed 18 Sept. 2017.

Glass House
The 1% Economy and the Shattering of the All-American Town

Author: Brian Alexander (b. 1959)
Publisher: St. Martin's Press (New York).
336 pp.
Type of work: Current affairs
Time: 1947–2016, primarily 2014–16
Locale: Lancaster, Ohio

Glass House *traces the rise and fall of an "all-American" corporate town through the complexities of the conjoined fates of the Anchor Hocking corporation and the town of Lancaster, Ohio. The narrative opens when town and corporation had a local and at least somewhat symbiotic relationship. Author Brian Alexander traces the economic, social, and psychological fallout for Lancaster following the shattering of this paradigm by international investment models.*

Courtesy of Macmillan

Principal personages

BRIAN GOSSETT, a Lancaster resident and employee of Anchor Hocking
CARL ICAHN, an investor and corporate raider
ISAAC J. COLLINS, the founder of Hocking Glass Company
J. RAY TOPPER, the chief executive officer (CEO) of Anchor Hocking from 1982 to 1987
LLOYD ROMINE, a local drug dealer
MARK KRAFT, a local drug dealer and addict
SAM SOLOMON, the CEO of Anchor Hocking from 2014 to 2015

The central protagonists of *Glass House: The 1% Economy and the Shattering of the All-American Town* are not people. Rather, they are a place (the city of Lancaster, Ohio) and a corporation (Anchor Hocking, inclusive of its many name changes). Having grown in Lancaster from its founding in 1905, Anchor Hocking remains the city's dominant economic force in the present day. A glass manufacturer, the corporation also lends its trade to the book's title, which plays on glass production, the collapse of American industry, and the concept of home.

Brian Alexander dispenses with the history of the symbiotic relationship between town and corporation in a single, foundational chapter. The balance of the book focuses on a shifting economic and social model that began to transform Anchor Hocking, along with much of the international world of finance, in the early 1980s. The principal chronological focus of the text takes place between 2014 and 2016, during which time a disastrous purchase of the company by Monomoy Capital Partners drastically depleted the financial resources of Anchor Hocking and degraded its physical plant. The corporation filed for bankruptcy in 2015, after more than a century of solid, if not always stellar, financial performance. Though Anchor Hocking survived the bankruptcy, Alexander leaves the reader uncertain of the company's future.

Anchor Hocking permeates *Glass House*, but the book is also concerned with the city of Lancaster, which Alexander dubs "the all-American town" in homage to a 1947 *Forbes* magazine issue that featured Lancaster as a model American town. As Alexander demonstrates, the original social contract between corporation and town meant that corporate leaders resided in, and invested in, the community. Schools were stable, and there were numerous outlets for social life and indicators of civic health. As the corporation gradually withdrew its economic footprint from the town, redirecting its wealth toward the world of New York City finance, Lancaster suffered. Schools collapsed, infrastructure began to fail, and the population of the town was subjected to the psychological effects of watching their home deteriorate, all while continuing to perform hard labor for the corporation.

During the period from 2014 to 2016, the years on which *Glass House* focuses, Lancaster was in the midst of an extreme drug epidemic that dominated all the resources of local law enforcement and drained the few remaining social support structures. Alexander weaves a complex investigative web, encompassing economics, personalities, and civic intrigue, in order to demonstrate how the free-market model of capitalism has unraveled his case-study town. Although the book is very specific to Lancaster, Ohio, Alexander's premise is that the story of this "all-American town" reflects the broader narrative of the United States. Lancaster is Alexander's hometown, so he is able to speak with trusted sources and get a deep perspective on the challenges faced by residents, but he is also far enough removed from the town's daily life to not be excessively biased by this personal association. Through the personal stories of Lancaster's (would-be) workers, Alexander is able to trace the plight of the American working family in light of the winner-take-all model of free-market capitalism in which they labor. His attention to the history of union representation for Anchor Hocking's employees also plays a key role in this narrative.

The social impact of economic models is at the heart of Alexander's analysis. This facet of his subject is generally addressed with journalistic clarity, through specific narratives of events or individual accounts of experiences, rather than through complex economic jargon. The exception to this is also a crucial framing chapter of the book—chapter 3, titled "Triggering Events"—which addresses a watershed moment for Anchor Hocking: investor Carl Icahn's 1982 purchase of 6 percent of the company's shares in a corporate raid aimed at furthering his agenda to increase corporations' profit margins for their investors. Although Anchor Hocking bought out Icahn, Alexander identifies this exchange as a turning point for Lancaster, noting that it caused panic in the corporate headquarters and put the company "'in play' by turning the old-time manufacturer to chum in shark-infested financial waters." A few years later, in 1987, another financial firm, Newell Corporation, purchased Anchor Hocking for $338 million. Arguably, Anchor Hocking would have faced these same pressures sooner or later, but the events that did transpire allow Alexander the opportunity to explore in somewhat greater depth the free-market models that were of such interest to Icahn and to the influential economic theorist Milton Friedman. Importantly, Alexander notes, Friedman "linked threats to the free market with existential threats to America itself," thus positing unregulated corporate profit seeking as in the national interest and opposition to it as unpatriotic.

As *Glass House* unfolds, the reader is able to explore how financial firms ran roughshod over this productive glass factory—exploiting its resources, forcing the factory to carry debt that was incurred in other branches of their investments, and levying fees, interest, and expertise charges that were oppressive for the company to service. All in all, the book reveals with dismal clarity how even a skilled factory worker has seen conditions, satisfaction, and reward for labor deteriorate since the 1980s, while financial investment firms have seen astronomical increases in wealth and virtually no controls. When Monomoy drives Anchor Hocking into bankruptcy, for example, the investment firm nevertheless makes vast profits and still maintains a controlling hold on the corporation after the completion of the bankruptcy proceedings.

In Alexander's narrative, the world of international finance is patently to blame for the degradation of Anchor Hocking and the collateral damage done to Lancaster. But these investment firms remain relatively anonymous in the account. Their records are difficult to crack because of various techniques used to maximize profit, minimize exposure, and obfuscate corporate relationships. Further, individual employees of the firms cannot be discussed with the depth and

Brian Alexander has written for numerous periodicals, including the New York Times, Science, Esquire, *and the* Atlantic, *and has been a contributing editor for* Wired *and* Glamour *magazines. In 2007, he was named a third-place winner of the John Bartlow Martin Award for Public Interest Magazine Journalism, awarded by Northwestern University's Medill School of Journalism. His previous books include* Rapture: How Biotech Became the New Religion *(2003) and* America Unzipped: In Search of Sex and Satisfaction *(2008).*

sensitivity that Alexander is able to award to Anchor Hocking employees—from the humblest position all the way up to the CEO—largely because these employees simply decline to speak with Alexander or answer his communications. Thus, while there is an unseen and poorly understood enemy in the account, the people of Lancaster become the primary interest of the narrative.

Alexander introduces a large number of Lancaster characters; indeed, perhaps too many for readers to effectively trace their stories and connect with each individual's role in the larger puzzle of the town. Common among them is a sensation of hopelessness, often paired with depression, and a feeling that the surrounding community has become unmoored. Though many of the figures depicted have multigenerational relationships with Lancaster, they seem uncertain of what the town continues to offer them. Nevertheless, their family bonds, lack of education, and limited resources prevent them from moving away. The social bonds of the town have completely collapsed between the generations. Among the younger citizens of Lancaster, drug use is rampant, adding a further layer of corrosion to society. Alexander gives particular attention to characters dealing drugs and also to those suffering from drug addiction, considering their roles within the complex set of unfortunate circumstances leading to the economic implosion of Lancaster. Of these stories, only one concludes on a positive note.

Generally, the reader is left with few windows for optimism, as the sun is clearly setting on this corporate town. Alexander characterizes Lancaster as a town that is too big to disappear completely as its corporate structure falters, but too small to easily re-create itself. While Lancaster's leaders attempt to remake the town as a tourist destination or a commuter bedroom community, the residents continue to suffer. The loss of Lancaster's working-class citizens is palpable throughout the book. In his conclusion, Alexander emphasizes that the tone of progress and urban reimagining fails to connect with the town's residents. He concisely states the central problem: "To so blithely dismiss the value of community was to pretend there was no loss. But there was, and the effects of that loss continued to ripple throughout the town." Although the future fate of Lancaster is unclear—it could successfully be reenvisioned, or it could degrade even further—Alexander emphasizes that the city will never be able to "recapture . . . the spirit of what it once was."

Because of this premise, reviewers have turned to *Glass House* as one source for understanding the 2016 political climate of the United States, a reality that lurks in the background of Alexander's final chapters. Yet the social and economic phenomena explored here far precede the contemporary social crisis in the United States and speak, instead, to economic and political decisions made over the last several decades—decisions at the national level that have contributed to the shattering of Lancaster. *Glass House* is a significant study for those interested in gaining a long view on the ongoing social, political, and economic changes in the United States, albeit through a localized lens. It will also have enduring value for its perceptive ability to lay bare the corrosive force of the unregulated financial market and for making a powerful economic case for the value of community investment.

Julia A. Sienkewicz

Review Sources

Review of *Glass House: The 1% Economy and the Shattering of the All-American Town*, by Brian Alexander. *Kirkus*, 23 Nov. 2016, www.kirkusreviews.com/book-reviews/brian-alexander/glass-house-economy/. Accessed 8 Nov. 2017.

Review of *Glass House: The 1% Economy and the Shattering of the All-American Town*, by Brian Alexander. *Publishers Weekly*, 28 Nov. 2016, www.publishersweekly.com/978-1-250-08580-1. Accessed 8 Nov. 2017.

Lowenstein, Roger. "The Death of the All-American Town." Review of *Glass House: The 1% Economy and the Shattering of the All-American Town*, by Brian Alexander. *The Wall Street Journal*, 17 Feb. 2017, www.wsj.com/articles/the-death-of-the-all-american-town-1487364666. Accessed 7 Nov. 2017.

Miller, Laura. "'This Is My *Town*.'" Review of *Glass House: The 1% Economy and the Shattering of the All-American Town*, by Brian Alexander. *The Slate Book Review*, 3 Feb. 2017, www.slate.com/articles/arts/books/2017/02/brian_alexander_s_glass_house_about_lancaster_ohio_reviewed.html. Accessed 7 Nov. 2017.
O'Kelly, Kevin. "*Glass House* Views the Rise and Fall of US Industrialism through One Town." Review of *Glass House: The 1% Economy and the Shattering of the All-American Town*, by Brian Alexander. *The Christian Science Monitor*, 23 Feb. 2017, www.csmonitor.com/Books/Book-Reviews/2017/0223/Glass-House-views-the-rise-and-fall-of-US-industrialism-through-one-town. Accessed 7 Nov. 2017.

Glass Houses

Author: Louise Penny
Publisher: Minotaur Books (New York). 400 pp.
Type of work: Novel
Time: Present day
Locales: Three Pines, Québec; Montréal, Québec

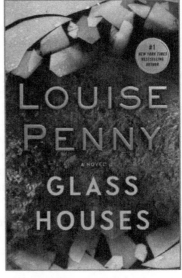

Armand Gamache is confronted with a murder in his small town of Three Pines, but murder is the least of his problems as he and his team plot to take down at least one major case of criminal activity in Québec.

Principal characters

ARMAND GAMACHE, chief superintendent of the Sûreté du Québec
REINE-MARIE GAMACHE, his wife
JEAN-GUY BEAUVOIR, his second-in-command and son-in-law
BARRY ZALMANOWITZ, a Crown prosecutor
KATIE EVANS, an architect
PATRICK EVANS, her husband
MAUREEN CORRIVEAU, a judge
ISABELLE LACOSTE, chief inspector of the homicide division
ANTON LEBRUN, a dishwasher at the local bistro
JACQUELINE MARCOUX, a pastry chef at the local bakery

Crime has returned to Three Pines, and Armand Gamache, the new chief superintendent of the Sûreté du Québec, is forced to look at his friends and neighbors differently. This thirteenth installment of Louise Penny's Chief Inspector Armand Gamache series features a mysterious murder in Three Pines, courtroom drama, and an investigation of corruption at the highest levels of government. Though *Glass Houses* can be read as a stand-alone book, the reader will benefit from familiarity with at least the two previous books, *The Nature of the Beast* (2015) and *A Great Reckoning* (2016), which establish the corruption that Gamache previously exposed in the Sûreté and explain how he came out of retirement.

Like many of the earlier novels in the series, *Glass Houses* is multilayered in its timeline, setting, and plot. The novel begins with Armand Gamache in a Montréal courtroom on a hot summer day, testifying in the case of the murder of architect Katie Evans in Three Pines the previous winter. This murder is not the main plot of the novel, but merely a thread in a twisted braid of suspense. The setting moves between the small village of Three Pines, the courtroom, and Gamache's offices in the city of

Montréal. Katie's murder is depicted in flashbacks. The town's church, St. Thomas, is added to the list of places that may be familiar to readers of the other books in the series, while the town center becomes shadowed by dark events. Three Pines also becomes the central location for the climactic action at the end of the novel.

This novel, like the previous books in the series, explores the issue of government corruption, but it also incorporates the topics of opioid addiction and drug trafficking. Though Gamache feels that the so-called war on drugs has been lost, he enlists leaders throughout his department in a fight to radically change the direction of the way that the drug-trafficking case is being handled. He and his allies—Jean-Guy Beauvoir, his second in command, and Isabelle Lacoste, the head of the homicide division—put their careers on the line in the battle, while still struggling with the decisions they must make; at one point, Beauvoir says to Gamache, "What's heading for the border isn't a weight, isn't a number. There's no measure for the misery that's heading our way. A slow and wretched death. . . . How many people, alive today, healthy today, will die, sir, or kill? Because of your 'rational' decision?" When Gamache discovers that Three Pines is a central location for the smuggling of dangerous drugs across the nearby Vermont border, he has even more motivation to stop the problem. Katie Evans's murder, the trial, Gamache's plot to save his country, and issues of conscience are intertwined in a complicated knot that will lead to what could be a tragic end.

Penny's skill in weaving together an engaging and suspenseful narrative is also demonstrated in her use of symbolism, the most notable example of this being the glass houses of the title. Katie Evans and her husband, Patrick, are both architects, best known for their designs of glass houses, and the glass houses that they and their friends live in are presented as revealing details about their lives in the search for Katie's murderer. More importantly, the symbol of the glass house is also used to represent the investigative branch of the Sûreté, and perhaps even the whole country; as Judge Maureen Corriveau struggles with her own conscience over understanding what Gamache and Barry Zalmanowitz, the chief Crown prosecutor, are doing with the trial, she muses, "Canada had a great reputation for law and order, as long as you didn't look under the table." Past scandal has left the public with a lack of faith in government leadership, and as Gamache and his team plot to win a battle against the insidiousness of the drug cartels, they build a house around themselves that seems too fragile to withstand the approaching storm.

There are several historical references that add depth to the story line. Readers learns about the *cobrador del frac*, a kind of debt collector in Spanish culture, of which there are two forms: the modern cobradors, dressed in suits, top hats, and gloves, who seek financial reparations; and the original cobradors, dressed in black robes that completely disguised their identities, who sought reparations for moral debts. These original cobradors, it is later revealed, sought not to exact revenge but rather "to accuse and expose. To act as a conscience." When a cobrador appears on the green in the center of Three Pines shortly before Katie's murder, the townspeople are agitated. Penny later foreshadows a second connection between the cobrador and Gamache's investigations: "The bell jar had expanded again, the cobrador's world was swelling, his dominion growing, while theirs seemed to be collapsing into itself." Penny also

Louise Penny is a former journalist who began writing fiction in her forties. Glass Houses *is the thirteenth novel in her Armand Gamache series, for which she has won numerous awards, including six Agatha Awards for best contemporary novel.*

weaves in details about the Nuremburg trials of Holocaust participants that followed World War II to expand on the theme of ethics and the conscience, specifically referencing Adolf Eichmann's defense that he was not responsible for the atrocities he committed because "he was just following orders." This comparison further complicates Gamache's scheme to stop the flow of dangerous drugs between Canada and the United States and challenges his conscience over the potential damage that will be done as he waits for the right time to act.

Penny continues to engage readers with her characterizations, both of figures from the previous books and of the new characters she introduces. Among these new characters are Anton and Jacqueline, two new Three Pines citizens who work in the local bistro and as the new pastry chef in the town bakery, respectively; these two likable characters seem to fit in well with Three Pines society, but they also bring mysterious backgrounds to the drama. Gamache's kindness is especially emphasized, but his willingness to sacrifice almost everything to bring an end to the war on drugs provides another layer of depth to this popular character. Additional details about his family life are explored, and Beauvoir, who is also his son-in-law, receives further character development as his faith in Gamache's plan is tested.

Though the heavy topics dealt with in the main plot—drug trafficking and murder—are treated with due seriousness, Penny does insert a few comedic moments to lighten the reading. Followers of the series will expect village poet Ruth and her duck Rosa to provide humor, and Penny does not disappoint. On one notable occasion, Gamache muses on the physical resemblance between Ruth and Rosa; later, he mentally draws parallels between Ruth and Beauvoir, amusing himself with the thought that his son-in-law "resemble[s] a drunken old woman." Other characters are similarly paired for comedic effect, as when Lacoste observes about Gamache and Beauvoir, "If ever two men were made for cahoots, it was these two. They were cahootites."

Glass Houses received generally positive reviews. Sandra C. Clariday wrote for *Library Journal*, "For devotees of the series and for those new to the magic, this thirteenth visit to Three Pines represents those elements most of us crave—safety, belonging, security, and friendship—despite a bit of murder and mayhem." The reviewer for *Publishers Weekly* wrote, "The familiar, sometimes eccentric, denizens of Three Pines and Gamache's loyal investigative team help propel the plot to an exciting, high-stakes climax." *Kirkus Reviews* also lauded the plotline, commenting, "While certain installments in Penny's bestselling series take Gamache and his team to the far reaches of Québec, others build their tension not with a chase but instead in the act of keeping still—this is one such book. The tension has never been greater, and Gamache has sat for months waiting, and waiting, to act, with Conscience watching close by." Fans of the series will appreciate the author's note at the end, in which Penny remarks on personal events that took place during her writing of the book and provides additional information on the history of the cobrador.

Theresa L. Stowell, PhD

Review Sources

Clariday, Sandra C. Review of *Glass Houses*, by Louise Penny. *Library Journal*, 1 Oct. 2017, p. 43. *Literary Reference Center*, search.ebscohost.com/login.aspx?direct=true&db=lfh&AN=125401500&site=lrc-live. Accessed 31 Jan. 2018.

Review of *Glass Houses*, by Louise Penny. *Kirkus Reviews*, 15 June 2017. *Literary Reference Center*, search.ebscohost.com/login.aspx?direct=true&db=lfh&AN=123542250&site=lrc-live. Accessed 31 Jan. 2018.

Review of *Glass Houses*, by Louise Penny. *Publishers Weekly*, 26 June 2017, pp. 154–55. *Literary Reference Center*, search.ebscohost.com/login.aspx?direct=true&db=lfh&AN=123774570&site=lrc-live. Accessed 31 Jan. 2018.

Stasio, Marilyn. "Mythic Revenge, a Mythic Film and Possibly Mythic Memories." Review of *Glass Houses*, by Louise Penny, et al. *The New York Times*, 1 Sept. 2017, www.nytimes.com/2017/09/01/books/review/crime-louise-penny-glass-houses.html. Accessed 31 Jan. 2018.

Goethe
Life as a Work of Art

Author: Rüdiger Safranski (b. 1945)
First published: *Goethe: Kunstwerk des Lebens*, 2013, in Germany
Translated from the German by David Dollenmayer
Publisher: Liveright (New York). 688 pp.
Type of work: Biography
Time: 1749–1832
Locales: Germany, Italy

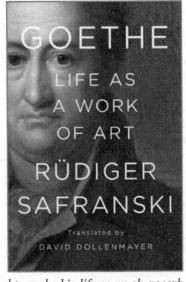

Courtesy of W.W. Norton

The distinguished German philosopher and biographer Rüdiger Safranski presents a comprehensive and compelling biography of Johann Wolfgang von Goethe. A multifaceted literary genius, over a long career Goethe produced novels, poetry, and plays, including his most celebrated masterpiece Faust *(1808–32). Safranski argues that Goethe worked to make his life as much a work of art as he did his writings.*

Principal personages

JOHANN WOLFGANG VON GOETHE, writer and statesman
KARL AUGUST, Duke of Saxe-Weimar-Eisenach, his longtime friend and employer
CHARLOTTE VON STEIN, his platonic friend
CHRISTIANE VULPIUS, his mistress and eventual wife
JOHANN GOTTFRIED HERDER, his friend and mentor; a philosopher
FRIEDRICH SCHILLER, his friend; a poet and playwright

Johann Wolfgang von Goethe defies easy categorization. He was a brilliant writer who, during a long life, poured out a seemingly endless succession of literary masterpieces that ranged from novels to plays to poetry of breathtaking beauty. Yet at the same time, Goethe embarked on a career of public service, serving Duke Karl August of Saxe-Weimar-Eisenach in a variety of capacities for most of his life. In addition, Goethe engaged in serious work in the natural sciences, studying and writing about plants, minerals, and light. Goethe was seen as a prodigy in his own day, helping ignite the cult of genius celebrated during the Romantic period. Today, it is easy to dismiss Goethe as a monument in German and European literature, more honored than read. Rüdiger Safranski takes up the challenge of reminding readers of the continuing relevance of the great German poet and statesman in his *Goethe: Life as a Work of Art* (2017; *Goethe: Kunstwerk des Lebens*, 2013).

Safranski is well suited to do this. Both a trained philosopher and an intellectual who has written biographies of great German thinkers and hosted a television show tackling philosophic issues, he expertly captures the inner world of a dynamic writer who, in his literary output, always sought to balance beauty and insight. Safranski is not interested in engaging in a historiographic debate with other biographers of Goethe. When writing his book, he largely ignored the vast secondary literature on Goethe and instead based his narrative and interpretations on a close reading of primary sources. Goethe left behind an enormous written record, not only his voluminous literary production, but thousands of letters and a detailed autobiography. Safranski makes brilliant use of this material, incorporating large amounts of it into his text and setting it off in italics instead of using the more cumbersome machinery of quotation marks and interrupting the flow of his narrative. The result is a surprisingly intimate account of the life of this great writer. Safranski is most interested in Goethe's inner life. While he adequately covers the details of his subject's public career, education, travels, publications, and service to the Duke of Weimar, Safranski the philosopher spends most of his hefty book exploring ideas. As the subtitle of his biography states, he believes that Goethe consciously shaped his life as a work of art. For Safranski, Goethe's life was a triumphant act of self-definition; succeeding in this, the writer, who was born during the Enlightenment, made a signal contribution to the increasingly individualistic Romantic period. This great artist, so deeply involved in giving his life aesthetic depth and form, in imbuing his existence with meaning, helped shape the emerging understanding of modern human beings—standing resolutely apart from both God and nature, establishing their own rules for life. Safranski presents Goethe as an exemplar who offered future generations an updated and compelling model of the good life.

Goethe was born in Frankfurt. His family belonged to the bourgeois upper class of the city; his father, a nonpracticing lawyer, held the honorable rank of imperial councilor. Frankfurt was a free imperial city of the Holy Roman Empire, and in his early days, Goethe was loyal to this increasingly ephemeral polity. He would never embrace nationalism and remained true to his early imperial predilections through his conception of himself as a man of the world. Goethe was trained to be a lawyer like his father, but his interests soon ran to poetry. As a result, his legal career was brief and undistinguished. Far different were his first forays into literature. Inspired by the adventures of a famous sixteenth-century German knight during the period of the Reformation, Goethe's play *Götz von Berlichingen* (1773) captured the imagination of audiences, who saw the eponymous hero as the embodiment of romantic individualism.

Goethe soon achieved even more sensational success. His novel *Die Leiden des jungen Werthers* (1774, *The Sorrows of Young Werther*) became an international best seller. The tale of a struggling artist whose love rejects him for a more conventionally prudent union with another man, the book partially mirrored Goethe's experience with depression and an unrequited romance. The protagonist of the novel goes far beyond Goethe's reaction to disappointment. Frustrated in love and overwhelmed by a *taedium vitae*, or a weariness of life, Werther shoots himself and dies while watched over by his grieving lover and her husband. This woeful but emotionally evocative tale resonated powerfully with a wide audience ready to slip the cultural restraints of the age of reason and embrace sensibility over sense. The book sold quickly, and had copyright laws been better, Goethe might immediately have become a wealthy man. Napoleon Bonaparte later told Goethe that he had read the novel seven times. Safranski dismisses the popular impression that *The Sorrows of Young Werther* set off a wave of suicides across Europe, but he discusses how the novel ignited the Sturm und Drang (storm and stress) movement in literature that heralded the coming of Romanticism. These works emphasized action and deep emotion. The Sturm und Drang writers also promoted the cult of genius, and for a time the creator of *The Sorrows of Young Werther* was their prime exhibit. Goethe distanced himself from what he saw as the enthusiastic excesses of these "stormy" authors.

In his midtwenties, Goethe was one of the most famous and respected writers in Germany. With this success, he sought activities in addition to writing. In 1775, he accepted the summons of Karl August, the young Duke of Saxe-Weimar-Eisenach. The duke was anxious to bring brilliant writers and thinkers to his small state. The poet Christoph Martin Wieland was his tutor. The presence of Goethe would help attract such luminaries as the philosophers Johann Gottfried Herder and Johann Gottlieb Fichte, as well as the poet and playwright Friedrich Schiller. The duke and Goethe became friends, and the young writer joined his young master in boisterous revels. But Goethe quickly became more than a courtier and playmate. In 1776, he was appointed to the duke's privy council. From that point on, he became an increasingly important minister of state. He acted as a diplomat, headed the duchy's War Commission, and supervised the highways and mines. Goethe would live in Weimar for the rest of his life, holding various offices, running the court theater for years, and serving as a trusted advisor to the duke. His official duties in the mines and elsewhere introduced Goethe to the serious study of the natural world. This would inspire him to publish a series of monographs on scientific subjects.

Rüdiger Safranski is a German philosopher, writer, and television host. He is the author of biographies of Friedrich Schiller, E. T. A. Hoffmann, Arthur Schopenhauer, Friedrich Nietzsche, and Martin Heidegger.

Goethe also continued to write poetry, plays, and novels. Though his governmental work in Weimar and his scientific investigations would sometimes take priority, his fertile genius never deserted a facile pen. Goethe was not someone who struggled with writer's block; writing came easily to him. When he worried that his bureaucratic duties were keeping him from finishing several works, a leave of absence in Italy from 1786 to 1788 enabled him to concentrate on his writing and absorb inspiration for new literary productions. Goethe often spent a long time bringing a work to completion, writing in spurts of activity amidst the varied interruptions of his busy life. The most famous instance of this is the inordinately protracted gestation and publication of *Faust* (1808–32). As early as 1772, Goethe had started writing *Faust*, a play that would become his masterpiece, and whose two parts he worked on for sixty years. Begun in his youth, he brought it to a conclusion as he neared his death.

Goethe lived through the tumult unleashed by the French Revolution. He accompanied the duke and a Prussian army in 1792 as it invaded France and attempted to crush the revolutionary regime. He experienced the French cannonade that turned back the Prussian forces and saved the French republic at the Battle of Valmy. Back home, he settled into domesticity with his mistress, Christiane Vulpius, whom he later married. He began an intense friendship with Friedrich Schiller that saw the men collaborate on many projects until Schiller's death in 1805. The next year the French arrived, as Napoleon routed Weimar's Prussian protectors. Goethe got along well with the French emperor and never shared the German nationalist passions that helped drive out the French in 1813. No more was he enthused by the liberalism and socialist idealism that began to challenge the restored monarchical order after the final defeat of Napoleon in 1815. Goethe was skeptical of political programs that he believed violated human nature and the lessons of history. He recognized that change was inevitable, and as an official himself, acknowledged that state action could ameliorate social problems. But he believed that gradual reform rather than revolution was the surest way forward.

Therefore, Goethe settled easily into the age of Klemens von Metternich, whose conservative policies he supported. He was equally aware of other forces transforming the world as he aged. Goethe lived into an era of increasingly dramatic economic and technological change. Before he died, railroads were beginning to transform travel and communications. In *Faust, Part Two*, Goethe has his hero save an empire's finances by manipulating its currency through an issue of paper currency. Goethe's Faust had become a capitalist who might have thrived speculating on a stock exchange. Having outlived most of his contemporaries, Goethe died not long after arranging a new complete edition of his works. He had prepared his own best monument.

Goethe was a man who lived his life most fully. Safranski helps his readers sense something of the awe that Goethe's contemporaries felt when confronted with a man who so completely embodied the classical ideal of the whole man. Implicit in Safranski's biography of the great writer is a challenge for even the least gifted to also, within their powers, make their lives works of art.

Daniel P. Murphy

Review Sources

Christensen, Bryce. Review of *Goethe: Life as a Work of Art*, by Rüdiger Safranski. *Booklist*, 15 Mar. 2017, www.booklistonline.com/Goethe-Life-as-a-Work-of-Art-Safranski-Rdiger/pid=8624154. Accessed 26 Feb. 2018.

Collins, Jeffrey. "The Genius of the Modern Age." Review of *Goethe: Life as a Work of Art*, by Rüdiger Safranski. *The Wall Street Journal*, 22 Sept. 2017, www.wsj.com/articles/the-genius-of-the-modern-age-1506108045. Accessed 26 Feb. 2018.

Hofmann, Michael. "He Built Roads. He Oversaw Mines. He Shrank the Deficit. He Was Johann Wolfgang von Goethe." Review of *Goethe: Life as a Work of Art*, by Rüdiger Safranski. *The New York Times*, 16 June 2017, www.nytimes.com/2017/06/16/books/review/goethe-biography-rudiger-safranski.html. Accessed 26 Feb. 2018.

Johnson, Daniel. "Getting to Grips with Goethe." Review of *Goethe: Life as a Work of Art*, by Rüdiger Safranski. *The New Criterion*, Sept. 2017, www.newcriterion. com/issues/2017/9/getting-to-grips-with-goethe-8759. Accessed 26 Feb. 2018.

Kirsch, Adam. "Design for Living." Review of *Goethe: Life as a Work of Art*, by Rüdiger Safranski. *The New Yorker*, 6 Nov. 2017, www.newyorker.com/magazine/2016/02/01/design-for-living-books-adam-kirsch. Accessed 26 Feb. 2018.

Mount, Ferdinand. "Super Goethe." Review of *Goethe: Life as a Work of Art*, by Rüdiger Safranski. *The New York Review of Books*, 21 Dec. 2017, www.nybooks. com/articles/2017/12/21/super-goethe/. Accessed 26 Feb. 2018.

Golden Hill
A Novel of Old New York

Author: Francis Spufford (b. 1964)
First published: 2016, in the United Kingdom
Publisher: Scribner (New York). 320 pp.
Type of work: Novel
Time: Largely 1746
Locale: New York City

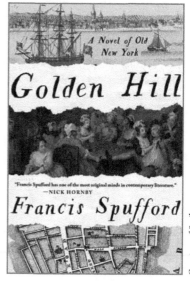

Francis Spufford's first novel, Golden Hill, *about power, artifice, and race, vividly conjures the city of New York in the years before the American Revolution.*

Principal characters
RICHARD SMITH, a young visitor from
    London
GREGORY LOVELL, a New York merchant
TABITHA, Lovell's daughter
SEPTIMUS OAKESHOTT, the New York governor's secretary

English writer Francis Spufford's debut novel, *Golden Hill: A Novel of Old New York*, is set in colonial New York City. (The title refers to an area in Lower Manhattan that became the site of a skirmish between British soldiers and the Sons of Liberty in 1770.) It is difficult for modern city dwellers to imagine the New York of 1746, which, as Spufford depicts it, more closely resembled a small town than a bustling international metropolis, but the author vividly conjures that world in language, sight, sound, and smell. Richard Smith, the twenty-four-year-old protagonist of *Golden Hill*, arrives from London as the book begins. He observes, appreciatively, the "bouquet" of New York as compared to the stench of old London: "A little fish, a little excrement; guts here, sh—— there; but no deep patination of filth, no cloacal rainbow for the nose in shades of brown, no staining of the air in sewer dyes." The authorial tone of this slightly bawdy description is indicative of the book as a whole. In an afterword, Spufford describes *Golden Hill* as a contemporary companion and homage to eighteenth-century works such as *Joseph Andrews* (1742), by Henry Fielding, and *The Adventures of David Simple* (1744), by Sarah Fielding. *Golden Hill* employs certain devices and affectations found in those novels; in addition to its comedy, social commentary, and swift and occasionally daring plot, the novel is written in the heightened voice of an eighteenth-century author—this affectation turns out, in the end, to be a clever device too.

Historical flourishes aside, the heart of *Golden Hill* lies in Smith's mysterious mission in the New York colony, the nature of which is a secret from everyone, including the reader, until the book's end. His legs still wobbling after months at sea, Smith presents himself at merchant Gregory Lovell's countinghouse door with a bill of exchange demanding a prodigious amount of money: over £1,700 in New York currency. Lovell is understandably suspicious. Smith, doing himself no favors, refuses to reveal his business with the money, but agrees to wait sixty days to claim it, long enough for more documentation to arrive from London to support his claim. Smith's attitude is strikingly reckless but also, in a contemporary reader's eyes, quintessentially American. "There's the lovely power of being a stranger," he tells Lovell, sounding like a colonial Jay Gatsby. "I may as well have been born again when I stepped ashore. You've a new man before you, new-made. I've no history here, and no character: and what I am is all in what I will be." In this picaresque tale, Smith's words prove ominous. Where there is great opportunity, there is also great danger; the subsequent events that unfold illustrate that Smith has no idea, at this point, what he has gotten himself into.

The most stunning achievement of *Golden Hill* is Spufford's attention to detail. For instance, Lovell wears a "bob-wig yellowed by tobacco smoke," and Tabitha, his sharp-witted and sometimes malicious daughter, stands uncomfortably in her elaborate dress at a party, "like a tall pole which in the wind happens to have become entangled in a cloth." His vision of old New York—lit by candles, cobblestones slick with rain—is similarly alive. He effectively conjures the blankets of snow that once buried the city in preindustrial days as well as the cozy, pine-wreathed Dutch celebration of Sinterklaas. In one early and harrowing scene, Spufford recreates the debauchery of Pope Day (or Guy Fawkes Day, as it was known in Great Britain), a celebration, then strongly anti-Catholic, in which revelers burn effigies of British Catholic dissident Guy Fawkes in huge bonfires in the street.

Smith watches the spectacle in wonder, but its undercurrent of violence alerts him to the frightening unknown of his journey and the strange new place where he has chosen to live. It occurs to him that there are thousands of miles of wilderness stretching westward in the darkness: "The awe and the fear of the New World broke in upon him. As if, till then, he had been inhabiting a little doll's house . . . and it proved to be standing all alone in the forests of the night; inches high, among silent, huge, glimmering trees." The scene turns ugly, but thanks to the help of the governor's secretary, Septimus Oakeshott, and his enslaved African servant Achilles, Smith narrowly avoids being carved alive by a butcher who accuses him of being a Papist. The derring-do of the men's escape—weaving through alleys, breaking into a house, and climbing ropes dangled from the top of a roof—alerts the reader that *Golden Hill* is also partly an adventure story.

Golden Hill balances comedy and tragedy, illustrating the artifice of New York (and, more broadly, the nascent United States). When Smith first walks the streets of the island of Manhattan, admiring its relatively pleasing smell and the visible health of its citizens, his gaze is interrupted by a gruesome sight in the city commons. Upon closer inspection, he discovers a row of rotting scalps nailed to a board. (The scalps belong to French traders who have infringed on English and Dutch land.) Just as quickly, Smith's eyes fall on an enslaved African man. Spufford, through the English eyes of Smith, emphasizes the absurdity of the colonists touting freedom and liberty while actively participating in the sale and exploitation of human beings. Glimpses at the horror of slavery build toward an important revelation. It is safe to say that Spufford's larger theme is something along the lines of things not always being what they appear on the surface.

Along those lines, performance is a recurring motif in the novel. Smith, who happens to be a former actor, performs the role (mostly poorly) of a beguiling stranger. Septimus, Tabitha, Achilles, and a fascinating woman of real theatrical gifts named Terpie have their own roles to play, as do the men and women in masks on Pope Day. Additionally, there is a literal performance, directed by Septimus and starring Smith and several other principal characters, of Joseph Addison's *Cato* (1713). The play, as Laura Miller noted in her review of *Golden Hill* for the *New Yorker*, is a specific choice; George Washington was rumored to have requested a performance of the piece for his troops at Valley Forge. The tragedy, about Cato the Younger's resistance to the tyranny of Julius Caesar, was enormously popular in its day because it captured the colonists' burgeoning desire for liberty. Meanwhile, the enslaved characters in the book watch the play from a bench in the back of the theater.

Golden Hill is Spufford's first full-length work of fiction. His previous books include the nonfiction works *I May Be Some Time: Ice and the English Imagination* (1996), about British arctic exploration; a childhood memoir and psychological exploration of children's books titled *The Child That Books Built: A Life in Reading* (2002); and *Red Plenty* (2010), a combination of fiction and nonfiction about the planned economy of the Soviet Union in the 1950s and 1960s, with chapters alternating between real and imagined characters as they struggle to achieve their version of Communist utopia. *I May Be Some Time*, like *Golden Hill*, explores the chasm between a romanticized ideal and reality. For the former, Spufford was given the 1997 Somerset Maugham Award for British writers under the age of thirty-five and was named the London Sunday Times Young Writer of the Year. His book *Unapologetic: Why, Despite Everything, Christianity Can Still Make Surprising Emotional Sense* (2012), is a defense of religion and a meditation on human suffering. Subject-wise, Spufford's interests are diverse. Dwight Garner, in his review of *Golden Hill* for the *New York Times*, compared his intellect to "a many-armed Hindu deity, able to pluck fruit and butterflies from anywhere on earth's most robust tall trees." But structurally, Spufford's work is characterized by deep research and unconventional storytelling.

Spufford's debut novel won three awards when it was first published in the United Kingdom in 2016: the Desmond Elliott Prize for debut novels, the Costa Award for first novel, and the Royal Society of Literature's Ondaatje Prize. It also received positive reviews from major publications. Garner, who had appreciated the inventiveness of Spufford's *Red Plenty* and named it one of his favorite books of 2012, was impressed by the author's fiction debut. He described it as "ebullient" and "freewheeling." Indeed, the book's first sentence—a galloping, half-page run-on that chronicles

> *Francis Spufford is an award-winning English author best known for his works of nonfiction, including* I May Be Some Time: Ice and the English Imagination *(1996),* The Child That Books Built: A Life in Reading *(2002), and* Red Plenty *(2010).* Golden Hill *is his first novel.*

Smith's arrival in New York—evokes these adjectives while ushering the reader into Spufford's fast-paced narrative.

Additionally, Miller appreciatively noted that, unlike *Golden Hill*'s eighteenth-century predecessors, the book is "trim rather than bulky, refrains from indulging in too many antique spellings, and tells its story with crafty precision." Still, a long chapter, written in the form of a letter from Smith to his estranged father, can grow tedious in its allegiance to a more archaic form of English. A reviewer for *Kirkus* gave the book a starred review, commenting on Spufford's "sure hand" as a storyteller and the "delightful twists" he plants throughout. A reviewer for *Publishers Weekly* was similarly impressed, as was Steven Poole for the *Guardian*, who concluded, "The whole thing, then, is a first-class period entertainment, until at length it becomes something more serious. The comedy gives way to darker tones, and Smith's secret is at last revealed—but the novel, most pleasingly, still has one more trick up its sleeve."

Molly Hagan

Review Sources

Garner, Dwight. "Review: Francis Spufford's First Novel is a Swashbuckling Tale." Review of *Golden Hill: A Novel of Old New York*, by Francis Spufford. *The New York Times*, 27 June 2017, www.nytimes.com/2017/06/27/books/review-golden-hill-francis-spufford.html. Accessed 22 Feb. 2018.

Review of *Golden Hill: A Novel of Old New York*, by Francis Spufford. *Kirkus*, 2 Apr. 2017, www.kirkusreviews.com/book-reviews/francis-spufford/golden-hill. Accessed 22 Feb. 2018.

Review of *Golden Hill: A Novel of Old New York*, by Francis Spufford. *Publishers Weekly*, 10 Apr. 2017, www.publishersweekly.com/978-1-5011-6387-6. Accessed 22 Feb. 2018.

Miller, Laura. "*Golden Hill*: A Crackerjack Novel of Old Manhattan." Review of *Golden Hill: A Novel of Old New York*, by Francis Spufford. *The New Yorker*, 3 July 2017, www.newyorker.com/magazine/2017/07/03/golden-hill-a-crackerjack-novel-of-old-manhattan. Accessed 22 Feb. 2018.

Poole, Steven. "*Golden Hill* by Francis Spufford Review—A Frolicsome First Novel." *The Guardian*, 1 June 2016, www.newyorker.com/magazine/2017/07/03/golden-hill-a-crackerjack-novel-of-old-manhattan. Accessed 22 Feb. 2018.

The Golden House

Author: Salman Rushdie (b. 1947)
Publisher: Random House (New York). 400 pp.
Type of work: Novel
Time: 2009–17
Locales: New York, New York; Bombay (now Mumbai), India

Set in the United States during the presidency of Barack Obama, Salman Rushdie's twelfth novel, The Golden House, *follows the fortunes of a real-estate developer from India as he and his sons relocate to Manhattan.*

Courtesy of Random House

Principal characters
NERO JULIUS GOLDEN, a wealthy, elderly Indian immigrant
VASILISA ARSENYEVA, his wife, a former Russian gymnast
PETRONIUS "PETYA" GOLDEN, his oldest son, autistic and often withdrawn
LUCIUS APULEIUS "APU" GOLDEN, his second son, an artist and foppish man-about-town
DIONYSIUS "D" GOLDEN, his rebellious younger son, half brother to the others
RIYA ZACHARIASSEN, D's girlfriend
RENÉ UNTERLINDEN, the narrator, an aspiring filmmaker and neighbor of the Goldens
SUCHITRA ROY, the narrator's girlfriend, also a filmmaker
MASTAN, a retired inspector with the Indian police force

In 2000, Salman Rushdie moved from London to the United States and settled in lower Manhattan, where he began at once to absorb the new culture. His first public response appeared in his eighth novel, *Fury* (2001), the story of a British academic of Indian extraction who tries to escape his personal demons by immersing himself in the public demons of America. Rushdie had been hounded by Islamic extremists after the publication of his fourth novel, *The Satanic Verses* (1988), and was forced to live under protective custody for a full decade. His tweets in the early days of Twitter identified him as a liberal intellectual—a one-time president of PEN American Center (from 2004 to 2006), the writers' advocacy group, and a strong supporter of the American Civil Liberties Union (ACLU)—though he was ready to criticize both groups over decisions that he considered dangerous. He posted his last tweet on the day of the 2016 presidential elections, after having cast his vote for Democratic candidate Hillary Clinton. He had seen the forces behind Donald Trump bubble up during the presidency of his predecessor, Barack Obama, but had not foreseen Trump's election victory. His new novel is deliberately set in the Obama era, spanning from the initial enthusiasm of the president's first term to its eventual demise.

In one sense, *The Golden House* is all about identity politics and its various manifestations: religious identity in India, national identity in England, and gender identity in the United States. One character works at what is called the Museum of Identity, from which she resigns when she concludes that the celebration of difference leads only to continual tearing of the social fabric. Other characters belong to one of two elite classes: the billionaire class, as in the case of the protagonist, Nero Golden, and his sons; or the class of superintellectuals, which includes members of the news media who interpret the world to their devoted followings. The young narrator, René Unterlinden, belongs to the latter group and aspires to document society from his perspective as a film buff who seems to have seen every classic film.

The main plot is remarkably simple. A wealthy real-estate developer in Mumbai, having lost his wife in the terrorist attacks of November 2008, decides to take his family

© Randall Slavin

Born in Bombay (now Mumbai) on the eve of India's independence, Salman Rushdie was educated in England and wrote his first novels about cultural tensions in the two countries. He won the 1981 Booker Prize for his second novel, Midnight's Children *(1981), and has won many other awards since then. He was knighted in 2007.*

to the United States and to establish a new identity for himself. Classically educated under the British raj, he renames himself after one of the Caesars—"Nero, of Caesar's house, last of that bloody line. . . . Me, I just like the name," he explains—and instructs his sons to likewise choose names from classical antiquity. He buys a large house in lower Manhattan in the MacDougal-Sullivan Gardens, so called because a whole block of houses looks in on a central garden. The family moves in on the day of President Obama's inauguration; once established, they get to know the narrator, a film-school graduate whose parents have recently died in a freak automobile accident. They take him in while he prepares his house for sale, and he becomes increasingly involved with the family and especially with the paterfamilias, whom he starts to see as the model character for a breakthrough film. In the central chapter, he agrees to father the child of Nero's new wife, a beautiful Russian immigrant who wants a child but knows her new husband is neither capable of begetting offspring—a fact revealed by recent medical testing—nor able to handle the news of his incapacity. At this point, René knowingly crosses the line between journalistic observer and participant. Of course, disaster awaits.

On the surface, *The Golden House* is a twenty-first-century version of *The Great Gatsby* (1925), F. Scott Fitzgerald's novel of great and dubious wealth in the Jazz Age. However, Rushdie is more of an *One Thousand and One Nights*–style novelist—as indicated by the title of his previous novel, *Two Years Eight Months and Twenty-Eight*

Nights (2015)—and the main plot tends to get submerged in a sea of stories swirling around and behind the principal characters. This can be a source of exuberance for some readers who appreciate Rushdie's wit and learning; others have said that they never get far in his longer novels, of which this fortunately is not one. Among the various subplots, Nero's two older sons, Petya and Apu, begin to spout the biases of the competing cable television news channels they watch; their younger brother, D, deals with transgender issues; and Nero himself makes leveraged investments as questionable as those of the new presidential contender. Other residents of the Gardens, even former renters, get their fifteen sentences of fame, the equivalent of Andy Warhol's proverbial fifteen minutes. As in Alfred Hitchcock's *Rear Window* (1954) and the many other films that René uses to explain the Goldens' world, Rushdie's side stories about American society are well researched and amusingly presented, but they do little to advance the main story. Meanwhile, in the background looms the Joker, who is at once the laughing villain of Batman cartoons and the wild-card presidential candidate.

The novel covers a period of about nine years, from January 2009 to late 2017, by which time René has finished his first film (also titled *The Golden House*), has entered it in a film festival, and is now preparing the filmscript for publication. Along the way, it documents the rise and fall of the dynasty, or house, that Nero Golden created and hoped would continue with his heirs. As Nero enters his eighties, his mind slips back from recent events to those of long ago and far away. He remembers the mafia boss who controlled business in Bombay, and he agrees to a visit from a retired policeman who once pursued them both. Before the visit, he feels the need to tell Riya, D's girlfriend who has since become his surrogate daughter, about his past business with the mafia boss, who led him from being a bagman for dirty money to "flipping" high-end real estate and laundering money in the process. It was all very fashionable, in the early days of Bollywood, when mobsters invested heavily in the film industry and were portrayed in many noir-style films. But it was also dangerous, as they leaned on each other, trying to extort promises and money. Even before the loss of his previous wife in a terrorist attack, Nero had good reason to relocate.

On the day of the 2016 election, René, seized by the confessional mood into which he is finally drawn, confesses his own secret to Nero: his parentage of the youngest Golden. The act leads to his absolute estrangement from both the Goldens and Suchitra, during which time he gets down to serious work on his documentary about the house of Golden. About a year into this estrangement, he begins meeting with Riya, an unexpected sympathetic ear; having been energized rather than defeated by the election results, she helps him realize that "America's secret identity wasn't a superhero. Turns out it was a supervillain. We're in the Bizarro universe and we have to engage with Bizarro-America to grasp its nature and to learn how to destroy it all over again. . . . And we have to engage with ourselves and understand how we became so f—— weak and apathetic and how to retool and dive back into the battle." After he subsequently reconciles with Suchitra, he embraces a larger vision, telling her that even then, "more than a year since the Joker's conquest of America . . . we were all still in shock and going through the stages of grief but now we needed to come together and set love and beauty and solidarity and friendship against the monstrous forces that faced us." She tells him to shut up and pulls him closer, and they end on a hopeful note.

Rushdie's endless spinning out of stories within the main story was a recurring theme in early book reviews. Some, such as Dwight Garner for the *New York Times* and Leo Robson for the *New Statesman*, suggested that the novel reads too much like the news or like a pastiche of Twitter posts while featuring a narrator who is less detached than Fitzgerald's and far less poetic. The more positive reviews seemed to appreciate most the satiric treatment of a highly leveraged real-estate developer from New York. In his defense, one might argue that Rushdie has created a protagonist who is both more humane and less narcissistic than the developer whom presidential historians are likely to describe.

Rushdie is not the first novelist to satirize the new American president and his world; the British satirist Howard Jacobson beat him to it with his novel *Pussy* (2017), published four months earlier. Jacobson's protagonist, Prince Fracassus, has a sort of verbal Tourette's syndrome, and he mangles what James Joyce once called the "jinglish janglage" as quickly as he slaps his name on luxury hotels in imaginary countries. Rushdie's Joker is never given a name or a central role in the action, but the Joker's contempt for the serving president, like his admiration for foreign oligarchs, is unmistakable. There is no suggestion that the sitting president's story will end as unhappily as that of Rushdie's expatriate financier. However, the very symmetries in *The Golden House* suggest that presidential cycles come and go, like the cycles of gods and heroes in the myths that give Nero Golden's story a larger human dimension, and that what has gone low in American life will one day go high.

Tom Willard

Review Sources

Athitakis, Mark. "In Salman Rushdie's *Golden House*, a Trump-Like Figure Rules the Manor." Review of *The Golden House*, by Salman Rushdie. *USA Today*, 5 Sept. 2017, www.usatoday.com/story/life/books/2017/09/05/salman-rushdies-golden-house-trump-like-figure-rules-manor/616279001/. Accessed 27 Dec. 2017.

Charles, Ron. "Salman Rushdie Launches a Novelistic Attack on Trump." Review of *The Golden House*, by Salman Rushdie. *The Washington Post*, 5 Sept. 2017, www.washingtonpost.com/entertainment/books/salman-rushdie-launches-a-novelistic-attack-on-trump/2017/09/05/9d871688-91d5-11e7-89fa-bb822a46da5b_story.html. Accessed 27 Dec. 2017.

Forna, Aminatta. "*The Golden House* by Salman Rushdie Review: A Parable of Modern America." Review of *The Golden House*, by Salman Rushdie. *The Guardian*, 16 Sept. 2017, www.theguardian.com/books/2017/sep/16/the-golden-house-salman-rushdie-review. Accessed 27 Dec. 2017.

Garner, Dwight. "Salman Rushdie's Prose Joins the Circus in *The Golden House*." Review of *The Golden House*, by Salman Rushdie. *The New York Times*, 4 Sept. 2017, www.nytimes.com/2017/09/04/books/review-golden-house-salman-rushdie.html. Accessed 27 Dec. 2017.

Robson, Leo. "*The Golden House* Is Salman Rushdie's Not-So-Great American Novel." Review of *The Golden House*, by Salman Rushdie. *The New Statesman*, 10 Sept. 2017, www.newstatesman.com/culture/books/2017/09/golden-house-salman-rushdies-not-so-great-american-novel. Accessed 27 Dec. 2017.

The Golden Legend

Author: Nadeem Aslam (b. 1966)
Publisher: Alfred A. Knopf (New York). 336 pp.
Type of work: Novel
Time: Present day
Locale: Zamana, Pakistan

Nadeem Aslam's new novel, The Golden Legend, *explores the bounds of human cruelty and compassion.*

Principal characters
NARGIS, a middle-aged architect with a dangerous secret
MASSUD, her husband and partner
HELEN, the daughter of their Christian servants
LILY, Helen's father, a rickshaw driver
GRACE, Helen's mother
AYSHA, the widowed daughter of a Muslim cleric
SHAKEEL, Aysha's brother-in-law

Courtesy of Knopf

British Pakistani novelist Nadeem Aslam's new novel, *The Golden Legend*, is set in Pakistan, in the fictional city of Zamana. There, a middle-aged couple, Nargis and Massud, lead a quiet life in a converted factory space, full of sunlight and books. This is a realistic tale, but Aslam offers readers a glimpse of the surreal imagery to come in the book's first pages. Helen, the teenage daughter of Nargis and Massud's Christian servants, admires the hovering forms of two structures, suspended from the ceiling. One is a miniaturized version of the Hagia Sophia, the other a version of the Great Mosque of Córdoba. The structures, which she refers to as cabins, are meant to be little study rooms, warm enough to read in during the winter months. Nargis and Massud's library is full of such delightful wonders, among them "the vertebrae of a whale from a bay in Antarctica" and "the earliest known photograph of a snowflake." A kind of surrogate daughter to the childless architects, Helen is free to explore this oasis of culture and learning, and like the small cabins in the room itself, it shields her from an ignorant and cruel world just outside the library's door. *The Golden Legend* begins just after the murder of Helen's mother, Grace. The killer has just gotten out of jail for good behavior, serving less than a year of time after memorizing the entire Qur'an. But Nargis and Massud cannot begin to contemplate this troubling news. They are scheduled to participate—another quasi-surreal image—in a mile-long human chain between one of Zamana's oldest libraries and its new quarters, which they have designed, the books being too sacred to risk coming in contact with something unclean in a truck or a car.

The chain is an emblem of Aslam's larger the theme, the beauty of human compassion and the free exchange of ideas, and because of that, also in keeping with this theme, it is subject to a random act of violence. A burly, white American man opens fire on two men in motorcycles who have stopped at his car window, and Massud is killed by a stray bullet.

Aslam's books have been celebrated and criticized for fusing poetic language and imagery with tales of horrific violence. In this regard, *The Golden Thread*, Aslam's fifth novel, is no exception. It was inspired, he said in a 2017 interview with Ben East for the *Guardian*, by the suspicion and mistreatment immigrants and refugees have been subject to in Britain, but also the deep intolerance of Pakistan, enshrined in the country's draconian blasphemy laws. "Earlier this year I saw a man wearing a T-shirt that said: 'Welcome to Britain, now fit in or f—k off.' That awful idea of only one God, one religion, one

Nadeem Aslam is a British Pakistani novelist. His other books include Season of the Rainbirds *(1993),* Maps for Lost Lovers *(2004),* The Wasted Vigil *(2008), and* The Blind Man's Garden *(2013). In 2014, he won a prestigious Windham-Campbell Prize for fiction for his body of work.*

© Eamonn McCabe

nation, one language that I explore in this book . . . well, it goes against everything I hold dear," he said. Aslam, the son of a Communist poet and film producer, was born in Pakistan but fled, with his family, to England after the rise of General Muhammad Zia-ul-Haq and the jihadis in the late 1970s. He was fourteen. His first novel, *Season of the Rainbirds* (1993), is set in a small Pakistani village. It won praise from the award-winning Indian novelist Salman Rushdie and was short-listed for the Whitbread first novel award. Aslam's second novel, *Maps for Lost Lovers* (2004), is set in the English community of Pakistani immigrants in which he lived during his teenage years, and centers on the murder of a young couple, an honor killing for living in sin. Aslam's novel, *The Wasted Vigil* (2008), is set in Afghanistan, as is his fourth novel, *The Blind Man's Garden* (2013); the latter follows two Pakistani brothers in the country in the months after the terrorist attacks on September 11.

Massud's death in *The Golden Legend*, though an accident, draws his family into a dangerous plot that costs them their tenuous peace. A menacing "soldier-spy" visits Nargis. He tells her that she must publicly forgive the American man for Massud's murder, accepting "blood money" in lieu of other punishment, to maintain the country's political relationship with the United States. Nargis, out of pride, does not want to do this, but the man makes clear, with terrible violence, that the choice was never hers to make. As a part of his threat, the man uses a scalpel to cut apart an old book in the house. It was the book Massud was holding when he died. It was also written by Massud's father. The nearly thousand-page tome, *That They Might Know Each Other*, is an encyclopedia of cultural exchange, "tracing the umbilical connections between places." The soldier-spy's coldly precise destruction of the book is thus fraught with symbolic weight, and seeming to recognize this, Nargis begins the task of sewing the book's pages back together again with golden thread. The act of doing this, of course, forms more "umbilical connections." She continues with this task even after she is forced from her home, due to events that comprise the book's second major plot line.

Lily and Helen, the father and daughter employed by Nargis, have never had it easy in Zamana. As Christians, they are subject to constant harassment and abuse enforced by Pakistani law. Lily, for instance, must carry his own cup for tea and water because no Muslim, even at a café, can touch a thing that a Christian might once have touched. Therefore, the reader can understand how truly dangerous it is when Lily begins an affair with the widowed daughter of a Muslim cleric. The widow, Aysha, lives at the mosque with her kindly father and her young son, who lost his legs when their former home was destroyed by an American drone. Aysha's husband, a devoted and radical Muslim, was killed in the blast. His brother, Shakeel, has come to her father's mosque to make sure Aysha does not marry again. Shakeel and his cronies have set the whole town on edge, critical as they are of the piety, or as they see it, lack of piety, of the Muslims there. They are largely responsible for the violent uprising that occurs the night Lily and Aysha's relationship is discovered. To protect Helen, Nargis and a young Kashmiri runaway named Imran, seek refuge on a small island. The setting is fable-like. Lara Feigel, who reviewed the book for the *Guardian*, even compared it to the magical island from William Shakespeare's *The Tempest*. The island is home to a mosque that Nargis and Massud designed many years before. The mosque and the island are abandoned now; a Hindu temple and a church were meant to be built beside it, symbols of religious tolerance, but after a murder in the mosque, the island's residents fled. The reader wishes that the three refugees could stay on the island forever, but like the other such symbols in Aslam's book, their idyll is not meant to last. Still, Helen and Imran have time to develop a tender romantic relationship, and Nargis does her best to shield them from the violence that surrounds them. Their plight emphasizes Aslam's most brutal point, about the necessity of maintaining hope in the face hopelessness. As Nargis observes early on, amid intolerance, cruelty, and greed, "these struggles of Pakistanis were not just about Pakistan, they were about the survival of the human race."

The Golden Thread was largely well-received by critics when it was published in 2017. Novelist Francine Prose, who reviewed the book for the *New York Times*, called it "powerful and engrossing," admitting that reading it felt like visiting a dystopian world. "Fortunately, 'The Golden Legend' is far more than the sum of the horrors it contains," she wrote. "Aslam . . . writes with great sensitivity and depth about the ways human beings behave under almost unimaginable pressure." *Kirkus Reviews* and *Publishers Weekly* gave the book a starred review, the latter calling it "exquisite" and "luminous." Feigel praised the book, but also offered a critique of its ambiguous world, hovering tonally between strict realism and magical realism. Aslam, Feigel wrote, is "writing a form of realism in which individual psychology is often secondary to larger symbolic structures and archetypes." Everything that happens, she continues, is "within the bounds of earthly possibility, if not within the bounds of credibility"—like, for instance, the coincidence of Massud acquiring his father's book or, as Prose pointed out, the use of thread to repair it, when it may have been more appropriate to use double-sided tape. These criticisms suggest ones that have been aimed at Aslam before. His poetry and his intent to illustrate real suffering are sometimes at odds. That being said, he makes an unusual stylistic decision at the end of the book. He introduces a true fantastical element that should seem unpleasantly jarring but manages to capture the intangible, and unknowable, feeling of exhilaration and sorrow experienced by one of the characters. This bold decision does more to communicate the energy that connects people, places, things, and memory than the golden thread at the heart of the novel.

Molly Hagan

Review Sources

Feigel, Lara. "The Golden Legend Review—Beauty and Pain in Pakistan." Review of *The Golden Legend*, by Nadeem Aslam. *The Guardian*, 28 Dec. 2016, www.theguardian.com/books/2016/dec/28/the-golden-legend-nadeem-aslam-review-pakistan. Accessed 25 Feb. 2018.

Garmeson, Laura. "The Golden Legend by Nadeem Aslam—Of Love and Loss." Review of *The Golden Legend*, by Nadeem Aslam. *Financial Times*, 13 Jan. 2017, www.ft.com/content/d063e9e6-d7f9-11e6-944b-e7eb37a6aa8e. Accessed 25 Feb. 2018.

Review of *The Golden Legend*, by Nadeem Aslam. *Kirkus Reviews*, 15 Feb. 2017, p. 1. *Literary Reference Center Plus*, search.ebscohost.com/login.aspx?direct=true&db=lkh&AN=121253277&site=lrc-plus. Accessed 25 Feb. 2018.

Review of *The Golden Legend*, by Nadeem Aslam. *Publishers Weekly*, 27 Feb. 2017, p. 70. *Literary Reference Center Plus*, search.ebscohost.com/login.aspx?direct=true&db=lkh&AN=121466679&site=lrc-plus. Accessed 25 Feb. 2018.

Prose, Francine. "Fleeing a Fictional World of Despots and Drones." Review of *The Golden Legend*, by Nadeem Aslam. *The New York Times*, 19 May 2017, www.nytimes.com/2017/05/19/books/review/the-golden-legend-by-nadeem-aslam.html. Accessed 25 Feb. 2018.

Goodbye, Vitamin

Author: Rachel Khong (b. 1985)
Publisher: Henry Holt (New York). 208 pp.
Type of work: Novel
Time: Present day
Locale: Southern California

Rachel Khong's debut novel, Goodbye, Vitamin, *chronicles a woman's year living at home with her parents after she breaks up with her longtime boyfriend and her father has been diagnosed with Alzheimer's disease.*

Principal characters
RUTH, a thirty-year-old who spends a year living with her parents after a breakup
HOWARD, her father, who is suffering from the early effects of Alzheimer's disease
ANNIE, her mother
BONNIE, her childhood best friend
LINUS, her younger brother

Courtesy of Henry Holt & Company, Inc.

Ruth has just turned thirty and recently gone through a painful breakup from her long-time boyfriend, Joel. Newly single, she returns home to Southern California to spend Christmas with her family instead of typically having gone to see her boyfriend's family in South Carolina for the holidays. While she describes that upon returning home, at least in terms of holiday traditions, "everything was the same," all is not well with her parents. Her mother, a proud home cook, has thrown away all her pots and pans, convinced that Ruth's father, Howard, who has recently been diagnosed with Alzheimer's disease, became sick from chemicals in their material. Giving in to her mother's encouragement, Ruth agrees to spend the following year living at home.

Rachel Khong's debut novel, *Goodbye, Vitamin*, is written like a diary, which proves to be an effective format for the minimalist action of the story that is meant to highlight the book's major themes, including identity, memory, and family relationships. In rather sparse but straightforward sentences, Ruth honestly records her days over the year she spends with her parents—going to the store, going to the library, patiently waiting for her father to emerge from his home office—and collects scraps of a similar diary her father kept when she was growing up. Khong includes actual excerpts from the notebook that her father presents Ruth with on Christmas morning, allowing for greater insight into both characters: "Today you had me excavate your nose, which you'd put corn into," one entry states. "Today you said, apropos of nothing, 'Good corpse, bad corpse,'" reads another. Other, more significant events come into play. Ruth and her father's teaching assistant, Theo, scheme to convince Howard that, contrary to the dean's original wishes, he will be teaching a seminar at the university where he was formerly employed (though the class would really be uncredited and unofficial). Ultimately, the class allows for other aspects of Howard's personality—his philandering, his periods of alcoholism—to surface, pushing Ruth to consider her father in all his complexity. Such struggles help to illustrate how Khong's short novel, both humorous and painful, is, overall, about family and what people strive to remember and choose to forget.

Khong is a writer and essayist who served as an editor for the now-defunct food magazine *Lucky Peach*. In a 2017 interview about the book for *Vogue*, she explained that she began writing *Goodbye, Vitamin*, her first novel, in 2010, a few years after graduating from college; she submitted a draft of it as her master's thesis. She continued to rewrite the book for many years, and eventually, her anguish with her failure to finish it became a part of the book itself. The novel, in its final iteration, takes an impressionistic form that Khong said was inspired by novels like Renata Adler's *Speedboat* (1976) and Joan Didion's *Play It as It Lays* (1970). These novels—and *Goodbye, Vitamin*—share particular themes. Adler and Didion, two deeply unique writers, value a cool-to-the-touch tone and precise sentence construction. Khong cultivates a lighter tone that serves as a kind of misdirection. Doree Shafrir, in her review of *Goodbye, Vitamin* for the *New York Times*, additionally noted Khong's ability to infuse the seemingly simple sentence structures of the diary format with meaning and impact because it is "told in a prose that is so startling in its spare beauty."

Goodbye, Vitamin is predominantly about memory, but it follows Ruth as she struggles to build an identity for herself. In brief asides, she paints a retrospectively troubling picture of her long-term relationship with Joel, who, at the beginning of the book, has dumped her unceremoniously. (They agree to move to a new apartment, but after their things are packed, he tells her she will move there alone.) She reveals that she dropped out of college to move with Joel to another city, eventually taking a job as an ultrasound engineer in San Francisco. The decision, made in the rush of new love, caused a rift between Ruth and her childhood best friend, Bonnie, an artist and hairdresser. Separated from the elements of her life that informed who she once was, a young Ruth, it seems, built herself around her relationship with Joel. Therefore, her return to her family home in Southern California is an act of rebirth. Who is Ruth, alone? She takes up her mother's mantle as family chef, and while her joyful kitchen experiments are a small part of the book, they are indicative of Ruth asserting herself as an individual, separate from both Joel and her family.

However, to establish who she is outside of her family, Ruth must reckon with the role she plays in her family as well. Her relationship with Joel allowed her to detach herself spiritually from her parents and brother, Linus. Without him, she must learn how to be a daughter again. Her memories of her father are happy, symbolized by one anecdote in which Howard and a young Ruth buy French fries to feed to a flock of hungry pigeons. This gentle image of Howard eludes Linus, who was a young teen when she went away to college and Howard began drinking again. Frequent benders, in Linus's recollection, led to fights, extramarital affairs, and threats of divorce. When

Courtesy of Andria Lo

Writer Rachel Khong is a former editor for the food magazine Lucky Peach. Goodbye, Vitamin *is her first novel.*

Linus and Ruth compare memories, she must reckon with a side of her father that she knew about but emotionally refused to acquaint herself with.

Clues from this period, cut short, it is suggested, surface with the onslaught of Howard's disease: signed divorce papers, never sent, locked in her father's desk drawer, and an unusual tension between Howard and a pretty, young graduate student. To be sure, in this case, Ruth was digging through her father's papers and pursued the history of the pretty grad student, but sometimes unwanted details assault her unbidden. At one point, she asks Howard to tell her the familiar story of how he and her mother met. He begins a tale, only for her to discover that he is describing the origin story of a woman with whom he had an affair. Still, she is determined to preserve what memories she can. Her diary—the book itself—is an act of love, a promise to keep both the good and the bad. She records Howard's triumphs but also, nearing the end of the book, the beginning of his sharp decline, as he throws dishes across the room and screams in confused terror. The doctor's directive, to wear light clothes instead of dark so as not to frighten the increasingly ill Howard, seems an elegant act of reverse mourning.

Goodbye, Vitamin was largely well reviewed and appeared on a number of year-end lists compiling the best books of 2017. Overall, critics praised Khong's tone, a tricky balance of dark humor and emotional honesty. As Sophie Browner, who reviewed the book for the *Los Angeles Review of Books*, wrote, the novel's driving premise—a history professor who is slowly losing his memory—could easily veer into sentimentality, but Khong ably avoids this. Criticisms of the novel were relatively minor. For example, Browner took issue with a few nagging narrative questions, such as how Ruth keeps managing to randomly and fortuitously run into people from her past. Another critique revolved around the elaborate mechanics of Howard's fake "class" requiring a heavy suspension of disbelief. However, as Browner notes, *Goodbye, Vitamin* includes moments that verge on the surreal. The novel itself, Browner wrote, becomes "infused with a kind of Alzheimer's logic." Early on, Ruth worries about her own memory, mistaking a trash can for a mail box, but elsewhere other things are askew. Howard keeps an aquarium filled with tiny plastic diving men but no fish and words are mistaken for other words, recalling passages of his diary chronicling Ruth's early development. Ruth's chronicle of her father's decline gives the novel its terrible symmetry: one diary accounts the acquisition of things while the other accounts their loss.

There are no hard and fast resolutions in *Goodbye, Vitamin*, suggesting the episodic nature of life while it is being lived. The book's structure is defined only by the chronology of the year over which it takes place. In this way, Khong fuses form and content, illustrating the unbridgeable chasm between recording a life and experiencing it. Short passages paint an impressionistic picture of Ruth's life, but in choosing to tell her story this way, Khong acknowledges the very thing that Ruth must reckon with: the impossibility of knowing a person completely. This concept is dramatized in Howard, of course, but also by the shadowy figure of Annie, Ruth's long-suffering mother. Much of Ruth's rebirth involves reconstructing a relationship with her mother that is defined by more than her own need. At a particularly low point, Ruth writes, "Here's the fear: she gave to us, and we took from her, until she disappeared." She also states, ruefully, "What imperfect carriers of love we are, and what imperfect givers." Her obsession with memory is really about attention and her inability to sufficiently pay it. She lives much of her year in close observation of her family and her own life as if paying a debt. What happened during all that time she was looking away? What are all the memories she will never have? She must let go of these questions to find peace.

Molly Hagan

Review Sources

Browner, Sophie. "The Mind Plays Tricks: Memory Loss and Nostalgia in Rachel Khong's *Goodbye, Vitamin.*" Review of *Goodbye, Vitamin*, by Rachel Khong. *Los Angeles Review of Books*, 18 Oct. 2017, lareviewofbooks.org/article/the-mind-plays-tricks-memory-loss-and-nostalgia-in-rachel-khongs-goodbye-vitamin. Accessed 8 Jan. 2018.

Review of *Goodbye, Vitamin*, by Rachel Khong. *Kirkus*, 2 May 2017, www.kirkusreviews.com/book-reviews/rachel-khong/goodbye-vitamin. Accessed 8 Jan. 2018.

Review of *Goodbye, Vitamin*, by Rachel Khong. *Publishers Weekly*, 29 May 2017, www.publishersweekly.com/978-1-250-10916-3. Accessed 8 Jan. 2018.

McAlpin, Heller. "*Goodbye, Vitamin* Is Sweet—But Not Sugarcoated." Review of *Goodbye, Vitamin*, by Rachel Khong. *NPR Books*, NPR, 12 July 2017, www.npr.org/2017/07/12/535799520/goodbye-vitamin-is-sweet-but-not-sugarcoated. Accessed 8 Jan. 2018.

Shafrir, Doree. "A Darkly Comic Novel about Turning 30 without Growing Up." Review of *Goodbye, Vitamin*, by Rachel Khong. *The New York Times*, 28 July 2017, www.nytimes.com/2017/07/28/books/review/goodbye-vitamin-rachel-khong.html. Accessed 8 Jan. 2018.

Grant

Author: Ron Chernow (b. 1949)
Publisher: Penguin Press (New York). Illustrated. 1104 pp.
Type of work: Biography
Time: 1822–1885
Locale: United States

Master biographer Ron Chernow takes on the life of Ulysses S. Grant, who rose from obscurity to lead the Union Army in the US Civil War and serve as president of the United States from 1869 to 1877, continuing a trend of positive reassessment of Grant's legacy.

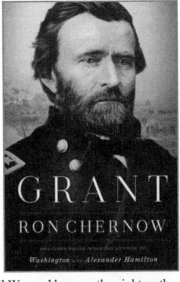

Courtesy of Penguin Press

Principal personages

ULYSSES S. GRANT, US Army officer who rose to command all Union troops in the Civil War and became the eighteenth president of the United States

JULIA GRANT, his wife

WILLIAM TECUMSEH SHERMAN, one of his most trusted commanders in the Civil War

JESSE ROOT GRANT, his father

JOHN RAWLINS, Union Army officer, his aide; briefly served as secretary of war in his first administration

ABRAHAM LINCOLN, sixteenth president of the United States under whom he served during the Civil War

ANDREW JOHNSON, Lincoln's vice president and the seventeenth US president; clashed with Grant over many issues during Reconstruction

ROBERT E. LEE, Confederate military leader

Chernow's massive biography of Civil War hero and US president Ulysses S. Grant is clearly in the revisionist and rehabilitative category. In this way it joins a trend among historians and some other biographers in which Grant's legacy has been reconsidered after decades of mostly mixed to negative public perception. For many, the standard interpretation of Grant's career has been to concede his importance as a military leader but view his presidency as a failure. Factors from the extensive corruption in his administration to his personal drinking problems undermined his achievements and damaged his reputation. Armed with extensive research, Chernow sets out to counter such claims and establish Grant as a flawed but deeply admirable American icon.

While Chernow is heavily sympathetic to his subject, he does not praise Grant artificially or universally. Even as he persuasively argues, for instance, that Grant had nothing to do with the political corruption surrounding him (and certainly did not personally profit from any of it), he is unsparing in his documentation of Grant's frequent naïveté. This was a problem throughout Grant's life—he was cheated on several occasions by business partners he had trusted, and betrayed by officers during his military career and by political appointees during his presidency. Throughout the book, Chernow portrays Grant's simple trust of people and reluctance to believe they had betrayed him, even in the face of mounting evidence, as a humanizing flaw. And while the author challenges established narratives, he also pulls no punches in going into considerable detail about some of the most controversial aspects of Grant's career, including his drinking and the charge that he was a "butcher" who carelessly sacrificed the lives of Union soldiers.

After an introduction and a series of maps, *Grant* is divided into four chronological parts. In Part one, subtitled "A Life of Struggle," in which Chernow covers Grant's early life, is relatively brief. His father, Jesse Root Grant, was a striving businessman, beginning with the operation of several tanneries. He had a penchant for braggadocio and self-promotion, which may have influenced his son's sense of modesty and reluctance to put himself forward. Like many young men, Grant went to the West Point military academy not because he longed for a military career, but simply for the free education. He graduated from West Point in 1843, and served in various posts until the outbreak of the war with Mexico in 1848. He served well in that war but without particular distinction, although his service as a quartermaster gave him an understanding of the problems of logistics that would later serve him well during the Civil War.

It is generally thought that problems with alcohol led to Grant's resignation from the army in 1854, and Chernow agrees that there is "overwhelming evidence" that this was the case. Indeed, Chernow addresses Grant's problems with alcohol as a major theme throughout the book. He argues that Grant should be seen as an alcoholic who simply could not use alcohol in moderation—a fact that he suggests Grant himself came to recognize. Chernow believes there was a distinct pattern to Grant's drinking episodes—they happened when he was lonely, bored, and away from his home or his regular headquarters of the moment, and when his "minders" (most importantly his staff officer, John Rawlins, and his wife, Julia) were not present to keep him on the "straight and narrow." Chernow suggests that accounts that fit this pattern may be accurate, and ones that do not can largely be discounted. Crucially, he argues that Grant's drinking never caused him to be absent at critical times when he was in command and never influenced his decisions in battle, and that Grant had largely conquered his alcohol problem by the time he became president.

Between the time Grant resigned from the army and the beginning of the Civil War, he was involved in several failing business ventures. He tried farming some acreage on his father-in-law's estate near St. Louis, Missouri, but gave up and sold his equipment and livestock after about two years. A real estate partnership in St. Louis lasted only a few months. When the war broke out, he was working as a clerk in one of his father's leather goods stores in Galena, Illinois. The coming of the Civil War, as Chernow suggests, "was about to rescue Grant from a dismal record of antebellum business failures."

Part two of the book is subtitled "A Life of War," referencing the fact that not only

© Beowulf Sheehan

Best-selling author Ron Chernow has won numerous honors, including the National Book Award for The House of Morgan *(1990), the Pulitzer Prize for* Washington: A Life *(2010), and a 2015 National Humanities Medal. He consulted on the Pulitzer-winning musical* Hamilton *(2015), based on his 2004 biography of Alexander Hamilton.*

did the Civil War occupy Grant's time and attention during this period, but that it truly changed the course of his life. Many who knew him before the war commented on the remarkable changes that war and high command wrought in Grant. Chernow argues that Grant excelled within a narrow range of skills and abilities: "Many major figures in history could have succeeded in about any environment, whereas Grant could only thrive in a narrower set of circumstances." His return to the army is portrayed as a turning point that came about almost by chance, as Grant was given a command in 1861 as the only local West Point graduate when President Abraham Lincoln called for volunteers to defend the Union.

Once allowed a chance to fight, Grant's rise to prominence was meteoric, going from a colonel to a major general in less than a year and winning the first significant Union victories of the war. After his successful 1863 siege of Vicksburg, Mississippi, he was in March 1864 given the newly revived rank of lieutenant general, which no one except George Washington had ever held. After receiving that promotion Grant was given command of all Union forces. Lincoln had watched Grant's rise through the officer's ranks with great interest, in part because Grant seemed to understand the central issue of winning the war in the same terms that Lincoln did—not by occupying Southern territory but by destroying Confederate armies. When Grant became general in chief, Lincoln backed him solidly and rarely second-guessed him, believing he had finally found the general who could win the war.

In many of Grant's Civil War battles, his Union forces emerged as victors even when they suffered more casualties than their Confederate opponents due to the strategic importance of the outcome. Grant understood the grim arithmetic of war—that the South would only be defeated by a long campaign of attrition, and that the Union had the manpower to replace casualties while the South did not. Still, Chernow believes that the common picture of "Butcher Grant," who cared little about the loss of life, is totally inaccurate. He cites military historians who have noted that Grant's armies tended to lose a smaller percentage of their men than his opponent's forces did, and fewer than most Civil War generals on either side. Even more convincingly, he includes many accounts of Grant reacting with deep emotion to the carnage left after a battle. "I have been called a butcher," Grant observed after the war's conclusion, as Chernow quotes. "But do you know I sometimes could hardly bring myself to give an order of battle. When I contemplated the death and misery that were sure to follow, I stood appalled."

The book's next section, "A Life of Peace," is dedicated mainly to Grant's two presidential terms. Following the end of the Civil War, Grant was a national hero, and after the assassination of Lincoln he was arguably the highest-profile leader in the country. As the North and South grappled with the challenges of Reconstruction, he was a natural choice to take the presidency after Lincoln's immediate successor, Andrew Johnson. Grant was elected by a wide margin in 1868, but his presidency would be troubled by frequent corruption scandals. Chernow challenges the image of the Grant administration as a failure, though he does not depart as far from the standard interpretations of previous historians as he does on other issues. He agrees with the general consensus that Grant himself was not corrupt, and that his principal fault was a naïve trust in people who betrayed him, even as the evidence against them became virtually impossible to ignore.

Perhaps the one area in which Chernow's views of Grant are too positive is in his consideration of Grant's role in Reconstruction. He gives plenty of evidence to prove that Grant became a true convert to the belief in emancipation and the goal of seeing that the freed slaves had all the rights of American citizens. Chernow especially credits Grant with virtually destroying the early manifestations of the Ku Klux Klan and winning the support of African American leaders. But the fact remains that terrorism by Southern whites eventually did reduce African Americans to second class citizenship and eliminated most black voting in much of the South. While the Klan may have been sidelined for a time, other paramilitary terror groups emerged that differed only in name. As political conditions changed in the North, toward the end of his second term Grant even refused to send federal troops to put down violence in Mississippi and South Carolina. While the ultimate failure of Reconstruction, as Chernow suggests, was not due to Grant's lack of effort, it was a failure nonetheless.

Chernow's book has received much critical praise, with many reviewers suggesting it stands as a definitive work on Grant. Several publications, including the *New York Times*, selected it as one of the top books of 2017. Critics compared *Grant* favorably to Chernow's other best-selling and award-winning biographies, including *Alexander Hamilton* (2004). In his review for *Slate*, for example, David Plotz suggested that Chernow had a harder task in this book than in writing about Hamilton, who was a blank slate to most readers, as the author had to "overcome a century of dishonest prejudice against Grant." Chernow's success in not only undoing misconceptions but also revealing new insights from his in-depth research once again proves his status as one of the preeminent biographers of his time.

Reviewers did find some faults with *Grant*. While admiring on the whole, T. J. Stiles remarked in a review for *The Washington Post* that "as a historian, Chernow proves somewhat uneven," noting some apparent factual errors and suggesting the book fails to reach the level of art. Other reviewers felt Chernow at times comes too close to apology in his effort to rehabilitate Grant's image. The book's meticulous detail—and corresponding page count—was also seen as a potential obstacle to some readers. Because of its length, this book may be one talked about more than read, but it is fascinating reading and well worth the effort of holding out to the end. It will also be a standard reference work, in part because of its detailed use of many primary sources, including the complete collection of Grant's writings completed in 2012.

Mark S. Joy, PhD

Review Sources

Duchschere, Kevin. Review of *Grant*, by Ron Chernow. *Minneapolis Star-Tribune*. 6 Oct. 2017, www.startribune.com/review-grant-by-ron-chernow/449664443/. Accessed 21 Feb. 2018.

Maslin, Janet. "In Ron's Chernow's 'Grant,' an American Giant's Makeover Continues." Review of *Grant*, by Ron Chernow. *The New York Times*, 10 Oct. 2017, www.nytimes.com/2017/10/10/books/review-grant-biography-ron-chernow.html. Accessed 21 Feb. 2018.

Plotz, David. "Give Me *Grant: An American Musical*." Review of *Grant*, by Ron Chernow. *Slate*, 2 Oct. 2017, www.slate.com/articles/arts/books/2017/10/grant_by_ron_chernow_reviewed_by_david_plotz.html. Accessed 21 Feb. 2018.

Stiles, T. J. "Chernow's Portrait of Grant as a Work of Literary Craftsmanship, If Not Art." Review of *Grant*, by Ron Chernow. *The Washington Post*, 6 Oct. 2017, www.washingtonpost.com/outlook/chernows-portrait-of-grant-as-a-work-of-literary-craftsmanship-if-not-art/2017/10/06/1139cbb2-9c89-11e7-9c8d-cf053ff30921_story.html. Accessed 21 Feb. 2018.

The Gulf
The Making of an American Sea

Author: Jack E. Davis (b. 1956)
Publisher: Liveright (New York). Illustrated. 608 pp.
Type of work: Environment, natural history, economics
Time: Prehistoric times–the present
Locales: The Gulf of Mexico and the United States

Historian Jack E. Davis provides an extensive commentary on the history of the Gulf of Mexico, focusing on the environmental impact of natural disasters, urban development, unregulated fishing and hunting, and industrial pollution on the region's natural resources.

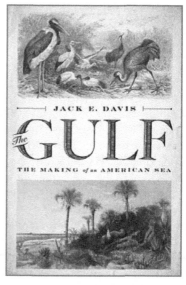

Courtesy of W.W. Norton

Principal personages

WALTER ANDERSON, a Mississippi artist
FRANK HAMILTON CUSHING, an anthropologist
JOHN D. MACDONALD, a crime fiction writer and environmental activist
EDWARD AVERY MCILHENNY, a business executive and conservationist
PÁNFILO DE NARVÁEZ, a Spanish conquistador
NASH ROBERTS, a New Orleans meteorologist
R. EUGENE TURNER, a marine scientist
DIANE WILSON, an environmental activist

The Gulf: The Making of an American Sea is one of those rare books that almost defies definition. One might best describe it as a biography of the Gulf of Mexico. Historian Jack E. Davis ranges widely across the disciplines of geology, marine science, ecology, history, and politics to create a comprehensive portrait of the Gulf that accounts for its development as a unique body of water that has supported human populations for millennia and one of the most diverse ecosystems on the planet. While Davis does a highly creditable job providing a primer on the geological factors that formed the Gulf and on the topography of its shoreline, his principal focus is on the people who have inhabited the region and their impact on this body of water. The real story Davis tells begins with the arrival of European explorers and adventurers. Motivated by the desire for wealth and zeal to spread Christianity among the native populations, these men brought with them prejudices that not only caused them to ignore the bounty of the region but also to put their own lives in grave danger. Among those whose adventures Davis profiles, the sixteenth-century conquistador Pánfilo de Narváez stands out. Authorized to colonize the territory of Florida, Narváez sailed from Spain with six hundred men, a formidable contingent certainly capable of subduing any opposition from poorly armed natives. Yet Narváez's expedition failed miserably, doomed by its leader's overconfidence and by the party's unwillingness to take advantage of the natural resources available to them. In waters where crabs, oysters, and fish were so abundant that they could be scooped from the sea, Narváez's men starved for lack of meat. They antagonized locals, who turned against them; eventually, the force was destroyed, and Narváez himself was lost at sea on a raft.

The history lesson continues through the next three centuries as other Europeans, notably English-speaking colonists who, after the American Revolution, made their way south in search of solitude or riches, took advantage of the natural bounty without regard for the sustainability of the Gulf's ecosystem. Vignettes on the founding of cities such as Tampa, Pensacola, and Destin pay tribute to the enterprising men and women who braved the elements—particularly storms and swarms of insects—to establish fishing communities and commercial ports in Florida, Alabama, Mississippi, Louisiana, and Texas. Chapters detail the development of sport fishing, beach-going, and leisure activities that transformed the sleepy backwaters and the coastline into bustling tourist destinations.

Although Davis does not dwell on any individual involved in the region's history, some are accorded more than a passing nod. Among these is Louisiana businessman Edward Avery McIlhenny, scion of the founder of a firm known worldwide for Tabasco sauce manufactured on Avery Island in southwest Louisiana. McIlhenny was responsible for establishing one of the first bird sanctuaries in the region, and though Davis admits that McIlhenny was also willing to allow hunting on his preserve, his efforts were important in saving the egret population. Davis also highlights the work of Frank Hamilton Cushing, an anthropologist whose work in Florida exploded myths about the region's American Indian population and helped highlight the area's important natural resources. One of Davis's more entertaining and even heartwarming accounts is a profile of Mississippi artist Walter Anderson, who spent a lifetime sketching and writing about the Gulf, particularly Mississippi's Horn Island, a barrier island miles offshore.

At the same time, however, Davis never misses a chance to point out the deleterious effects of many ventures on the flora and fauna of the Gulf region. His chapter on the decimation of Florida's bird population, given the ironic and somewhat macabre title "Birds of a Feather, Shot Together," is rife with examples of human greed trumping respect for other creatures. While the killing of millions of birds took place far from population centers, the driving force for the mass slaughter lay hundreds of miles away, in the nation's urban centers. The mania to decorate ladies' hats with elegant plumes from wading birds that teemed along the coastline and in adjacent marshes prompted hunting sprees that decimated many species. Similarly wanton overfishing nearly wiped out the tarpon population, as people took to the water in chartered boats to strive for the right to brag at having caught the largest of these magnificent game fish.

The damage done to the Gulf region during the first four centuries by Europeans and then Americans pales beside that wreaked on the area in the twentieth and twenty-first centuries by the greatest villains in Davis's book: big oil and its corporate cousins, the natural gas and petrochemical industries. Davis details in graphic language, supported by staggering statistics, the catastrophic effects (especially in Louisiana and Texas as well as the Gulf itself) of activities by companies bent on extracting natural resources and turning them into commodities for which there seems to be an ever-increasing demand by Americans (and people around the world). Davis lays bare oil companies' fallacious claims that the huge derricks erected offshore are good for the environment because they attract marine life. His counterargument stresses the lasting effects from the loss of marshlands that have, until the twenty-first century, served as barriers against the storms that periodically sweep inshore from the Gulf. He catalogs the loss of aquatic animals whose numbers have dropped precipitously during the twentieth century. He intones a litany of oil spills, explosions, and other accidents that have harmed animal and human life alike.

Jack E. Davis, a professor of history at the University of Florida, previously authored Race against Time: Culture and Separation in Natchez since 1930 *(2001) and* An Everglades Providence: Marjory Stoneman Douglas and the American Environmental Century *(2009). He received the 2017 Kirkus Prize for nonfiction for* The Gulf: The Making of an American Sea.

The final section of the book provides a kind of status report on the pollution of the Gulf and its estuaries. As Davis acknowledges, no one entity is to blame—yet there is plenty of blame to go around. Industries as far away as the Midwest have, for decades, used these waters as dumping grounds for waste products. Agricultural interests have enhanced crop growth by using chemical fertilizers, some of which end up in rainwater that runs off into rivers and streams that empty into the Gulf. Chemical treatment of lawns by the growing number of people who have moved to the region to take advantage of its temperate climate (and in many cases low taxes) have exacerbated the problems caused by agribusiness, as runoff into sewer systems combines with that from farms and ranches and the toxic effluents from petrochemical plants to create huge "dead zones" where no marine life can survive. Davis adds his voice to the chorus of environmental activists calling for swift and decisive action to halt this pollution.

Nevertheless, Davis's account is not one-sidedly pessimistic. His book is filled with stories of people whose love for the Gulf has made them champions against unchecked spoliation of its beauty and fecundity. One early rabble-rouser in the environmentalist camp was the novelist John D. MacDonald, a transplanted northerner who settled in Sarasota where, when not writing the at least seventy books for which he is known by millions of fans of mysteries and thrillers, he spent considerable time lobbying against rampant development that he saw destroying the pristine ecosystems he had come to love. Less polemic but equally determined to highlight the alarming state of the Gulf's ecosystems, acclaimed marine biologist and environmentalist R. Eugene Turner is repeatedly cited for his work in calling to account those responsible for callous industrial, commercial, and residential development.

Another crusader in the cause of environmental sanity who gets considerable attention is Diane Wilson, the Texas shrimping company owner who turned activist against the petrochemical companies that were polluting the waters around her home and causing thousands of her neighbors to become ill. Although Wilson has been an eloquent spokesperson for her cause in books such as *An Unreasonable Woman: A True Story of Shrimpers, Politicos, Polluters, and the Fight for Seadrift, Texas* (2005), Davis weaves her story deftly into a larger account of the struggles by environmentalists to take on industries that he says have long been cozy with local and state government officials, often because oil, natural gas, and petrochemical executives promise jobs to citizens and revenues to the states' coffers. The irony, Davis points out, is that these jobs do irreparable harm to places where these people and their ancestors have lived in harmony with nature for centuries.

While Davis is certainly exercised by humanmade catastrophes, he is keenly aware that the Gulf region has also been affected repeatedly by natural disasters. Chief among them are the hurricanes that either sweep in from the Atlantic or form in the Gulf itself. Some of Davis's finest writing is devoted to describing the impact of these monster storms. In what seems an inspired decision, he chooses not to focus on Katrina, the 2005 hurricane that caused massive flooding in New Orleans, Louisiana, perhaps because that storm has already been the subject of several studies. Instead, he offers a detailed account of Hurricane Audrey, a 1957 storm that took upward of four hundred lives in southwest Louisiana. Piecing together first-person accounts of those who survived the winds and floodwaters that ravaged Cameron Parish, Davis offers poignant insights into the effects that nature has had on those who live and work along the Gulf Coast. Focusing on Audrey also gives Davis the opportunity to profile another legend in the region, New Orleans meteorologist Nash Roberts. Alone among forecasters, Roberts accurately predicted the track of Audrey, challenging the "wisdom" of national weather agencies that insisted the storm would make landfall west in Texas or farther east along the Louisiana-Mississippi border. Roberts's ability to combine state-of-the-art technology with more traditional forecasting methods—principally reports from fishing captains at sea—made him the most respected weatherman in the region, so much so that, when national broadcasts made predictions about future storms such as Betsy (1965) and Camille (1969), locals would withhold judgment, asking instead, "What does Nash say?"

This mixture of personal profile, local anecdotes, scientific description, and historical narrative make *The Gulf* an interesting read for many beyond the academic community of which Davis is a member. Hence, his pleas for responsible treatment of the region's resources will reach a wider audience than the typical academic book would. At the same time, readers who simply want to acquire a greater understanding about one of America's most colorful and intriguing regions will learn much from Davis's well-researched chronicle, and his lively style will keep them entertained—two qualities that mark *The Gulf* as an exceptional book sure to enjoy a long shelf life.

Laurence W. Mazzeno

Review Sources

Bancroft, Colette. "Review: Jack E. Davis' *The Gulf* Is an Enthralling History of the Gulf of Mexico." Review of *The Gulf: The Making of an American Sea*, by Jack E. Davis. *Tampa Bay Times*, 2 Mar. 2017, www.tampabay.com/features/books/review-jack-e-davis-the-gulf-an-enthralling-history/2315014. Accessed 20 Dec. 2017.

Connors, Philip. "The Gulf of Mexico in the Age of Petrochemicals." Review of *The Gulf: The Making of an American Sea*, by Jack E. Davis. *The New York Times*, 26 May 2017, www.nytimes.com/2017/05/26/books/review/gulf-making-of-an-american-sea-jack-davis.html. Accessed 20 Dec. 2017.

Review of *The Gulf: The Making of an American Sea*, by Jack E. Davis. *Kirkus*, 16 Jan. 2017, www.kirkusreviews.com/book-reviews/jack-e-davis-8/the-gulf. Accessed 20 Dec. 2017.

Review of *The Gulf: The Making of an American Sea*, by Jack E. Davis. *Publishers Weekly*, 23 Jan. 2017, www.publishersweekly.com/978-0-87140-866-2. Accessed 20 Dec. 2017.

Half-Light
Collected Poems 1965–2016

Author: Frank Bidart (b. 1939)
Publisher: Farrar, Straus Giroux (New York). 736 pp.
Type of work: Poetry, autobiography

Half-Light: Collected Poems 1965–2016 *presents Frank Bidart's previous eight books of poems with selected new work, along with interviews, establishing the trajectory of the award-winning poet's career.*

Frank Bidart is widely regarded as one of the most important American poets of the past fifty-plus years. *Half-Light: Collected Poems 1965–2016* brings together eight previous volumes of Bidart's poetry and includes a collection of new poems as well as interviews with Mark Halliday, Adam Travis, and Shara Lessley that date from 1983 to 2013. This expansive collection, an impressive achievement that records the growth and development of Bidart's career, was chosen for the 2017 National Book Award in poetry.

As Bidart has explained in various interviews, and as his work demonstrates, he is a poet with a special interest in verbal and visual rhythms. The placement of words, phrases, and lines on the page are almost as important to him as the contents or meanings of the poems themselves. In fact, the meanings and effects of Bidart's poems cannot be separated from their technical details, especially the use of white space on the page to indicate sounds and silences heard in the inner ear. Consider, for example, the opening lines of the poem titled "Old and Young," which begins the section Thirst (New Poems, 2016):

> If you have looked at someone in
> a mirror
> looking at you in the mirror
>
>
> your eyes meeting
> there
> not face to face

*

backstage as you
prepare
for a performance

This sentence goes on and on: not a single comma, semicolon, or period interrupts its flow as the speaker piles detail on top of detail, phrase on top of phrase, to create a rhythm that eventually becomes almost hypnotic. The poem's point is increasingly deferred and postponed so that reading the text becomes a process almost impossible to stop once one has started. This is a technique Bidart uses in many of his works, especially his latest works: they are poems meant to be heard as much as be read, but the placement of words on the mostly blank pages is meant to guide that imaginative hearing. There are also many other subtleties in the movements from line to line, as in the emphatic placement of "a mirror" in the second line, the emphatic echo of that word at the end of the third line, the emphatic isolation of "there," and the understated (but still literally and figuratively pronounced) rhyme of "there" and "prepare," and so on. Bidart is well known for his poetic monologues such as in the poems "Herbert White" or "Ellen West," that include transgressive content such as necrophilia and anorexia, but for the most part his poems depend not on sensational topics or imagery, but on their visual and auditory techniques to capture and hold a reader's attention.

At the same time, the contents of the poems are themselves often moving, even in the abstract. As Major Jackson noted in his review for the *New York Times*, Bidart's poetry "over five decades has volubly modeled a wholly new approach to autobiographical material, chiefly by giving voice to the inner travails of other people's lives, both real and imagined." For example, in the poem "Half-Light," the speaker recalls a time of furtive, drunken intimacy with a male friend from undergraduate days:

Parallel. We lay in parallel furrows.

—That suffocated, fearful
look on your face.

Jim, yesterday I heard your wife on the phone
tell me you died almost nine months ago.

In interviews, such as in his 1999 *Chicago Review* session with Andrew Rathmann wherein Bidart spoke of the artist and poet Joe Brainard with whom had a deep friendship, Bidart has memorably expressed the notion of not having regrets, and certainly this poem illustrates that idea. These are often poems in this collection that look back wistfully on the past, celebrating the possibilities it offered while regretting how many of those possibilities went unfulfilled. Bidart, one of the most important of all the twentieth century's "confessional" poets, is in now his late seventies, and part of the value of his collected work is to provide the reader with a perspective on life from the long view, from an extended vantage point. But the poems enduring value results

Courtesy James Franco

Frank Bidart is the author of numer-
ous books of poetry, beginning with
the publication of Golden State *(1973).*
Half-Light: Collected Poems 1965–2016
won the 2017 National Book Award.
Other honors include a Lila Wallace–
Reader's Digest Foundation Writers'
Award (1991); the American Academy of
Arts and Letters Morton Dauwen Zabel
Award for Poetry (1995); and the Poetry
Society of America's Shelley Memorial
Award (1997). In 2007 Bidart received
the prestigious Bollingen Prize for Po-
etry.

from the methods Bidart uses to compose
them, not simply from what is said. In "Half-
Light," for example, there are many accomplished effects, ranging from the subtle to the
surprising. The single, emphatic word "parallel," for instance, instantly catches readers
off guard but then is immediately explained.
The ensuing reference to "parallel furrows"
(the speaker and his friend are lying out in a
remote field, in the darkness of night, with
only stars above) makes perfect everyday
sense but also, in retrospect, foreshadows
parallel graves. The tone of pastoral pleasure
is immediately complicated by the "suffocated, fearful" look on Jim's face. But then
comes the sudden, abrupt shift to news that
Jim, many decades later, has passed away.

Nothing prepares readers for the transition from youthful dalliance to the friend's
final absence, and the speaker is even more
stunned than his audience. Details mentioned
in passing—especially the reference to "your
wife"—imply much but remain understated.
The speaker addresses Jim as if Jim were still
alive (as, in a sense, he is: in the speaker's
memory and imagination and now in this
poem itself). The final quoted lines are especially poignant, but much of their power
depends on the skill with which they are
phrased, especially the use of emphatic repetition. This poem exemplifies many of
the talents for which Bidart is justly praised: conversational plain-spokenness; ready
accessibility; an emphasis on personal experience that also somehow seems universal;
and, above all, the careful attention he pays to subtleties of rhythm. Little wonder,
then, that Bidart chose this work as the title poem for a volume summing up his entire
career. He is a poet whom many readers can easily understand, but whom many other
poets will value for the details of his careful craftsmanship.

The subjects, like the powers, of Bidart's poems are varied. In "End of a Friendship," for instance, he immediately takes an openly political stance, offering phrasing
shocking in the ways it describes the brutality of American colonialists in their treatment of Native Americans. But this part of the poem is powerful not because of the descriptions alone but because of the subtlety with which those descriptions are phrased
and, especially, for the skill with which the phrases are laid out on the page. Yet the
poem soon metamorphoses, as its title suggests, into an extended meditation on Bidart's long, important, but ultimately broken friendship with Robert Lowell, his mentor

and substitute father. Here again the poetry is personal and confessional, and it is also, importantly, personal from the perspective of an aging man. Bidart has emphasized, in various interviews, that his verse is often rooted in his own personal experience, that its purpose is not only to give voice to his own life but, in doing so, to give voice to life itself. Thus, this poem is not only about his broken friendship with Lowell but also about *any* broken friendship, just as the poem's lines about Bidart's parents will seem relevant to anyone's relations with his or her parents.

Similarly, "Sum" will seem relevant to anyone aging and nearing death, but it will seem so less because of the subject matter itself than because Bidart uses vivid imagery and haunting sounds to imply whatever message the poem has to offer about mutability, as in these closing lines:

> Each morning you wake to long slow piteous
> swoops of sound, half-loon, half-dog.
>
> He is wandering in the yard.
>
> The dog at eighteen who at sixteen began protesting each dawn.

Here, again, is the note repeated throughout the final poems: the note of approaching finality—the note of looming death. But here, too, is Bidart's gift for engaging the inner ear, for playing with gaps in spacing, for ending with a line that suggests much more than it openly states. The dog becomes the symbol of the speaker, but the speaker avoids any hint of sentimentality, whether in depicting himself, or in depicting the dog.

As Christopher Spaide suggested in his review of this collection for the *Yale Review*, the book could be "read as a single seven-hundred-page poem, reprising the same obsessions over its fifty-year composition." In any era when so much poetry can seem either merely prosy, or impenetrably arcane, or overtly propagandistic, or simply playful and ultimately empty, Bidart offers poems that are rich in every respect: in obvious meaning, in subtle implication, and especially in skill with which the words are summoned up and laid out on the page.

Robert C. Evans, PhD

Review Sources

Als, Hilton. "Frank Bidart's Poetry of Saying the Unsaid." Review of *Half-Light: Collected Poems 1965–2016*, by Frank Bidart. *The New Yorker*, 11 Sept. 2017, www.newyorker.com/magazine/2017/09/11/frank-bidarts-poetry-of-saying-the-unsaid. Accessed 30 Jan. 2018.

Jackson, Major. "Five Decades of Frank Bidart's Verse, From Masks to Self-Mythology." Review of *Half–Light: Collected Poems 1965–2016*, by Frank Bidart. *The New York Times*, 4 Oct. 2017, www.nytimes.com/2017/10/04/books/review/frank-bidart-half-light-poems.html. Accessed 30 Jan. 2018.

Spaide, Christopher. "Poetry in Review: *Half-Light: Collected Poems, 1965–2016,* by Frank Bidart. Review of *Half-Light: Collected Poems 1965–2016*, by Frank Bidart. *The Yale Review*, yalereview.yale.edu/poetry-review-half-light-collected-poems-1965-2016-frank-bidart. Accessed 30 Jan. 2018.

Teicher, Craig Morgan. Review of *Half-Light: Collected Poems 1965–2016*, by Frank Bidart. *Publishers Weekly*, Aug. 2017, www.publishersweekly.com/978-0-374-12595-0. Accessed 30 Jan. 2018.

Vendler, Helen. "The Tragic Sense of Frank Bidart." Review of *Half-Light: Collected Poems 1965–2016*, by Frank Bidart. *The New York Review of Books*, 26 Oct. 2017. www.nybooks.com/articles/2017/10/26/tragic-sense-of-frank-bidart/. Accessed 30 Jan. 2018.

Hallelujah Anyway
Rediscovering Mercy

Author: Anne Lamott (b. 1954)
Publisher: Riverhead Books (New York).
192 pp.
Type of work: Memoir, philosophy, religion
Time: Present day
Locale: San Francisco Bay Area, California

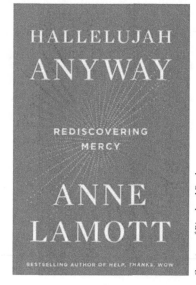

Courtesy of Riverhead Books

Using examples from her own life and those of her family and friends, Anne Lamott explores the concept of mercy as a way to understand one's place in an increasingly complex world, discover one's spiritual identity, and allow the transformative power of forgiveness to bring healing to one's life and the lives of loved ones.

Principal personages
ANNE LAMOTT, the author
SAM LAMOTT, her son
KENNETH LAMOTT, her father
ANN, her ninety-two-year-old friend
JAY, Ann's son, who died by suicide

"Mercy" is a word that does not appear often in the lexicon of popular culture. Instead, such terms as "empowerment," "leverage," and "proactive" populate the jargon of social media, political speeches, personal interaction, and work environments. If words reflect values, then where do patience, peace, humility, and service fit in? Is it possible to cultivate such traits in an age where self-worth is measured in "likes"? In her book *Hallelujah Anyway*, Anne Lamott suggests that practicing mercy toward others, as well as toward oneself, may loosen the grip of the self-absorption and self-centeredness that characterize contemporary society.

What is mercy? The *Merriam-Webster Dictionary* defines it as "compassion or forbearance shown especially to an offender or to one subject to one's power" and "a blessing that is an act of divine favor or compassion." In Judaism, Christianity, and Islam, mercy is viewed as intrinsic to the relationship between God and humankind. God shows love and compassion to people who are inherently sinful and do not deserve such consideration, and God expects the same from his followers. Lamott offers a simpler, to-the-point definition of mercy, writing, "Mercy is radical kindness."

Lamott's collection of nine essays takes its title from Candi Staton's 2012 gospel song. Faith and hope infuse Staton's lyrics: "Praise him till your blessings come down / Praise him till your situation turns around / You gotta lift up your voice and say /

Hallelujah anyway." Lamott writes that she chose Staton's song as the title of her book because in spite of life's challenges, mercy and love carry people through difficult times even when the world seems cold and heartless. Lamott explains, "Hallelujah that in spite of it all, there is love, there is singing, nature, laughing, mercy." In addition to Staton's song, the "North Star" that guides Lamott's reflections is a passage from the Old Testament prophet Micah who admonishes, "What doth God require of thee but to do justice and to love mercy, and to walk humbly with thy God?"

It will come as no surprise to readers familiar with Lamott's work that she launches her exploration of mercy by quoting a Bible verse. In the early 1980s, she began to walk her rocky road to faith after experiencing what she claims was a spiritual encounter with Jesus. At the time, her life revolved around drugs and alcohol. She began attending a Presbyterian church in Marin City, California, because she was drawn to the music. However, the pastor's sermons and the love shown to her by the members of the congregation led her to surrender her life to Christ. Her first spiritual memoir, *Traveling Mercies* (1999), details her conversion. Others followed as she progressed in her journey, including *Plan B* (2005), a collection of essays on faith, and *Help, Thanks, Wow* (2012), a book on prayer. In her signature style, she interweaves her observations on faith with humorous and sometimes acerbic anecdotes about her dysfunctional family, her ambivalent relationship with her parents, her insecurities concerning her physical appearance, the trials and joys of single parenthood, and struggles with aging. Never preachy or openly evangelistic, she focuses on what faith can teach about life's difficulties and how it can ultimately bring healing to one's deepest wounds.

Writers often seek healing and transformation through the power of words. For example, David Brooks comments on his reason for writing his book *The Road to Character* (2015): "I wrote it, to be honest, to save my own soul." Lamott also uses writing as a way to work out her salvation as she grapples with difficult and painful situations. In an interview, she noted that when she reads a book that reflects an honest, authentic view of life, she feels "rich and profoundly relieved to be in the presence of someone who will share the truth with me, and throw the lights on a little, and I try to write these kinds of books. Books, for me, are medicine." In candidly writing about her own human frailties, personal disappointments, and resentments, she connects with readers on an emotional level, which is one of the reasons her books consistently top the best-seller lists.

Throughout her career, Lamott has wrestled on the page with coming to terms with her unconventional early life. She does so again in *Hallelujah Anyway*. In a chapter titled "Life Cycles," she somewhat petulantly compares her own dysfunctional family to the "three or four people I've ever known" who came from happier backgrounds. As Lamott writes, "My intimate friends have always been the children of absent parents, alcohol, faithlessness, hickory switches, and manic depression." She is resentful that her childhood experiences robbed her of innocence. She goes on to describe the tug of war between parents and their children; "life in the shrapnel field" of adolescence when children lose "contact with our innately merciful selves"; the longing for a mate; and finally, her experiences as a single mother. At every stage, she is aware that at any moment, loss and disappointment can endanger hopeful expectations. It is during these

Courtesy of Sam Lamott

Anne Lamott is the best-selling author of several nonfiction books, including Help, Thanks, Wow *(2012),* Some Assembly Required *(2012),* Stitches *(2013), and* Small Victories *(2014), as well as several novels, including* Imperfect Birds *(2010). She is also a past recipient of a Guggenheim Fellowship and an inductee to the California Hall of Fame.*

fragile times that mercy—radical kindness to oneself and others—is most necessary. At the end of the chapter, she shares a story about how she and her son, Sam, were briefly estranged when he took issue with a snippy remark she made about a celebrity transgendered person. Eventually she and Sam were reconciled, and through that reconciliation she realizes that "extending mercy had cost him, and extending mercy to myself cost me even more deeply, and it grew us both."

Even a small act of mercy has the power to bring comfort during a trying time. Ironically, Lamott is reminded of this fact not in a religious setting but in a mall, an iconic establishment of modern consumerism. She has just had an argument with Sam and is seeking distraction by browsing the aisles of a high-end store that is filled with pricey clothes, furniture, and knickknacks. But her shopping excursion cannot supply what she really needs—Sam's forgiveness. Collapsing into a comfortable chair, she calls an old friend for support. Suddenly she feels somebody by her side. It is a store attendant who, noticing her fatigue, brings her a small cup of water. The simple, unexpected act of kindness coupled with her friend's encouragement amounts to "a glut of mercy."

One of Lamott's most moving meditations is inspired by grief. In the fifth chapter, titled "Impatiens," she poses a difficult question: "How—if we are to believe that there is meaning in our brief time here on earth, that mercy is the ground of our being and love is sovereign—do we explain childhood cancer, earthquakes, addiction? Where is mercy in a beloved's suicide?" Exploring the age-old conundrum of why God allows suffering, she turns to the New Testament story of Jesus raising his friend Lazarus from the dead recounted in the Gospel of John. Irritated with Jesus for delaying his arrival at Lazarus's tomb, Lamott does not let him off the hook. She takes Jesus to task for getting "pissy" when Martha and Mary, the "ultimate believers," are upset because he did not come in time to save their brother, and she accuses him of not "hearing the humanity" of the grief-stricken sisters. But the lesson she draws from this story is that in spite of the temporary animosity between them, Mary, Martha, and Jesus remain committed to their friendship and their love for one another. It is in this commitment that she discerns another "definition" of mercy: "Mercy means, I don't run away from this, and go shopping. . . . I stay."

Her commentary on the resurrection of Lazarus leads to a poignant present-day story of another death—one where Lamott discovers mercy "in a beloved's suicide."

After Jay, the younger son of her ninety-two-year-old friend Ann, dies by suicide, Lamott and three others remain with Ann during the ensuing week. They are there when Jay's body lies in a closed casket at the funeral home awaiting cremation, and they help Ann prepare for Jay's memorial service a week later. In reflecting on Jay's suicide, Lamott reveals another, darker side of mercy. She notes that Jay was at the mercy of a "bad brain," and that "mercy has claws, too, that don't easily let go." Although Lamott mostly focuses on the redemptive, transformative aspects of mercy, she sometimes hints at its ambiguities and reminds readers that "God doesn't give us answers. God gives us grace and mercy."

Lamott often revisits subjects that have troubled her over the years. Her "frizzy" hair and her relationship with her father, Kenneth, are two of these topics. In past memoirs, when she returns to the feelings of rejection associated with her appearance and her father, she peels back new layers of understanding but never seems to get to the core cause of her pain. In the last chapter of *Hallelujah Anyway*, she goes deeper into her past to hunt for new insights. She tells the story of a time she accompanied Kenneth to the beach on a fishing trip when she was five. She tells of the joy she feels as she explores the weeds and bugs while her father and another man fish. In the course of their conversation, Kenneth's fishing buddy looks at her and uses a racial slur to describe her unruly hair. But instead of defending his daughter, her "civil-rights-marching" dad laughs—and she is stung by his reaction. She feels betrayed and "attacked." She carries her pain through adulthood, long after her father passes away. The biblical story of Joseph's betrayal by his brothers and the guidance of her therapist help her to better understand that everyone is flawed. The realization of this shared brokenness causes her to see the incident in a new light. She grasps that her father viewed the fisherman as harmless and was not colluding with him but understanding him. Because she is finally able to extend mercy and forgiveness to her father, she is able to release her resentment and anger.

Some reviewers have been critical of *Hallelujah Anyway* as a loose collection of rambling essays that does not effectively communicate what mercy really is. Is it love? Forgiveness? Tolerance? Compassion? Nonjudgmental acceptance of oneself and others? In Lamott's big-tent view, each of these virtues, when practiced with a sincere heart, is a facet of the "radical kindness" that the world sorely needs.

Pegge Bochynski

Review Sources

Arnett, Ray. Review of *Hallelujah Anyway: Rediscovering Mercy*, by Anne Lamott. *Library Journal*, vol. 142, no. 3, 15 Feb. 2017, pp. 92–94.

Bauer, Anne. "*Hallelujah Anyway*: Anne Lamott's Conflicted Message for a Conflicted Nation." Review of *Hallelujah Anyway: Rediscovering Mercy*, by Anne Lamott. *The Washington Post*, 30 Mar. 2017, www.washingtonpost.com/entertainment/books/hallelujah-anyway-anne-lamotts-conflicted-message-for-a-conflicted-nation/2017/03/28/6102faec-1011-11e7-9d5a-a83e627dc120_story.html. Accessed 6 Oct. 2017.

Review of *Hallelujah Anyway: Rediscovering Mercy*, by Anne Lamott. *Kirkus*, 1 Feb. 2017, www.kirkusreviews.com/book-reviews/anne-lamott/hallelujah-anyway. Accessed 6 Oct. 2017.

Review of *Hallelujah Anyway: Rediscovering Mercy*, by Anne Lamott. *Publishers Weekly*, 13 Feb. 2017, www.publishersweekly.com/978-0-7352-1358-6. Accessed 6 Oct. 2017.

Heitman, Danny. "*Hallelujah Anyway* Celebrates All in Life That Is Worthy of Praise." Review of *Hallelujah Anyway: Rediscovering Mercy*, by Anne Lamott. *The Christian Science Monitor*, 24 Apr. 2017, www.csmonitor.com/Books/Book-Reviews/2017/0414/Hallelujah-Anyway-celebrates-all-in-life-that-is-worthy-of-praise. Accessed 6 Oct. 2017.

The Hearts of Men

Author: Nickolas Butler (b. 1979)
Publisher: Ecco (New York). 400 pp.
Type of work: Novel
Time: 1962, 1996, and 2019
Locale: Northern Wisconsin

This novel of three generations of boys and men at a summer camp in northern Wisconsin paints a picture of evolving American notions of masculinity.

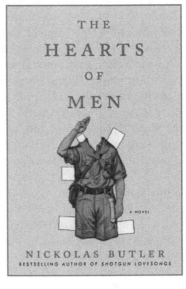

Courtesy of Ecco

Principal characters

NELSON DOUGHTY, an earnest Boy Scout who grows up to serve in Vietnam, then returns to run the summer camp he attended as a child
JONATHAN QUICK, his lifelong friend
WILBUR WHITESIDE, camp director
TREVOR QUICK, Jonathan's son
RACHEL QUICK, Trevor's widow, who is raising their son alone
THOMAS QUICK, Trevor's son

The Hearts of Men is a novel that explores how boys across three generations learn to become men during their summers spent at a Wisconsin Boy Scout camp. Nickolas Butler has created a beguiling, interlocking structure for his second novel; its three parts are set at the same scout camp in 1962, 1996, and 2019, respectively. Characters who are adolescents in the first part become middle-aged parents in the second part, and, old men in the final part. Each successive generation struggles to raise a new generation of boys. Butler is unflinching in his portrayal of the cruelties that boys and men can inflict on one another. Yet he is, at the same time, fundamentally optimistic about an individual's capacity to live by a moral code and to instill this code in others.

The first part of the novel is titled "Summer, 1962: The Bugler." The title refers to Nelson Doughty, a young man who excels at scouting but who is spurned by his fellow scouts. At Camp Chippewa, he is the first boy up each morning, as punctilious in his playing of reveille on his bugle as he is in earning the merit badges that will make him an Eagle Scout. In the opening scene, set in the town of Eau Claire, Nelson's parents throw him an elaborate birthday party. They have invited his entire scout troop, and yet no one shows up. Nelson cries, his parents argue, and his abusive father is on the verge of beating his son when an older Boy Scout, Jonathan Quick, arrives and salvages the party. Jonathan is everything Nelson is not: handsome, popular, loved by other boys. He has come to the party out of a sense of duty, the reader surmises, but Jonathan nevertheless is Nelson's savior and is the closest thing the younger boy has to a friend.

Nelson and Jonathan's complex relationship will span the next fifty-odd years and will be the cord that ties together the three parts of Butler's novel.

During the week that Nelson spends at summer camp, his triumphs and struggles are thrown into sharper contrast. Although Nelson's father, Clete, attends the camp as a chaperone, he is distant from his son. It is the camp director, Wilbur Whiteside, who sees in Nelson great potential and who mentors and encourages him. A decorated World War I veteran, Wilbur is a paragon of scouting virtues and a role model to Nelson and the other boys. Yet the old man is not entirely what he seems. In a flashback to his war years, the reader learns that Wilbur survived the battlefield because he lay in the mud, playing dead for three days. Wilbur's personal history is only one part of a larger pattern of deception. Nelson prizes the bugle that his grandfather, another World War I veteran, allegedly took as a trophy from a dead German soldier. But Wilbur explains to Nelson that the horn is not a military model—and that his grandfather's story may be equally suspect.

Early in the novel and in the week of camping, Wilbur warns the campers, counselors, and fathers that he knows of "clandestine meeting . . . vulgar happenings . . . disturbingly uncouth behavior." Nelson will be witness to some of this: when he tracks a group of boys who are setting out into the woods at night after curfew, they ransack his tent and smash up his beloved bugle. Wilbur turns to Nelson specifically for help in rooting out the corruption among his staff, saying, "Son, you help me locate this evil, I'll make sure you are promoted to camp counselor next year." It is a morally questionable proposition on the old man's part. Nelson is young and lonely enough that he agrees readily to this offer, which will set in motion forces that shape much of the rest of his life.

Meanwhile, Nelson is subjected to a particularly cruel punishment by the other campers. In one harrowing scene, he is lowered into a latrine to retrieve a nickel after his troop loses a bet to another troop; Jonathan alleviates his torture somewhat but is also shown to be partly complicit in it. This scene has led several reviewers, including Darin Strauss in his review for the *New York Times*, to compare Butler's novel to *The Lord of the Flies*. The perennial message is that, left to their own devices, boys can have a bottomless appetite for cruelty. In descending into the latrine, Nelson sheds some of his innocence and faith.

This process continues in the next few days, when Nelson discovers where the counselors have been holding their clandestine meetings. They have been drinking, smoking, and watching pornographic movies at an abandoned site a few miles away from camp, and the boy leads a furious Wilbur to break up their party. Counselors are fired, campers are sent packing, and the week of scout camp ends in general chaos. This chaos continues back at the Nelson household, where Clete accuses his son of being "a snitch," and after a violent altercation with Nelson's mother, Dorothy, Clete leaves his family for good. This first part of the book concludes with Nelson calling Wilbur for help, and Wilbur takes him in. In an image that runs throughout the book, Nelson hangs up the phone and feels himself being swept away by events and by time itself.

The next part of the book leaps forward thirty-five years, to the summer of 1996. A middle-aged Jonathan Quick takes his son, Trevor, to spend a week at Jonathan's old Boy Scout camp. Camp Chippewa has been renamed Camp Whiteside, in honor of the old scoutmaster, and Nelson is now its director. Where Jonathan has become rich by going into the family trucking business, Nelson, we learn, attended a military academy (with Wilbur's help), joined the Green Berets, and served in Vietnam. This part of the novel revolves around a single evening, in which Jonathan, a hard-drinking, womanizing cynic, tries to puncture his son's steadfast virtuousness. Jonathan worries that Trevor is too dependent on his girlfriend, Rachel. He wants his son to "go to Baskin-Robbins and try all the flavors. . . . Why, oh, *why* would a sixteen-year-old boy lock into vanilla for the rest of his life?" Jonathan therefore arranges a particularly awkward dinner on the evening before camp starts, with Trevor, Nelson, and—to Trevor's horror—his mistress. It is a tumultuous evening for Trevor, as his father introduces him to the girlfriend that he did not know existed, and announces that his marriage to Trevor's mother is coming to an end. Driven by a complex of conscious and subconscious motivations, Jonathan is driving a wedge between Trevor and his mother, his teenage girlfriend, and women as a whole. He is ushering his son out of innocence and into a jaded manhood. Nelson serves as an important foil throughout this evening. Trevor idealizes the camp director, who has emerged from his tumultuous childhood and adolescence as a tough, principled, virtuous man, who is nonetheless haunted by his wartime experiences. As he becomes a man, Trevor will have to navigate between the two contrasting models of masculinity that these two men, his father and Nelson, represent.

This part of the novel feels particularly freewheeling and fresh. Whereas Butler clearly needed to research and reconstruct the opening section of the book, set as it is before he was born, the second part feels more of his own time, and hence more natural in its cadences. Butler has said that this episode is autobiographical, as his own father staged much the same scene, introducing his son to his mistress over dinner. After dinner, Jonathan and Nelson take Trevor to a strip club, where he meets a young woman who does, in fact, challenge his steadfast devotion to Rachel. The next morning, a downcast and hungover Trevor calls his mother. He wants desperately to be back home, and, one imagines, to have back the more innocent relationship he had the day before to his mother and to Rachel. Of course, he can say none of this; his father has been successful in separating him from the women in his life, and he assures his mother, emptily, that "we're fine . . . we're all just fine."

The third section of the book, set in the near future of 2019, finds Rachel, now Trevor's widow, taking their teenage son, Thomas, to Camp Whiteside. Scouting, which in many ways is an institution well past its prime, proves a surprisingly powerful lens for Butler to direct at present-day issues, ranging from social media to rape culture. Nelson is grappling with these issues; like Wilbur before him, he has become an old man struggling to shepherd one last generation of boys to manhood. Befuddled by the boys' addiction to their screens and their indifference to nature, Nelson confides to Rachel that this will be his last summer at the camp. In a sign of the times, this section of the novel is punctuated by the occasional text message exchange. Yet the biggest issue raised in this chapter is one that runs through the novel as a whole: What does it mean to be a man? There has always been a strain of toxic masculinity running through the camp, but in some ways, it takes on its most acute form in the twenty-first century. Trevor himself looms over this section of the novel, standing as both a paragon and a victim of masculine ideals. A decorated Special Forces veteran who served in Afghanistan, he died in a movie theater parking lot, shot by a drunk patron who felt disrespected by Trevor's asking him to quiet down during the show.

Rachel is independent and supremely competent, and has tried her best to raise Thomas—a reluctant camper, at best—in a way that respects his father's ethos. She is the only woman in attendance at camp, and some of her interactions with the boorish, misogynistic fathers border on the cartoonish. One father is crude and homophobic, a mouthpiece for angry white men. Another father, Dr. Platz, is urbane and smooth talk-

Nickolas Butler is a graduate of the University of Wisconsin–Madison and the Iowa Writer's Workshop, and is the author of the short-story collection Beneath the Bonfire, *and the novels* Shotgun Lovesongs *and* The Hearts of Men.

ing, but is equally vile in his attitudes toward women and in his predatory nature. At points, Rachel's interactions with these men can read like a rehashed think-piece rather than like glimpses of real people interacting with each other. Rachel herself is a compelling character, but she reads at times like an ideal man's ideal woman. She is characterized a few too many times by her love of strong coffee, and is defined a little too roundly by her devotion to Trevor's memory. As Dr. Platz emerges as a true villain, it falls to Nelson and Thomas to save Rachel from him. In a section of the novel that is very much an exploration of modern ideas of gender and power, it is a little disappointing to find the book's one independent woman relegated to the role of damsel in distress. This, perhaps, is a pitfall of Butler's three-part structure: it creates in the early sections of the book a series of programmatic expectations that the author is compelled to deliver on in later sections. Some of what unfolds in the novel's final section therefore feels inevitable, not because of the motivations and actions of its characters, but because of the structural imperatives and symmetries of the overarching narrative. But these are, in the end, minor flaws in what is otherwise a remarkably gripping and relevant book. *The Hearts of Men* is an ambitious, thoughtful novel that offers a kaleidoscopic view of generations of American notions of masculinity.

Matthew J. Bolton

Review Sources

Cole, Tom, and Nicole Cohen. "What's Inside 'The Hearts of Men'? A New Novel Forages for Answers." Review of *The Hearts of Men*, by Nickolas Butler. *All Things Considered*, National Public Radio, 10 Mar. 2017, www.npr.org/2017/03/10/518877262/whats-inside-the-hearts-of-men-a-new-novel-forages-for-answers. Accessed 7 Feb. 2018.

Nathans-Kelly, Steve. "Nickolas Butler Talks Family Secrets and the Rust Belt in *The Hearts of Men*." *Paste Magazine*, 10 Mar. 2017, www.pastemagazine.com/articles/2017/03/nickolas-butler-hearts-of-men.html. Accessed 7 Feb. 2018.

Strauss, Darin. "Heroes Meet at a Boy Scout Camp out of William Golding." Review of *The Hearts of Men*, by Nickolas Butler. *The New York Times*, 8 Mar. 2017, www.nytimes.com/2017/03/08/books/review/hearts-of-men-nickolas-butler.html. Accessed 7 Feb. 2018.

Her Body and Other Parties

Author: Carmen Maria Machado
Publisher: Graywolf Press (Minneapolis).
  245 pp.
Type of work: Short fiction
Time: Present day
Locales: Various

Her Body and Other Parties is the debut short story collection from award-winning writer Carmen Maria Machado. At its center is the experience of the female body, which Machado reclaims for women through explorations of psychological, social, and sexual themes. Each story is fantastical, eerie, and steeped in the supernatural, offering a startlingly original voice.

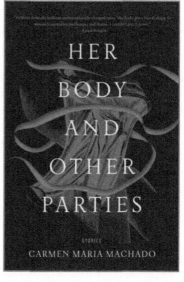

Courtesy of Graywolf Press

Her Body and Other Parties is the haunting debut book from Carmen Maria Machado, collecting stories including some of her most acclaimed pieces previously published in various literary periodicals. The eight fable-like works that comprise the book all delve into the terror women can feel living in a world that often sees them more as objects to be conquered or targets for violence than people with basic rights like safety, autonomy, or even life. As the title suggests, Machado's primary way of examining this concept is through the visceral experience of the body, which in the case of women is often violated or appropriated, yet also capable of wonder and joy. This grounding in the physical gives rise to a complexity of psychological and social themes that further makes the collection a timely cultural commentary.

Through the course of the eight stories, Machado leads readers through a spectrum of female experience. The diverse settings and plots show that despite best intentions, it is frequently impossible to ever find oneself completely at ease in a moment. The pieces frequently evoke aspects of fairy tales or other folk stories, capturing such tales' deep, universal cultural meanings and built-in morals. By exploring and busting open the fairy tale genre—the kinds of stories engrained in women from a young age—Machado reveals the unease women can often feel in the world. She does not see the stories children are told as pure innocent entertainment, but neither does she see them as sinister. Rather, she seems to view them as early warnings for the young about what is to come in life. She applies these same themes to her own stories with sophistication.

The collection's opening story, "The Husband Stitch," is named after a rumored procedure administered to some women following childbirth that is meant to benefit the man, rather than help the woman who has just given birth. The female narrator of

Courtesy of Tom Storm Photography

Carmen Maria Machado has had short fiction and essays published in Granta, *the* New Yorker, *and* Gulf Coast, *as well as in numerous anthologies. A graduate of the Iowa Writers' Workshop, she has served as a writer in residence at the University of Pennsylvania, among other residencies and fellowships.*

the story is eventually given such a "husband stitch," though it is not the base of violence bestowed on her. The story also adapts the well-known horror tale about a woman who always wears a mysterious ribbon around her neck, which her husband is never allowed to untie. In Machado's version, the ribbon-wearing woman and her eventual husband meet at a party as teenagers and fall in love almost immediately. Though curious about the ribbon, the man is able to resist his desire to remove it as the couple satisfy their sexual desires, marry, and settle into a seemingly happy life. Tension around the ribbon increases over the years, however, as he begins to feel she is keeping him in the dark about one of her deepest secrets. Happy to please him in any other way, she wants to keep this one secret for herself.

Interspersed within the narrative are the narrator's summaries of fairy tales, urban legends, and fables in which women are mistrusted, subjected to violence, or are part of a mystery. One such interlude discusses the story of a woman supposedly raised by wolves, and who was said to have been later spotted raising wolf cubs. The narrator comments that she likes to believe the feral woman bore the cubs herself. Another narrated story-within-the-story is about a woman who pleases her abusive husband with her cooking skills. One day she accidentally eats the entirety of a piece of liver intended for dinner that night. Desperate and without any money to buy a replacement, she goes to the local mortuary and removes the liver of a newly deceased woman to cook. That night as she lies in bed with her husband, heavy footsteps lumber down the hall, and when the door swings open, the woman sees what she first believes to be the ghost of the corpse whose liver she stole. However, she then feels the sticky wetness of blood on the sheets next to her, and realizes she is bleeding from the hole where she removed her own liver.

The use of these mini stories helps Machado to make a larger point with her narrative, which itself is quite simple and sticks to quaint details about childbearing, weddings, drifting apart, and growing old together. At the story's end, the woman's husband begs to remove the ribbon, and she finally says he can, before telling him that she has always loved him more than anything. What happens next is a mystery that both reflects the nature of classic horror tales and reinforces the deeper social themes at play. In many ways, the power of stories is the story's central message.

The following story, "Inventory," is narrated by a woman inventorying everyone she has had sexual encounters with throughout her life, as meanwhile a deadly pandemic spreads. As she attempts to move further away from the infected areas, she comes across characters who are also plotting their escape. Machado humanizes their struggle by writing about these moments of connection between the characters.

The story's main character, who is unnamed like many of the others in the book, begins her sexual history in her youth. High school escapades follow before she gets into deeper connections, and sometimes not, in college. From the beginning, the encounters vary between men and women, illustrating Machado's skill in depicting LGBTQ characters. One of the core strengths of *Her Body and Other Parties* is the author's ease in writing frankly and beautifully about sex. While Machado has also written pure erotica under a pseudonym, these stories are not necessarily erotic. Rather, they reveal a keen understanding of how people find emotional connection in sexual situations, and show how pleasure is usually connected to something deeper within a character.

As the world withers around her, the narrator in "Inventory" continues to find connection with those she encounters. Machado moves the plague plotline along by revealing the symptoms of the disease, and in sometimes moving detail. In one instance, the protagonist falls in love with a woman who comes across her cabin in Maine, and they begin to live together. However, one day they both notice symptoms in the new lover, and the narrator must look into her eyes to see if the virus has taken hold. When it is revealed that it has, the protagonist flees to an island where she is completely isolated, and the story ends.

The centerpiece of the collection is arguably "Especially Heinous," a novella-length story that reimagines the descriptions of each episode from the first twelve seasons of the long-running police procedural television series *Law & Order: Special Victims Unit*. Machado creates characters named "Benson" and "Stabler" who both are and are not the same characters as the stars from the series. Told in lyrical prose and creepy detail, "Especially Heinous" reveals what exposure to violence on a regular and intimate basis can do to a human, while also examining the ways women and men are affected differently.

As the "series" progresses, Benson begins to experience a haunting by young women with bells for eyes. The women are the victims of violent attacks who demand that Benson avenge their deaths. Each night, as Benson sleeps alone in her apartment— Benson being alone is also a theme in this story—she awakes in the middle of the night to the women, or has vivid dreams about them. Sometimes she allows the girls access to her body, and they control her during her trips out of the house. Stabler, meanwhile, projects the violence around him onto his wife and daughters, entertaining sometimes paranoid delusions about the safety of each, or pausing for a moment when it seems that his daughters have passed some sort of poignant milestone he was not prepared for. When shadow versions of the two characters show up, named Henson and Abler, the four characters surround each other in their storylines to surreal effect. The district attorney, who is in love with Benson, ends up dating Henson, and Abler stalks Stabler's family. The effect is dizzying and increasingly absurd, a perfect opportunity to showcases the strangeness and strength of Machado's writing skills.

The collection's final story, "Difficult at Parties," centers on a woman who is recovering from a violent sexual assault. Her boyfriend, Paul, tries to help her to hold her life together, but she has an increasingly difficult time adjusting. She regularly has fits in her sleep, and cannot connect with others. In an attempt to deal with her trauma and improve her relationship with Paul, the woman begins to order pornography to her house. The DVDs show up—"adult films for loving couples"—but as she watches them, she begins to hear the inner thoughts of the actors. The dialogue she picks up, especially from the females on screen, is filled with desperation, which the protagonist herself feels regarding her recovery from the attack.

Machado has frequently been compared to other surrealist writers like Kelly Link, and she cites writers like Shirley Jackson and Ray Bradbury as major influences on her work. Her skill at blending horror, science fiction, and other genres drew positive critical attention as her stories appeared in various publications, but it took the release of this collection to bring her a new level of popular attention. *Her Body and Other Parties* met with instant success, with reviewers almost unanimously praising it as an incredibly assured debut book. It was nominated for the National Book Award and the Kirkus Prize, and won the Bard Fiction Prize. Despite being released by a small publisher, the book went into its third printing almost immediately following publication.

Reviewers especially praised the way in which Machado reclaims the experience of women. Many commented on how she provokes discussion and examination of social norms by building upon the framework of folk stories. In a review for the *New York Times*, Parul Sehgal noted, "Machado is fluent in the vocabulary of fairy tales—her stories are full of foxes, foundlings, nooses and gowns—but she remixes it to her own ends. Her fiction is both matter-of-factly and gorgeously queer." That ability to transcend genre, to combine theory and storytelling, is not one seen too often, and in Machado's case, it is exciting to imagine what she will dream up next to follow such an exciting and enchanting debut.

Melynda Fuller

Review Sources

Review of *Her Body and Other Parties*, by Carmen Maria Machado. *Kirkus*, 20 June 2017, www.kirkusreviews.com/book-reviews/carmen-maria-machado/her-body-and-other-parties/. Accessed 13 Dec. 2017.

Quinn, Annalisa. "'Her Body and Other Parties:' Be Your Own Madwoman." Review of *Her Body and Other Parties*, by Carmen Maria Machado. *NPR*, 8 Oct. 2017, www.npr.org/2017/10/08/553978325/-her-body-and-other-parties-be-your-own-madwoman. Accessed 13 Dec. 2017.

Robins, Ellie. "Carmen Maria Machado's 'Her Body and Other Parties' Reclaims the Female Body in Subversive, Joyful Ways." Review of *Her Body and Other Parties*, by Carmen Maria Machado. *Los Angeles Times*, 29 Sept. 2017, www.latimes.com/books/jacketcopy/la-ca-jc-carmen-maria-machado-20170929-story.html. Accessed 13 Dec. 2017.

Rooney, Kathleen. "Carmen Maria Machado's Debut Collection Thrills." Review of *Her Body and Other Parties*, by Carmen Maria Machado. *Chicago Tribune*, 10 Oct. 2017, www.chicagotribune.com/lifestyles/books/

sc-books-her-body-other-parties-carmen-machado-1011-20171009-story.html. Accessed 13 Dec. 2017.

Sehgal, Parul. "Fairy Tales about the Fears Within." Review of *Her Body and Other Parties*, by Carmen Maria Machado. *The New York Times*, 4 Oct. 2017, www. nytimes.com/2017/10/04/books/review-her-body-and-other-parties-carmen-maria-machado.html. Accessed 13 Dec. 2017.

Heretics

Author: Leonardo Padura (b. 1955)
First published: *Herejes*, 2013, in Spain
Translated from the Spanish by Anna Kushner
Publisher: Farrar, Straus and Giroux (New York). 544 pp.
Type of work: Novel
Time: Mid-seventeenth century to the early twenty-first century
Locales: Havana, Cuba; Miami, Florida; Kraków, Poland; Amsterdam, Dutch Republic (now the Netherlands)

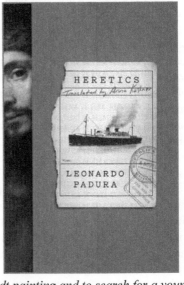

Courtesy of Macmillan

Part history, part mystery, the English translation of the complex, multilayered Heretics *follows the fortunes of a Jewish family in Havana, Cuba, where former policeman Mario Conde is asked to help track a lost Rembrandt painting and to search for a young woman gone missing.*

Principal characters

MARIO CONDE, a private detective and former policeman
TAMARA VALDEMIRA, his longtime lover
ELIAS KAMINSKY, his client, a large, ponytailed Cuban American painter in search of information
DANIEL KAMINSKY, Elias's father, a Jew sent from Poland to Cuba to escape the Nazis
JOSEPH KAMINSKY, a.k.a. Pepe the Purseman, Daniel's uncle and unofficial guardian, a Cuban resident
MARTA ARNÁEZ, Daniel's Catholic Cuban wife, Elias's mother
CARIDAD SOTOLONGO, a voluptuous mixed-race single mother who becomes Joseph's lover and later wife
RICARDO KAMINSKY SOTOLONGO, Joseph's adopted child, Caridad's son, who became a doctor
YADINE KAMINSKY, Ricardo's emo granddaughter
REMBRANDT VAN RIJN, a.k.a. The Maestro, a renowned seventeenth-century Dutch painter
ELIAS AMBROSIUS MONTALBO DE ÁVILA, a young Jew in seventeenth-century Amsterdam with painterly aspirations
MANUEL "MANOLO" PALACIOS, a police major, Conde's former assistant investigator

The good news for fans of Leonardo Padura's Mario Conde novels is that the Cuban former policeman and private detective has returned to undertake baffling new investigations. The bad news is that Conde, last seen in *La neblina del ayer* (2005; *Havana Fever*, 2009), is absent for a significant portion of the far-reaching, sometimes meandering narration of *Heretics*.

As in the previous novel, Conde in *Heretics* is living a precarious, feast-or-famine existence as partner with colorful entrepreneur Yoyi the Pigeon in a used-book business. As in all five earlier entries in the series, beginning with his introduction in *Pasado Perfecto* (1991; *Havana Blue*, 2007), Conde enjoys an on-and-off romantic relationship with lovely, lively Tamara Valdemira. He relies, as always, on the advice, camaraderie, and support of a faithful cadre of longtime friends, acquaintances, and former colleagues—disabled Skinny Carlos (not so skinny anymore), information-gatherer Rabbit, Protestant convert Candito the Red, and Manuel Palacios, his former underling, now a police major. Conde smokes and drinks to excess when he can afford it and cares for an omnivorous dog, Garbage II.

Mostly, Conde broods. For hours at a time he contemplates the contradictory character of Havana: a contrast featuring luxurious mansions of the super-rich and tumbledown hovels of the ultra-poor, an environment torpid during the fierce heat and humidity of the day, a simmering sea of exciting and often outré social life in the cool shadows of the night. Conde muses about freedom, a scarce commodity under Cuba's repressive socialist government, and other philosophical topics of universal concern. He bemoans the effects of aging that slow him physically and mentally and that undermine his deep-seated machismo. And occasionally, he is offered the opportunity to practice the unique set of skills that make him effective at what he does: determination, honesty, and an understanding of human nature. Conde knows how to ask pertinent questions, follow promising leads, and connect diverse pieces of data to produce reasonable solutions to problems.

In *Heretics*, Conde faces a conundrum so complicated that the novel must be divided into several parts. In part 1, "The Book of Daniel," Conde is approached in 2007 by a ponytailed Cuban American artist, Elias Kaminsky. Elias has come to Conde on the recommendation of Andrés, the detective's physician friend who departed Cuba for Miami many years before. Elias begins to tell Conde the poignant story of his Jewish forebears.

In 1938, Elias's father, Daniel, then a boy, was sent from Poland to Havana, where his uncle Joseph was already living. The following year, the rest of the Kaminsky family—father, mother, and daughter—arrived by ship, the MS *Saint Louis*, a real vessel that contained more than nine hundred Jews fleeing the Nazi regime. The passengers were not allowed to disembark (and were likewise later turned away from the United States). While at anchor outside Havana, the shipbound Kaminskys attempted to sell a precious heirloom, an authenticated Rembrandt painting that had been in the family for almost three hundred years, in order to buy documents permitting them to stay in Cuba. They were unsuccessful in their effort, and the ship eventually was forced to return to Europe, and many of the passengers, including the Kaminsky family, perished in concentration camps. Young Daniel, already safe in Cuba, afterward became the ward of his taciturn, religious uncle Joseph, a leather worker. Meanwhile, the valuable painting vanished, and only in the twenty-first century did it turn up again, at a London auction house, where its sale was halted pending legal action. Elias wants Conde to take on a pair of tasks. First, he wants the detective to find out what happened to the painting between the times it disappeared and reappeared. Second, he wants to know whether his father, as rumored, killed someone before fleeing Cuba for Miami in 1958. Elias will pay Conde one hundred dollars per day—a windfall for the often-destitute detective.

Conde begins investigating by visiting the home where the late Daniel and Joseph once lived. He canvasses the neighborhood in search of anyone who remembers the Jewish refugees, but most people he encounters are too young and the area is greatly changed. Conde visits Jewish cemeteries and finds Joseph's tombstone, which bears the following words: "Believed in the sacred. Violated the law. Died without feeling any remorse." In the course of his search, Conde discovers that Daniel was involved in anti-Batista revolutionary activities with several native-born Cubans before relocating to Miami. This leads him to the home of a surviving former rebel, aging Roberto Fariñas, who shows Conde a letter from Daniel's widow, Marta. This points the detective in a new direction: toward Dr. Ricardo Kaminsky, the grown adopted son of Joseph, who gives him a key piece of information.

After a promising start, *Heretics* hits a wall in part 2, "The Book of Elias." This section retreats to seventeenth-century Amsterdam, Dutch Republic, where it serves as a link between the preceding and following parts. Those nearly 150 pages focus on a young Jew, conveniently also named Elias: Elias Ambrosius Montalbo de Ávila. Elias is willing to risk ouster from the relatively safe haven of Amsterdam (called "New Jerusalem" by many members of his faith) through the heresy of becoming a painter. He knows if he is discovered practicing art he will incur the wrath of the Jewish community by violating sacred law concerning idolatry, which forbids the representation of "men, animals and objects from the sky, sea or earth." Elias eventually connects clandestinely—working in a janitorial capacity—with the city's most famous artist, Rembrandt van Rijn, who teaches the young man to paint and uses him as a model for preliminary studies for a well-known work. There is much to latch onto. The story gives details of Rembrandt's sometimes turbulent life, provides glimpses of Amsterdam in the mid-seventeenth century not long after coffee drinking and tobacco smoking became popular fads, and touches on a real-life self-proclaimed messiah operating in the Middle East, Sabbatai Zevi, who stirred many Jews to become zealous followers. However, despite such points of interest, "The Book of Elias" feels overwritten and seems interminable. The emphasis here is on mental, rather than physical action, and nothing much happens. Worse, as far as holding the attention of the reader, the language employed becomes languorous, almost soporific, with lengthy narrative passages unbroken by dialogue and almost uninterrupted by paragraph indentations. On a random page, for example, the word count is more than 440 largely multisyllabic words, divided into only eleven sentences, a difficult level of readability.

Luckily, in part 3, "The Book of Judith," Conde returns, Padura brings back the brusque, straightforward phrasing, and the landscape of the alternately exciting and depressing modern setting of Havana continues to be painted, as in part 1. In this section, the detective embarks on a fresh investigation generated by Ricardo Kaminsky's granddaughter Yadine, a member of a self-destructive urban tribe known as emos. Yadine wants him to find her missing friend Judith "Judy" Torres, since the police, under Conde's former colleague Manuel Palacios, have been unable to discover her whereabouts. The novel finishes with a coda, titled "Genesis," which brings the story of the Rembrandt painting up to date with fresh information and ends with what could serve as Conde's epitaph: "The only thing that really belongs to you, is your freedom of choice."

With more layers than a *mille-feuille* pastry, *Heretics* is a long, sometimes difficult read demanding patience, though whether the payoff is worth the effort is ultimately up to the individual. In a carefully constructed novel where everything counts, Padura lays out several themes in the front matter with a quote about the meaning of life from the Talmud, plus standard (from the Greek, meaning "to choose") and Cuban (describing difficult political or economic situations) definitions of "heretic." Both concepts of heresy figure prominently throughout: the Jews as heretics

Courtesy of Héctor Garrido

Cuban journalist and fiction writer Leonardo Padura published his first novel in 1988, and in 1997 released the first of six Mario Conde novels. He won the Premio Hammett of the International Association of Crime Writers three times, the Raymond Chandler Prize in 2009, Cuba's National Prize for Literature in 2012, and the Princess of Asturias Literature Award in 2015.

to Christians across many centuries of history; the idolaters and messiah-believers as heretics to Orthodox Jews; the rebels as heretics to the Cuban regime, itself heretical to Communism; the emos as heretics to the Havana community at large. A related subtext deals with the blind hatred fomented by perceived heresy, which often results in the commission of unspeakable acts of savagery in the name of religion.

Similarly related is the theme of displacement as exemplified throughout history, whereby successful Jews, viewed with envy by less successful Gentiles, were denounced and falsely accused of horrific crimes (such as the sacrifice of Christian children for some unspecified ritual), resulting sometimes in their massacre, sometimes in their expulsion. Some Jews, as Padura notes, accepted their fate as the will of God and submitted to torture and death. Others, more pragmatic or with stronger survival instincts, converted to Christianity. Still others emigrated elsewhere and over time reestablished themselves, only to see the same process, with the same awful choices—die, change, or leave—be repeated.

Despite its flaws—a by-product of a series that has, in six entries produced at irregular intervals over nearly three decades, progressed from relatively short, no-frills police procedurals to lengthy, freeform explorations of existential issues—*Heretics* has much to recommend it. Mario Conde continues to excel as an outstanding and believable character: a vulnerable human, sorrowed by the depravity of others and wracked with doubt, who is a unique product of his time and place. It will be fascinating to see what Leonardo Padura plans next for his resolute Cuban detective.

Jack Ewing

Review Sources

Fifer, Elizabeth. Review of *Heretics*, by Leonardo Padura. *World Literature Today*, Sept. 2017, www.worldliteraturetoday.org/2017/september/heretics-leonardo-padura. Accessed 2 Feb. 2018.

Livingstone, Josephine. "A Crime Novelist Investigates Cuba's Polyphonic Past." Review of *Heretics*, by Leonardo Padura. *New Republic*, 26 Apr. 2017, newrepublic.com/article/142266/crime-novelist-investigates-cubas-polyphonic-past. Accessed 2 Feb. 2018.

Murphy, Siobhan. Review of *Heretics*, by Leonardo Padura. *The Times* [London, UK], 25 Mar. 2017, www.thetimes.co.uk/article/heretics-by-leonardo-padura-trans-anna-kushner-kkf06kn25. Accessed 2 Feb. 2018.

Schleier, Curt. "*Heretics*, Stories from Cuba." Review of *Heretics*, by Leonardo Padura. *Hadassah Magazine*, Aug. 2017, www.hadassahmagazine.org/2017/08/03/heretics-stories-cuba. Accessed 2 Feb. 2018.

History of Wolves

Author: Emily Fridlund (b. 1979)
Publisher: Atlantic Monthly Press (New York). 288 pp.
Type of work: Novel
Time: Present day
Locale: Northern Minnesota

Linda is a teenager living in a nontraditional home in northern Minnesota with people who may or may not be her birth parents. When new neighbors move into a house across the lake, she seeks to belong to a family that looks safe on the outside. As her relationship with the family grows, however, she comes to realize that not all is as it seems.

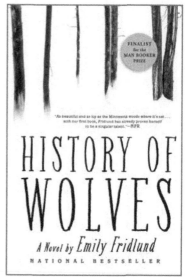

Courtesy of Grove Atlantic

Principal characters

MADELINE FURSTSON, a.k.a. Linda, a somewhat awkward teenage girl
PATRA GARDNER, her new neighbor
PAUL GARDNER, Patra's four-year-old son
LEO GARDNER, Patra's husband and Paul's father
ADAM GRIERSON, Linda's eighth-grade history teacher
LILY HOLBURN, an acquaintance of Linda's from school

History of Wolves is the debut novel from author Emily Fridlund, who subsequently published a short-story collection titled *Catapult* (2017). In addition to being short-listed for the 2017 Man Booker Prize, the novel was the American Booksellers Association's number-one Indie Next List pick for January 2017 and a Barnes & Noble Discover Great New Writers selection for spring 2017, and the first chapter won a 2013 McGinnis-Ritchie Award for fiction after its publication in the *Southwest Review*. Still, at times, *History of Wolves* reads less like a novel than an extended short story, a format with which the author seems more at home.

Death is one of the major focuses of the novel. The story is told in retrospect, as the narrator, named Madeline but more often called Linda, recalls her teenage years; it begins with her memory of her four-year-old neighbor, Paul Gardner, plopping onto her lap, secure in his expectation of her acceptance. "It's strange, you know?" she muses in this opening scene. "It's marvelous, and sad too, how good it can feel to have your body taken for granted." In the very next line (following a section break), she reveals that Paul is now dead. Paul's death seems to have been the one defining element of her life, leaving her fighting to understand herself and those around her in its wake.

Tied in with Paul's death is an exploration of the meaning of God and the problems of a religion that refuses to acknowledge the importance of professional medical care.

Paul's death is the direct result of his being denied medical care despite slow-growing evidence that something is wrong with the child. Patra, his mother, knows that she should seek a doctor's opinion, and she steps out to do so at several points, but her husband's adherence to Christian Science keeps her from following through with the care that could have saved her child even hours before his death. After the loss of their child, her husband, Leo, seemingly ignores the fact that his religious beliefs were the cause of Paul's spiraling health, while Patra convinces herself that she cannot be held accountable for not stepping up and making sure her son was safe. Even Linda wrestles with guilt over Paul's death, as she knew that his symptoms were serious but did not go to authorities to report it. Though she cognitively understands that her fifteen-year-old self could not have changed the situation, her adult psyche still battles with almost unrelenting grief.

As the teenage Linda struggles with understanding her own reaction to Paul's death, she reveals her childlike desire for normalcy in her family life. Raised in a former commune by people whom she is not sure are even her biological parents, Linda knows poverty and discomfort. Her relationship with her father is planned; from early childhood, she carefully insinuates herself into his routines, listening to baseball with him on Sundays and learning to clean fish and chop wood to make his life easier. Her relationship with her mother is more problematic, and Linda never truly understands how to connect with the woman who raised her. Since her own family life is, in Linda's eyes, strained, she seeks a place in what she sees as a normal family. So, when Patra and Leo build a house across the lake from her home, Linda regularly sits on the roof of the shed and watches them through binoculars, fascinated by the attention the couple bestows on four-year-old Paul. Before long, Leo has left to work in Hawaii, and Linda meets Patra and Paul on the road to town. She befriends the lonely young mother and child, beginning to babysit for Paul and becoming a central figure in their lives. She moves to the sidelines of the little family, however, when Leo returns after a prolonged absence. Though the older man accepts her presence, he does not want her around as much as Patra did, and Patra herself has changed with her husband home.

Sexuality is a central theme in the novel. It begins with Mr. Grierson, the replacement for the former eighth-grade history teacher, Mr. Adler, who died in front of his students. Mr. Grierson comes blowing into town, bigger than life. His enthusiasm for history subtly affects Linda, and when he asks her to be his student volunteer for a local contest, she jumps into the project, preparing a treatise on the history of wolves. Mr. Grierson confuses Linda with invitations to come to his classroom after school to discuss his teaching, as if she were an adult who could relate to his insecurity in his profession. This sexual confusion culminates on the way home from the presentation, when Linda awkwardly offers herself to her teacher. His gentle rejection of her advances ironically precedes the revelation that he was fired from his previous teaching position for sexual behavior with students. Though he is quickly removed from Linda's school and disappears, he remains a fascination for the girl into her adulthood, even after she has a steady boyfriend.

The sexuality of young people in Linda's community is referenced with a calm nonchalance. When Linda and Paul meet a girl in the park, Linda thinks, "She could have

Courtesy of Doug Knutson

Emily Fridlund has published short stories in a number of journals and in her short-story collection Catapult *(2017). She has won several awards for her work and holds a PhD in literature and creative writing from the University of Southern California.* History of Wolves *is her first novel.*

been any one of the Karens in my class a few years down the line, and when I realized this I wanted to laugh but not because it was funny. The girls who stuck around Loose River after high school were always having babies and getting married at eighteen, then moving into their parents' basements or backyard campers. That's what happened if you were pretty enough to be a cheerleader, but not smart enough to go to college." Later, Linda learns that one of her own classmates has created an elaborate scheme to hide her own pregnancy, and she admires the girl for her ingenuity in attempting to escape this fate.

While openly attracted to and sexually involved with men, Linda experiences a somewhat confusing sexual attraction to women as well. This begins with Lily Holburn, an acquaintance from school. Lily is a popular girl whom Linda has known all her life. Linda's descriptions of Lily are flattering and often sexual, as when she narrates, "Without saying a word, Lily could make people feel encouraged, blessed. She had dimples on her cheeks, nipples that flashed like signs from God through her sweater." Here, as she does throughout the novel, Linda uses Lily as a basis of comparison for herself, saying in the next breath, "I was flat chested, plain as a banister. I made people feel judged." The focus on Lily's physical attributes continues throughout the novel, and Linda seeks Lily out on numerous occasions, especially after Lily accuses Mr. Grierson of inappropriate sexual behavior. Patra is more clearly the focus of Linda's confused fascination, which culminates on the night that Paul dies. After falling asleep on the couch beside Patra, Linda awakes early and watches the woman sleep. She recalls, "Later, it would be impossible for me to tell anyone of the happiness of those hours, the exquisite sweetness of sitting there with her asleep beside me on the couch." Though these somewhat contradictory interactions with Lily and with Patra do not lead to anything more, they leave Linda confused and torn about her own feelings, questioning the relationships that she imagined around these women.

Ultimately, Linda seeks relationships to help alleviate the loneliness that permeates the lives of most of the characters in the novel. From the isolated setting of Linda's home, a five-mile walk from a small town in northern Minnesota, to her aging commune leader mother's constant need for reassurance that she is no worse than anyone else, solitude is a final central theme of the novel. Labeled "Commie" or "Freak" by her classmates, Linda does not have any close friends her own age, so when Patra, who is left in the Minnesota woods with only a young child for company, opens her home to the teen, the two temporarily bond in a strangely comforting way. Loneliness also follows Lily, Mr. Grierson, and a number of other minor characters, adding to the haunted quality of Linda's life.

One notable aspect of Fridlund's novel is the organization. The story jumps around throughout Linda's life, with the earliest recollections being of herself as a three-year-old child in the commune her parents started, then moving up to her eighth-grade year, following her fifteenth year, and jumping around adulthood experiences ranging from her early twenties to her late thirties. Presented sometimes in full chapters and sometimes in single paragraphs, these snapshots of Linda's life flow in an almost stream-of-consciousness presentation that does not follow any chronological pattern. The lack of transitions between these jumps in time showcases the further challenges Linda continues to face as a result of Paul's death at an influential point in her teen years.

Fridlund's debut novel has received acclaim from most review sources. In his review of the novel for *Booklist*, Michael Cart described the writing as "beautiful throughout" and "a triumph of tone and attitude." Leslie Patterson, reviewing it for *Library Journal*, commended Fridlund's talent for "getting inside the head of an unhappy youth and revealing how neglect and isolation scar a child for life"; the reviewer for *Publishers Weekly* concluded, "Fridlund has elegantly crafted a striking protagonist whose dark leanings cap off the tragedy at the heart of this book, which is moving and disturbing, and which will stay with the reader."

Though the reception was generally positive, some reviewers had reservations. Patterson warned that "this first novel, as cold and bleak as a Minnesota winter, may be too dark for some readers." Jennifer Senior, in her review for the *New York Times*, found it to be less than satisfying, claiming that the late reappearance of characters from the award-winning first chapter is "disorienting, strained," and arguing that while the novel "contains the kernels of many possible novels, with lots of larger ideas to plumb," those ideas are not fully developed, resulting in an ultimately underwhelming reveal.

Still, whatever it may lack in narrative structure, the book would be a worthwhile read for those who appreciate what Senior described as Fridlund's "unusual" voice and her ability to "create a moody, slate-gray sense of place." Fred Melnyczuk, reviewing the novel for the *Financial Times*, praised Fridlund's success in "mak[ing] likeable that most unlikeable creature—the teenager," and noted that while "the reader may feel a slight aimlessness. . . . Fridlund is a fine writer and her work is cut through with moments of sparse beauty." Adult readers may strongly relate to and sympathize with the thirty-seven-year-old narrator who looks back on her haunting youth.

Theresa L. Stowell, PhD

Review Sources

Cart, Michael. Review of *History of Wolves*, by Emily Fridlund. *Booklist*, 15 Oct. 2016, www.booklistonline.com/History-of-Wolves-Emily-Fridlund/pid=8291031. Accessed 6 Sept. 2017.

Review of *History of Wolves*, by Emily Fridlund. *Publishers Weekly*, 3 Oct. 2016, www.publishersweekly.com/978-0-8021-2587-3. Accessed 6 Sept. 2017.

Hustad, Megan. "A Novel's Sheltered Girl Seeks Her Identity among Messed-Up Adults." Review of *History of Wolves*, by Emily Fridlund. *The New York Times*, 6 Jan. 2017, www.nytimes.com/2017/01/06/books/review/history-of-wolves-emily-fridlund.html. Accessed 6 Sept. 2017.

Melnyczuk, Fred. Review of *History of Wolves*, by Emily Fridlund. *Financial Times*, 1 Sept. 2017, www.ft.com/content/314b7920-8d8c-11e7-a352-e46f43c5825d. Accessed 6 Sept. 2017.

Patterson, Leslie. Review of *History of Wolves*, by Emily Fridlund. *Library Journal*, 1 Nov. 2016, p. 74.

Senior, Jennifer. "Review: A Teenager Bears Witness to Backwoods Intrigue in *History of Wolves*." Review of *History of Wolves*, by Emily Fridlund. *The New York Times*, 4 Jan. 2017, www.nytimes.com/2017/01/04/books/review-history-of-wolves-emily-fridlund.html. Accessed 6 Sept. 2017.

Hit Makers
The Science of Popularity in an Age of Distraction

Author: Derek Thompson (b. 1986)
Publisher: Penguin (New York). 352 pp.
Type of work: Media, sociology

In Hit Makers: The Science of Popularity in *an Age of Distraction, Derek Thompson explores the multitude of factors that make a work of art, a piece of technology, or a trend popular.*

What makes something popular? That question has long plagued those who create, market, and sell products or content of any sort, and anyone confronted with an omnipresent song, film, or trend, might wonder just why that specific cultural artifact has become a hit when countless similar—and possibly even superior—examples have not. In *Hit Makers: The Science of Popularity in an Age of Distraction*, journalist Derek Thompson presents numerous examples of popular works and trends and explores the many factors that contributed to their popularity, including luck, repeated public exposure, and an appealing mixture of the new and the familiar. Thompson focuses primarily on examples originating in the twentieth and twenty-first centuries, in which modern mass media plays an outsize role. However, he also cites a variety of trends and works of art and media—such as nineteenth-century German composer Johannes Brahms's lullaby "Wiegenlied"—that became hits centuries before technologies such as television or the internet could have given them a boost. Indeed, Thompson indicates that the concept of a work becoming extremely popular—often described in the early twenty-first century as "going viral"—is far from new and that the questions surrounding the mechanics of popularity are as enduring as many of humankind's most popular creations.

Thompson details the origins of "Wiegenlied" and his own childhood connections to the German lullaby at the start of his introduction to *Hit Makers*. He then goes on to explore how the popularity of the song in both Europe and the United States ties into the book's core concerns and conclusions. He explains that *Hit Makers* seeks to answer two basic questions: "What is the secret to making products that people like—in music, movies, television, books, games, apps, and more across the vast landscape of culture?" and "Why do some products fail in these marketplaces while similar ideas catch on and become massive hits?" In regard to "Wiegenlied," Thompson posits that the song's popularity was in part the result of its blending of the new and the familiar: its basic melody and lyrics were both taken from earlier works but combined in a new manner and context by Brahms. Carried to the United States by German-speaking

Courtesy of Penguin Press

immigrants during the late nineteenth century and passed down through family networks, "Wiegenlied" traveled far beyond its originating point and attained widespread distribution. Thompson highlights that phenomenon, noting that while technology such as the internet has changed the means of distribution dramatically, the process of a work becoming popular is often heavily reliant on introducing it into an existing social network through which it can then spread.

Following its introduction, *Hit Makers* is divided into two parts. The book's first section, "Popularity and the Mind," explores the psychological factors at play in the phenomenon of popularity. Thompson first explores the concepts of exposure and familiarity, which he argues can be key to ensuring the popularity of a work. Establishing a pattern that he continues throughout the book, Thompson switches between recounting anecdotes that reflect his point and research that supports it, introducing readers to the quantitative data as well as interesting stories. Many of the examples focus on well-known historical or contemporary figures, while also examining the roles of lesser-known individuals in their popularity.

The first chapter, "The Power of Exposure," focuses initially on the work of the nineteenth-century impressionist painters, whose popularity can largely be traced back to one man: the painter and art collector Gustave Caillebotte. Upon Caillebotte's death in the 1890s, he bequeathed his collection of art, which included paintings by impressionists such as Claude Monet and Edgar Degas, to a major French museum. Although the French artistic elite disapproved of impressionism during Caillebotte's lifetime, displaying his collection of paintings in a museum granted them not only legitimacy but also extensive exposure. Thompson explains that according to studies conducted by Cornell University researcher James Cutting, people tend to prefer paintings that they have seen before over paintings with which they are unfamiliar. Study subjects typically show a preference for famous paintings over their lesser-known counterparts, but when repeatedly exposed to less famous paintings, subjects' appreciation for those works increases. In light of such findings and others, Thompson explains that people generally prefer shapes, images, words, and sounds that are familiar over those that are not. Works that become popular, then, are often familiar to their audience in structure, narrative, or other characteristics.

Despite the human preference for familiarity, however, Thompson notes that solely being familiar is not the key to a work's success. He devotes several chapters to discussing how people in general prefer creations that are largely familiar but are also new or unfamiliar in some way. He presents a variety of examples, including the work of twentieth-century designer Raymond Loewy, who created iconic designs for organizations such as Coca-Cola and NASA. Thompson explains that Loewy's design philosophy was based on the motto MAYA, or most advanced yet acceptable. Devoted to innovation, Loewy understood that failing to present advanced designs would be inadequate, but designs that were too difficult for the public to understand would be similarly unacceptable. Work that fell in the middle ground between those two points would be most successful.

In addition to discussing Loewy's contributions, Thompson raises examples of popular works such as the films in the original Star Wars trilogy, which blended a variety of time-tested archetypes and film genres in a new way that appealed to a broad audience. While Thompson largely focuses on specific artistic or technological creations, he also delves into broader trends such as trends in first names. Building on his ongoing discussion of familiarity and popularity, he suggests that many people seek out what he terms "Goldilocks names," which are neither so uncommon that they are strange nor so familiar that they are overused.

In the second section of *Hit Makers*, "Popularity and the Market," Thompson delves further into the forces that make a creation popular not only with individuals but also within the broader market. Just as Caillebotte's decision to collect impressionist art and ensure its preservation led to the popularization of that art, Thompson argues, the unexpected intervention of a third party has played a substantial role in the popularization of a variety of other major cultural artifacts. The 1954 song "Rock Around the Clock," for instance, received significant promotion by its record label upon its initial release but failed to become a hit. However, Thompson explains, the song became a favorite of a nine-year-old California boy named Peter Ford, whose actor father, Glenn, was set to star in the 1955 film *Blackboard Jungle*. When the film's director was searching for a rock and roll song to include at the beginning of the film, Ford recommended "Rock Around the Clock," which ultimately played during *Blackboard Jungle*'s opening credits. Reintroduced to audiences in a new context, "Rock Around the Clock" went on to become one of the most popular rock and roll songs of all time. Thompson argues that the success of "Rock Around the Clock" illustrates the important role that the means of distribution can play in making a work popular, noting that the song's catchiness alone was unable to render it a hit upon its initial release.

One of the book's other particularly interesting observations comes in chapter 8, "The Viral Myth," which features discussions of such varied topics as the 2011 romance novel *Fifty Shades of Grey* and so-called viral videos about malaria and the Ugandan guerilla leader Joseph Kony. In the chapter, Thompson works to dismantle the widely discussed concept that a trend or creation can go viral—that is, spread from person to person like a virus. Thompson notes that while going viral is often used as the explanation for a trend or work's abrupt rise to popularity, such popularization is in fact often the result of the artifact in question being broadcast to a large audience by a relatively small group of influential figures, such as celebrities with large followings on the social media platform Twitter. Rather than being spread through one-to-one interactions, Thompson explains, they are spread through one-to-one-million broadcasts. Although they interact with the works they promote in a new and decidedly twenty-first-century manner, online influencers essentially fill the role previously filled by figures like Ford and Caillebotte.

Throughout *Hit Makers*, Thompson makes it clear that in many, if not all, cases, popular culture is not a meritocracy. Works of art and media, technological innovations, and trends do not rise to popularity thanks solely to their quality and superiority within their respective fields. At the same time, he does not suggest that quality does not matter. Rather, the popularity of a particular cultural artifact is based on the complex intersections of a variety of factors, which may include its quality, blending of the familiar and unfamiliar, and promotion by influential figures within a particular online or in-person social network. For would-be hit makers, Thompson's findings may be frustrating yet valuable, calling attention to the seemingly arbitrary yet potentially surmountable hurdles that stand between them and widespread recognition. Over the course of the book's twelve chapters and four interludes, *Hit Makers* provides an engaging overview of many of the scientific, social, and economic factors that play into whether a work, invention, or trend becomes popular. As a journalist, Thompson writes well for a general audience, and he strikes a comfortable balance between anecdotal evidence and scientific research without becoming dry or overly academic in tone. The book's extensive sources, which include conversations and interviews with many of the relevant individuals as well as a variety of published works, are documented in the book's end matter and provide a useful starting point for readers interested in delving deeper into the hard science that underlies many of Thompson's key points.

Courtesy of Emersson Barillas

Derek Thompson is a senior editor of the Atlantic *and a contributor to a variety of radio and television news programs.* Hit Makers: The Science of Popularity in an Age of Distraction *is his first book.*

Reviews of *Hit Makers: The Science of Popularity in an Age of Distraction* were largely positive. The anonymous reviewer for *Kirkus*, for example, characterized the book as a "well-considered" overview that may help readers better understand the forces underlying their own cultural experiences. Critics particularly appreciated Thompson's discussions of major pop-cultural touchstones such as Star Wars and "Rock around the Clock" alongside lesser-known figures such as Caillebotte and Loewy. Indeed, the *Guardian*'s Steven Poole noted that Thompson himself presents a work that is both familiar and new, building on earlier work by writers such as Malcolm Gladwell while also devoting attention to further research and interviews with experts in the relevant fields. Although some reviewers identified minor flaws in Thompson's writing and approach—Poole noted in his review that the author "sometimes slips himself into the zombie semantics of marketing speak"—critics generally found *Hit Makers* to be an engaging and informative contribution to the ongoing discussion surrounding the mechanics and implications of popularity in media and culture.

Joy Crelin

Review Sources

Review of *Hit Makers: The Science of Popularity in an Age of Distraction*, by Derek Thompson. *Kirkus*, 8 Dec. 2016, www.kirkusreviews.com/book-reviews/derek-thompson/hit-makers/. Accessed 28 Nov. 2017.

Holahan, David. "New Book *Hit Makers* Hits All the Right Notes." Review of *Hit Makers: The Science of Popularity in an Age of Distraction*, by Derek Thompson. *USA Today*, 5 Feb. 2017, www.usatoday.com/story/life/books/2017/02/05/hit-makers-the-science-of-popularity-in-an-age-of-distraction-book-review/97061624/. Accessed 28 Nov. 2017.

"The Magic of Making Hits." Review of *Hit Makers: The Science of Popularity in an Age of Distraction*, by Derek Thompson. *The Economist*, 16 Mar. 2017, www.economist.com/news/books-and-arts/21718855-psychology-behind-and-economics-pop-culture-magic-making-hits. Accessed 28 Nov. 2017.

Poole, Steven. "*Hit Makers* by Derek Thompson Review—How Things Become Popular." Review of *Hit Makers: The Science of Popularity in an Age of Distraction*, by Derek Thompson. *The Guardian*, 22 Feb. 2017, www.theguardian.com/books/2017/feb/22/hit-makers-by-derek-thompson-review. Accessed 28 Nov. 2017.

The Holocaust
A New History

Author: Laurence Rees (b. 1957)
Publisher: PublicAffairs (New York). 552 pp.
Type of work: History
Time: 1919–45
Locales: Germany, France, and Poland

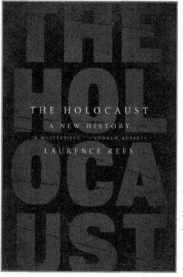

*The result of nearly a quarter century of re-
search by British historian Laurence Rees,
The Holocaust: A New History offers a complete chronological history of the systematic
extermination of more than six million people
at the hands of Adolf Hitler's Nazi regime.*

Courtesy of PublicAffairs

Principal personages

ADOLF HITLER, leader of the Nazi Party,
dictator of Germany, and architect of the
Holocaust

ADOLF GEMLICH, a German soldier in World War I

DIETRICH ECKART, an anti-Semitic playwright and poet, cofounder of the German
Workers' Party

ALBERT WIDMANN, a German SS officer and chemist who helped create the Nazis'
involuntary euthanasia program

JOSEF MENGELE, a German SS officer and physician who conducted deadly experiments on prisoners at Auschwitz

Laurence Rees, the former head of BBC History and creative director of history programs for the BBC, is widely considered an authoritative voice on the events of World
War II. He is the creator of the educational website WW2History.com, which offers
video and audio testimony from eyewitnesses on both sides of the conflict, and has
produced several documentaries on the war, including *The Nazis: A Warning from
History* (1997), *Auschwitz: The Nazis and the "Final Solution"* (2005), and *The Dark
Charisma of Adolf Hitler* (2012). Over the years, Rees had amassed hundreds of hours
of interviews with Holocaust survivors, as well as with members of the Nazi Party
who authorized and even committed the atrocities. These interviews formed the foundation of what would become *The Holocaust: A New History*.

The book follows a chronological path, tracing the origins of the Holocaust back
to a letter written by Adolf Hitler in 1919. Embittered, angry, and humiliated over the
German army's defeat in World War I (in which he served on the western front and at
the Battle of the Somme, as well as other engagements), Hitler wrote to a fellow soldier, Adolf Gemlich, and laid the blame for Germany's rout almost squarely at the feet

of the Jewish people. He believed that the Jewish race was inferior to those of German descent and that they harbored a lust for money that weakened the German resolve. This letter, Rees notes, would form the foundation of Hitler's virulent anti-Semitism, which he would expand on in his book *Mein Kampf* (1925–26) and which would ultimately result in his attempted genocide of the Jewish people.

Rees goes on to explain that Hitler's hatred of Jews, while extreme, had its roots in the German *Völkish* movement, which grew out of some Germans' deep love for their country and their roots and espoused not only a strong sense of nationalism but also an almost mystical connection to the so-called fatherland. This connection led to the notion that those with "pure" German blood were superior to those without. The *Völkish* movement, Rees notes, would become very important to Hitler and his fellow Nazis.

Having established the roots of the anti-Semitism that fueled the Holocaust, Rees then delves into the birth of the Nazi Party, outlining the relationship between Hitler and Dietrich Eckart, a playwright and an alcoholic who often espoused anti-Jewish views in his works. Eckart belonged to the Thule Society, a radical group of anti-Semites who preached hatred against the Jewish people and required its members to have no Jewish blood. Hitler, Rees writes, was enamored of Eckart and was especially taken by his anti-Jewish rhetoric. Eckart and Hitler were also both members of the German Workers' Party, which was later renamed the National Socialist German Workers' Party, known colloquially as the Nazi Party. For the party, Hitler designed a new logo, a black swastika in a white circle against a red background.

Rees goes on to illustrate Hitler's increasing influence in the party as well as the increasingly anti-Jewish stance evident in his speeches. In addition to railing against Jews, Hitler filled his speeches with words about national pride and the strength of the German people. He told the German public that the problems they were facing were not their fault and was keen to tell them whose fault he thought those problems actually were. These words rallied more Germans to his cause.

Rees then talks about Hitler's prison sentence, the result of a failed coup by the Nazi Party in Bavaria in 1923. During his time in prison, Hitler penned *Mein Kampf* (My struggle), the book that fully outlined his ideology and shaped the direction the Nazi Party would take upon his release in 1924. Following his release, Hitler continued his rise to power, although he tempered his speeches to focus less on the Jewish people and more on the pride of the German people. However, his anti-Semitic beliefs were still there, and Rees observes that when Hitler was elected chancellor of Germany on January 30, 1933, he was finally able to put them into practice.

Rees continues to detail Hitler's consolidation of power and the beginning of his ultimate plan to purge the Jewish people from the world. Rees talks about the anti-Semitic legislation that Hitler passed, such as the Law for the Restoration of the Professional Civil Service, which called for civil service officers who were of "non-Aryan" descent ("Aryan" being a catch-all term for German racial superiority) to be removed from office. Rees goes on to describe the day-to-day life of German Jews under the new regime. Business owners, such as the Jewish owner of a cigarette factory in Stuttgart whose business was ruined when dealers told him they could no longer carry his cigarettes, suffered greatly. At schools, lessons in biology were reworked to teach students that Jews were of a different race altogether from Germans.

As time went on, Rees writes, the grip of the Nazi Party continued to grow and, with it, the uneasiness of the Jewish people. In 1933, shortly after Hitler's rise to the chancellorship, the first concentration camp opened at Dachau. Shockingly, these concentration camps were not hidden and were even written about openly in newspapers around the world. Rees quotes an excerpt from the January 1, 1934, edition of the UK *Guardian* that describes the living conditions and the brutal methods of torture that were occurring at Dachau.

At this time, Hitler was beginning to amass an army outside of the paramilitary Stormtroopers he had employed since his earliest days with the Nazi Party. He withdrew Germany from the League of Nations and, in 1935, put forth the Anglo-German Naval Agreement, which allowed him to build a German fleet comparable to the British Navy. This agreement was in violation of the Versailles Treaty and set the stage for his eventual invasion of Poland four years later.

The invasion of Poland was the beginning of Hitler's full-scale persecution of the Jews, setting into motion not only World War II but a racially motivated war that would claim six million lives. Rees offers firsthand accounts of life in the ghettos, small sections of towns and cities across occupied Europe in which Jewish people were forced to live. He offers testimony from Max Epstein, then the fifteen-year-old son of a prosperous businessman who was forced into a one-room apartment in the Lodz ghetto. Max talks about how the move sapped his father's will to live, while he and his mother tried to find a way to make the best of their circumstances.

Rees also discusses how Hitler's plan for extermination did not just target Jewish people. Hitler and his Nazi regime ordered the deaths of disabled children, which were recorded as being the result of disease. The efficiency of these killings led Hitler to propose a similar extermination of physically and mentally disabled adults. He turned to Albert Widmann, a chemist, who suggested the use of carbon monoxide gas, which could be "discharged into the wards at night and thus 'euthanize' the mental patients." He later conducted an "experiment" in which he pumped carbon monoxide into a fake shower room under the guise of having the patients shower. This was, along with the continued victories of Hitler's armies across Europe, a key development in the Holocaust.

Laurence Rees is a British historian and documentary filmmaker who has won numerous awards for his books and documentaries about World War II. The Holocaust: A New History *is his ninth book.*

As the book goes on, Rees starkly describes life (and death) in the Nazi death camps, where mass murder was carried out at an efficient, industrial pace. He offers small details that illuminate the suffering on a human level, such as the children who peer into a latrine at the Beaune-la-Rolande internment camp, where French Jews would await transport to Auschwitz, and see shiny items glittering amidst the waste, wedding rings hidden there by wives who had to surrender their jewelry.

The book also does not shy away from the more terrible aspects of the Holocaust, discussing how, in concentration camps such as Treblinka, the Nazis' *Schutzstaffel* ("protection squad," abbreviated SS) troops were capable of murdering up to seven thousand Jews per day. He talks about how people living nearby could not escape the smell of burning corpses and how new arrivals to the camps saw hundreds of corpses piled atop one another.

Rees also devotes a chapter of the book to the network of Polish concentration camps collectively known as Auschwitz. He details the horrific medical research conducted by Josef Mengele, the Nazi doctor whose genetic experiments on unwilling prisoners, particularly twins and triplets, made him one of the most infamous names in the history of the Holocaust. However, Rees does not dwell on Auschwitz, or the horrors perpetrated there, in favor of offering a more detailed and complete picture of the Holocaust. Auschwitz tends to be the focal point of many studies and conversations about the Holocaust and concentration camps, but in *The Holocaust*, it is a piece of a larger whole. Throughout the book, Rees uses interviews culled from his years as a television producer and documentarian to offer insight into the Holocaust from those who lived it, from prisoners to the Nazis themselves.

There are hopeful stories in the book as well, even amid the atrocities that are taking place. In the chapter titled "Oppression and Revolt," Rees recounts the uprising at Treblinka in August 1943, in which a number of Jewish prisoners managed to arm themselves and storm the main gate. Seventy prisoners escaped in the chaos.

Rees concludes *The Holocaust: A New History* with an examination of the final days of Adolf Hitler and the Nazi regime. He notes that even as the Allied forces began their advance toward Berlin in the waning days of 1944, Hitler continued to launch into anti-Jewish tirades, although his audience was swiftly dwindling. He also recounts a story of New Year's Day 1945, when, following an announcement from Hitler that their enemies were not far from Auschwitz, SS troops decided to escape the area rather than murder the remaining prisoners. Rees discusses Hitler's suicide on April 30, 1945, and how, even at the end of his life, he was still railing against the Jewish people. The book ends on a bittersweet note, with the camps being liberated but many of the Jewish people, having lost everything over the past decade, not knowing where to go. Rees closes with a quote from a former prisoner, Giselle Cycowicz, who says that even seventy years later, she still cannot get over the evil she witnessed.

The Holocaust: A New History earned strong praise from critics. Reviewing the book for the *Guardian*, Nikolaus Wachsmann wrote, "What distinguishes [*The Holocaust*] is not an original interpretation, but its approach. Rees is a gifted educator, who can tell a complex story with compassion and clarity, without sacrificing all nuances. It is this quality that makes his book one of the best general introductions to the Holocaust." Saul David, in his review for the *Telegraph*, was even more laudatory, describing the book as a "unique" and "brilliant new history" and noting that it "is not a book for the faint-hearted. Some of the first-hand testimony is both shocking and heart-rending. Yet it has important things to say about human nature—what our species is capable of doing if not prevented by civilized laws—and demands to be read."

The Holocaust is one of the most documented, discussed, and recounted events in human history. As such, one might wonder what a book such as *The Holocaust: A New History* can bring to the conversation that is new and different. However, Rees manages to assemble the narrative of the greatest atrocity in recent memory in a way that is both accessible and compelling. It will likely stand the test of time as one of the more definitive accounts of the Holocaust.

Jeremy Brown

Review Sources

Cronin, Joseph. Review of *The Holocaust: A New History*, by Laurence Rees. *Reviews in History*, Oct. 2017, www.history.ac.uk/reviews/review/2176. Accessed 11 Dec. 2017.

David, Saul. "*The Holocaust* by Laurence Rees Is the Best Single-Volume Account of the Atrocity Ever Written." Review of *The Holocaust: A New History*, by Laurence Rees. *The Telegraph*, 13 Feb. 2017, www.telegraph.co.uk/books/what-to-read/holocaust-laurence-rees-best-single-volume-account-atrocity. Accessed 11 Dec. 2017.

Review of *The Holocaust: A New History*, by Laurence Rees. *Kirkus Reviews*, 1 Apr. 2017, p. 181. *Academic Search Complete*, search.ebscohost.com/login.aspx?direct =true&db=a9h&AN=122253082&site=ehost-live. Accessed 11 Dec. 2017.

Sexton, David. Review of *The Holocaust: A New History*, by Laurence Rees. *London Evening Standard*, 19 Jan. 2017, www.standard.co.uk/lifestyle/books/the-holo-caust-a-new-history-by-laurence-rees-review-a3445386.html. Accessed 11 Dec. 2017.

Wachsmann, Nikolaus. "*The Holocaust* by Laurence Rees Review: The Voices of Victims and Killers." Review of *The Holocaust: A New History*, by Laurence Rees. *The Guardian*, 26 Jan. 2017, www.theguardian.com/books/2017/jan/26/the-holocaust-laurence-rees-review. Accessed 11 Dec. 2017.

Wilson, Gary. Review of *The Holocaust: A New History*, by Laurence Rees. *LSE Review of Books*, London School of Economics and Political Science, 20 June 2017, blogs.lse.ac.uk/lsereviewofbooks/2017/06/20/book-review-the-holocaust-a-new-history-by-laurence-rees. Accessed 11 Dec. 2017.

The Home That Was Our Country
A Memoir of Syria

Author: Alia Malek (b. 1974)
Publisher: Nation Books (New York). 352 pp.
Type of work: Memoir
Time: 1950s–present day
Locale: Damascus, Syria

Award-winning journalist Alia Malek chronicles her family history through several generations while depicting the history of Syria during the same periods.

Principal personages
ALIA MALEK, the author
SALMA, her maternal grandmother
SHEIKH ABDELJAWWAD AL-MIR, her great-grandfather
LAMYA, her mother

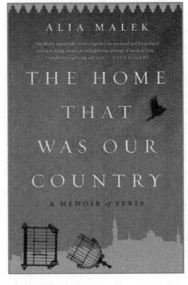

Courtesy of PublicAffairs

Journalist Alia Malek's book *The Home That Was Our Country: A Memoir of Syria* combines family and national history, leading up to the devastating war that, in seven years, displaced twelve million Syrians and killed more than 470,000 people. Malek was born in Baltimore, Maryland, shortly after her parents emigrated from Syria in the early 1970s. She became a civil rights lawyer, working for a nonprofit in the West Bank before joining the Department of Justice (DOJ) in 2000. She left the DOJ after the run-up to the invasion of Iraq and moved to Lebanon. However, her dream was to make a life in Syria, surrounded by extended family members. After growing up primarily with her parents and siblings, day-to-day life with aunts, uncles, and cousins held a special allure for her. In April 2011, during the wake of the Arab Spring, a series of uprisings across the Middle East and North Africa, she moved to Damascus with plans to renovate a family apartment and chronicle the birth of a new Syria. Her experience living in Syria—she left in 2013—inspired her memoir.

Malek is also the author of *A Country Called Amreeka: Arab Roots, American Stories* (2009), which is about Arab Americans and their relationships with their countries of origin. *The Home That Was Our Country* is organized with a similar approach, though for Malek, the content is now personal. She writes of the nostalgia her parents have for their country and of her early memories of Syria, where she spent her first summers. She longs for a culture and family history she only partially knows.

The central figure of Malek's memoir is her beloved maternal grandmother, Salma. Salma's father, a wealthy businessman named Sheikh Abdeljawwad al-Mir, was born near Hama in 1889, during the reign of the Ottoman Empire. Salma was born when

Syria was under French rule. Growing up, she worshipped her charismatic father and brothers, sometimes to the detriment of her relationship with her mild-mannered husband and children. Like Abdeljawwad, she was enterprising and resourceful. After moving to Damascus, she settled in the 1950s in an apartment building called the Tahaan. She became a social power broker, hosting frequent salons with the elite but also demonstrating generosity toward any poor person who knocked on her door.

Malek describes the Tahaan of the 1950s and 1960s in loving detail, from the exact layout of the rooms as they were inhabited by Salma and her growing family to the descriptions of the merchants selling tiny cucumbers on the street. Neighbors greeted one another other each day, exchanging pleasantries from balcony to balcony, and Salma, her ubiquitous cigarette dangling from her lips, enforced a strict schedule for washing the stairs between each floor. This was the warm and familial world in which Lamya, Malek's mother, grew up. But outside of the comforting rhythms of life in the Tahaan, Syria struggled to assert itself as a nation in a series of coups. Malek notes that in Salma and her husband's first year of marriage, the Syrian government was overthrown three times. After a brief interval during which Syria joined Egypt to become the United Arab Republic (UAR), the nationalist Ba'th Party began its rise to power. Describing the nuances of this period is a difficult task, but using the perspective of her family members, Malek brings that history to life.

While each subsequent coup swept an ideologically distinct party into power, Malek writes, the mechanisms of the coups themselves were dully familiar. In 1970, when former Syrian defense minister Hafez al-Assad assumed power, Malek's family had little reason to believe he would remain in power any longer than any ruler that had come before him. The same year, Salma offered the apartment in the Tahaan to a famous, but poor, songwriter until he could afford to rent his own apartment. Salma's family was moving into a house elsewhere in the city, and Salma assumed that the songwriter would be gone within a year or two. However, the renter refused to leave and was protected by a law put into place by al-Assad. Al-Assad's regime also remained entrenched. Malek's parents finally reclaimed the apartment in 2004, and in 2011, she returned to Syria and began the task of renovating it. By then, al-Assad's son, Bashar, was the president of Syria. Like his father, Bashar al-Assad maintained a tight grip on Syrian society. Malek's family, she notes, lived in fear of the *mukhabarat*, the Syrian secret police, warning Malek that the "walls have ears."

During this period, the Arab Spring began. In Tunisia and Egypt, ordinary people were gathering in the streets, demanding revolution. Then, in Da'ara, a southern city near Jordan, a group of schoolboys scrawled graffiti on a wall, mimicking the phrases they had heard on the news. The regime's security forces arrested the boys—who ranged in age from ten to fifteen years old—for their prank and tortured them. The mutilated corpse of one boy, thirteen-year-old Hamza Ali al-Khateeb, was delivered to his parents' doorstep as a warning. The boys' arrest sparked protests in Da'ara, where the regime opened fire on the crowd. In a disorienting juxtaposition in the book, these events happen as Malek and her mother hire a contractor and go about mundane errands. The disconnect is not lost on her mother, who begs Malek to move back to the United States. But Malek is resolute in her desire to remain in Syria, even as the regime's attacks intensify and an armed resistance forms. Malek's extended family worries about her. She has told them that she is living in Syria to write a book about Salma, which is only partly true; she is also writing about the resistance for American news outlets such as the *New York Times*. She knows that her work puts her family in danger, but for two years she decides to continue.

The resistance Malek chronicles is one of the finest aspects of *The Home That Was Our Country*. Thousands of ordinary Syrians risk incredible danger to run supplies and medical aid to cities under siege in an underground network from Damascus to Homs. The group, Malek notes, had tried working openly only to be violently repressed by the regime. The man who introduces Malek to the network—she gives him the code name "Mustache"—tells her, "They [the regime] want to get rid of the idea that the people can help each other. They don't want there to be solidarity among the Syrian people." From resistance efforts to the neighbors of varying religions and ethnicities living in the old Tahaan, Malek's book is a rich illustration of this solidarity. Malek also chronicles the psychological toll of the war's brutality. In one chapter, she attends a group therapy meeting in which participants create characters to critique the regime or speak openly about the future. It is worth noting that Syrians initially demanded

Alia Malek is a Syrian American journalist and civil rights lawyer.

reform—not revolution. In the game, participants challenge each other to name their dreams for Syria, but one woman is too exhausted to fathom the nature of the question. "It's hard for us to dream given what we are seeing," she says. "My biggest dream is for the killing to stop; I can't dream past this."

Malek, fearing for the safety of her family, finally left Syria in 2013. Though her book offers little resolution, it does raise pointed questions about power and complicity. Members of her family offer a loud defense of the regime, and she spends much time contemplating why. Does her family truly believe the regime—which insists that the violence is the work of foreign agents—or are they parroting the lies they hear out of fear? (The walls still have ears, after all.)

When two cars bombs explode in Damascus, Malek's uncle is strangely "euphoric," she writes. The bombs could plausibly have been the work of terrorists, supporting the regime's claim. He was not alone in his vindication, she writes: "If the regime wasn't lying to us, then we couldn't be blamed for our submission." The moment, a critical turning point in the violence, powerfully illustrates the various ways in which the regime suppresses its people and robs them of their agency, and even their humanity. The "shame" of living under the regime, Malek writes, is being "both victim and bystander." In many ways, she herself feels complicit with the regime, walking past the austere offices of the *mukhabarat* in her neighborhood each day. She later discovers there is a torture chamber in that building's basement, in which young men are hung upside down and beaten for hours. Her personal anguish leads her to a poem by the South African poet Breyten Breytenbach, and in quoting it the reader cannot help but be implicated as well. "The two of you, violator and victim (collaborator! violin!) are linked, forever perhaps, by the obscenity of what has been revealed to you, by the sad knowledge of what people are capable of. We are all guilty."

In recent years, numerous personal narratives that chronicle the war in the Middle East have been published in English. Malek's book was called "one of the finest examples of this new testimonial writing" by the reviewer Eliza Griswold for the *New York Times*. Other reviewers have cited that Malek's ability to draw from the interpersonal dramas within the family makes the book engaging. At the same time, the reviewer Marcia Lynx Qualey, writing for the *National*, found that some of the "historical insertions are so scrupulous they become dry."

Molly Hagan

Review Sources

Donoghue, Steve. "*The Home That Was Our Country* Recalls Syria As It Once Was." Review of *The Home That Was Our Country*, by Alia Malek. *The Christian Science Monitor*, 14 Feb. 2017, www.csmonitor.com/Books/Book-Reviews/2017/0214/The-Home-That-Was-Our-Country-recalls-Syria-as-it-once-was. Accessed 6 Oct. 2017.

Griswold, Eliza. "Two Testimonials Shed Light on Syrian Life and Death." Review of *The Home That Was Our Country*, by Alia Malek, and *We Crossed a Bridge and It Trembled*, by Wendy Pearlman. *The New York Times*, 19 July 2017, www.nytimes.com/2017/07/19/books/review/alia-malek-the-home-that-was-our-country-wendy-pearlman-we-crossed-a-bridge-and-it-trembled-syria-memoir-oral-history.html. Accessed 6 Oct. 2017.

Review of *The Home That Was Our Country*, by Alia Malek. *Kirkus Reviews*, 15 Dec. 2016, vol. 84, no. 24, p. 122.

Review of *The Home That Was Our Country*, by Alia Malek. *Publishers Weekly*, 9 Jan. 2017, pp. 59–60.

Qualey, Marcia Lynx. "Book Review: Alia Malek's *The Home That Was Our Country* Mirrors the Tragedy of Syria." Review of *The Home That Was Our Country*, by Alia Malek. *The National*, 14 Feb. 2017, www.thenational.ae/arts-culture/book-review-alia-malek-s-the-home-that-was-our-country-mirrors-the-tragedy-of-syria-1.89125. Accessed 6 Oct. 2017.

Homesick for Another World

Author: Ottessa Moshfegh (b. 1981)
Publisher: Penguin Press (New York). 304 pp.
Type of work: Short fiction
Time: Present day
Locale: United States

Courtesy of Penguin Press

Homesick for Another World *is a collection of fourteen stories by Ottessa Moshfegh. Set in various locations across the United States, the collection offers an intimate view of the lives of misfits—both average people and those who defy public convention. From chronic gamblers to the newly divorced or widowed to the elderly and lonely, Moshfegh's characters are at once extraordinary and relatable.*

In *Homesick for Another World*, Ottessa Moshfegh's first collection of short stories, no one quite fits. A school teacher with a steady, stable job cannot stay sober and spends her time between classes sleeping off her hangover in a closet, zipped up in a sleeping bag; a regular at a casino–internet café pines for a lonely-seeming woman who answers the phone and counts out cash for patrons; a successful, handsome man with a drinking problem in his mid-twenties finds himself in the throes of an encounter with a local woman and a sex toy. In each of these cases, the characters themselves resonate so strongly because of their ordinariness—a piece of each is recognizable in one's everyday life—but the real brilliance of the stories is in the details, particularly the time and attention Moshfegh has put into showing the reader how otherworldly these characters are, and ultimately every person one may encounter.

The collection opens with the story "Bettering Myself," a story about a thirty-year-old alcoholic Catholic schoolteacher, Miss Mooney, who has an uncomfortably close relationship with some of her students. The reader learns that her classroom is in the old library, that she vomits every morning when she arrives at school, that she is divorced and dating someone who is still in college, that she enjoys giving sex advice to her students, and that she has a habit of staying up all night drinking, sometimes out with friends, sometimes at home. The ironic tone of the story's title is clear once the plot begins to form. Moshfegh is much more interested in the current state of the human condition and in how those who cannot conform find ways to thrive in their desperate, but not entirely disastrous, lives. For example, in "Bettering Myself," the reader sees a woman who seemingly once had it together in the traditional sense—married, holding a steady job—but has since deviated from that path to the one she is seen on now. However, Moshfegh is not there to say which life is the best lived. The reader is never told whether Miss Mooney was happier before. Mooney still calls her ex-husband incessantly, and at one point the two meet for dinner and he asks her to stop, but it is unclear whether her problems led to the breakup or the breakup led to her problems. As with the other stories in this collection, the reader is forced to assess the current state of a character's life rather than speculate, and that practice is what leads to the development of empathy and curiosity for this strange set of stories and characters.

The following story, "Mr. Wu," follows a man who is clearly isolated and lonely but also unsure how to connect with other people, besides the prostitutes he regularly visits. As the story of Mr. Wu progresses, one of the overlying themes of the collection quickly emerges: the burden of dealing with a human body. Not long after Mr. Wu has declared that he is in love with the attendant at the arcade he regularly visits to gamble and use the internet and secured a date with her anonymously by finding her cell phone number and sending a series of texts, he becomes horrified by her body. He sits in the arcade scrutinizing the face he once loved, analyzing the gunk around her eyes and the heaviness of her makeup. He imagines her taking part in sexual acts he sees as horrific. Still, he plans to show up on the night of their blind date, when he will stand in the lamplight and she in the shadows so she can decide if she likes him or not. However, before the date happens, Mr. Wu visits a prostitute and acts out some of the acts he has imagined the arcade woman taking part in, and suddenly he is free from his feelings of disgust. In his review for the *New York Times*, critic Dwight Garner wrote of the book's characters, "Moshfegh's men and women cannot quite cope with this world. They are desperate and lonely and estranged. They want to tear the pain from their hearts, and it is less complicated to void their stomachs. Our empathy for them blends with disgust, which is nearly the definition of the grotesque in literature."

That feeling of disgust is what provides the most compelling thread through the collection. Moshfegh's characters are plagued by poor teeth and bad hygiene (in the story "The Locked Room," a teenage girl describes the taste of her boyfriend's kisses as reminiscent of excrement, and the reader sees him sitting on a couch squeezing pimples as the two wait to be freed). Characters have leaky colonoscopy bags, rashes that never seem to fade, and weak stomachs that threaten to empty their contents at every turn. Unsavory men pursue equally unsavory women, but no one seems to be able to see their own place in the order of things. It is Moshfegh's skill at describing such unfortunate characters in great detail that allows them to remain compelling.

In an essay for the *Los Angeles Review of Books*, W. S. Lyon wrote, "But [the stories] also insist upon the collision of memory and desire, drawing with a razor's edge the boundaries between solitude and isolation, allowing the narrator to move between Moshfegh's frank, gorgeous sentences and her wide, uncompromising authorial gaze. Nothing escapes her. And the great pleasure of the book is watching Moshfegh lend her enormous gifts to each of her alternately charming and repulsive protagonists, regardless of how terrible their ways." Lyon was writing in response to the heavy attention put on the more salacious details of the book, explaining why the characters are able to transcend those details. Two stories that exemplify this are "The Beach Boy," in which

Courtesy of Krystal Griffiths

Ottessa Moshfegh is the author of three books, including the 2015 novel Eileen, *which was short-listed for the Man Booker Prize and won the PEN/Hemingway Award. She has received a Pushcart Prize, an O. Henry Award, and the Plimpton Discovery Prize, along with a grant from the National Endowment for the Arts.*

a middle-aged man suddenly finds himself widowed after a tropical vacation with his wife, and the final story, "A Better Place," which is set in an unnamed town where a brother and sister are attempting to escape their current circumstances through murder. Essentially, they are trying to go home to the place where they feel they belong.

The beginning of "The Beach Boy" finds couple John and Marcia at dinner in New York City with two of their friends as they recount a trip to an island getaway. They are particularly interested in describing the beggars and men on the beach who proposition tourists for sex. That night, after the pair returns home to their comfortable apartment, Marcia complains of a headache. She lies on the couch and dies suddenly and quietly. John sleeps next to her, falling asleep during the movie they were to watch, only to realize she is dead the following morning. After the funeral, as John begins to adjust to life without Marcia, he has film developed from their trip. In one of the last images, a single eye peers out from the bottom with a dark landscape above it. John suspects this is the eye of one of the beach boys and begins to question Marcia's fidelity to him, thus inspiring him to take a trip back to the island to find the man with whom he believes she had a brief affair. This story takes its departure from the others as it focuses on the psychological messiness all humans deal with and the pain they unintentionally inflict upon each other. In John, the story has a character who is mundane—he is a dermatologist without any of the habits or attributes of his fellow characters in the collection—but whose seemingly stable life was precariously balanced at best. After losing Marcia, John is forced to ask himself if the years spent with her were the best for him and what he has lost following her death.

This psychological unease is mirrored in the collection's final story, "A Better Place." Waldemar and Urszula, a brother and sister living in a nondescript but presumably European environment, are literally homesick for another world. They talk and conspire endlessly about how they will get back to that world and how they will travel together. They both believe that they must find the one person they are meant to kill, and once that person is dead they will be allowed to jump through a hole to their home. Urszula decides she has found her person in Jarek Jaskolka, a man who assaults young girls. "'Jarek Jaskolka,' I whisper to remind myself that I will soon be far away from the place and all its horrors. Every time I say the name out loud, my head feels a little better," Urszula says at one point. After the tumultuous journey through the lives of the previous thirteen stories, one can understand Urszula's exhaustion with the world and her desire to escape, and it is her singular ambition that adds a resonance to the story and those that came before it. Readers have been forced to ask themselves over and over again who actually belongs in the world, and Urszula's answer is "no one," which provides a sense of comfort and horror all its own.

Melynda Fuller

Review Sources

Garner, Dwight. "'Homesick for Another World,' Food (and Bodily Functions) for Thought." Review of *Homesick for Another World*, by Ottessa Moshfegh. *The New York Times*, 14 Feb. 2017, www.nytimes.com/2017/02/14/books/homesick-for-another-world-ottessa-moshfegh.html. Accessed 25 Sept. 2017.

Schappell, Elissa. "The Art of Disgust: Ottessa Moshfegh's 'Homesick for Another World' Teeters between Bold and Bukowski." Review of *Homesick for Another World*, by Ottessa Moshfegh. *Los Angeles Times*, 19 Jan. 2017, www.latimes.com/books/jacketcopy/la-ca-jc-ottessa-moshfegh-20170119-story.html. Accessed 25 Sept. 2017.

Lorentzen, Christian. "Ottessa Moshfegh's Book Homesick for Another World Revels in Flawed Characters." Review of *Homesick for Another World*, by Ottessa Moshfegh. *Vulture*, 10 Feb. 2017, www.vulture.com/2017/02/ottessa-moshfeghs-homesick-for-another-world-book-review.html. Accessed 25 Sept. 2017.

Clanchy, Kate. "Homesick for Another World by Ottessa Moshfegh Review—Absorbing Short Stories from the Author of Eileen." Review of *Homesick for Another World*, by Ottessa Moshfegh. *The Guardian*, 20 Jan. 2017, www.theguardian.com/books/2017/jan/20/homesick-for-another-world-by-ottessa-moshfegh-review. Accessed 25 Sept. 2017.

Lyon, W. S. "Razor-Thin Boundaries." Review of *Homesick for Another World*, by Ottessa Moshfegh. *Los Angeles Review of Books*, 2 June 2017, lareviewofbooks.org/article/razor-thin-boundaries-a-review-of-homesick-for-another-world-by-ottessa-moshfegh. Accessed 25 Sept. 2017.

A Horse Walks into a Bar

Author: David Grossman (b. 1954)
First published: *Sus echad nichnas lebar*, 2014, in Israel
Translated from the Hebrew by Jessica Cohen
Publisher: Alfred A. Knopf (New York). 208 pp.
Type of work: Novel
Time: 2014
Locale: Netanya, Israel

David Grossman's award-winning novel A Horse Walks into a Bar *presents an aging, bitter Jewish stand-up comedian in what may be his final performance: an unforgettable routine that covers a gamut of topics, from the consideration of what is humorous to the nature of guilt and remembrance.*

Principal characters

DOVALEH "DOV" GREENSTEIN, a fifty-seven-year old Israeli stand-up comedian
AVISHAI LAZAR, his childhood friend, now a retired judge; the narrator
AZULAI, a.k.a. Euryclea, a.k.a. Pitz, a small woman who knew Dov in his youth
HEZKEL GREENSTEIN, his father
SARAH GREENSTEIN, his mother
YOAV, the owner of the nightclub where Dov performs

A Horse Walks into a Bar—first published in 2014 and translated from Hebrew into English in 2017—is quite different from the typical novel. The entire book unfolds in present tense, laid out like the prose rendition of a two-hour performance by a comedian who is only sporadically humorous but increasingly cynical and unhinged, as observed and documented by a member of the audience. There are no chapter divisions, only periodic brief pauses, like deep breaths, indicated by double-spaced gaps in the continuous narrative. This unusual, claustrophobic structure draws the reader into the experience of the performance, adding to the power of the story that unfolds.

The sense of claustrophobia is reinforced by the extremely limited setting: virtually the whole novel takes place in the comedy venue, a small basement nightclub in Netanya, Israel. The audience represents a cross-section of the community: blue-collar workers, soldiers, blue-haired old ladies, well-dressed couples, androgynous bikers, English-speaking immigrants, and others out for a night of entertainment. The date is August 20, 2014, a fact established by the comedian, who notes soon after his entrance that it is his fifty-seventh birthday. It quickly becomes clear that this will be no ordinary night of comedy.

The entertainer is Dovaleh G, also known as Dov Greenstein, who has a small following of faithful fans. The epitome of a neurotic comedian, he shambles onto a stage empty except for a large copper urn in the background, a blackboard on an easel, and an overstuffed armchair. Dov is short, scrawny, wears large eyeglasses, and sports a miniscule braid. He is dressed in a strange ensemble that contrasts with the audience's generally more restrained garments: T-shirt, red suspenders, ripped jeans, and platform cowboy boots decorated with silver stars. Dov sets the confrontational tone of the evening with his opening line, intentionally confusing Netanya with a smaller town. The joke gets some laughs from the audience, but it is immediately clear that Dov is no comic genius. In fact, it appears that he has other intentions for the night than entertaining.

These intentions relate to Dov's past, and there are two audience members who knew him earlier in life. One is the narrator of the story, Avishai Lazar. A retired district judge about the same age as Dov, he is still mourning the death of his beloved, much younger wife three years earlier. Though he does not appreciate stand-up comedy, he is there at the behest of Dov, who phoned weeks earlier to request his presence. Though Avishai did not initially remember Dov, as they talked memories came flooding back: the two men were childhood acquaintances, even friends, forty years earlier. When Avishai asks why Dov wants him at his performance, the comedian answers he has followed Avishai's career and wants the former judge to see him and tell him afterward what he saw. Essentially, Dov wants to be judged. Although Avishai is highly uncomfortable at first, as the evening wears on he begins to relax and even enjoy himself for the first time since his wife died. He also throws himself into his appointed task, jotting notes on a stack of bar napkins for later discussion. Dov, onstage, notices and appreciates Avishai's commitment.

Also present during Dov's routine is Azulai, a tiny manicurist and alleged medium in her early fifties with a speech impediment and orthopedic shoes. She too was acquainted with Dov in her youth and remembers him fondly for cheering her up after she was bullied. He dried her tears by turning upside down and walking on his hands, a tactic he frequently employed to surprise and disarm the boys who cruelly picked on him. Azulai seeks to find that kind young boy within the bitter man on stage.

The thrust of the story is Dov's monologue, variously delivered in conversational language, whispers, or shouts in a style ranging from refined to crude. His act at first primarily consists of jokes (some tired, some funny, some raunchy) and quick physical impersonations of types of people. Interspersed are rapid-fire one-liners, mostly stale topical comments or groaners based on Jewish stereotypes, since nightclub owner Yoav prefers to avoid conflict-laden political subjects. More insults fly, aimed both at hecklers and more randomly at individual audience members' characteristics, such as one woman's grotesquely obvious plastic surgery. Woven throughout are rambling, disjointed, tangential fragments of stories—digressions that invariably end with the refrain: "Where was I?"—touching upon problems that pervade Dov's life (three failed marriages, five estranged children, complications from prostate cancer). The crowd's reactions vary from belly laughs to boos to stunned silence.

Courtesy of Michael Lionstar

*David Grossman launched his literary
career in 1982 after working in radio
and serving in the Israeli military, finding international success with fiction,
nonfiction, drama, and children's literature alike. His numerous honors include the Sapir Prize, the Bialik Prize,
the Wingate Prize, and the Man Booker
International Prize.*

The atmosphere in the nightclub changes dramatically when Dov's act steers more and more into a long, rambling story about his youth. The account fills in Dov's backstory and his connection to Avishai, but like the rest of the novel, it is told through the comedian's monologue from the judge's perspective—not as a true flashback—creating a unique dynamic for the reader. The audience in the novel, however, becomes more and more frustrated with Dov's disjointed manner and apparent self-therapy. People turn against him as he fails to entertain, heckling him and walking out. Unfazed, he notes the departures with chalk marks on the onstage blackboard but continues his story.

The major past events that Dov relates happened after he was sent away to Israel's compulsory youth military training, where Avishai also served. During their time there, Avishai witnessed Dov being mercilessly bullied—stuffed in a duffle bag and tossed back and forth, for example—but did nothing to prevent it. Sitting in the audience, Avishai reflects on his own guilt. However, Dov's story is about something else: he was sent home from the military camp for a family funeral, but nobody informed him who had died—his mother, his father, or both parents. He was transported to Jerusalem in a military truck driven by a soldier soon to compete in a military joke-telling competition and practices his jokes on his passenger. The humor served as a welcome distraction to young Dov, but it is clear that the bizarre and tragic trip had a deep effect on him. The memories cause adult Dov to feel guilty all over again, and he viciously punches himself on stage, breaking his glasses and bloodying his own nose.

The audience—and the reader—is also subjected to Dov's interspersed accounts of his parents, Hezkel and Sarah Greenstein. These glimpses reveal their strengths and weaknesses and make them realistic and sympathetic. Sarah, a Holocaust survivor, suffered from deep psychological problems. To boost her spirits, young Dov for years put on complete nightly costumed shows with songs, comedy sketches, and impersonations, using a broomstick as a pretend microphone. Sarah would watch for a time, showing little reaction, then suddenly dismiss him. Hezkel, on the other hand, was ambitious and strict, beating his son regularly. Such personal, detailed recollections greatly displease Dov's audience, leading almost everyone to leave. Yet a few remain to hear the end of the story.

Back in the thread of Dov's youth, the journey to Jerusalem becomes more bizarre after the driver stops to pick up his sister and her newborn baby. The surreal experience, filtered through layers of narrative, effectively moves the novel along. Tension increases as the truck speeds toward the city and Dov—along with the remaining nightclub audience and the reader—look forward with dread to the revelation of who has died. It is that moment, Dov notes, when life became poisoned for him, and the narrative holds meaning at both personal and societal levels.

A remarkably affecting, uniquely structured accomplishment in storytelling, *A Horse Walks into a Bar* gathers up threads that author David Grossman has woven into his other work. The difficulty of transition from youth into adulthood, for example, was a major theme in such novels as *The Book of Intimate Grammar* (1991), *The Zigzag Kid* (1994), and *Someone to Run With* (2000). The linked issues of loss and grief, components of *To the End of the Land* (2008) and *Falling out of Time* (2014), are likewise explored. The lingering aftereffects of the Holocaust, which forever damaged Dov's mother, are also examined in Grossman's *See Under: Love* (1986).

Grossman's works have been translated into over thirty languages, and the success of the original Hebrew version of *A Horse Walks into a Bar* made it another logical candidate for the international market. Although the English translation (by Grossman's frequent translator Jessica Cohen) was published three years after the original, critical attention was no less enthusiastic. Reviewers almost universally praised the book's unique structure, technical accomplishment, and concise style. Many noted the skillful use of the rhythms of stand-up comedy, as well as the blend of genuine humor, Dov's bad jokes, and other emotions such as sadness and hope. Reflecting the rave reviews, *A Horse Walks into a Bar* was awarded the prestigious Man Booker International Prize in 2017.

Jack Ewing

Review Sources

Alvarez, Rafael. Review of *A Horse Walks into a Bar*, by David Grossman. *Washington Independent Review of Books*, 17 May 2017, www.washingtonindependentreviewofbooks.com/index.php/bookreview/a-horse-walks-into-a-bar-a-novel. Accessed 13 Nov. 2017.

Balint, Benjamin. "From Shtick to Striptease: An Israeli Tragi-Comedy with Universal Import." Review of *A Horse Walks into a Bar*, by David Grossman. *Haaretz*, 15 June 2017, www.haaretz.com/life/books/.premium-1.768748. Accessed 13 Nov. 2017.

Greenblatt, Stephen. "The King of the Bitter Laugh." Review of *A Horse Walks into a Bar*, by David Grossman. *The New York Review of Books*, 20 Apr. 2017, www.nybooks.com/articles/2017/04/20/david-grossman-king-of-bitter-laugh/. Accessed 13 Nov. 2017.

Sansom, Ian. "*A Horse Walks into a Bar* by David Grossman Review—Serious Portrait of a Shocking Standup." Review of *A Horse Walks into a Bar*, by David Grossman. *The Guardian*, 20 Sept. 2017, www.theguardian.com/books/2016/dec/09/a-horse-walks-into-a-bar-by-david-grossman-review. Accessed 13 Nov. 2017.

Shteyngart, Gary. "Is This Mic On?: A Stand-Up Comedian Wrestles with His Country and His Soul." Review of *A Horse Walks into a Bar*, by David Grossman. *The New York Times*, 27 Feb. 2017, www.nytimes.com/2017/02/27/books/review/horse-walks-into-a-bar-david-grossman-.html. Accessed 13 Nov. 2017.

House of Names

Author: Colm Tóibín (b. 1955)
Publisher: Scribner (New York). 288 pp.
Type of work: Novel
Time: Antiquity
Locale: Greece

House of Names, *the award-winning Irish author Colm Tóibín's 2017 novel, is a reimagining of an ancient Greek myth.*

Principal characters
CLYTEMNESTRA, queen of Mycenae
AGAMEMNON, king of Mycenae
ELECTRA, daughter of Clytemnestra and Agamemnon
ORESTES, son of Clytemnestra and Agamemnon
IPHIGENIA, daughter of Clytemnestra and Agamemnon

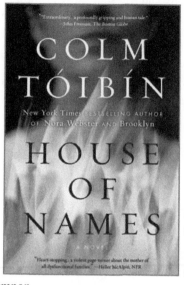

Courtesy of Scribner

In his 2017 novel *House of Names*, Colm Tóibín retells and embellishes a classic Greek myth. Told from three perspectives, the novel describes a family torn apart by murder and vengeance. The first narrator, the queen Clytemnestra, avenges her husband's deception after he lured her beautiful daughter Iphigenia to her death after promising her a wedding to the young hero Achilles. At the behest of the gods, King Agamemnon sacrifices his daughter in return for a fair wind, which he needs to set sail for the Trojan War. An enraged Clytemnestra bides her time. When Agamemnon returns to Mycenae, victorious after the war and with the young and beautiful concubine Cassandra on his arm, she murders him and Cassandra on the same night. This family tragedy, in both the myth and Tóibín's saga, has one more bloody plot point. Heaping vengeance upon vengeance, Clytemnestra's children Electra and Orestes scheme and carry out the murder of their mother. Tóibín's novel combines various versions of this gruesome tale—including that of Aeschylus's trilogy the *Oresteia* (458 BCE); Euripides's *Electra* (ca. 418 BCE) and *Iphigenia in Aulis* (ca. 410 BCE); and Sophocles's *Electra* (ca. 410 BCE)—while also taking liberties with particular details, such as Orestes's mysterious disappearance between Iphigenia's murder and the murder of his mother. Tóibín plumbs the psychological depths of these larger-than-life characters to explore how violence begets violence, and how revenge can be limitlessness.

Tóibín wrote in a 2017 article for the *Guardian* that he was inspired to tell this particular story because it reminded him of the violent ethno-nationalist conflicts that occurred in Northern Ireland in the period of the 1960s to the 1990s. "[N]o event was isolated," he wrote. "Each murder or set of murders seemed to have been inspired by a previous one, each atrocity appeared to be in retaliation for something that had occurred the week before." In *House of Names*, Tóibín draws on images from that period, including one from a particularly grisly massacre in Kingsmill in County Armagh in 1976. Tóibín interviewed a survivor, Alan Black, ten years after the event. Black had survived the execution-like killing by pretending to be dead. Tóibín evokes this image in *House of Names*, when one character hides beneath a pile of dead bodies, hoping to fool her executioners. Tóibín was particularly interested in the lives of the shadowy, unknown men who committed such murders, and who were likely living normal lives years after the fact. Tóibín has explained that he drew on various images of cruelty—the violent members of the terrorist group ISIS on one hand, and the stylish first family of Syria, Bashar al-Assad and his clan, who appeared in *Vogue* magazine, on the other.

Tóibín is an award-winning Irish author perhaps best known for his novel *Brooklyn* (2009), which was adapted for film in 2015. *Brooklyn* is about a young Irish girl from county Wexford (Tóibín's familial home) who reluctantly agrees to move to New York City in 1951. That book sprang from an anecdote Tóibín once heard about a mother whose children had moved to Brooklyn. His semiautobiographical 2014 novel *Nora Webster* is about an Irish widow (loosely based on Tóibín's mother) and her children in the 1960s. Tóibín has also been known to explore, in fiction, the lives of historical figures. His 2004 novel *The Master* imagines several years in the life of legendary author Henry James. Edging closer to the territory of *House of Names*, Tóibín's novella *The Testament of Mary* (2012) imagines an elderly Virgin Mary looking back on her life. Tóibín envisions her as being exhausted and bitter over the life and spectacular death of her son.

Connecting many of Tóibín's novels is the theme of an abiding interest in mothers. His own mother was a central, though largely silent, figure in his life after the death of his father when Tóibín was twelve. His book *Mothers and Sons* (2006) explores this complex familial relationship in nine short stories. Like Tóibín's memories of his mother, characters in his work are shaped as much, if not more, by the things they do not say as by the things they do. Tóibín continues to explore this idea, through the lens of an ancient Greek family, in *House of Names*.

The slow realization of her husband's intent is the excruciating event of the book's first section. Clytemnestra, her daughter Iphigenia, and her young son, Orestes, have arrived at the place where Agamemnon's troops are camped, expecting Iphigenia to be married to the young warrior Achilles. No one seems to want to be the first person to tell Clytemnestra, or rather, confirm for her, her husband's true intention, least of all Agamemnon himself. In one scene, the king plays with Orestes, mock sword fighting with the boy in an effort to avoid his wife's questioning gaze. "Agamemnon did not glance at me now, nor did he look at Iphigenia," she says. "The longer his jousting went on, the more I realized that he was afraid of us, or afraid of what he would have to say to us when it stopped." Agamemnon's cowardice regarding the murder of his daughter unhinges Clytemnestra. She becomes a calculating vortex of rage, scheming with her lover, Aegisthus, to kill Agamemnon upon his return. Tóibín chooses to dramatize the poor relationship between Clytemnestra and her other daughter, Electra, in the wake of Iphigenia's death. The murder makes an atheist of Clytemnestra,

Courtesy of Brigitte Lacombe

Colm Tóibín is an award-winning Irish novelist best known for his books such as Brooklyn *(2009) and* Nora Webster *(2014).*

but makes Electra all the more pious. The girl sides with her father, believing that if the gods truly demanded her sister's death, there was nothing else he could have done to stop it. The period between Iphigenia's death and Clytemnestra's murder of Agamemnon is shaped by Clytemnestra's desire to reach out to her other daughter, and her profound inability to do so.

Clytemnestra's is the most arresting voice in Tóibín's novel, perhaps because she has the clearest motivation. After her father's death, Electra schemes to relinquish power from her mother and Aegisthus. Her story line is defined by palace intrigue as guards and royals form and break alliances, creating underground networks of power. Sections that feature Orestes are told in the third person. Orestes is eight years old when Iphigenia is killed. Soon after her death, Aegisthus arranges to have him kidnapped. The boy is led to a strange house populated with young boys too fearful to speak to one another. This section of the narrative seems, as Daniel Mendelsohn pointed out in his review for the *New Yorker*, strangely anachronistic. Their imprisonment, he wrote, "feels suspiciously like a Catholic reform school." Regardless, Orestes and his friends, Leander and Mitros (both conjured by Tóibín), soon make their escape, finding refuge on the farm of an elderly woman. The boys work the land for her and grow from preteens into young men. Orestes and Leander form a deep friendship that Tóibín suggests is also sexual. In Tóibín's telling, Orestes's love for his friend drives him to commit murder, but this explanation for Orestes's behavior is not fully plausible. The elements of Orestes's story, taken all together, make him a captivating character, but Tóibín's rendering may feel incomplete for some readers.

House of Names received fair reviews from critics, including ancient Greek scholars Mary Beard, who reviewed the book for the *New York Times*, and Mendelsohn. Both seemed to enjoy parsing Tóibín's engagement with his source material. Each wrote about their pleasure in Tóibín's maneuvering in regard to a particular episode of the story, in which Orestes returns to Mycenae and must prove his identity to his sister, Electra. In Aeschylus's telling, Orestes gives her a lock of his hair as proof. This moment became so well known among Greek audiences that Euripides parodied the scene in his telling, choosing to have Electra express bewilderment at the idea that a lock of hair could serve as a form of identification. Tóibín seems to reference this "recognition scene," as Beard called it, in a scene where Leander must convince his family of his identity. Of course, most readers will not be so familiar with previous versions of the myth. Most readers will approach the novel with a sketchy memory of the story and a capacity to be surprised by Tóibín's telling of it.

As a novel read without a full understanding of the mythic framework, *House of Names* has moments of success as well as moments of failure. There are passages that illuminate the complex interior lives of Tóibín's characters—in her *New York Times* review of the novel *Brooklyn*, Liesl Schillinger memorably called Tóibín a "patient fisherman of submerged emotions"—but there are also passages that seem to hold the characters at arms' length, collapsing them back into myth. Tóibín's setting is likewise sketchily drawn, emerging only in snatches (like the farmhouse or the troop encampment), making it difficult to imagine the world of the story. "It was as if," Mendelsohn wrote in his *New Yorker* review, "[Tóibín] had pored over Joseph Campbell's *The Power of Myth* but never thought to pick up *Everyday Life in Ancient Greece*." Still, Tóibín never loses sight of his original aim. Though the novel as a whole might seem "tonally disjointed," as the reviewer for *Kirkus* wrote, the author accurately "captures the way that corruption breeds resentment and how resentment almost unstoppably breeds violence."

Molly Hagan

Review Sources

Beard, Mary. "A Pair of Updated Greek Tragedies Startle Us Anew." Review of *House of Names*, by Colm Tóibín, and *Bright Air Black*, by David Vann. *The New York Times*, 11 May 2017, www.nytimes.com/2017/05/11/books/review/house-of-names-colm-toibin-bright-air-black-david-vann.html. Accessed 10 Jan. 2018.

Charles, Ron. "Colm Tóibín's *House of Names* Gives Voice to a Furious Mother." Review of *House of Names*, by Colm Tóibín. *The Washington Post*, 2 May 2017, www.washingtonpost.com/entertainment/books/colm-toibins-house-of-names-gives-voice-to-a-furious-mother/2017/05/01/eddc845c-2b77-11e7-be51-b3fc6ff-7faee_story.html. Accessed 10 Jan. 2018.

Clanchy, Kate. "*House of Names* by Colm Tóibín Review—Greek Myths Made Human." *The Guardian*, 27 May 2017, www.theguardian.com/books/2017/may/27/house-of-names-colm-toibin-review. Accessed 10 Jan. 2018.

Review of *House of Names*, by Colm Tóibín. *Kirkus*, 7 Mar. 2017, www.kirkusreviews.com/book-reviews/colm-toibin/house-of-names/. Accessed 10 Jan. 2018.

Review of *House of Names*, by Colm Tóibín. *Publishers Weekly*, 13 Mar. 2017, www.publishersweekly.com/978-1-5011-4021-1. Accessed 10 Jan. 2018.

Mendelsohn, Daniel. "Novelizing Greek Myth." Review of *House of Names*, by Colm Tóibín. *The New Yorker*, 31 July 2017, www.newyorker.com/magazine/2017/07/31/novelizing-greek-myth. Accessed 10 Jan. 2018.

How Emotions Are Made
The Secret Life of the Brain

Author: Lisa Feldman Barrett (b. 1963)
Publisher: Houghton Mifflin Harcourt (Boston). Illustrated. 448 pp.
Type of work: Science

How Emotions Are Made: The Secret Life of the Brain is a summation of the groundbreaking research of Dr. Lisa Feldman Barrett, an expert in neuroscience and psychology. It is her first nonacademic book.

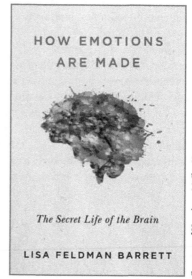

Courtesy of Houghton Mifflin Harcourt

In science, the long-held view of human emotion has been that there is a small, universal set of feelings that everyone is born with. That is to say, the brain is prewired with neurons that, when triggered by an event, produce the appropriate emotion. This theory posits that because emotions are locatable entities within the brain, everyone experiences and conveys joy, anger, disgust, surprise, and fear in the same way. In her groundbreaking book *How Emotions Are Made: The Secret Life of the Brain*, neuroscientist and psychologist Dr. Lisa Feldman Barrett challenges this widely accepted belief, arguing that emotions are not hardwired into humans but are in fact constructed over time as a result of a person's unique experiences, including cultural experiences.

A dramatic break from established scientific thought, *How Emotions Are Made* is an exciting work of nonfiction thanks to its revolutionary conclusion: humans are not necessarily at the behest of their emotions; instead, the phrase that Barrett strategically repeats throughout the book is that "you are an architect of your experience." The narrative path that she takes to reach such a bold concept is straightforward and singularly focused.

The book's first three chapters provide context by introducing the history and science of emotion. Barrett describes how, for years, it was believed that each emotion had a "fingerprint," or a distinct pattern of physical changes in the face, brain, and body. However, when she began a quest to define each emotion's fingerprint, she discovered that variation was actually the norm—different people undergo different physical changes when experiencing the same emotion. In other words, the facial expressions and body language associated with specific feelings such as fear or anger are not universal, as was previously believed. This discovery convinced her that a new theory on emotion was needed and led her to explore the theory of "constructed emotion," or the idea that a person's brain tells them how to feel by using past experiences to interpret current sensory experiences.

One of the unique qualities of Barrett's writing is her willingness to display humility. The author is quick to discuss experiments that went wrong or produced inconclusive results, and she does not hesitate to give credit to others when it is due. She never, for example, tries to claim the theory of constructed emotion as her own. Where the book's first section focuses on her own research and conclusions, Barrett shifts her focus in the middle section to well-established neuroscientific processes, which she uses to contextualize the relatively new theory of constructed emotion. She goes to great lengths to explain the different parts of the brain and how they work in tandem to process information and generate emotions. She is careful and patient in the way that she presents this information to readers; each piece of decidedly complex and esoteric knowledge builds on the previous one in a sequential manner intended to maximize readers' overall comprehension.

As the first two-thirds of the book focus on the science of emotion, *How Emotions Are Made* occasionally feels dense and overwhelming. To support the central theory of constructed emotion, Barrett weaves into these chapters an esoteric range of evidence, from descriptions of psychological and physiological phenomena to Charles Darwin's theory of evolution to examples of real-life emotional experiences. While this is interesting content, the book is perhaps most fascinating in its final chapters, where Barrett makes a case for the significance of her hypothesis. Here, the author illustrates what it would mean for society if everyone accepted that human emotion is not a hardwired biological function, but rather something the brain generates and reconfigures over time. Adopting the perspective of a psychologist, she argues that if emotions are constructed spontaneously, then human beings can potentially learn how to control them. This, in turn, would allow people to mitigate the detrimental effects of disorders such as depression and anxiety.

In addition to providing insight into ways that people could improve their mental health, Barrett also explores the impact that controlled emotions would have on child rearing, personal relationships, and even the law. To this end, she uses the example of the Boston Marathon bomber Dzhokhar Tsarnaev, who was sentenced to death in 2015 because most of the jury at his trial felt that his face showed no remorse. If it became widely accepted that not everyone physically expresses emotion the same way, then it is possible that juries might set the fate of defendants completely differently. Ultimately, Barrett succeeds in conveying the big-picture implications of her work in an exciting way.

How Emotions Are Made is enjoyable largely thanks to its narrative style. Barrett does not write in stilted declaratives, as one might in a dissertation or textbook. At first glance, this stylistic choice could be attributed to the fact that her hypothesis has yet to be accepted as fact. However, the prose and tone appear more reflective of Barrett's desire to write a book about research that would be easily understood by the public. To that end, she takes readers along step by step through the process that she embarked on in order to arrive at her conclusion. She shifts back and forth between first- and second-person pronouns, which allows her to both describe her findings and instruct readers on how they should view the research process. This, combined with her tendency to use idioms and casual language while discussing the scientific process, helps

How Emotions Are Made maintain a somewhat conversational tone, thereby ensuring that a book about a potentially controversial topic feels welcoming.

It is decidedly not easy to write a science book for the general public, but Barrett takes great pains to make her work accessible to readers of all backgrounds. In addition to a conversational writing style, she also uses photographs and diagrams to supplement and explain her complex theory, and she regularly employs amusing anecdotes as tools to illustrate complicated neurological phenomena while engaging the reader. At one point, for example, she argues that the brain constructs emotion by using past experiences to give meaning to the present moment—a process known as "simulation." To explain how simulation works, she uses the example of her daughter's twelfth birthday party, which was a "gross foods" party. The cheese on the pizza was dotted with green food coloring to make it look moldy, and the white grape juice was served in medical urine sample cups. Many of the party guests gagged even though they were in on the joke and knew that the food was perfectly safe to consume. Barrett explains that their brains were recalling previous experiences with the same imagery, and these memories were triggering the emotional response of disgust. Ultimately, it is this type of funny, relatable anecdote that helps readers understand the fundamental concepts of *How Emotions Are Made.*

How Emotions Are Made makes for an interesting addition to the canon of popular science books. Thanks to its subject matter, it is likely to be compared to works such as David Eagleman's *The Brain: The Story of You* (2015) and Antonio Damasio's *Descartes' Error: Emotion, Reason, and the Human Brain* (1994). Stylistically, however, *How Emotions Are Made* is more similar to zoologist Sy Montgomery's best-selling book *The Soul of an Octopus: A Surprising Exploration into the Wonder of Consciousness* (2015). While Montgomery's prose is arguably more poetic than Barrett's, both

Lisa Feldman Barrett is a University Distinguished Professor of Psychology at Northeastern University. Her work on emotion in the brain earned her a National Institutes of Health (NIH) Director's Pioneer Award in 2007.

books are written from the first-person perspective of the scientist, with a bifurcated focus on both the author's data and her research process.

Reviews of *How Emotions Are Made* have been mixed. Although Barrett has been praised for her revolutionary theory and supporting research, she has also been criticized for not sufficiently tailoring the information to the average reader. This is evident in the review of the book for *Publishers Weekly*, which concluded, "The book is a challenging read and will offer the most rewards to researchers already familiar with the longstanding and apparently still unresolved arguments about what emotions are." Despite the fact that Barrett is an excellent writer who clearly attempted to deliver her findings in layman's terms, it is a valid concern that *How Emotions Are Made* often feels like a book for experts. Still, curious and determined readers will glean new knowledge from it as long as they are prepared for something more challenging than a typical popular science book.

Perhaps the most cutting criticism of *How Emotions Are Made* came from fellow neuroscientist Jay Hosking, writing for the *Globe and Mail*. In his review of the book, Hosking argued that Barrett's hypothesis is bold but ultimately poorly supported by her writing, claiming that "too often the answers in *How Emotions Are Made* are dissatisfying, vague or entirely absent." It can be argued that, given Hosking's background, he simply felt that Barrett failed to provide the amount of evidence typically expected of a member of the scientific community; in this context, his complaint feels subjective, and one that will not necessarily apply to everyone who endeavors to read *How Emotions Are Made*. It is likely that many other readers will feel that Barrett excels at explaining the research and reasoning behind her arguments. Such was the case for the reviewer for *Kirkus Reviews*, who called the book a "highly informative, readable, and wide-ranging discussion."

Criticisms aside, *How Emotions Are Made* is one of the most important books of the year simply for the dialogue it will jump-start within science and mental health communities. In addition to being well written and informative, it is a highly compelling work that will inspire readers from all backgrounds to learn methods for better understanding and controlling their emotions. In turn, this could lead to higher-quality lives—ones that are not dictated by the ubiquitous misconception that humans are at the mercy of raw emotion. While it has yet to be determined whether or not Barrett's theory will be accepted and established as fact, at the very least, *How Emotions Are Made* marks an exciting new shift in the direction in which neuroscience and psychology research are headed.

Emily Turner

Review Sources

Hosking, Jay. "Lisa Feldman Barrett's *How Emotions Are Made* Reviewed: Provocative Theory Falls Flat." Review of *How Emotions Are Made: The Secret Life of the Brain*, by Lisa Feldman Barrett. *The Globe and Mail*, 31 Mar. 2017, www.theglobeandmail.com/arts/books-and-media/book-reviews/lisa-feldman-barretts-how-emotions-are-made-reviewed-a-provocative-theory-that-falls-flat/article34516679/. Accessed 10 Jan. 2018.

Review of *How Emotions Are Made: The Secret Life of the Brain*, by Lisa Feldman Barrett. *Kirkus Reviews*, 18 Jan. 2017, www.kirkusreviews.com/book-reviews/lisa-feldman-barrett/how-emotions-are-made/. Accessed 10 Jan. 2018.

Review of *How Emotions Are Made: The Secret Life of the Brain*, by Lisa Feldman Barrett. *Publishers Weekly*, 12 Dec. 2016, www.publishersweekly.com/978-0-544-13331-0. Accessed 10 Jan. 2018.

The Hungry Brain
Outsmarting the Instincts That Make Us Overeat

Author: Stephan J. Guyenet
Publisher: Flatiron Books (New York). Illustrated. 304 pp.
Type of work: Science

In The Hungry Brain: Outsmarting the Instincts That Make Us Overeat, *Stephan J. Guyenet explains the complex brain processes that cause humans to overeat and, in many cases, develop obesity.*

According to neuroscientist and science writer Stephan J. Guyenet, in 1960, one-seventh of adults in the United States were obese by twenty-first-century standards. Fifty years later, in 2010, one-third of American adults had obesity. That dramatic increase in the prevalence of obesity among American adults has been attributed to many different factors, including many late twentieth- and early twenty-first-century professions being sedentary, fast-food restaurants proliferating, and high-calorie ingredients such as high-fructose corn syrup becoming popular. As convincing as such arguments may be, however, Guyenet asserts that such explanations fail to tell the whole story. Rather, the increased prevalence of obesity in the United States and elsewhere is the result of a collection of nonconscious, concrete brain processes that encourage overeating, promote high-calorie foods over their lower-calorie counterparts, and otherwise sabotage conscious, abstract efforts to lose or maintain weight. In *The Hungry Brain: Outsmarting the Instincts That Make Us Overeat*, Guyenet explores such processes in detail, explaining how different areas of the brain and the functions they control contribute to the development of obesity. A former postdoctoral researcher at the University of Washington, Guyenet spent many years studying the neurobiological processes underlying obesity and is particularly well suited to compiling and interpreting decades of research conducted by leading experts, presenting readers not only with a new understanding of obesity but also practical strategies for preventing it.

Guyenet begins *The Hungry Brain* with an introduction explaining that despite the US government's release of dietary guidelines in 1980, US residents have since become more obese. He notes that although some individuals have argued that the guidelines themselves and their specific food recommendations contributed to the rise in obesity, he disagrees with that idea. Rather, he argues, human beings' eating behavior—and the corresponding development of obesity—is governed largely not by conscious and rational decisions about what to eat, but by brain processes originating in humankind's early evolutionary history. Traits that benefit members of hunter-gatherer societies, such as the instinctual ability to seek out calorie-dense food and eat as much as is available in times when food is scarce, are largely irrelevant and even harmful in industrialized societies where wide varieties and large quantities of food are available. Guyenet describes this conflict between nonconscious processes and the realities of industrialized twenty-first-century society as an evolutionary mismatch. The human brain, he argues, still operates in the mode of early humans but is doing so in a world where the eating habits it prompts may be detrimental.

After explaining his core thesis, Guyenet discusses several different brain systems that can cause humans to overeat and contribute to obesity. The first, the reward system, resides in an area of the brain called the basal ganglia and causes humans to seek out foods that contain specific nutritional elements, including fat and sugar. When a person is exposed to cues related to such foods—for instance, by smelling or seeing them—the brain guides the person to eat those foods and reinforces that doing so was good. The next system, based in the orbitofrontal cortex and ventromedial prefrontal cortex, is called the economic choice system and helps human beings decide between multiple options and determine the best choice in a situation. When an individual is presented with foods from which to choose, the economic choice system seems to prioritize food that is more caloric and pushes the person to choose those foods. This tendency, Guyenet notes, results from the historically beneficial nature of high-calorie and calorie-dense foods. In times when food was scarce, eating the rare calorie-dense foods available was key to survival. In the twenty-first century, however, calorie-dense foods are widely available, and the brain urges humans to eat them in large quantities.

Guyenet next describes the lipostat system, which regulates the appetite and prevents weight loss through hormones such as leptin, before describing the satiety system, which controls feelings of hunger and fullness. Although the satiety system typically causes a person to feel full after eating an adequate amount, it can at times limit a person's feeling of satiety when the person eats food that the reward system deems particularly rewarding. Although Guyenet describes the functions of the reward, economic choice, lipostat, and satiety systems broadly, he acknowledges that different people's brain processes vary somewhat based on genetic factors. While genes will not make a person obese on their own, they have the capacity to make an individual more susceptible to the brain's cues to overeat. In addition to brain processes specifically related to the appetite and the drive to seek out and consume food, Guyenet also discusses how strains on the body and mind can trigger people to overeat. He devotes a chapter to sleep, noting that when people do not get enough sleep or sufficiently restorative sleep, they become more likely to overeat in response to food cues. He further explains that stress, which is linked to the threat-response system overseen by the brain's amygdala, affects the levels of hormones linked not only to appetite but also to an increase in body fat.

Although the human body's nonconscious impulses can seem insurmountable, Guyenet remains optimistic that people who know about the brain and body's functions can overcome some of the processes in play. In the final chapter, "Outsmarting the Hungry Brain," he proposes various tactics for overcoming the nonconscious processes that promote overeating and obesity. He argues that the US government could prevent obesity by levying taxes on high-calorie foods, decreasing subsidies for crops used to make fattening food products, increasing subsidies for lower-calorie crops, and regulating food advertising so that the public is not bombarded with the food cues such advertisements create. Although he acknowledges that the food industry has made limited efforts already through programs such as the Children's Food and Beverage Advertising Initiative, which regulates food advertising aimed at children, Guyenet asserts that further work is needed. Moving on, he presents steps that he states can help individuals overcome the brain processes that drive them to overeat. He advises individuals to reduce exposure to food cues, eat foods that promote satiety, and avoid highly rewarding calorie-dense foods. Guyenet likewise calls attention to the importance of getting sufficient sleep, maintaining a basic level of physical activity, and reducing stress in one's daily life.

Throughout *The Hungry Brain*, Guyenet works to make complex scientific concepts accessible to readers. He describes topics such as innate food preferences and aversions, the functions of chemicals such as leptin and dopamine, and adiposity in a clear, understandable, and pleasurable manner. The numerous accompanying charts, graphs, and other images, many of them created by science illustrator Shizuka N. Aoki, helpfully illustrate the book's key points and support the author's assertions. Overall, Guyenet maintains a conversational and engaging tone, rendering topics that might otherwise seem dry and boring thoroughly entertaining. An extensively researched work, *The Hungry Brain* compiles many years of study on the underlying causes of obesity into a single, concise text. Guyenet draws heavily from published scientific papers, conversations with experts, and statistical data, and his sources are meticulously catalogued in the notes that follow the text, providing a useful starting point for readers interested in learning more about the subjects he discusses in the book.

In addition to researching through traditional means for *The Hungry Brain*, Guyenet went so far as to conduct experiments on himself so that he could examine his own brain's responses to food. In chapter 7, "The Hunger Neuron," he recounts his experience having his brain scanned with a magnetic resonance imaging (MRI) machine at the University of Washington. Using functional MRI, the University of Washington researchers observed and measured Guyenet's brain activity while he looked at three sets of images: images of high-calorie "junk foods," images of healthy low-calorie foods, and images of non-food objects. The researchers determined that his brain responded strongly to the images of high-calorie foods, causing areas of the brain that control the dopamine system to light up in the scans when he looked at those images. To illustrate his discussion of the experiment, Guyenet includes images of his own brain scans, enabling readers to see the noticeable differences between his brain's responses to images of high- and low-calorie foods. Guyenet's decision to include images of his own brain also demonstrates his commitment to explaining complex systems to his readers and underscores the near-universality of the brain processes at hand: even Guyenet, an experienced obesity researcher

Stephan J. Guyenet is an obesity and neuroscience researcher, science and health writer, and consultant. The Hungry Brain is his first book.

with a doctorate in neuroscience, is subject to the nonconscious siren song of potato chips.

The critical response to *The Hungry Brain* was largely positive, with reviewers praising Guyenet's clear and informative examination of the processes underlying the human relationship with food. In a review for the *New York Times*, Judith Newman described the book as an "essential" text for those interested in the scientific areas Guyenet describes. As well as praising the book's content, critics widely appreciated Guyenet's tone and conversational manner of writing about complex scientific topics. *The Hungry Brain* was similarly well received by more science-focused publications. In a review for the website of the British Association for Psychopharmacology, Ravi Das described Guyenet's argument as "logical, convincing, and accessible." While Das notes that the book cannot cover all the "complexities and nuances" at play in the development of obesity, he appreciates Guyenet's willingness to acknowledge that research is ongoing and that further factors may yet to be discovered.

Joy Crelin

Review Sources

Das, Ravi. Review of *The Hungry Brain: Outsmarting the Instincts That Make Us Overeat*, by Stephan J. Guyenet. *British Association for Psychopharmacology*, 31 Mar. 2017, www.bap.org.uk/articles/book-review-the-hungry-brain. Accessed 31 Oct. 2017.

Review of *The Hungry Brain: Outsmarting the Instincts That Make Us Overeat*, by Stephan J. Guyenet. *Kirkus Reviews*, vol. 84, no. 24, 15 Dec. 2016, p. 115. *Literary Reference Center Plus*, search.ebscohost.com/login.aspx?direct=true&db=lkh&AN=122749137&site=lrc-plus. Accessed 31 Oct. 2017.

Review of *The Hungry Brain: Outsmarting the Instincts That Make Us Overeat*, by Stephan J. Guyenet. *Publishers Weekly*, vol. 263, no. 50, 5 Dec. 2016, p. 63. *Literary Reference Center Plus*, search.ebscohost.com/login.aspx?direct=true&db=lkh&AN=120042217&site=lrc-plus. Accessed 31 Oct. 2017.

Newman, Judith. "And a Thinner New Year: Five New Books about Food and Diets."' Review of *The Hungry Brain: Outsmarting the Instincts That Make Us Overeat*, by Stephan J. Guyenet, et al. *The New York Times*, 28 Dec. 2016, www.nytimes.com/2016/12/28/books/review/new-books-about-food-and-diets.html. Accessed 31 Oct. 2017.

310

I Was Told to Come Alone
My Journey behind the Lines of Jihad

Author: Souad Mekhennet (b. 1978)
Publisher: Henry Holt (New York). 368 pp.
Type of work: Current affairs, history, memoir
Time: Twentieth and twenty-first centuries
Locales: Europe, the Middle East

In I Was Told to Come Alone: My Journey behind the Lines of Jihad, *author Souad Mekhennet discusses her development as a reporter focusing on Islamist extremism, the various major stories she has covered, and the disturbing future that may await a world in which violent jihadism is far from defeated.*

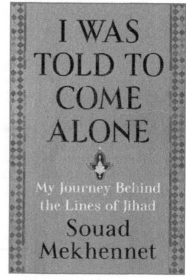

Courtesy of Henry Holt & Company, Inc.

Principal personages

ABU MALEEQ, a.k.a. Denis Cuspert, a German rapper turned terrorist
OSAMA BIN LADEN, former leader of al-Qaeda
MICHAEL MOSS, an American journalist
MOHAMMED EMWAZI, a.k.a. Jihadi John, a terrorist famous for on-camera beheadings
ABU MUSAB AL-ZARQAWI, an early leader of al-Qaeda in Iraq

As its title and subtitle suggest, Souad Mekhennet's book *I Was Told to Come Alone: My Journey behind the Lines of Jihad* is more a memoir than a detailed analysis of Islamist extremism. Anyone approaching the book looking for probing insights into the nature of the violent jihadist threat may be disappointed, because the volume is more about Mekhennet's adventures as a reporter than about what makes terrorists tick. Mekhennet does reinforce narratives that are by now familiar—some Muslims, especially in the Middle East and Europe, have been bothered enough by perceived racism or unfair treatment, or by Western hypocrisies or military interventions in their holy lands, to take up arms or cut off heads to oppose those they consider infidels—but she also explores the feelings of powerlessness and alienation at the root of this narrative, humanizing her subjects without downplaying the horrific results of their actions. She is, throughout her book, a passionate defender of universal human rights, equally willing to criticize both Western failings and violent perversions of Islam. But she is also honest enough to admit that if she criticizes some Islamists too openly, her life may be at risk, and she offers enough evidence to make many readers wonder whether multiculturalism, especially as conceived of in western Europe, can ever truly succeed.

Born in Germany to parents who had emigrated from Morocco and from Turkey, Mekhennet benefited from the freedoms available in the West. But she was also, like many immigrants in many nations, exposed to the unfairness that often results from being a member of a minority culture. "To rise in my home country as a Muslim migrant, or even as the child of migrants," she writes, "you have to toe the line and praise Europe's progressiveness. If you criticize the government too loudly or raise serious questions about anything from foreign policy to Islamophobia, the backlash can be intense." Mekhennet clearly values the freedoms she grew up with in Germany, especially her freedoms as a woman, but she also wants her readers to know about the pain-inducing distrust, dismissal, and prejudice that Muslims encounter in Western nations. Beyond being unfair, she argues, this distrust is counterproductive: the more discrimination Muslims suffer in the West, the more alienated they feel, and the more vulnerable they are to the

Courtesy of Ben Kilb

Souad Mekhennet is an important journalist who has broken significant stories for such US outlets as the New York Times *and the* Washington Post.

desire to lash out against that sense of alienation with potentially catastrophic violence.

Anyone interested in journalism in general, and the growing role of women and minorities in journalism in particular, will find Mekhennet's book especially fascinating. Readers will learn the ins and outs of undercover reporting; of setting up clandestine interviews with dangerous figures; of the bonds that develop between writers, editors, and other writers; and of the need to establish facts while also keeping the need to achieve exclusives in mind. Mekhennet, for instance, was the first journalist to determine the true identity of Mohammed Emwazi, the infamous black-masked Islamic State of Iraq and Syria (ISIS) butcher previously known only as "Jihadi John." She feared that if she published her story too soon, a captive of ISIS might be publicly beheaded in retaliation; yet at the same time, she worried that if she did not publish, the BBC, which had also been working on the story, might break the news before her. Eventually, her story was published, just in time to beat the competition. Why it was worth publicizing Emwazi's true identity at that particular point in time, and posing any risk at all to any hostages, is not entirely clear, although bragging rights and professional advancement seem to be part of the explanation.

Mekhennet, who can trace her family tree all the way back to the Prophet himself, seems to have the uncanny ability to be just about anywhere, and to get to know just about anyone, connected with the rise of Islamic terrorism. Beginning as a "stringer," or freelance journalist, she soon became affiliated with some of the world's most important newspapers, including the *New York Times* and the *Washington Post.* Her descent from the Prophet, her knowledge of Arabic and other Middle Eastern languages, her appealing personality, and, yes, even her gender helped her win the trust of many jihadists who are usually not especially interested in talking to Western journalists.

(Several of these "sheikhs" actually tried to court Mekhennet or convince her to sign up for marriage as an additional wife.)

Mekhennet comes across, in this book, as an exceptionally brave person whose wit, tact, manners, intelligence, and assertiveness often kept not only her but especially her Western male colleagues from serious harm. Some of the humor in this often-humorous book occurs when men who cannot speak Arabic have no idea how close they are coming to being kidnapped, tortured, or beheaded. Meanwhile, the many sheikhs Mekhennet meets often have surprisingly good senses of humor. They obviously get a kick out of teasing the attractive woman journalist, and she (often wisely) laughs right along.

There are times, however, when some readers will wish the book were not as long as it is. All the minor details of making contacts, establishing relationships, arranging secret meetings, sending and receiving text messages, and talking to colleagues and terrorists are reported in great detail. Mekhennet assumes that many readers will be interested in practically everything she has ever said or done, and perhaps she is right. But for any readers approaching the book for insights into what to expect in the future (rather than what happened in one journalist's past), this leisurely pace can be a bit frustrating. Mekhennet herself is always at the center of the stage, and some readers may wish that the story were more about others than about herself. It is easy to imagine how this book would have worked most successfully as a series of articles in the *New Yorker* rather than as a sustained narrative sandwiched between two covers. Like many examples of the now-old "New Journalism," this is a work in which the reporter is as much the story as the story itself.

Still, parts of this book are genuinely intriguing. Notable among these are the parts near the end in which Mekhennet discusses the massive wave of immigration to western Europe that followed the rise of ISIS in the Middle East. Germany, Mekhennet's home country, famously welcomed the refugees (three million of them) with open arms; Chancellor Angela Merkel even invented the catchy slogan *Wir schaffen das* ("We will manage it," or "We can do it") to proclaim Germany's determination to make the refugees feel at home. This is where Mekhennet's narrative takes a truly unsettling turn. "As I read German media accounts and listened to the politicians talk," she writes, "I sensed a completely uncritical euphoria about the newly arrived foreigners." Having once been a kind of foreigner in Germany herself, Mekhennet is unusually well positioned to assess the wisdom of Merkel's moves. What she writes, based on her firsthand reporting, is disturbing.

Mekhennet comments that she "knew this would be a perfect opportunity for all kinds of jihadi groups to send recruits to Europe, where they could operate as sleeper cells." When she visited Austrian train stations, she "began to see signs that this was already happening." Merkel's speeches were often understood, throughout the Islamic world, as open invitations to head to Germany: "People from all over North Africa, the Middle East, and even South Asia flew to Turkey, destroyed their passports, and joined the flood of refugees." Often these faux refugees, many of them young men, tried to pass themselves off as new arrivals from war-torn Syria, but Mekhennet, with her knowledge of specific Arabic accents and dialects, could immediately tell that they were lying. She reports that, according to one Austrian security official she spoke to, "there were thriving black markets for Syrian passports in Croatia, Serbia, Hungary, and Austria, in addition to Turkey"; in fact, she notes, "there were enough pretenders that the true Syrians began to complain about the false Syrians, saying that opportunists such as [them] would quickly wear out their welcome, if they hadn't already."

Even many of the legitimate refugees, she says, came looking mainly for the free benefits Germany could provide. "Some of these conversations tried my patience," she recalls. "When I asked, here and there, if they would agree to work for the benefits they received, I sometimes heard answers like, 'I don't want my wife or daughter to work.'" (Mekhennet's own father and mother had gladly worked not only at their jobs but also at trying to fit into German society.) When bureaucrats claimed that most of the "refugees" were highly educated, Mekhennet was skeptical. "That wasn't what I saw at the train stations," she writes. "Most of the Syrians I met were farmers or laborers. . . . That wasn't a problem in itself, but politicians and the media were telling a very different story." She "also met some migrants who said they'd lived under ISIS and liked it," who were coming solely for "the job opportunities."

Ironically, then, Mekhennet, who earlier complained about being discriminated against as a Muslim in Germany, now provides ammunition that will be used to discriminate against a new wave of Muslims in Germany and the rest of Europe. That, of course, is very far from her intent. She wants people to live in peace and tolerate each other's differences. In fact, by the end of the book, she is basically wishing that some sort of Western liberalism can prevail throughout the world. Mere democracy, in which the majority rules, sometimes absolutely, finally seems less appealing to her than "a code of universal values" that might preserve the rights of minorities of various kinds, including the rights of the actual majority of human beings: women.

Yet Mekhennet provides little hope that this wish might be fulfilled. Her comments on the "Arab Spring," which quickly turned into an Arab nightmare, are chastening, and her book's final pages are extremely unsettling—especially when she suggests that the Iranian nuclear deal, designed to strengthen the hands of Iranian moderates, may actually backfire, strengthening Islamic extremists instead. Like her comments about the mass immigration of refugees, this is not the sort of thing one might have expected from such a book. But whatever bad things may happen in the future, Mekhennet will be ideally positioned, in many different ways, to cover them, explain them, and produce a grim sequel to this gloomy, grisly volume.

Robert C. Evans, PhD

Review Sources
Donoghue, Steve. "*I Was Told to Come Alone* Is One Reporter's Up-Close Look at Jihad." Review of *I Was Told to Come Alone: My Journey behind the Lines of Jihad,* by Souad Mekhennet. *The Christian Science Monitor,* 14 June 2017, www. csmonitor.com/Books/Book-Reviews/2017/0614/I-Was-Told-To-Come-Alone-is-one-reporter-s-up-close-look-at-jihad. Accessed 12 Jan. 2018.

Review of *I Was Told to Come Alone: My Journey behind the Lines of Jihad*, by Souad Mekhennet. *Kirkus Reviews*, 15 Apr. 2017, p. 63. *Academic Search Complete*, search.ebscohost.com/login.aspx?direct=true&db=a9h&AN=122748722&site=ehost-live. Accessed 12 Jan. 2018.

Review of *I Was Told to Come Alone: My Journey behind the Lines of Jihad*, by Souad Mekhennet. *Publishers Weekly*, 24 Apr. 2017, p. 82. Academic Search Complete, search.ebscohost.com/login.aspx?direct=true&db=a9h&AN=122683206&site=ehost-live. Accessed 12 Jan. 2018.

Okeowo, Alexis. Review of *I Was Told to Come Alone: My Journey behind the Lines of Jihad*, by Souad Mekhennet. *The New Yorker*, 20 June 2017, www.newyorker.com/books/page-turner/souad-mekhennet-i-was-told-to-come-alone-my-journey-behind-the-lines-of-jihad. Accessed 12 Jan. 2018.

The Idiot

Author: Elif Batuman (b. 1977)
Publisher: Penguin Press (New York). 432 pp.
Type of work: Novel
Time: 1995
Locales: Boston, Paris, Hungary, Turkey

In The Idiot, *Elif Batuman crafts a semi-autobiographical saga about love, language, and the frustrations and musings, exhilarations and self-innovations that are characteristic of coming-of-age transitions.*

Principal characters
SELIN KARADAĞ, an eighteen-year-old Turkish American girl
IVAN, her love interest, a Hungarian graduate student in mathematics at Harvard
SVETLANA, her friend from Russian class at Harvard

THE IDIOT

ELIF BATUMAN

A NOVEL

Courtesy of Penguin Press

Love, with all its sundry conditions, whether obsession or infatuation, mania or depression, has always seemed to be literature's central subject. And despite love's status as one of the most notable characteristics of the human experience, the psychology of love is no easy thing to define. Psychoanalyst Sigmund Freud likened its effects to those of hypnosis, discovering alongside it an attendant ambivalence due to its ideal nature. Likewise, writer Roland Barthes once reiterated: "Love at first sight is a hypnosis: I am fascinated by an image." But perhaps it was French writer Stendhal (Marie-Henri Beyle) who took up the most admirable approach to the matter in his 1822 book *On Love*, the first part of which yields a systematic analysis and taxonomy of four types of love. They are enumerated as follows: physical love, which is purely sexual and lust-driven; vanity love, instrumental for social climbers wanting to marry into the higher echelons of class society; love as a social game, a type of love bereft of passion; and finally, passionate love, which Stendhal identified as the finest and purest of the four types. In Elif Batuman's first novel, *The Idiot* (2017), protagonist Selin Karadağ is in love. Or so she thinks. If one were to place her amorous feelings on a Stendhalian spectrum, they would perhaps fall somewhere between passionate and dispassionate.

It is 1995 and Selin, an only child of Turkish immigrants, is eighteen years old, a freshman at Harvard University, and the self-aware narrator of a story about love. Much like Batuman's previous work, an essay collection, *The Possessed: Adventures with Russian Books and the People Who Read Them* (2010), *The Idiot* is a realistic narrative crafted in prose that is incisive, sharpened by the journalistic adroitness of a skilled and attentive reporter. In *The Idiot*, Batuman has sketched a deliberate account of Selin's meandering reflections on what it is like for her to transition into young adulthood. It is a personal story inflected by the relative novelty of the internet and email— by love, language, and books. Selin refers to Dostoevsky, Chekhov, Gogol, Camus, Pasternak, Balzac, Tolstoy, Nabokov, and others. But little is said substantively about these masters of the writing craft, the literary productions that have clearly left an indelible impression on her and encouraged her to explore the possibility of becoming a writer herself. On one hand, Selin's narration presents a traditional coming-of-age saga with Selin and her college friends, such as the sophisticated Svetlana, engaged in the usual rites of passage that lead to young adulthood. On the other hand, the character of Selin is drawn from Batuman's own experiences as a student at Harvard, where she studied Russian literature and encountered the internet at

Courtesy of Beowulf Sheehan

Elif Batuman is a staff writer at The New Yorker *and the author of* The Possessed: Adventures with Russian Books and the People Who Read Them *(2010). She is the recipient of a Whiting Award in Nonfiction (2010) and the inaugural* Paris Review Terry Southern Prize for Humor.

the close of the twentieth century. Selin's bookish introspection and how the growing use of technology is used to communicate add to the realistic narrative voice that Batuman has created for her character.

Continually locked in the reflective patterns of a raw and brainy pensiveness, borne along by unswerving literary ambitions and brief spells of dry wit, Selin is carving out a path in life, at times clumsily, at other times with tact. All the while she is trying to stay true to her sense of self. The problem, however, is that for Selin a "true" sense of self is, just like the "true" meaning of love, not always clear and distinct. It is often caught up in the opacity of its own stubborn discursiveness, inarticulacy, and dumb silence. Her awkward conduct frequently vacillates between low affect and academic dispassion. And she is often reluctant and apprehensive about interacting with other human beings. But it all makes sense. Selin is at a time in her life when almost everything is utterly uncanny, alienating, and transformative. Change plays out all around her on several different levels. And this only vexes the status of her ambiguous courtship with Ivan, a Hungarian student who studies math, whom she meets in Russian class, and with whom she thinks she has fallen in what sometimes feels to her like a clear-cut case of unrequited love.

The novel is structured in two parts. The first part concerns Selin's fall and spring semesters as an undergrad, giving a loose chronological structure to her detailed accounts of her daily routines and habits. The second part of Batuman's novel, subdivided into June, July, and August, takes place during the following summer when

Selin travels to Hungary, not only to teach English in a small Hungarian village, but also to follow Ivan. Throughout the course of the year, Selin goes from exchanging emails with him, waxing philosophical about books, existentialism, math, and language, to meeting his parents and spending an ambiguously romantic night with him at his childhood home in Hungary.

Anecdotal, meticulous, and at times tedious, *The Idiot* is both a chronicle of Selin's life in all its daily activities, and a love story inspired by her understanding of the romantic poetry of courtly love. What keeps *The Idiot* separate from the Provençal literature of twelfth-century southern France, however, is, among other things, its difficulty in distinguishing who is courting whom. Selin discovers that unfortunately Ivan has a girlfriend and wonders whether they have broken up and where she herself might fit in his romantic world. This problem is not made easier by Selin's excruciating self-awareness and awkwardness. She feels more comfortable communicating with Ivan through email than in the real world. Selin is at once retreating into, and recoiling from, both her own sense of self and a love that she is not so sure she has to offer to someone who may not be so sure he wants it. For critic Elaine Margolin, Batuman's novel "mirrors a growing and upsetting trend among so many young people who seem to have given up on the possibility of love and jubilation and euphoria before they have even tasted it." Add to Margolin's concerns that, for the reader, Selin's motivations are difficult to understand despite the easiness of Batuman's prose. Although Selin's character exhibits little to no affect, there is nonetheless plenty of meaningful value structured into her story. Selin not only reports the world as it is, she also lays it bare to the reader through her thoughts and feelings. There is a romantic quality to such symmetry, as Batuman balances Selin's objective reporting on what is going on outside and inside her own mind.

Reviewers have commented on the humor conveyed by Selin's naïve yet literary introspection as she experiences the world. Sloane Crosley of *Vanity Fair* called the book a "Masterly funny debut novel . . . erudite but never pretentious." A reviewer for the *Boston Globe* remarked on its "cutting satire of academia, a fresh take on the epistolary novel."

Frank Joseph

Review Sources

Feigel, Lara. "The Idiot by Elif Batuman Review—Books v. the World." Review of *The Idiot*, by Elif Batuman. *The Guardian*, 16 June 2017, www.theguardian.com/books/2017/jun/16/idiot-elif-batuman-review-life-lived-through-russian-novel. Accessed 20 Oct. 2017.

Garner, Dwight. "Review: Elif Bauman's *The Idiot* Sets a Romantic Crush on Simmer." Review of *The Idiot*, by Elif Batuman. *The New York Times*, 28 Feb. 2017, www.nytimes.com/2017/02/28/books/review-elif-batuman-idiot.html. Accessed 20 Oct. 2017.

Illingworth, Dustin. "Elif Batuman Turns Her Gifts to Fiction in *The Idiot*." Review of *The Idiot*, by Elif Batuman. *Los Angeles Times* 17 Mar. 2017, www.latimes.

com/books/jacketcopy/la-ca-jc-batuman-idiot-20170314-story.html. Accessed 20 Oct. 2017.

Review of *The Idiot*, by Elif Batuman. *Kirkus Review*, 6 Dec. 2016, www.kirkusreviews.com/book-reviews/elif-batuman/the-idiot/. Accessed 20 Oct. 2017.

Margolin, Elaine. "Elif Batuman's *The Idiot*." Review of *The Idiot*, by Elif Batuman. *The Washington Post*, 1 Mar. 2017, www.washingtonpost.com/entertainment/ books/elif-batumans-the-idiot/2017/03/01/ae9b5860-fdf3-11e6-8ebe-6e0dbe4f2b-ca_story.html. Accessed 20 Oct. 2017.

Schwartz, Madeleine. "Reality Fiction: Depicting 'The World as It Is'." Review of *The Idiot*, by Elif Batuman. *Harvard Magazine*, March–April 2017, harvardmagazine.com/2017/03/reality-fiction. Accessed 20 Oct. 2017.

Ill Will

Author: Dan Chaon (b. 1964)
Publisher: Ballantine Books (New York).
496 pp.
Type of work: Novel
Time: 1983–2014
Locales: Cleveland Heights and other communities in Ohio; St. Bonaventure, Nebraska; Gillette, Wyoming; Chicago, Illinois

Courtesy of Ballantine Books

An unsettling thriller spanning three decades, Ill Will *concerns two disturbing sets of events separated by thirty years: a mass murder in Nebraska and a series of drowning deaths in Ohio, both possibly the result of satanic rituals. The novel delves into the nature of memory, the definition of sanity, and the issue of trust.*

Principal characters

DR. DUSTIN TILLMAN, a psychologist
KATELYNN "KATE" TILLMAN, his cousin, with whom he grew up
WAVERNA "WAVE" TILLMAN, a.k.a. Galadriel Bluecloud, his cousin, Kate's twin
RUSSELL BICKERS, a.k.a. Rusty Tillman, his adopted older brother
JILL BELL TILLMAN, his wife, a lawyer
AARON TILLMAN, his younger son, a heroin addict
DENNIS TILLMAN, his older son, a college student
AQIL OZOROWSKI, his patient, a policeman on medical leave
BRUCE "RABBIT" BEREND, Aaron's friend, also a heroin addict
XZAVIOUS REINBOLT, a.k.a. Amy, Rabbit's friend

A hallmark of literature is the skillful construction of a standout opening line, a memorable, quotable beginning meant to draw the reader into the ensuing narrative. Classic opening lines usually have at least one purpose. "Call me Ishmael," from Herman Melville's *Moby-Dick* (1851), raises an immediate question: Is Ishmael an alias? "It was the best of times, it was the worst of times," from Charles Dickens's *A Tale of Two Cities* (1859), hints at a story built around contrasts. "Last night I dreamt I went to Manderley again," from Daphne du Maurier's *Rebecca* (1938), suggests that what follows may be partly illusion. "It was a bright cold day in April, and the clocks were striking thirteen," from George Orwell's *Nineteen Eighty-Four* (1949), introduces an element of unreality, something beyond the usual.

Only time will tell if Dan Chaon's *Ill Will* is similarly destined to become a classic, but its hardworking first line transmits considerable information, including the establishment of tone, rhythm, theme, and time of year: "Sometime in the first days of November the body of the young man who had disappeared sank to the bottom of the river." This irresistible opening—Who was the young man? What happened to him?—pays off its promise by leading quickly and naturally into the introduction of protagonist Dustin Tillman. A psychologist in his early forties, Dustin has been drifting aimlessly along, with no more volition than a corpse, and he is on the cusp of great changes in his life.

Married, living in Ohio, and the father of two teenaged sons, Dustin is a character who represents the nexus of two significant events, one in the distant past and one in the present. In 1983, when he was thirteen and living in rural Nebraska, he and his twin cousins Kate and Wave found all four of their parents—Dustin's mother and father, Colleen and Dave, and those of the twins, Vicki and Lucky—shot to death. At the trial that followed, a severely upset and confused Dustin testified against his troubled older foster brother, Rusty. On the strength of Dustin and Kate's sketchy testimonies, Rusty was convicted of the seemingly occult-inspired murders and sentenced to life in prison. In the present, the adult Dustin has been drawn into the investigation of a possible series of satanic cult murders by a patient of his, Aqil Ozorowski, who is on psychological leave from the Cleveland police department. The victims, all young male college students, each went missing over the course of a decade and were subsequently found dead, with elevated blood alcohol levels, in various local bodies of water. Despite tantalizing evidence that the deaths are connected, law enforcement has dismissed them all as tragic accidental drownings, the unfortunate consequence of a wave of collegiate binge drinking.

Though Dustin has misgivings about Aqil's theory of the crimes—he believes Aqil's theory may be a case of apophenia, a human tendency to find connections among random events—he is eventually enticed into participating in Aqil's obsession. Research into the deaths offers Dustin a welcome distraction from his myriad other problems: his beloved wife of twenty years, Jill, is dying of cancer; he is losing touch with his sons, Dennis and Aaron; and, in a retrial, Rusty has been acquitted of the murders he supposedly committed and has been released from prison after serving almost thirty years behind bars. The dramatic stakes are clearly raised: Will Rusty seek vengeance against Dustin, whose testimony originally helped convict him?

Dustin, whose perspective dominates much of the narration of *Ill Will*'s multiple parts, is a highly unreliable narrator, a unique variation on the theme of the psychologist being more disturbed than his patients. After the murders of his parents and his aunt and uncle, Dustin underwent extensive therapy, which may not have been as effective as hoped. He later majored in psychology as a college student to better understand abnormal behavior. His doctoral dissertation concerned cults and repressed memories surrounding the 1980s-era phenomenon of alleged satanic ritual abuse, wherein it was widely believed that there were sinister cults everywhere performing horrible rites on innocent victims—allegations that have since been largely discredited. Despite the therapy, his education, and his profession as a specialist in hypnotherapy, Dustin is

© Ulf Andersen

The Delaney Professor of Creative Writing at Oberlin College, Dan Chaon published his first short-story collection, Fitting Ends, *in 1995; his first novel,* You Remind Me of Me, *was published in 2004. He was a finalist for the National Book Award in fiction for his short-story collection* Among the Missing *(2001) and was awarded a 2006 Arts and Letters Award in literature by the American Academy of Arts and Letters. His stories have been widely anthologized.*

still traumatized by what happened in 1983. His continued confusion, suggested by typographic lacunae (blank spaces) that appear in the book and by his frequent inability to complete thoughts, is compounded by a flawed memory that makes him increasingly doubt what he thinks, or knows, or believes. As the story progresses, Dustin's grasp on reality becomes more tenuous, and this, too, is reflected on the page: halfway through the novel, pages begin to be divided into halves vertically, then into quarters, then into sixths, and finally into eighths, an evocative text design intended to depict Dustin's splintering thoughts.

Further complicating the story are the other narrators—Aaron, Kate, Wave, Rusty, and Dennis, all members of the extended Tillman family—who are likewise unreliable, for different reasons. Aaron, Dustin's younger son, is a heroin addict and a practiced liar; though he is supposed to be enrolled in classes at Cleveland State, he is in fact using the tuition money his father has given him to buy drugs from the shady characters who gather at the House of Wills, a former funeral home that has become a center for drug use. Aaron has also committed a major sin of omission: he has not told his father that he has been in regular contact with his Uncle Rusty via cell phone and Skype. Despite these character flaws, he exhibits some of his father's investigative traits. After being informed that his friend and fellow addict Bruce "Rabbit" Berend has been found dead, Aaron begins his own investigation to seek the truth. He acquires Rabbit's cell phone and begins checking his late friend's contacts, in the process venturing into dangerous territory.

Dustin's cousin Kate, who also narrates parts of the novel, has her own challenges with reliability. Before and after the murders of their parents, she and the younger Dustin shared a twin bed in a mobile home, creating a sexual frisson between them that simultaneously drove a wedge between Kate and her twin sister, Wave. In one section, Kate confesses to taking drugs and performing rituals in a cemetery just before the murders in Nebraska. Wave, who shortly afterward moved away from her sister, became a recluse, and adopted the alias Galadriel Bluecloud, briefly contributes to the narrative, disputing some of Kate's possibly faulty recollections.

Perhaps the most illuminating narrative voice is that of fifty-year-old ex-convict Rusty. After his release from prison following his belated acquittal, he travels from Nebraska to Chicago, where he lands menial work at a restaurant and lodging at a second-rate hotel. Rusty, who has the misspelled legend REMEMEMBER tattooed prominently across his throat, reminisces about being abused as a child by one of his mother's boyfriends. His mother, who was incarcerated for prostitution and drugs when Rusty was five, was later killed in prison, making him an orphan. Though Rusty was a prime suspect in the 1983 murders, in part because he was the only survivor when his previous foster family was killed in a mysterious house fire, he maintains that he never killed anyone. He does, however, admit to having committed several aberrant actions, among them doing numerous drugs, sexually abusing and tormenting young Dustin, and killing baby rabbits with a rock in a fake occult ritual. Though Rusty is bitter about being falsely accused and spending much of his adult life in prison, he is apparently too dispirited to do anything about the injustice he has suffered. He can only tally mental lists of people he would like to murder—Dustin, Wave, himself— while bemoaning the unfairness of being a potential murderer who was incarcerated before he could kill.

Ill Will is a fascinating, complex, multilayered work with much to recommend it. The disquieting story repurposes autobiographical details from the author's own life (the memory of growing up in a small town in Nebraska; the joy of fathering two sons; the grief of losing his wife, fellow writer and teacher Sheila Schwartz, to cancer in 2008). Told in short chapters, like snapshots, the novel flashes forward and backward, in first or third person, threading psychological themes among motifs of lying and keeping secrets that play with the reader's perceptions to generate a growing sense of unease. With great skill, Chaon relentlessly creates networks of conflict that collectively build suspense to the breaking point. As a result, readers will not soon forget the overall effect of *Ill Will*: a glimpse of unspeakable evil operating in an overpowering atmosphere of impending doom.

Jack Ewing

Review Sources

Brundage, Elizabeth. "Dan Chaon's Latest Takes on Satanism, Suspicious Deaths and a Faltering Family." Review of *Ill Will*, by Dan Chaon. *The New York Times*, 24 Mar. 2017, www.nytimes.com/2017/03/24/books/review/ill-will-dan-chaon. html. Accessed 20 Dec. 2017.

Charles, Ron. "Dan Chaon's *Ill Will* Is the Scariest Novel of the Year." Review of *Ill Will*, by Dan Chaon. *The Washington Post*, 6 Mar. 2017, www.washington-post.com/entertainment/books/dan-chaons-ill-will-is-the-scariest-novel-of-the-year/2017/03/06/1ba3cc8c-fe8d-11e6-8f41-ea6ed597e4ca_story.html. Accessed 20 Dec. 2017.

DeAngelo, Dominic. "Dan Chaon's Latest Book, *Ill Will*, Is a Disturbing Read." Review of *Ill Will*, by Dan Chaon. *Pittsburgh Post-Gazette*, 12 Mar. 2017, www. post-gazette.com/ae/books/2017/03/12/Dan-Chaon-s-latest-book-Ill-Will-is-a-disturbing-read/stories/201703120054. Accessed 20 Dec. 2017.

Preziosi, Dominic. "Lie, Memory." Review of *Ill Will*, by Dan Chaon. *Commonweal*, 10 July 2017, www.commonwealmagazine.org/lie-memory. Accessed 20 Dec.

2017.

Upchurch, Michael. "A Rust Belt Gothic of Murdered Parents, a Jailed Adopted Brother, and Suspicious Drownings." Review of *Ill Will*, by Dan Chaon. *The Boston Globe*, 3 Mar. 2017, www.bostonglobe.com/arts/books/2017/03/02/ rust-belt-gothic-murdered-parents-jailed-adopted-brother-and-suspicious-drownings/1OLEBKI8sHaZLQToIWAjVI/story.html. Accessed 20 Dec. 2017.

Wiersema, Robert J. "Dan Chaon's *Ill Will* Follows a Broken Man as His Life Takes Another Sharp Turn into the Darkness." Review of *Ill Will*, by Dan Chaon. *National Post*, 10 Mar. 2017, nationalpost.com/entertainment/books/book-reviews/ dan-chaons-ill-will-follows-a-broken-man-as-his-life-takes-another-sharp-turn-into-the-darkness. Accessed 20 Dec. 2017.

Imagine Wanting Only This

Author: Kristen Radtke (b. 1987)
Publisher: Pantheon (New York). 288 pp.
Type of work: Memoir, graphic novel
Time: 2000s
Locales: Chicago, Iowa, Kentucky, various
international locations

Imagine Wanting Only This is a graphic memoir by debut author Kristen Radtke. When Radtke's beloved uncle dies suddenly while she is in college, she becomes obsessed with the presence of ruins both metaphorical and literal. Through explorations of the recent and ancient past and communities touched by the impermanence of the landscapes around them, she attempts to discover the origin of her own obsession with these places.

Courtesy of Pantheon

Principal personages

KRISTEN, a college-aged woman studying to become a writer
UNCLE DAN, her favorite uncle
ANDREW, her college boyfriend
MARY HELEN, her best friend in graduate school
MOM, her mother

Many graphic memoirs have enjoyed enthusiastic readerships and become standards for the genre; Alison Bechdel's *Fun Home* (2006), Art Spiegelman's *Maus* (1980–91), and Marjane Satrapi's *Persepolis* (2000–2003) are three that come immediately to mind. While *Imagine Wanting Only This*, the debut work from Kristen Radtke, may not find itself in the upper echelons of graphic memoir fame as of yet, it is a worthy addition to the genre. Radtke has worked as an illustrator, a writer, and an editor, and her stark illustration style enhances the subjects of ruined landscapes and faraway travels that are central to her memoir. Through touching portraits of beloved friends and family members and dreamlike illustrations of disparate places such as Gary, Indiana; Iceland; the Philippines; and her home in Wisconsin, Radtke tells the story of a beloved uncle, Dan, who was born with a heart defect and dies prematurely. Her uncle's untimely death worries Kristen, the eponymous protagonist of the story, who fears that she may have inherited a heart defect herself. It also leaves her with a budding obsession with abandoned places and the people who were once, or still are, tied to them. Radtke's memoir focuses on her personal journey from self-assured college student to stumbling graduate student, and then to full-fledged adult.

At the memoir's start, a young Kristen, no more than five or six years of age, is shown with her Uncle Dan, introducing him as a wrestler who runs around the front yard in a garbage bag to sweat off more weight. Dan, a volunteer firefighter, is the person who taught Kristen to be curious about the world. In one poignant sequence, he takes her out to a field, covering her eyes until they arrive. When she is allowed to look, hundreds of fireflies fill the field in front of her, and her face is shown to be filled with wonder. Throughout this prologue, Radtke allows the reader to get to know Dan to set the stakes for the loss that Kristen is soon to encounter, but the effect is not overly saccharine, as might be expected when dealing with childhood and a lost relative. Rather, it enables the reader to see Kristen develop into a thoughtful narrator who will carry the story through the book's remaining pages.

A careful threading of themes contributes to the success of *Imagine Wanting Only This*. Rather than throwing the reader headfirst into the untimely death of her uncle, Radtke introduces the reader to her own character, now a sophomore who is studying art at a Chicago college. The first panel of chapter 1 opens as Kristen and Andrew, her college love interest, are driving to Gary, Indiana, which they have heard described as "post-apocalyptic." Their sensibilities toward ruin are similar, and they are soon driving down the abandoned streets of the town, where they find a derelict cathedral near the city's center. Kristen and her camera are inseparable—she has told Andrew that they should create an installation artwork out of the imagery they find in Gary—and she takes shot after shot of the space before stumbling on a pile of photographs of a young man. The photos of this unknown person are everywhere, and she decides to collect them and take them home with her.

Radtke allows these photos to stand in for Kristen's obsession with impermanence and her restless need for connection with the world around her, a device that feels natural rather than contrived. When Kristen discovers that the photographs were taken by a man who was killed on the train tracks nearby and his friends have created a makeshift shrine at the cathedral—his favorite place to shoot photos—she feels more closely tied to him, while at the same time also burdened by guilt. She wonders if she has somehow meddled in the young man's afterlife by altering his shrine. The photos remain in a bag in her closet until after graduation, when she takes them with her as she travels abroad to work as an au pair.

Kristen becomes fixated on abandoned places, indulging in a pastime that has become something of a cliché today, with many people traveling to places such as Detroit to photograph the empty and crumbling spaces of a once-thriving city. Her obsession begins as she and her mother are driving to her uncle's funeral; just as she is struggling with how to account for the loss she has suffered and to preserve the memory of an impermanent body and being—her uncle's—she sees the abandoned factories and decaying houses that once held life of their own. The alienating effect of the merging of these images is produced seamlessly, particularly as the reader learns that Kristen is also dealing with her own heart condition and the knowledge that the organ could fail her someday, as it has others in her family.

It is when dealing with ruins, however, that Radtke is at her weakest. In one sequence, while still a graduate student, Kristen returns home to her crumbling house in Iowa City from a trip abroad with her best friend, Mary Helen. The pair has just traveled through Asia, visiting Singapore, Macau, the Philippines (where they visited the island of Siquijor after touring World War II ruins in Corregidor), and the killing fields of Phnom Penh. When Kristen lands in Detroit, a sequence of frames shows her standing in front of a window at the airport as she challenges, "So tell me then what is so perverse in these empty high-rises. In these calcifying rust-belt cities." In the following frames, as she returns to her apartment in Iowa City, she continues her inquiry into desolation and abandonment. "Tell me what in these rotting hallways," she says as she enters her apartment building and finds a letter from Andrew, now her ex-boyfriend. "Tell me what in these bedrooms that look too much like your own." Radtke's sentiment is clear: ev-

© Greg Salvatori

Author and illustrator Kristen Radtke is the art director and New York editor of the Believer *magazine.* Imagine Wanting Only This *is her first book.*

eryone experiences loss, whether a loss of life, loved ones, home, or community. What is less clear is whether Radtke and her alter-ego narrator understand the varying types of human suffering that lead to such loss. Can the killing fields of Phnom Penh be compared equitably to a rundown house in Iowa City? At a temple in Laos, Kristen comments that the burning candles look like those she and her family lit for her grandmother. The connections Radtke attempts to make are meant to create a feeling of universality around the losses everyone encounters, but the delivery is filled with an unenlightening naïveté.

As Kristen continues to indulge her obsession with ruined places, her mother finds an obsession of her own: family genealogy. It seems that everyone has been affected deeply by the heart disease that kills members of their family, and looking to the past has become a salve for Kristen's mother as well as for Kristen herself. "I think she liked that the puzzles were solvable, the fact that she could search for a connection and find that connection marked in tangible, real-life stone," Kristen says of her mother's new hobby, which includes traveling to graveyards and combing through online records. This is of course in contrast to Kristen's interests, which involve finding the abstract connections across all humankind.

Yet Kristen is not immune to the allure of a tangible personal connection. At one point her mother uncovers a story in their family history about a nun named Adele Briese who saved her entire parish in Peshtigo Harbor, Wisconsin, from a devastating fire in the 1800s. When Adele was in her late twenties, she began to see apparitions of the Virgin Mary, and she soon became a devout follower. When the fire swept across the church property, Adele marched around the perimeter of the church holding a crucifix. "And apparently, the church was the only thing that didn't burn down for thousands and thousands of acres," Kristen narrates. As she sits in her Iowa City apartment with Mary Helen, she wonders less about the supernatural theme of Adele's story and more about what would have happened if the area had not been razed, if it had been allowed to grow into a city like Minneapolis or Detroit. "In truth, I didn't care that much about Adele, what she had done or not done," Kristen says. "But I loved the mythology of it all. She gave me a connection to the fire that made me feel like I had some right to the story."

The book's culmination comes as Kristen finds herself living in Louisville, Kentucky, isolated and depressed. For the first time in her life, she cannot find her place in the landscape. She decides to visit her dead uncle's wife, Sonia, who lives in Colorado; she also wants to visit the abandoned Colorado mining town of Gilman. In Gilman she finds more unanswered questions, but they feel satisfying nonetheless. While visiting a woman with close family ties to the mines, Kristen asks if she was sad when she had to leave the area when the mines closed. The woman replies, "It's simple. When one mine closed, we went to another." When Kristen is finally faced with the people she has spent the book mythologizing, the answer is quite different from what she imagined.

Imagine Wanting Only This is intrepid in its longing and sense of adventure, but it falls short when attempting to investigate and answer some of the larger philosophical questions that are presented in its pages. Met with mixed reviews from outlets such as the *Atlantic*, the *Chicago Tribune*, and NPR, the book is engaging on many levels, but some of the finer points of Kristen's deeper understanding of her spiritual quest prevent it from resonating deeply. Still, through a mastery of the graphic memoir form, haunting illustrations, and an ear for storytelling that is somehow rich and sparse simultaneously, Radtke has woven a memorable tale worthy of exploration.

Melynda Fuller

Review Sources

Adhikari, Arnav. "A Graphic-Novel Memoir That Tangles with the Puzzle of Existence." Review of *Imagine Wanting Only This*, by Kristen Radtke. *The Atlantic*, 18 Apr. 2017, www.theatlantic.com/entertainment/archive/2017/04/a-graphic-novel-memoir-that-tangles-with-the-puzzle-of-existence/523359/. Accessed 20 Aug. 2017.

Hart, Michelle. "Lineage of Restless Women: On Kristen Radtke's *Imagine Wanting Only This*." Review of *Imagine Wanting Only This*, by Kristen Radtke. *The Millions*, 23 May 2017, www.themillions.com/2017/05/lineage-of-restless-women-on-kristen-radtkes-imagine-wanting-only-this.html. Accessed 20 Aug. 2017.

Hunter, Greg. Review of *Imagine Wanting Only This*, by Kristen Radtke. *The Comics Journal*, 26 July 2017, www.tcj.com/reviews/imagine-wanting-only-this/. Accessed 20 Aug. 2017.

Kephart, Beth. "*Imagine Wanting Only This*: Devastating Graphic Memoir Features 'Ruins' of Gary, Ind." Review of *Imagine Wanting Only This*, by Kristen Radtke. *Chicago Tribune*, 12 Apr. 2017, www.chicagotribune.com/lifestyles/books/

ct-imagine-wanting-only-this-kristen-radtke-books-0416-20170412-story.html. Accessed 20 Aug. 2017.

Lehoczky, Etelka. "Wanting More from *Imagine Wanting Only This*." Review of *Imagine Wanting Only This*, by Kristen Radtke. *NPR*, 22 Apr. 2017, www.npr. org/2017/04/22/523586347/wanting-more-from-imagine-wanting-only-this. Accessed 20 Aug. 2017.